# Government Procedures and Operations

snova
New York

# Government Procedures and Operations

**Social Security Insights: Legislation, Coverage, and Financial Health**
Gina P. King (Editor)
ISBN: 979-8-89530-483-9
eBook ISBN: 979-8-89530-511-9

**The Roles of the FDA, CDC and PSR in Food Safety**
Ricardo A. Martin (Editor)
ISBN: 979-8-89530-364-1
eBook ISBN: 979-8-89530-394-8

**Parental Rights in the Face of Government Interference**
Louis Bray (Editor)
ISBN: 979-8-89530-315-3
eBook ISBN: 979-8-89530-343-6

**The Financial Surveillance of Americans' Private Data**
Shawn S. Neumann (Editor)
ISBN: 979-8-89530-179-1
eBook ISBN: 979-8-89530-198-2

**The Biden Administration's Overreach**
David D. Chaney (Editor)
ISBN: 979-8-89530-219-4
eBook ISBN: 979-8-89530-280-4

**The Internal Revenue Service: Federal Taxes, Corporate Taxes, Tax Credits and Tax-Advantaged Accounts**
Jonas S. Nørgaard (Editor)
ISBN: 979-8-89530-242-2
eBook ISBN: 979-8-89530-299-6

**More information about this series can be found at**
https://novapublishers.com/product-category/series/government-procedures-and-operations/

**Jolene Rivera**
Editor

# The National Flood Insurance Program (NFIP)

**Background, Reforms and Affordability**

snova
New York

**Library of Congress Cataloging-in-Publication Data**

ISBN: 979-8-89530-612-3

*Published by Nova Science Publishers, Inc. † New York*

# Contents

# Preface

The National Flood Insurance Program (NFIP) was established by the National Flood Insurance Act of 1968 (NFIA). The general purpose of the NFIP is both to offer primary flood insurance to properties with significant flood risk, and to reduce flood risk through the adoption of floodplain management standards. Communities volunteer to participate in the NFIP in order to have access to federal flood insurance, and in return are required to adopt minimum standards.

## Chapter 1

# Introduction to the National Flood Insurance Program (NFIP)*

**Diane P. Horn**
**and Baird Webel**

## Summary

The National Flood Insurance Program (NFIP) was established by the National Flood Insurance Act of 1968 (NFIA; 42 U.S.C. §4001 et seq.) and was most recently reauthorized to September 2024, through a series of short-term reauthorizations. The general purpose of the NFIP is both to offer primary flood insurance to properties with significant flood risk, and to reduce flood risk through the adoption of floodplain management standards. Communities volunteer to participate in the NFIP in order to have access to federal flood insurance, and in return are required to adopt minimum standards.

The NFIP is managed by the Federal Emergency Management Agency (FEMA), through its subcomponent the Federal Insurance and Mitigation Administration (FIMA). FEMA manages a Risk Mapping, Assessment and Planning (Risk MAP) process to produce Flood Insurance Rate Maps (FIRMs). Depicted on FIRMs are Special Flood Hazard Areas (SFHAs), which are areas exposed to a 1% or greater risk of annual flooding. FIRMs vary in age across the country, and are updated on a prioritized basis. The Risk MAP process provides extensive outreach and appeal opportunities for communities. Updating a community's FIRMs can take three to five years or more. Participating communities must adopt a flood map and enact minimum floodplain standards to regulate development in

* This is an edited, reformatted and augmented version of Congressional Research Service Publication No. R44593, updated April 2, 2024.

In: The National Flood Insurance Program (NFIP)
Editor: Jolene Rivera
ISBN: 979-8-89530-612-3

the SFHA. FEMA encourages communities to enhance their floodplain standards by offering reduced premium rates through the Community Rating System (CRS). FEMA also manages a Flood Mitigation Assistance (FMA) grant program using NFIP revenues to further reduce comprehensive flood risk. Participating communities that fail to adopt FIRMs or maintain minimum floodplain standards can be put on probation or suspended from the NFIP. In communities that do not participate in the NFIP, or have been suspended, individuals cannot purchase NFIP insurance. Individuals in these communities also face challenges receiving federal disaster assistance in flood hazard areas.

NFIP insurance uses one of three types of Standard Flood Insurance Policies (SFIPs). SFIPs have maximum coverage limits set by law. Any federal entity that makes, guarantees, or purchases mortgages must, by law, require property owners in the SFHA to purchase flood insurance, generally through the NFIP. In moderate risk areas, community members may purchase Preferred Risk Policies (PRPs) that offer less costly insurance. The day-to-day sale, servicing, and claims processing of NFIP policies are conducted by private industry partners. Most policies are serviced by companies that are reimbursed through the Write Your Own (WYO) Program.

The premium rate for most NFIP policies is intended to reflect the true flood risk. However, Congress has directed FEMA to subsidize flood insurance for properties built before the community's first FIRM (i.e., the pre-FIRM subsidy). In addition, FEMA "grandfathers" properties at their rate from past FIRMs to updated FIRMs through a cross-subsidy. These subsidies are being phased out under FEMA's new rating approach, known as Risk Rating 2.0.

Congress has provided appropriations to the NFIP for some of the cost of Risk MAP. Congress also authorizes the use of premium revenues for other NFIP costs, including administration, salaries, and other expenses. NFIP premiums also include other charges, such as a Federal Policy Fee, a Reserve Fund assessment, and a surcharge to help fund the NFIP. In October 2017, Congress cancelled $16 billion of NFIP debt, making it possible for the program to pay claims for Hurricanes Harvey, Irma, and Maria. The NFIP currently owes $20.525 billion to the U.S. Treasury, leaving $9.9 billion in borrowing authority from a $30.425 billion limit in law. This debt is serviced by the NFIP and interest is paid through premium revenues.

After September 30, 2024, key authorities of the NFIP, such as the authority to issue new insurance contracts, will expire if they are not reauthorized by Congress.

## Introduction

The National Flood Insurance Program (NFIP) was created by the National Flood Insurance Act of 1968 (NFIA).[1] Since the end of FY2017, 30 short-term NFIP reauthorizations have been enacted (see *Table 6*). The NFIP is currently authorized until September 30, 2024.[2]

The last long-term reauthorization of the NFIP was by the Biggert-Waters Flood Insurance Reform Act of 2012 (hereinafter BW-12),[3] from July 6, 2012, to September 30, 2017. Congress amended elements of BW-12, but did not extend the NFIP's authorization further, in the Homeowner Flood Insurance Affordability Act of 2014 (HFIAA).[4] The NFIP is managed by the Federal Emergency Management Agency (FEMA), through its subcomponent the Federal Insurance and Mitigation Administration (FIMA). As of February 29, 2024, the NFIP had over 4.7 million flood insurance policies providing over $1.3 trillion in coverage. The program collects about $4.6 billion in revenue from policyholders' premiums, fees, and surcharges.[5] Nationally, as of March 2024, over 22,000 communities in 56 states and jurisdictions participated in the NFIP.[6] According to FEMA, the NFIP's flood management standards have saved the nation almost $2.4 billion annually in flood losses avoided.[7]

This report provides introductory information on key components of the NFIP, ranging from floodplain mapping to the standard flood insurance forms. This report will be updated as significant revisions are made to the NFIP through legislation or administrative action.

---

[1] Title XIII of P.L. 90-448, as amended, 42 U.S.C. §4001 et seq.

[2] P.L. 118-47.

[3] Title II of P.L. 112-141.

[4] P.L. 113-89.

[5] Statistics on the NFIP policy and claims are available from FEMA, *The Watermark: National Flood Insurance Program Financial Statements*, at https://www.fema.gov/flood-insurance/work-with-nfip/watermark-financial- statements, and from FEMA's website at https://nfipservices.floodsmart.gov//reports-flood-insurance-data.

[6] Detailed information about which communities participate and where is available from the Community Status Book, found on FEMA's website at https://www.fema.gov/flood-insurance/work-with-nfip/community-status-book.

[7] U.S. Congress, Senate Committee on Banking, Housing, and Urban Affairs, *Reauthorization of the National Flood Insurance Program, Part II*, Statement of David Maurstad, Deputy Associate Administrator for Insurance and Mitigation, Federal Insurance and Mitigation Administration, FEMA, 117th Cong., 1st sess., June 17, 2021, p.2, https://www.banking.senate.gov/imo/media/doc/Maurstad%20Testimony%206-17-21.pdf.

## Purpose of the NFIP

In the original NFIP statute, Congress stipulated that "a program of flood insurance can promote the public interest by providing appropriate protection against the perils of flood losses and encouraging sound land use by minimizing exposure of property to flood losses."[8] Congress had found that post-disaster flood losses, and the subsequent federal disaster relief assistance to help communities recover from those flood losses, had "placed an increasing burden on the Nation's resources" and that as a matter of national policy "a reasonable method of sharing the risk of flood losses is through a program of flood insurance which can complement and encourage preventive and protective measures."[9] At the time of establishment of the NFIP, as is generally still the case today, it was found that "many factors have made it uneconomic for the private insurance industry alone to make flood insurance available to those in need of such protection on reasonable terms and conditions."[10]

Thus, the NFIP essentially has two interrelated policy purposes that can be summarized as

1. to provide access to primary flood insurance, thereby allowing for the transfer of some of the financial risk of property owners to the federal government, and
2. to mitigate and reduce the nation's *comprehensive* flood risk[11] through the development and implementation of floodplain management standards.

A core design feature of the NFIP is that communities are not required to participate in the program by any law or other regulation.[12] Rather, communities in the United States voluntarily participate in the NFIP generally

---

[8] See 82 Stat. 573 for text in original statute (§1302(c) of P.L. 90-448). This language remains in statute (see 42 U.S.C.§4001(c)).

[9] See 82 Stat. 573 for text in original statute (§1302(a) of P.L. 90-448). This language remains in statute (see 42 U.S.C.§4001(a)).

[10] See 82 Stat. 573 for text in original statute (§1302(b)(1) of P.L. 90-448). This language remains in statute (see 42U.S.C. §4001(b)(1)).

[11] In the context of this report, *comprehensive* flood risk means that the risk includes both financial risk (i.e., physical damage to property), but also the risk to human life.

[12] 44 C.F.R. §59.1 defines community as any State or area or political subdivision thereof, or any Indian tribe or authorized tribal organization, or Alaska Native village or authorized native organization, which has authority to adopt and enforce flood plain management regulations for the areas within its jurisdiction.

as a means of securing access to the primary flood insurance offered by the NFIP. Essentially, the NFIP is structured so that the availability of primary flood insurance through the NFIP (purpose #1 from above) is tied to the adoption and enforcement of floodplain management standards by participating communities (purpose #2). FEMA is only allowed to provide flood insurance to "those States or areas (or subdivisions thereof)" where "adequate land use and control measures" have been adopted that "are consistent with the comprehensive criteria for land management and use developed" by the NFIP.[13] Thus, communities that participate in the NFIP, and therefore whose residents may access the NFIP's primary flood insurance, also adopt through local or state laws minimum floodplain management standards that are described in FEMA regulations.

## Reduction of Comprehensive Flood Risk

The NFIP accomplishes the goal of reducing comprehensive flood risk primarily by requiring participating communities to

- collaborate with FEMA to develop and adopt flood maps called Flood Insurance Rate Maps (FIRMs), and
- enact minimum floodplain standards based on those flood maps.

In addition, premiums collected from the sale of insurance in the NFIP finance a Flood Mitigation Assistance (FMA) grant program that reduces overall flood risk. This section of the report briefly discusses each of these means of reducing comprehensive flood risk.

### Risk Mapping, Assessment, and Planning (Risk MAP) and Flood Insurance Rate Maps (FIRMs)

FEMA is responsible for undertaking Flood Insurance Studies (FISs) nationwide to identify areas within the United States having special flood, mudslide, and flood-related erosion hazards; assess the flood risk; and designate insurance zones.[14] FEMA develops, in coordination with

[13] 42 U.S.C. §4012(c)(2).
[14] See 42 U.S.C. §4101 and 44 C.F.R. Part 65.

participating communities, flood maps called FIRMs using these FISs that depict the community's flood risk and floodplain. In BW-12, Congress revised the authorities of FEMA as it relates to flood hazard mapping to formally establish what FEMA has called the Risk Mapping, Assessment and Planning (Risk MAP) process.[15] Though formally authorized in BW-12, FEMA started the Risk MAP process at the request of Congress in 2009.[16] While FEMA is largely responsible for the creation of the FIRM, the community itself must pass the map into its local or state law in order for the map to be effective.

### *Flood Zones*

An area of specific focus on the FIRM is the Special Flood Hazard Area (SFHA). The SFHA is intended to distinguish the flood risk zones that have a chance of flooding during a "1 in 100-year flood" or greater frequency. This means that properties in the SFHA have a risk of 1% or greater risk of flooding every year. Table 1 shows flood-risk zones that are depicted on the FIRMs.

Zones A (A1-30), AE, AH, AO, V, VE, VO, and V1-30 constitute the designated SFHA on the community's FIRM. V zones are distinguished from A zones in that V zones are subject to wave action (i.e., coastal flooding). Two other designations for classifying zones in the SFHA are the Zone AR, which is an area where a levee or similar structure is determined not to provide sufficient flood protection, but is undergoing restoration; and the Zone A99, an area where a federal flood protection structure is under construction to provide the necessary flood protection standard.

**Table 1.** Flood Zones as Depicted on Flood Insurance Rate Maps (FIRMs)

| Zone Symbol | Description |
|---|---|
| A | Area of special flood hazard without water surface elevations determined. |
| A1-30, AE | Area of special flood hazard with water surface elevations determined. |

---

[15] §100216 of P.L. 112-141, 126 Stat. 927, as codified at 42 U.S.C. §4101b.

[16] Congress called for the creation of a new five-year National Flood Map Maintenance Plan for FY2010-FY2014 in the Explanatory Statement which accompanied the Department of Homeland Security Appropriations Act, 2009 (P.L. 110-329). For the initial Risk MAP plan, see FEMA, *Risk Mapping, Assessment, and Planning (Risk MAP) Multi-Year Plan: Fiscal Years 2010-2014*, March 16, 2009, at http://www.fema.gov/media-library-data/20130726-1650-20490- 4732/fema_risk_map_plan.pdf.

| Zone Symbol | Description |
|---|---|
| AO | Area of special flood hazards having shallow water depths and/or unpredictable flow paths between 1 and 3 feet |
| A99 | Area of special flood hazard where enough progress has been made on a protective system, such as dikes, dams, and levees, to consider it complete for insurance rating purposes. |
| AH | Areas of special flood hazards having shallow water depths and/or unpredictable flow paths between 1 and 3 feet, and with water surface elevations determined. |
| AR | Area of special flood hazard that results from the decertification of a previously accredited flood protection system that is determined to be in the process of being restored to provide base flood protection. |
| V | Area of special flood hazards without water surface elevations determined, and with velocity, that is inundated by tidal floods (coastal high hazard area). |
| V1-30, VE | Area of special flood hazards, with water surface elevations determined and with velocity, that is inundated by tidal floods (coastal high hazard area). |
| VO | Area of special flood hazards having shallow water depths and/or unpredictable flow paths between 1 and 3 feet and with velocity. |
| B, X | Areas of moderate flood hazards or areas of future-conditions flood hazard. |
| C, X | Area of minimal hazards. |
| D | Area of undetermined, but possible, flood hazards. |
| M | Area of special mudslide (i.e., mudflow) hazards. |
| N | Area of moderate mudslide (i.e., mudflow) hazards. |
| P | Area of undetermined, but possible, mudslide hazards. |
| E | Area of special flood-related erosion hazards. |

Source: Adapted from 44 C.F.R. §60.3 by CRS.

### *Updating Flood Maps*

Flood maps adopted across the country vary considerably in age and in quality. While some FIRMs may have last been developed and adopted by a community in the 1980s, especially in rural areas of the country, most communities will have maps adopted within the past 15 to 20 years.[17] All official FIRMs can be accessed, and are searchable by address and location, on a FEMA website called the Map Service Center,[18] and modern FIRMs can be digitally viewed via the Geographic Information System in the National Flood Hazard Layer.[19]

There is no consistent, definitive timetable for when a particular community will have their maps revised and updated. FEMA uses a process called the Coordinated Needs Management Strategy to prioritize, identify, and track the lifecycle of mapping needs of Risk MAP.[20] Generally, flood maps may require updating when there have been significant new building developments in or near the flood zone, changes to flood protection systems (e.g., levees and sand dunes), and environmental changes in the community. Because of the variability in how and when a FIRM is updated, for example, one community may be undergoing the process of updating its map while a neighboring community is not, and one community may have had its map last updated in 2020 while a neighboring community had its last revised in 2005, etc.

There are statutory guidelines for how FEMA is allowed to develop new FIRMs for a community. These guidelines require, for example, FEMA to conduct extensive communication and outreach efforts with the community during the mapping process and include various minimum waiting periods after intermediary steps are taken in the process.[21] In addition, during this process, communities are asked to submit pertinent data concerning their flood hazards, flooding experience, mitigation plans to avoid potential flood hazards, and estimates of historical and prospective economic impacts flooding has had on the community.[22] Generally, FEMA seeks to make the Risk MAP process a collaborative process with local communities to

---

[17] By law, FEMA is required to "assess the need to revise and update all floodplain areas and flood risk zones" every five years, but not necessarily update the maps. See 42 U.S.C. §4101(e).

[18] See the Map Service Center website at https://msc.fema.gov/portal/home. In addition, one can review the last revision date of a community's Flood Insurance Rate Map (FIRM) in the Community Status Book found at https://www.fema.gov/flood-insurance/work-with-nfip/community-status-book.

[19] For more on the NFHL, and directions for accessing it, see FEMA's website at https://www.fema.gov/flood-maps/tools-resources/flood-map-products/national-flood-hazard-layer.

[20] For more, see FEMA, *Coordinated Needs Management Strategy*, at https://www.fema.gov/flood-maps/tools-resources/risk-map/coordinated-needs-management-strategy.

[21] See, for example, 42 U.S.C. §4101b(d)(1) and 42 U.S.C. §4104.

[22] See, for example, 44 C.F.R. §66.1.

encourage a joint sense of "ownership" of the maps. There are also legal requirements allowing communities and individuals to appeal during the process of updating FIRMs.[23] This appeal process now includes the option, first authorized in BW-12, for communities to appeal to a Scientific Resolution Panel regarding a proposed FIRM.[24]

In BW-12, Congress reestablished and reauthorized a council called the Technical Mapping Advisory Council (TMAC).[25] The TMAC is broadly authorized to review and recommend improvements to how FEMA produces and disseminates flood hazard, flood risk, and flood map information.[26] In particular, the TMAC is authorized to recommend to FEMA "mapping standards and guidelines for—(A) flood insurance rate maps [FIRMs]; and (B) data accuracy, data quality, data currency, and data eligibility."[27] Currently, the TMAC estimates that the production of a new or revised FIRM is designed to take three to five years under the Risk MAP program, but can often take as long as six and a half years or longer.[28] The TMAC has suggested that the ideal Risk MAP project timeline is 25 months.[29]

### *Map Corrections*

After a map is finalized and adopted by a community, it can still be revised to correct for errors in map accuracy. To correct these inaccuracies, FEMA allows individuals and communities to request letters amending or revising the flood map. In general, two primary circumstances may result in changes to the flood map. First, the natural elevation of property may be incorrectly accounted for on a FIRM, and that natural elevation is such that the property

---

[23] Primarily, see 42 U.S.C. §4104(c)-(g).

[24] §100218(a) of P.L. 112-141, 126 Stat. 930, as codified at 42 U.S.C. §4104-1. For more on the Scientific Resolution Panel, see the Panel's website at http://www.floodsrp.org/.

[25] Section 100215, Title II of P.L. 112-141, 126 Stat. 924, as codified at 42 U.S.C. §4101a. Congress originally authorized the creation of the Technical Mapping Advisory Council (TMAC) in 1994 (see §576 of P.L. 103-325, 108 Stat. 2280). However, in that originating statute, the TMAC was required to terminate "5 years after the date on which all members of the Council have been appointed." BW-12 did not include a termination clause for TMAC, thus making it permanent. BW-12 describes the conditions for membership, pay, and other matters relating to the operations and structure of the TMAC.

[26] For a list of duties, see 42 U.S.C. §4101a(c).

[27] 42 U.S.C. §4101a(c)(2).

[28] For further details on the remapping process, see Section 4.4.2 in Technical Mapping Advisory Council, *Annual Report, 2015*, December 2015, pp. 4-55, and the section on Process, in Technical Mapping Advisory Council, *National Flood Mapping Program Review,* June 2016, pp. 13-17, both at https://www.fema.gov/flood-maps/guidance-partners/ technical-mapping-advisory-council.

[29] Ibid. See Figure 4-10.

should not be considered part of the SFHA. Generally, in this circumstance, an individual or community may request a Letter of Map Amendment (LOMA).[30] Second, a community may feel that a physical development in the community has resulted in a reduction of the flood risk for areas previously mapped in the floodplain. Generally, in this circumstance, the community may request a Letter of Map Revision (LOMR).[31] In either a LOMA or LOMR, the decision to correct a map must be based on scientific information validating the inaccuracy of the current map. In most circumstances, the cost of requesting the map correction is borne by the community or individual.[32]

## State and Local Land Use Controls

As authorized in law, FEMA has developed a set of minimum floodplain management standards that are intended to

1) constrict the development of land which is exposed to flood damage where appropriate,
2) guide the development of proposed construction away from locations which are threatened by flood hazards, (3) assist in reducing damage caused by floods, and (4) otherwise improve the long-range land management and use of flood-prone areas.[33]

Communities are required to adopt these minimum floodplain management standards in order to participate in the NFIP.[34] FEMA has set forth the minimum standards it requires for participation in the NFIP in federal regulations.[35] Though the standards appear in federal regulations, the standards only have the force of law because they are adopted and enforced

[30] For more on LOMAs, see 44 C.F.R. Part 70, or FEMA's website at https://www.fema.gov/glossary/letter-map- amendment-loma.

[31] For more on LOMRs, see 44 C.F.R. Part 72, or FEMA's website at https://www.fema.gov/flood-maps/change-your- flood-zone/loma-lomr-f.

[32] For detailed information on the process of revising and amending NFIP maps, please see FEMA, *Appeals, Revisions, and Amendments to National Flood Insurance Program Maps: A Guide for Community Officials*, December 2009, at https://www.hsdl.org/?abstract&did=30227.

[33] 42 U.S.C. §4102(c).

[34] 42 U.S.C. §4022(a)(1).

[35] See 44 C.F.R. Part 60, particularly 44 C.F.R. §60.3.

by a state or local government. Key conditions of the NFIP minimum standards include, among many other conditions, that communities

- require permits for development in the SFHA;
- require elevation of the lowest floor of all new residential buildings in the SFHA to or above the Base Flood Elevation (BFE);[36]
- restrict development in the regulatory floodway to prevent increasing the risk of flooding; and
- require certain construction materials and methods that minimize future flood damage.[37]

Legal enforcement of the floodplain management standards is the responsibility of the participating NFIP community. However, FEMA, often in cooperation with state governments, will conduct community assistance visits (CAVs) to monitor how and if a community is adequately enforcing its floodplain ordinances.[38] Two previous reviews commissioned by FEMA on community enforcement of minimum floodplain standards have estimated that the nationwide rate of community compliance with the standards is 70% to 85%,[39] and that between 58% and 70% of buildings are built in full compliance

---

[36] The Base Flood Elevation (BFE) is the water-surface elevation of the base flood, which is the 1%-annual-chance flood, commonly called the 100-year flood. The probability is 1% that rising water will reach BFE height in any given year. The depth of the base flood is calculated by subtracting the ground elevation from the BFE.

[37] For more on the NFIP minimum floodplain standards, see, for example, FEMA, *NFIP Floodplain Management*, at https://www.fema.gov/floodplain-management-requirements and selected other sources: Christopher P. Jones, William L. Coulbourne, and Jamie Marshall, et al., Evaluation of the National Flood Insurance Program's Building Standards: Prepared as part of the 2001-2006 Evaluation of the National Flood Insurance Program, American Institutes of Research, October 2006, at https://www.fema.gov/sites/default/files/2020-07/ fema_nfip_eval_building_standards.pdf.
Association of State Floodplain Managers, *A Guide for Higher Standards in Floodplain Management*, March 2013, at https://s3-us-west-2 amazonaws.com/asfpm-library/General/Higher_Standards_Floodplain_Management_ASFPM_2013.pdf.

[38] For more information on CAVs, see FEMA, *Guidance for Conducting Community Assistance Contacts and Community Assistance Visits*, F-776, April 2011, at https://s3-us-west-2.amazonaws.com/asfpm-library/Mentoring/FEMA_2011_guidance_conducting_community.pdf.

[39] A community was estimated to be compliant with the floodplain management standards if it had no program deficiencies or violations or if it addressed them satisfactorily within two years [following a community assistance visit]. As another way of gauging overall community compliance, FEMA and state personnel were asked in interviews to give estimates of the proportion of compliant communities in their 'territories.' Their responses ranged from 0 percent compliant for some areas to 100 percent for others, but averaged to 78 percent compliant, the median of the range calculated from existing records. See

with the standards.[40] A community that has been found failing to enforce the floodplain management standards may be placed on probation and ultimately suspended from the NFIP (as discussed later in this report).[41] As these standards are just *minimum* requirements, states and communities can elect to adopt higher standards as a means of mitigating flood risk. In addition, FEMA operates a program, called the Community Rating System, to incentivize NFIP communities to adopt more rigorous floodplain management standards (also discussed later in this report).[42]

## Flood Mitigation Assistance Grants

To reduce comprehensive flood risk, FEMA also operates a Flood Mitigation Assistance (FMA) Grant Program that is funded through revenue collected by the NFIP.[43] The FMA Program[44] awards grants for a number of purposes, including state and local mitigation planning; the elevation, relocation, demolition, or flood proofing of structures; the acquisition of properties; and other activities.[45] FMA grants are only available to communities which participate in the NFIP, to assist in efforts to reduce or eliminate flood damage

---

Jacquelyn L. Monday, Kristen Y. Grill, and Paul Esformes, et al., *An Evaluation of Compliance with the National Flood Insurance Program Part A: Achieving Community Compliance*, American Institutes of Research, Prepared as part of the 2001-2006 Evaluation of the National Flood Insurance Program, November 2006, p. x, at https://www.fema.gov/sites/default/files/2020-07/fema_nfip_eval_community_compli ance_a.pdf.

[40] Margaret L. Mathis and Suzanne Nicholson, *An Evaluation of Compliance with the National Flood Insurance Program Part B: Are Minimum Building Requirements Being Met?*, Dewberry, Prepared as part of the 2001-2006 Evaluation of the National Flood Insurance Program, October 2006, p. viii, at https://www.fema.gov/sites/default/files/2020-07/fema_nfip_eval_community_comp liance_b.pdf.

[41] See the "Nonparticipating Communities and Community Suspension" section of this report.

[42] See the "Community Rating System" section of this report.

[43] 42 U.S.C. §4104c.

[44] In BW-12, Congress mandated that the grant assistance previously delivered by the Repetitive Flood Claims (RFC) and the Severe Repetitive Loss (SLR) grant programs should be unified into a single program, Flood Mitigation Assistance (FMA), by rescinding the authorization for the SLR program and the RFC program. See Sections 100225(b)-(c) of P.L. 112-141, respectively.

[45] For additional information on the FMA Program, see 44 C.F.R. Part 78, and FEMA's website at https://www.fema.gov/grants/mitigation/floods.

to buildings and structures insurable under the NFIP, particularly repetitive loss[46] and severe repetitive loss[47] properties.

The FMA Program has $800 million available for FY2023.[48] FMA funding is available until it is expended, so in certain years the amount awarded may exceed the amount authorized by Congress in an appropriation act for a specific fiscal year.[49]

***Infrastructure Funding for Flood Mitigation***

The Infrastructure Investment and Jobs Act[50] appropriated $3.5 billion for the FMA program, with $700 million for each of FY2022 to FY2026. This represents a significant increase in the amount of funding available for flood mitigation, and the first time that funding has been appropriated for the FMA program. The first project to be funded with the IIJA funding was the Swift Current Initiative, which was intended to expedite FMA awards after a flooding event and reduce the complexity of the application process, with the goal of obligating FMA dollars for NFIP-insured and substantially damaged properties as quickly and equitably as possible after a flood. Swift Current allocated $60 million to Louisiana, Mississippi, New Jersey, and Pennsylvania. These states were selected because they were affected by Hurricane Ida and had the highest repetitive loss and severe repetitive loss of NFIP-insured unmitigated properties, and the highest total insurance claims within their respective FEMA regions.[51] Swift Current FY2022 obligated $40.3 million of the total $60 million within a year of the Notice of Funding

---

46 42 U.S.C. §4121(a)(7) defines repetitive loss structure as a structure covered by a contract for flood insurance that— a) has incurred flood-related damage on 2 occasions, in which the cost of repair, on the average, equaled or exceeded 25 percent of the value of the structure at the time of each such flood event; and b) at the time of the second incidence of flood-related damage, the contract for flood insurance contains increased cost of compliance coverage.

47 Severe repetitive loss properties are those that have incurred four or more claim payments exceeding $5,000 each, with a cumulative amount of such payments over $20,000, or at least two claims with a cumulative total exceeding the value of the property. See 42 U.S.C. §4014(h) and 44 C.F.R. §79.2(h).

48 See FEMA, *Notice of Funding Opportunity (NOFO) Fiscal Year 2023 Flood Mitigation Assistance*, at https://www.grants.gov/web/grants/view-opportunity.html?oppId=350564.

49 For additional information on how the FMA program is financed, see the "Appropriations and Offsetting Receipts" section of this report.

50 P.L. 117-58.

51 FEMA, *Eligibility for Current Initiative*, https://www.fema.gov/grants/mitigation/floods/swift-current/eligibility.

Opportunity.[52] $300 million is available for Swift Current in FY2023.[53] Applicants (state, tribe, or territory [STT]) must have received a major disaster declaration for a flood-related disaster between June 1, 2023, and May 31, 2024. Additionally, one of the following criteria must be met:

1) The STT has at least $1 million in prior NFIP claims from June 1, 2022, to disasters declared before May 31, 2024; or
2) The STT has 500 or more NFIP claims in a declared flood-related disaster event from June 1, 2022, to May 31, 2024.
3) The applicant is a tribal nation or territory applying directly to FEMA.[54]

## Primary Flood Insurance Through the NFIP

### Standard Flood Insurance Policies (SFIPs)

FEMA has considerable discretion under the law to craft the details of the flood insurance policies it sells through the NFIP.[55] Currently, there are three policies that the NFIP uses to sell primary flood insurance—the Dwelling, the General Property, and the Residential Condominium Building Association policy forms. Collectively, these Standard Flood Insurance Policies (SFIPs) appear in regulations, and coverage qualifications are generally equivalent.[56] Table 2 displays the maximum available coverage limits for SFIPs by occupancy type. These coverage amounts are set by law.[57] Policyholders are able to elect coverage for both their building property and separate coverage for contents. Renters may obtain contents-only coverage.

---

[52] Email from FEMA Congressional Affairs Staff, June 30, 2023.

[53] FEMA, *Swift Current*, https://www.fema.gov/grants/mitigation/flood-mitigation-assistance/swift-current.

[54] FEMA, "Biden-Harris Administration Announces Second Round of Funding to Mitigate Repetitive Flooding," press release, November 14, 2023, https://www.fema.gov/press-release/20231113/biden-harris-administration-announces- second-round-funding-mitigate.

[55] 42 U.S.C. §4013(a).

[56] See 44 C.F.R. Part 61, Appendix A. Copies of the policy forms are also available on FEMA's website at https://www.fema.gov/flood-insurance/find-form.

[57] 42 U.S.C. §4013(b).

**Table 2.** Maximum available coverage limits for SFIPs by occupancy type

| | Occupancy Type | | |
|---|---|---|---|
| Policy Coverage Type | 1-4 Family | Other Residential | Nonresidential Business, other Nonresidential |
| Combined Building/Contents | $250,000/$100,000 | $500,000/$100,000 | $500,000/$500,000 |
| Contents Only | $100,000 | $100,000 | $500,000 |

Source: FEMA, Flood Insurance Manual, 3. How to Write, revised October 2020, p. 3-3, at https://www.fema.gov/sites/default/files/2020-09/fema_flood-insurance-manual-full-edition_april-oct2020.pdf.

Because SFIP coverage limits are often less than the value of a structure or the value of the property's contents, policyholders can obtain excess flood insurance to cover losses beyond the coverage limit. However, such excess coverage is not sold by the NFIP, and can only be purchased through the private insurance market.

Within the SFIPs sold by the NFIP, there are numerous policy exclusions that are often not understood by policyholders. For example, SFIPs do not provide coverage for alternative living expenses (e.g., the cost of staying in a hotel while a house is being repaired) or business interruption expenses, and SFIPs have limited coverage of basements or crawlspaces.[58] In addition, the SFIP does not cover damage caused by earth movement, including landslides.[59]

## Mandatory Mortgage Purchase Requirement

In a community that participates or has participated in the NFIP, owners of properties in the mapped SFHA[60] are required to purchase flood insurance as

---

[58] For a basic guide to coverage under the SFIP, see FEMA, *Summary of Coverage*, at https://agents.floodsmart.gov/sites/default/files/fema_NFIP-summary-of-coverage_brochure_09-2021.pdf.

[59] The exclusion for earth movement was particularly contentious in the aftermath of Hurricane Sandy. For a basic discussion, see Lloyd Dixon, Noreen Clancy, and Bruce Bender, et al., *Flood Insurance in New York City Following Hurricane Sandy*, RAND Corporation, October 2013, at http://www.rand.org/pubs/research_reports/RR328.html.

[60] For additional information on the Special Flood Hazard Area, see the "Risk Mapping, Assessment, and Planning (Risk MAP) and Flood Insurance Rate Maps (FIRMs)" section of this report.

a condition of receiving a federally backed mortgage. By law and regulation, federal agencies, federally regulated lending institutions, and government-sponsored enterprises must require these property owners to purchase flood insurance as a condition of any mortgage that these entities make, guarantee, or purchase.[61] Examples of the types of lenders that are mandated to issue regulations requiring the purchase of flood insurance related to mortgages include

- federal agency lenders, such as the Department of Veterans Affairs, or
- the government-sponsored enterprises (GSEs), Federal National Mortgage Association (Fannie Mae) and Federal Home Loan Mortgage Corporation (Freddie Mac), or
- federally regulated lending institutions, such as banks covered by the Federal Deposit Insurance Corporation (FDIC) or the Office of the Comptroller of the Currency (OCC).[62]

Property owners falling under this mandate may purchase flood insurance through the NFIP, or through a private company, so long as the private flood insurance provides "flood insurance coverage which is at least as broad as the coverage provided under a [SFIP] ... including when considering deductibles, exclusions, and conditions offered by the insurer."[63]

The implementation of this requirement has proved challenging, with the responsible federal regulators (the Federal Reserve, Farm Credit Administration, Federal Deposit Insurance Corporation, National Credit Union Administration, and Comptroller of the Currency) issuing two separate Notices of Proposed Rulemaking (NPRM) addressing the issue in October

---

[61] 42 U.S.C. §4012a.

[62] 42 U.S.C. §4012a(b)(1)-(3). For examples of regulations and policies implementing this provision, see 12 C.F.R. Parts 12 and 339 for regulations for the OCC and FDIC, respectively, or Federal National Mortgage Association (Fannie Mae), *Servicing Guide, Part B-3-07: Flood Insurance Requirements*, 2019, available at https://selling-guide.fanniemae.com/Selling-Guide/Origination-thru-Closing/Subpart-B7-Insurance/Chapter-B7-3-Property-and-Flood-Insurance/1032999711/B7-3-07-Flood-Insurance-Coverage-Requirements-08-07-2019.htm.

[63] 42 U.S.C. §4012a(b). For additional information on private flood insurance, see CRS Insight IN10450, *Private Flood Insurance and the National Flood Insurance Program (NFIP)*, by Baird Webel and Diane P. Horn; and CRS Report R45242, *Private Flood Insurance and the National Flood Insurance Program*, by Diane P. Horn and Baird Webel.

2013[64] and November 2016.[65] The crux of the implementation issue can be seen as answering the question of who would judge whether specific policies met the "at least as broad as" standard and what criteria would be used in making this judgment? The uncertainty as to whether particular private policies would meet the standard has been seen as "at odds with" greater private participation in the flood insurance marketplace.[66]

On February 12, 2019, the regulators announced a final rule[67] implementing the BW-12 "requirement that regulated lending institutions accept private flood insurance policies." The rule took effect on July 1, 2019. Of particular note, the rule

- "allows institutions to rely on an insurer's written assurances in a private flood insurance policy stating the criteria are met; [and]
- clarifies that institutions may, under certain conditions, accept private flood insurance policies that do not meet the Biggert-Waters Act criteria."

The rule does not apply directly to other federal agencies, nor to the GSEs, which would be subject to separate rulemaking. On November 23, 2020, the Department of Housing and Urban Development released a proposed rule on the acceptance of private flood insurance for Federal Housing Administration-insured mortgages.[68] The proposed rule is similar, but not identical, to that put into place by federal regulators in 2019. The rule has not yet been finalized.

Not all mortgages in the SFHA are affected by this mandatory purchase requirement. For example, a personal mortgage loan between two private parties (such as between family members), or a mortgage issued by a private

---

[64] Department of the Treasury, Federal Reserve System, Federal Deposit Insurance System, Farm Credit Administration, National Credit Union Administration, "Loans in Areas Having Special Flood Hazards," 78(210) *Federal Register* 65107-65142, October 30, 2013.

[65] Department of the Treasury, Federal Reserve System, Federal Deposit Insurance System, Farm Credit Administration, National Credit Union Administration, "Loans in Areas Having Special Flood Hazards—Private Flood Insurance," 81(215) *Federal Register* 78063-78080, November 7, 2016.

[66] See, for example, the response on behalf of the National Association of Insurance Commissioners to the proposed rulemaking on "Loans in Areas Having Special Flood Hazards—Private Flood Insurance," January 6, 2017, at https://www.naic.org/documents/government_relations_comment_letter_federal_banking_private_flood_insurance.pdf.

[67] Department of the Treasury, Federal Reserve System, Federal Deposit Insurance System, Farm Credit Administration, National Credit Union Administration, "Loans in Areas Having Special Flood Hazards," 84(34) *Federal Register* 4953-4975, February 20, 2019.

[68] Department of Housing and Urban Development, "Acceptance of Private Flood Insurance for FHA-Insured Mortgages," 85 *Federal Register* 226, November 23, 2020.

mortgage company that is not then sold on the secondary market to a bank or entity like Fannie Mae, may not require flood insurance. Even if they are not technically required to mandate flood insurance by federal law, the issuing party may still require it as a means of financially securing the property. While the exact percentage of total mortgages requiring flood insurance is unknown, one study suggested at least 77% of all mortgages in SFHAs in 2003 would be subject to the requirement.[69]

Despite the mandatory purchase requirement, not all covered mortgages carry the insurance as dictated. There are no official statistics available from the federal mortgage regulators responsible for implementation of the mandate and no recent reports on compliance with the mandatory purchase requirement. A 2006 study of national compliance with the MPR suggested that compliance rates may have been as low as 43% in some areas of the country (the Midwest), and as high as 88% in others (the West).[70] In a 2013 analysis done following Hurricane Sandy, one study found that approximately 65% of properties in New York City required to have insurance through their mortgage had such insurance.[71] A 2017 study of flood insurance in New York City by the same authors reassessed the 2013 data and suggested that the estimate in their earlier study may have slightly overstated the actual take-up rate, which the 2017 study estimated at 61%. The later study found that compliance with the mandatory purchase requirement by properties in the SFHA with mortgages increased from 61% in 2012 to 73% in 2016. The later study also argued that findings for properties without mortgages indicate the effectiveness of the mandatory purchase requirement, as the 37% take-up rate for properties without mortgages in the SFHA was similar to take-up rates

---

[69] The 77% figure was estimated using the overall percentage of mortgages held by parties subject to the mortgage requirement, and likely is subject to a degree of error. See Richard J. Tobin and Corinne Calfee, *The National Flood Insurance Program's Mandatory Purchase Requirement: Policies, Process, and Stakeholders*, American Institutes for Research, Prepared as part of the Evaluation of the National Flood Insurance Program, March 2005, p. 31, available at https://www.fema.gov/sites/default/files/2020-07/fema_nfip_eval_mandatory_purchase_requirement.pdf.

[70] Lloyd Dixon, Noreen Clancy, and Seth A. Seabury, et al., *The National Flood Insurance Program's Market Penetration Rate: Estimates and Policy Implications*, RAND Corporation, prepared as part of the Evaluation of the National Flood Insurance Program, February 2006, p. 23, available at https://www.rand.org/content/dam/rand/pubs/technical_reports/2006/RAND_TR300.pdf.

[71] Lloyd Dixon, Noreen Clancy, Bruce Bender, et al., *Flood Insurance in New York City Following Hurricane Sandy*, RAND Corporation, 2013, p. 15, available at http://www.rand.org/pubs/research_reports/RR328.html.

outside the SFHA (37% for properties with mortgages and 32% for properties without mortgages).[72]

The escrowing of insurance premiums may increase compliance with the mandatory purchase requirement. Federal mortgage regulators have required the escrowing of flood insurance premiums on certain mortgages in compliance with regulations issued after changes to the law made in 1994.[73] Expanding upon existing requirements, Section 100209 of BW-12,[74] as subsequently revised by Section 25 of HFIAA,[75] has required that regulated lenders start escrowing flood insurance for all mortgages, except if the lending institution is under a regulated size or the loan is a subordinate to another loan. This broader implementation of the escrowing provision began in January 2016, per law and regulations.[76] This requirement may increase compliance with the MPR, but no data on this are available.

## Flood Insurance Policies Outside the Special Flood Hazard Area

FEMA encourages the purchase of policies for properties outside the SHFA both to reduce the financial flood risk of a broader group of individuals, and to expand the policy base of the NFIP writ large, thus improving the fiscal soundness of the NFIP portfolio. Flood insurance is optional for properties outside the SFHA regardless of whether they have a federally backed mortgage.

However, as there is still a risk of flooding outside the SFHA, members of NFIP participating communities with property located in the B, C, or X

[72] Lloyd Dixon, Noreen Clancy, and Benjamin M. Miller, et al., *The Cost and Affordability of Flood Insurance in New York City: Economic Impacts of Rising Premiums and Policy Options for One- to Four-Family Homes*, RAND Corporation, March 2017, pp. 15-18, https://www.rand.org/pubs/research_reports/RR1776.html.

[73] P.L. 103-325, §523; 108 Stat. 2258.

[74] P.L. 112-141, §100209; 126 Stat. 920.

[75] P.L. 113-89, §25 128 Stat. 1030.

[76] See 42 U.S.C. §4012a(d)(1), and the final rule of Office of the Comptroller of the Currency, Treasury; Board of Governors of the Federal Reserve System; Federal Deposit Insurance Corporation; Farm Credit Administration; National Credit Union Administration, "Loans in Areas Having Special Flood Hazards," 80 *Federal Register* 43216, July 21, 2015. For a full explanation of how escrowing had previously worked prior to BW-12, and for how it is being required following BW-12 and HFIAA, see the notice of proposed rulemaking from the federal agency regulators at Office of the Comptroller of the Currency, Treasury; Board of Governors of the Federal Reserve System; Federal Deposit Insurance Corporation; Farm Credit Administration; National Credit Union Administration, "Loans in Areas Having Special Flood Hazards," 79 *Federal Register* 64518, October 29, 2014.

Zones of a FIRM may voluntarily purchase a lower-cost policy, which was until 2022 known as a Preferred Risk Policy (PRP). The PRP classification was retired under Risk Rating 2.0,[77] but owners of low-risk properties can still purchase flood insurance.

## Increased Cost of Compliance (ICC) Coverage

The NFIP requires most policyholders[78] to purchase what is in effect a separate insurance policy to offset the expense of complying with more rigorous building code standards when local ordinances require them to do so. This increased cost of compliance coverage is authorized in law, and rates for the coverage, as well as how much can be paid out for claims, are set by FEMA.[79] Congress has capped the amount that can be paid for ICC coverage at $75.[80] The ICC policy has a separate rate premium structure, and provides an amount up to $30,000 in payments for certain eligible expenses.[81]

For example, when a building is determined by a community to be substantially damaged[82] following a flood, floodplain management standards adopted by local communities can require the building to be rebuilt to current floodplain management requirements, even if the property previously did not need to do so. For instance, the new compliance standard may require the demolition and elevation of the rebuilt building to above the BFE. An ICC claim may then be submitted by the policyholder to offset the cost of complying with the elevation standard. FEMA also makes ICC coverage available if a building has been declared a repetitive loss by a community's floodplain management regulations.[83] However, not all participating NFIP communities have or enforce a "repetitive loss provision" that records,

---

[77] When a PRP policy is renewed under Risk Rating 2.0, its premium will begin increasing until it reaches the full risk- based rate. See National Flood Services, *Risk Rating 2.0: What Is Changing*, https://nationalfloodservices.com/wp-content/uploads/2021/06/Risk-Rating-2.0-What-is-Changing.pdf.

[78] For example, ICC coverage is not required on condominium units and content-only policies.

[79] 42 U.S.C. §4011(b).

[80] Ibid.

[81] For example, for ICC premiums, see FEMA, *Flood Insurance Manual, Appendix J: Rate Tables*, p. J-19, revised October 2020, at https://www.fema.gov/sites/default/files/2020-09/fema_flood-insurance-manual-full-edition_april- oct2020.pdf.

[82] 44 C.F.R. §59.1 defines "substantial damage" as damage of any origin sustained by a structure whereby the cost of restoring the structure to its before damaged condition would equal or exceed 50% of the market value of the structure before the damage occurred.

[83] 42 U.S.C. §4011(b)(1).

declares, and mandates improvements to properties that have experienced repetitive loss. Thus, certain structures that have experienced repetitive loss may not be eligible for ICC payments.[84]

FEMA has not implemented ICC coverage for two conditions that they are authorized to do so by law. These two conditions are for properties that have sustained flood damage on multiple occasions, if the Administrator determines that it is cost-effective and in the best interests of the NFIP, and for properties for which an offer of mitigation assistance is made under various federal assistance programs.[85] FEMA's decision not to implement these provisions has provoked criticism from some stakeholders of the NFIP.[86]

## Servicing of Policies and Claims Management

While FEMA provides the overarching management and oversight of the NFIP, the bulk of the day-to-day operation of the NFIP, including the marketing, sale, writing, and claims management of policies, is handled by private companies. This arrangement between the NFIP and private industry is authorized by statute and guided by regulation.[87] There are two different arrangements that FEMA has established with private industry. The first is the Direct Servicing Agent, or DSA, which operates as a private contractor on behalf of FEMA for individuals seeking to purchase flood insurance policies directly from the NFIP.[88] The second arrangement is called the Write- Your-Own (WYO) Program, where private insurance companies are paid to directly write and service the policies themselves. With either the DSA or WYO Program, the NFIP retains the actual financial risk of paying claims for the policy (i.e., underwrites the policy), and the policy terms and premiums are the same.

---

[84] For additional information on repetitive loss and repetitive loss provisions, see FEMA, *Increased Cost of Compliance (ICC) Coverage*, at https://www.fema.gov/floodplain-management/financial-help/increased-cost-compliance.

[85] See 42 U.S.C. §4011(b)(3) and (4).

[86] See, for example, Association of State Floodplain Managers (ASFPM), *A Vision for Implementing ICC as it Exists in Law Today*, February 29, 2016, at https://www.floods.org/whats-new/in-case-you-missed-it-asfpms-vision-for-implementing-icc-as-it-exists-in-law-today/.

[87] See primarily 42 U.S.C. §4081 and §4018, and 44 C.F.R. Part 62.

[88] The current Direct Servicing Agent is a company called National Flood Services, who were awarded the contract in October 2020. See https://nationalfloodservices.com/press/nfs-awarded-nfip-direct-service-provider-contract/.

Currently, approximately 12.4% of the total NFIP policy portfolio is managed through the DSA, and 87.6% of NFIP policies are sold by the 48 companies participating in the WYO Program.[89] Over the years, the balance between the number of policies serviced by the WYO Program or the DSA has evolved, with the WYOs covering approximately 50% of policies in 1986, and approximately 97% of policies in 2008.[90] Because most purchasers of the NFIP policies never interface directly with a FEMA representative, and only deal with a WYO company or the DSA, they may not be aware that they are actually purchasing insurance from FEMA.

Companies participating in the WYO Program are compensated through a variety of methods, as summarized in *Table 3.* The Government Accountability Office (GAO) and Department of Homeland Security, Office of the Inspector General (DHS IG) have produced a number of reports investigating how much the WYOs were compensated for the services they provided in support of the NFIP.[91] In BW-12, Congress required FEMA to develop and issue a rulemaking on a "methodology for determining the appropriate amounts that property and casualty insurance companies participating in the Write Your Own program should be reimbursed for selling, writing, and servicing flood insurance policies and adjusting flood insurance claims on behalf of the National Flood Insurance Program."[92] This rulemaking was required within a year of enactment of BW-12.[93] FEMA published an Advanced Notice of Proposed Rulemaking (ANPR) to revise the compensation structure of the WYOs on July 8, 2019.[94] GAO reported that FEMA officials said that they would complete an annual analysis of WYO

---

[89] Email correspondence from FEMA Congressional Affairs staff, December 15, 2023. A list of companies participating in the WYO Program is available at https://nfipservices.floodsmart.gov/wyo-program-list.

[90] For additional background on the estimates and history of the WYO Program, see, respectively, U.S. Government Accountability Office, *Private Companies' Participation in the Write Your Own Program*, RCED-87-108, May 29, 1987, at http://www.gao.gov/products/RCED-87-108, and U.S. Government Accountability Office, *Opportunities Exist to Improve Oversight of the WYO Program*, GAO-09-455, August 2009, at http://www.gao.gov/products/GAO-09-455.

[91] For example, see U.S. Government Accountability Office, *Opportunities Exist to Improve Oversight of the WYO Program*, GAO-09-455, August 2009, at http://www.gao.gov/products/GAO-09-455 and DHS Office of Inspector General, *FEMA Does Not Provide Adequate Oversight of Its National Flood Insurance Write Your Own Program*, OIG-16-47, March 8, 2016, at https://www.oig.dhs.gov/assets/Mgmt/2016/OIG-16-47-Mar16.pdf.

[92] P.L. 112-141, §100224; 126 Stat. 936.

[93] BW-12 required the rulemaking to be completed by July 6, 2013.

[94] Federal Emergency Management Agency, "National Flood Insurance Program (NFIP); Revisions to Methodology for Payments to Write Your Own (WYO) Companies," 84(130) *Federal Register* 32,371-32,379, July 8, 2019.

data by the end of FY2020 and that they were reviewing comments received in response to the July 2019 notice.[95] Since the ANPR, FEMA has reviewed the public comments received and engaged the RAND Corporation to conduct research and analysis. RAND's work is informing FEMA's development of a new WYO compensation methodology, which FEMA is still in the process of developing.[96]

**Table 3.** Types of compensation for WYO companies

| Compensation Type | Description |
|---|---|
| Operating and Administrative Expenses | Reimbursement of marketing, operating, and administrative expenses. |
| Commission Allowance | Allowance to meet commissions or salaries of insurance agents. |
| Growth Bonus | Increase in compensation dependent on the extent to which the Company meets the NFIP marketing goals. |
| Allocated Loss Adjustment Expenses (ALAE) | Standard amount of compensation for each individual claim. |
| Unallocated Loss Adjustment Expenses (ULAE) | General overhead (indirect expenses) for settling losses. |
| Special Allocated Loss Adjustment Expenses (SALAE) | Direct expenses that are above what is covered by ALAE. |

Source: Table 1 of DHS Office of Inspector General, FEMA Does Not Provide Adequate Oversight of Its National Flood Insurance Write Your Own Program, OIG-16-47, March 8, 2016, p. 3, at https://www.oig.dhs.gov/assets/Mgmt/2016/OIG-16-47-Mar16.pdf. This replicated table is based on the OIG's analysis of the subsidy arrangement.

Following Hurricane Sandy, there were concerns raised regarding the possible systematic underpayment of claims for flood losses through the NFIP.[97] As a result of these issues, FEMA carried out a process by which Hurricane Sandy survivors could resubmit their NFIP claims to be reevaluated

---

[95] U.S. Government Accountability Office, *Priority Open Recommendations: Department of Homeland Security*, GAO-20-355PR, April 23, 2020, p. 9, https://www.gao.gov/assets/710/706532.pdf.

[96] Email correspondence from FEMA Congressional Affairs staff, December 15, 2023.

[97] For an analysis of the claims issues following Hurricane Sandy, see U.S. Congress, Senate Committee on Banking, Housing, and Urban Affairs, *Assessing and Improving Flood Insurance Management and Accountability in the Wake of Superstorm Sandy*, prepared by Majority Staff Report, 114th Cong., 1st sess., June 22, 2015, at https://www.banking.senate.gov/download/majority-staff-shelby-flood-insurance-report-2015.

by FEMA. FEMA reviewed the resubmitted claims and provided additional claim payments to those deemed warranted in the review, and concluded the Sandy Claims Review Process on March 1, 2018.[98] As of January 29, 2018, approximately 85% of policyholders who requested a review had received additional payments, resulting in approximately $258.6 million in additional claims payments. The remaining 15% of reviewed files received no additional payment.[99] In addition, FEMA settled and litigated lawsuits initiated by claimants following Hurricane Sandy, with 1,631 of the 1,633 court cases settled, resulting in approximately $164 million in settlement payments.[100] The Sandy claims review process was concluded on March 1, 2018.

## Pricing and Premium Rate Structure

Except for certain subsidies, flood insurance rates in the NFIP are directed to be "based on consideration of the risk involved and accepted actuarial principles,"[101] meaning that the rate is reflective to the true flood risk to the property. Essentially, FEMA uses several basic characteristics to classify properties based on flood risks. Structures are evaluated by their specific risk zone on a FIRM, the elevation of the structure relative to the Base Flood Elevation (BFE) in each risk zone, and occupancy type (e.g., single family, other residential, nonresidential, and mobile/manufactured homes), along with other specific determinants of risk. In addition, the premium structure includes estimates for the expenses of the NFIP, including servicing of policies. A detailed discussion of the premium rate structure of the NFIP, and how or why it is and is not actuarially sound, is beyond the scope of this report. However, additional resources exist to assist Congress with this issue.[102]

---

[98] FEMA published a series of fact sheets about the Sandy claims review and legal settlements, which since August 2016 have been called Sandy Claims Review Decision Fact Sheets.

[99] Department of Homeland Security Office of Inspector General, *Unsupported Payments Made to Policyholders Who Participated in the Hurricane Sandy Claims Review Process*, OIG-18-38, Washington, DC, January 24, 2018, https://www.oig.dhs.gov/sites/default/files/assets/2018-01/OIG-18-38-Jan18.pdf.

[100] Ibid.

[101] 42 U.S.C. §4014(a)(1).

[102] See, for example, CRS Report R45999, *National Flood Insurance Program: The Current Rating Structure and Risk Rating 2.0*, by Diane P. Horn; Office of Inspector General, Department of Homeland Security, *FEMA Is Not Effectively Administering a Program to Reduce or Eliminate Damage to Severe Repetitive Loss Properties*, OIG-20-68, Washington, DC, September 8, 2020, pp. 1-34, https://www.oig.dhs.gov/sites/default/files/assets/2020-09/OIG-20-68- Sep20.pdf; several reports from GAO, including U.S. Government Accountability Office, *National Flood Insurance Program: Fiscal*

### *Pre-FIRM Subsidy*

While most premium rates in the NFIP are intended to represent the full flood risk of a given structure, Congress has directed FEMA *not* to charge actuarial rates for properties that were constructed or substantially improved before December 31, 1974, or before the date upon which FEMA has published the first Flood Insurance Rate Map for the community, whichever was later.[103] Therefore, by statute, premium rates charged on structures built before they were first mapped into a flood zone that have not been substantially improved, known as pre-FIRM structures, are allowed to have lower premiums than what would be expected to cover predicted claims. The availability of this pre-FIRM subsidy was intended to allow preexisting floodplain properties to contribute in some measure to prefunding their recovery from a flood disaster instead of relying solely on federal disaster assistance. In essence, the flood insurance could distribute some of the financial burden among those protected by flood insurance and the public.

As of October 2023, approximately 15% of NFIP policies received a pre-FIRM subsidy.[104] Historically, the total number of pre-FIRM policies is relatively stable, but the percentage of those policies by comparison to the total policy base has decreased.[105] The pricing subsidy for pre- FIRM policies is progressively being phased out of the NFIP, as was initially required under Section 100205 of BW-12, as revised by Sections 3 and 5 of HFIAA.[106] Under

---

*Exposure Persists Despite Property Acquisitions*, GAO-20-508, June 2020, pp. 1-50, https://www.gao.gov/assets/710/707821.pdf; U.S. Government Accountability Office, *High-Risk Series: Substantial Efforts Needed to Achieve Greater Progress on High-Risk Areas*, GAO-19+157SP, March 2019, pp. 111-114 and 272-274, https://www.gao.gov/ assets/700/697245.pdf; U.S. Government Accountability Office, *Flood Insurance: Comprehensive Reform Could Improve Solvency and Enhance Resilience*, GAO-17-245, April 2017, pp. 1-58, https://www.gao.gov/ assets/690/ 684354.pdf; U.S. Government Accountability Office, *Continued Progress Needed to Fully Address Prior Recommendations on Rate-Setting Methods*, GAO-16-59, March 2016, at http://www. gao.gov/assets/680/675855.pdf/; National Academies of Sciences, *Affordability of National Flood Insurance Program Premiums: Part 1*, 2015, Chapter 3, National Flood Insurance Pricing, Policies, and Premiums, http://www.nap.edu/ catalog/21709/ affordability-of-national-flood-insurance-program-premiums-report-1; Congressional Budget Office, *The National Flood Insurance Program: Factors Affecting Actuarial Soundness*, November 2009, https://www.cbo.gov/sites/default/files/ cbofiles/ftpdocs/ 106xx/doc10620/11-04-floodinsurance.pdf.

[103] 42 U.S.C. §4015(c).

[104] Email correspondence from FEMA Congressional Affairs staff, December 15, 2023.

[105] For an historical prospective on the percentages of subsidized policies in the NFIP, see Figure 1 of U.S. Government Accountability Office, *Flood Insurance: More Information Needed on Subsidized Properties*, GAO-13-607, July 2013, p. 7, at http://www.gao.gov/assets/ 660/655734.pdf.

[106] P.L. 112-141, 126 Stat. 917; and P.L. 113-89, 128 Stat. 1021-1022; respectively.

current law, all premiums for pre-FIRM properties will eventually reach actuarially sound rates (i.e., the rate equivalent structures pay without the subsidy, reflecting true flood risk), but at a different pace of phaseout depending on the property type. *Table 4* provides an adaptation of a table from GAO regarding the multifaceted phaseout of the pre-FIRM subsidy following BW-12, as revised by HFIAA. In summary, HFIAA slowed the rate of phaseout of the pre-FIRM subsidy for most primary residences, but retained the pace of the phaseout of the subsidy from BW-12 for business properties and secondary homes. In addition, HFIAA created a minimum and maximum increase in the amount for the phaseout of pre-FIRM subsidies for all primary residences of 5%-15% annually. Unless otherwise noted, the percentage increases are based on the current premium (e.g., a 15% annual increase from the prior year premium), rather than the percentage difference between the current premium and the actuarial rate (i.e., a rate increase of 25% does not mean the pre-FIRM subsidy is eliminated in four years).

**Table 4.** Phaseout of NFIP Pre-FIRM premium subsidy following legislation

| Annual Rate of Phaseout | | |
|---|---|---|
| Property Type or Circumstance | *After BW-12* | *After HFIAA (current)* |
| Primary residence | | |
| and all other properties not included in other categories | Five-year phaseout starting after property is identified on new FIRM[a] | 5-15%[b] |
| purchased after July 6, 2012 | Eliminated immediately | Reinstated, 5-15%[b] |
| not insured by NFIP as of July 6, 2012 | Eliminated immediately | Reinstated, 5-15%[b] |
| Nonprimary residence | 25% | 25% |
| Nonresidential properties other than business properties[c] | 25% | 5-15%[b] |
| Business properties | 25% | 25% |
| Property with severe repetitive loss[d] | 25% | 25% |
| Property with substantial cumulative damage[e] | 25% | 25% |
| Property with substantial damage or improvement after July 6, 2012[f] | 25% | 25% |
| Owner let NFIP policy lapse | Eliminated immediately[g] | Eliminated immediately[h] |
| Prospective insured who refuses to accept offers for mitigation assistance[i] | Eliminated immediately | Eliminated immediately |

Source: CRS analysis of P.L. 112-141 and P.L. 113-89. Adapted from Figure 3 from U.S. Government Accountability Office, Forgone Premiums Cannot Be Measured and FEMA Should Validate and

Monitor Data System Changes, GAO-15-111, December 2014, p. 10, at http://www.gao.gov/assets/670/667413.pdf.

Notes:

[a] All properties with subsidies not being phased out at higher rates or already eliminated were required to begin paying actuarial rates following a five-year period, phased in at 20% a year, after a revised or updated flood insurance rate map (FIRM) was issued for the area containing the property. Thus, this provision would have gradually eliminated both pre-FIRM and grandfathering subsidies for all properties before being struck by the Homeowner Flood Insurance Affordability Act of 2014 (HFIAA; P.L. 113-89). See Section 100207 of P.L. 112-141, 126 Stat. 919.

[b] HFIAA permits individual property increases of up to 18%, but limits the rate class increases to 15% per year. See 42 U.S.C. §4015(e).

[c] Prior to BW-12, FEMA did not distinguish business properties from other nonresidential properties such as houses of worship, nonprofits, and schools. In order to implement the requirement that business properties should have their rates phased out at 25% annually, FEMA needed to increase all nonresidential properties at that rate. However, with greater distinguishing between property types possible with new data, and phaseout rate increases being capped by HFIAA, nonresidential properties other than business properties are now having their subsidies phased out at 5%-15% instead of 25%. For more discussion on this issue, see U.S. Government Accountability Office, Status of FEMA's Implementation of the Biggert-Waters Act, as Amended, GAO-15-178, February 2015, p. 22, at http://www.gao.gov/products/GAO-15-178, and FEMA, April 1, 2019 and January 1, 2020 Program Changes, WYO Program Bulletin W-15046, Attachment A, at https://nfipservices.floodsmart.gov/sites/default/files/w-18021a.pdf.

[d] Severe repetitive loss properties are those that have incurred four or more claim payments exceeding $5,000 each, with a cumulative amount of such payments over $20,000; or at least two claims with a cumulative total exceeding the value of the property. See 42 U.S.C. §4014(h) and 44 C.F.R. §79.2(h).

[e] Any property that has incurred flood-related damage in which the cumulative amounts of payments under the NFIP equaled or exceeded the fair market value of such property. See 42 U.S.C. §4014(a)(2)(C).

[f] Any property that has experienced or sustained substantial damage exceeding 50% of the fair market value or substantial improvement exceeding 50% of the fair market value. See 42 U.S.C. §4014(a)(2)(E). Section 100205(a)(1)(A) of BW-12 (P.L. 112-141, 126 Stat. 917) originally set the substantial improvement amount at 30%, but HFIAA raised the percentage to 50% of fair market value.

[g] As required by Section 100205(a)(1)(B) of BW-12 (P.L. 112-141, 126 Stat. 917), only for NFIP policies that lapsed in coverage as a result of the deliberate choice of the policyholder. If a policy lapses for other reasons, rate increases of 25% may have applied if the policy qualifies under one of the other property categories.

[h] FIAA revised the condition for policy lapse to be for NFIP all policies that lapsed in coverage unless the decision of the policyholder to permit a lapse in coverage was as a result of the property covered by the policy no longer being required to retain such coverage. For any policy that lapses but is not automatically charged full-risk rates, rate increases of 25% or 5% to 15% may apply if the policy qualifies under one of the other categories stated above. See 42 U.S.C. §4014(g)(1).

[i] Any prospective insured who refuses to accept any offer for mitigation assistance by FEMA (including an offer to relocate), including an offer of mitigation assistance following a Stafford Act major disaster; or in connection with a repetitive loss property or a severe repetitive loss property. See 42 U.S.C. §4014(g)(2).

### *Newly Mapped Subsidy*

Congress introduced a new form of subsidy in HFIAA, for owners of properties newly mapped into a SFHA.[107] The newly mapped procedure applies to properties previously in zones B, C, X, D, AR, or A99 (see *Table 1*), which are newly mapped into a SFHA on or after April 1, 2015, if the applicant obtains coverage that is effective within 12 months of the map revision date. The newly mapped procedure does not apply to properties mapped into a SFHA by the initial FIRM for a community entering the NFIP, and certain properties may be excluded based on their loss history.[108] The rate for eligible newly mapped properties is equal to the (now discontinued) PRP rate, but with a higher Federal Policy Fee,[109] for the first 12 months following the map revision. After the first year, the newly mapped rate will begin its transition to a full-risk rate, with annual increases to newly mapped policy premiums calculated using a multiplier that varies by the year of the map change.[110] Annual increases are restricted to no more than 18% per year. As of October 2023, about 7% of NFIP policies received a newly mapped subsidy.[111]

### *Grandfathering Cross-Subsidy*

Using the authority to set rate classes for the NFIP and to offer lower than actuarial premiums,[112] FEMA allows property owners to maintain their old flood insurance rate class if their property is remapped into a new flood rate class. This practice is colloquially referred to as "grandfathering," "administrative grandfathering," or the "grandfather rule" and is separate and distinct from the pre-FIRM subsidy.[113] To understand the grandfather rule,

---

[107] P.L. 113-89, §6; 128 Stat.1028, as codified at 42 U.S.C. §4015(i).

[108] For properties which are excluded from, or ineligible for, the newly mapped subsidy, see FEMA, *Flood Insurance Manual, 3. How to Write*, revised October 2020, pp. 3-40 to 3-48, https://www.fema.gov/sites/default/files/2020-09/fema_flood-insurance-manual-full-edition_april-oct2020.pdf.

[109] The Federal Policy Fee (FPF) pays for certain administrative expenses of the NFIP, including some of the costs of mapping. The FPF is $47 for all policies other than residential condominium buildings with more than 20 units, for which the FPF is priced based on the number of units. See FEMA, *Flood Insurance Manual, 3. How to Write*, revised October 2022, pp. 3-50 and 3-51, https://www.fema.gov/sites/default/files/documents/fema_nfip-flood-insurance-full- manual_102022.pdf.

[110] FEMA, *Attachment A: April 1, 2019 and January 1, 2020 Program Changes: A Summary*, at https://nfipservices.floodsmart.gov/sites/default/files/w-18021a.pdf.

[111] Email correspondence from FEMA Congressional Affairs staff, December 15, 2023.

[112] 42 U.S.C. §4013(a).

[113] For a full description, see FEMA, *NFIP Grandfathering Rules for Agents*, March 2016, at https://www.fema.gov/media-library-data/1488482596393-dcc52e6c120c9327dcd75f1c08e802e4/GrandfatheringForAgents_03_2016.pdf.

consider a hypothetical property X that is currently mapped into one flood zone (e.g., Zone AE), and is built to the proper building code and standards. If property X then is remapped to a new flood zone (e.g., Zone VE) and has maintained continuous insurance coverage under the NFIP, the owner of property X can pay the flood insurance rate and premium based on the prior mapped zone (i.e., pay the AE rate instead of the higher VE rate). A policyholder with a property may also be grandfathered if the elevation of a base flood is changed in a map, but the property itself does not change flood zones.[114]

Congress eliminated the practice of offering grandfathering to policyholders after new maps were issued in BW-12, but then subsequently reinstated the practice in HFIAA.[115] As of October 2023, about 15% of NFIP policies were grandfathered.[116]

FEMA does not consider the practice of grandfathering to be a subsidy for the NFIP, per se, because the discount provided to an individual policyholder is cross-subsidized by other policyholders in the NFIP. Thus, while grandfathering does intentionally allow grandfathered policyholders to pay premiums that are less than their known actuarial rate, the discount is offset by others in the same rate class as the grandfathered policyholder. FEMA tries to recoup lost revenue by charging higher rates for other policies in the SFHA. It is not clear, however, whether the NFIP is increasing other SFHA policy premiums by an amount equal to the discount from other NFIP risk-based rates that are being paid by the grandfathered properties.[117]

### *Community Rating System*

Through a program called the Community Rating System (CRS), FEMA encourages communities to improve upon the minimum floodplain management standards that are required to participate in the NFIP. The CRS

---

[114] For a description of the types of grandfathering, see National Academies of Sciences, *Affordability of National Flood Insurance Program Premiums: Part 1*, 2015, p. 43, at http://www.nap.edu/catalog/21709/affordability-of-national-flood-insurance-program-premiums-report-1.

[115] P.L. 112-141, §100207 amended the law to require that when a property has a revised or updated flood rate class with a new flood map, the "risk premium rate charged for flood insurance on such property adjusted to accurately reflect the current risk of flood to such property" (126 Stat. 919), thus eliminating the ability to grandfather. This provision was struck by P.L. 113-89, 4; 128 Stat. 1022.

[116] Email correspondence from FEMA Congressional Affairs staff, December 15, 2023.

[117] National Academies of Sciences, *Affordability of National Flood Insurance Program Premiums: Part 1*, 2015, p. 43, at http://www.nap.edu/catalog/21709/affordability-of-national-flood-insurance-program-premiums-report-1.

program, as authorized by law, is intended to incentivize the reduction of flood and erosion risk, as well as the adoption of more effective measures to protect natural and beneficial floodplain functions.[118] FEMA awards points that increase a community's "class" rating in the CRS on a scale of 1 to 10, with 1 being the highest ranking. Points are awarded for an array of improvements for how the community informs its public on flood risk; maps and regulates its floodplain; reduces possible flood damage; and provides immediate warnings and responds to flooding incidents.[119] Starting at Class 9, policyholders in a CRS community receive a 5% discount on their SFIP premiums, with increasing discounts of 5% per class until reaching Class 1, and at that level, policyholders can receive a 45% discount on their SFIP premiums.

Under Risk Rating 2.0, these discounts are available to all policyholders in the community.

In order to participate in the CRS program, a community must apply to FEMA and document its creditable improvements through site visits and assessments. As of October 2023, 1,505 communities participate in the CRS program, which represents approximately 6.6% of the total number of communities in the NFIP.[120] Information on how highly rated a community is available online.[121]

The CRS discount is cross-subsidized and shared across all SFIP policies on a state basis. At a national level, the average CRS discount is 13.8% of total full risk premium in CRS-participating communities. To offset the CRS discounts, the NFIP applies a premium load across all policies in each state, in both CRS and non-CRS communities. When a community's CRS discount is lower than the average discount in that state, it could result in the CRS load being higher than the CRS discount being offered in that community. This situation would occur only in states with a high proportion of CRS-participating communities with high CRS discounts.[122]

---

[118] 42 U.S.C. §4022(b)(1).

[119] For a full listing of possible creditable activities in the Community Rating System (CRS), see FEMA, *NFIP Community Rating Coordinator's Manual 2017*, at https://www.fema.gov/sites/default/files/documents/fema_community-rating-system_coordinators-manual_2017.pdf.

[120] See FEMA, *Community Rating System*, https://www.fema.gov/floodplain-management/community-rating-system.

[121] See FEMA, *Community Rating System Eligible Communities*, tes/default/files/documents/fema_crs_eligible- communities_oct-2023.pdf.

[122] Email correspondence from FEMA Congressional Affairs staff, December 15, 2023.

### *Affordability Study and Framework*

Congress has expressed concern related to the perceived affordability of flood insurance premiums. In BW-12, Congress required FEMA to commission a study with the National Academy of Sciences (NAS) regarding participation in the NFIP and the affordability of premiums. The Affordability Study was not finished by its original deadline (270 days following enactment of BW-12). Congress amended the authorization for the Study while also extending the deadline in HFIAA.[123] The NAS Affordability Study report was published in two parts.[124] In HFIAA, Congress also required FEMA to develop a Draft Affordability Framework "that proposes to address, via programmatic and regulatory changes, the issues of affordability of flood insurance sold under the National Flood Insurance Program, including issues identified in the affordability study."[125] Due 18 months following the submission of the Affordability Study, the deadline for the Framework, based on FEMA's stated date of submittal of the Affordability Study, was September 10, 2017.[126] FEMA published their Affordability Framework on April 17, 2018.[127]

FEMA does not currently have the authority to implement an affordability program, nor does NFIP's current rate structure provide the funding required to support an affordability program. If an affordability program were to be funded from NFIP funds, this would require either raising flood insurance rates for NFIP policyholders or diverting resources from another existing use.

Alternatively, an affordability program could be funded fully or partially by congressional appropriation.[128]

---

[123] See P.L. 112-141, §100236; 126 Stat. 957; as amended by P.L. 113-89, §16; 128 Stat. 1026.

[124] See National Research Council of the National Academies, *Affordability of National Flood Insurance Program Premiums: Report 1*, 2015, at http://www.nap.edu/catalog/21709/affordability-of-national-flood-insurance-program-premiums-report-1; and National Research Council of the National Academies, *Affordability of National Flood Insurance Program Premiums: Report 2*, 2016, at http://www.nap.edu/catalog/21848/affordability-of-national-flood- insurance-program-premiums-report-2.

[125] §9(a) of P.L. 113-89, 128 Stat. 1024.

[126] §9(c) of P.L. 113-89, 128 Stat. 1024. FEMA has stated it officially submitted the Affordability Study on March 10, 2016 (email correspondence with FEMA Congressional Affairs staff, March 10, 2016). However, Part 2 of the Affordability Study was available from the NAS website on December 11, 2015.

[127] FEMA, *An Affordability Framework for the National Flood Insurance Program*, Washington, DC, April 17, 2018, at https://www.fema.gov/sites/default/files/2020-05/Affordability_april_2018.pdf.

[128] For additional information on NFIP affordability, see CRS Report R47000, *Options for Making the National Flood Insurance Program More Affordable*, by Diane P. Horn.

***Risk Rating 2.0***

FEMA has introduced a new rating system known as Risk Rating 2.0,[129] which represents the biggest change to the way the NFIP calculates flood insurance premiums since its inception.[130] The new rates went into effect on October 1, 2021, for new NFIP policies and went into effect on April 1, 2022, for existing policyholders.[131] Under the change, premiums for individual properties are tied to their actual flood risk and flood zones are no longer used in calculating a property's flood insurance premium, in contrast to the legacy rating system in which properties with the same NFIP flood risk were charged the same rates. Under Risk Rating 2.0 the premium is calculated based on the specific features of an individual property. Risk Rating 2.0 incorporates a broader range of flood frequencies and sources, such as pluvial flooding, than the legacy rating system, which only considered the potential for coastal storm surge and fluvial (river) flooding.

However, flood zones will still be used for floodplain management purposes, and the boundary of the Special Flood Hazard Area will still be required for the mandatory purchase requirement. Risk Rating 2.0 continues the overall policy of phasing out NFIP subsidies, but cannot increase rates annually beyond the caps on annual premium increases which are set in statute[132] (see *Table 4).*

## Nonparticipating Communities and Community Suspension

FEMA enforces two regulatory conditions—probation and suspension—for removing a participating community from the NFIP. Whether or not a particular community has either been placed on probation or suspended can be found using the NFIP's Community Status Book.[133] Notably, a community cannot be removed from the NFIP because of increased or excess flood insurance claims and losses. Rather, probation and suspension only occur if

---

[129] For additional information on Risk Rating 2.0, see CRS Report R45999, *National Flood Insurance Program: The Current Rating Structure and Risk Rating 2.0*, by Diane P. Horn, and CRS Insight IN11777, *National Flood Insurance Program Risk Rating 2.0: Frequently Asked Questions*, by Diane P. Horn.

[130] See FEMA, *Risk Rating 2.0: Equity in Action*, at https://www.fema.gov/flood-insurance/risk-rating.

[131] Ibid.

[132] 42 U.S.C. §4015(e).

[133] See FEMA's website for the Community Status Book at https://www.fema.gov/flood-insurance/work-with-nfip/community-status-book.

the community fails to uphold its obligations related to floodplain management.

A community can be placed on probation by FEMA if it is found that it is failing to adequately enforce the floodplain management standards it has adopted. As established by regulations, probation can result in a fee of $50 being charged to all policyholders in the community while the community is given time to rectify FEMA's concerns regarding their implementation of the floodplain management standards. Ultimately, if the community does not correct its cited deficiencies after given time periods described in regulations, the community will be suspended from the NFIP by FEMA.[134]

A community can also be involuntarily suspended from the NFIP for either

- failing to adopt an approved floodplain map and an approved set of floodplain management standards within the time periods required by regulations; or
- repealing or revising its floodplain management standards to a level below the minimum standards set forth in regulations.[135]

A suspended community may be reinstated to the NFIP once the relevant errors or deficiencies provoking the suspension have been resolved to meet FEMA's specification.

Communities that have been suspended or those communities that do not participate in the NFIP can face significant consequences. Primarily, members of these communities are not able to purchase primary flood insurance through the NFIP, which may result in significant uninsured property risk in that community. However, communities may elect not to participate in the NFIP because they have very little flood risk to begin with, given their particular geography or climate.

In addition, if a community does not participate in, or has been suspended from, the NFIP but has been previously mapped by FEMA for flood hazards, it is difficult for the community and policyholders to access other forms of federal assistance for areas in the floodplain.[136] For example, by law, no

---

[134] For additional details on probation, see 44 C.F.R. 59.24(b) and (c).

[135] See 44 C.F.R. §59.24(a) and (d).

[136] For more on how individuals may receive assistance following a flood, see CRS Report R44808, Federal Disaster Assistance: The National Flood Insurance Program and Other Federal Disaster Assistance Programs Available to Individuals and Households After a

federal assistance may be provided for acquisition or construction purposes in an area that has been identified as having special flood hazards unless the property is covered by flood insurance.[137] Likewise, federally backed mortgages still require flood insurance for properties in the SFHA, so these property-owners would be required to obtain such insurance in the private market. A community is allowed to leave the NFIP at its will, but the potential consequences of that decision are similar to those if the community has been suspended.

## Funding

The funding for the NFIP is primarily maintained in an authorized account called the National Flood Insurance Fund (NFIF).[138] Generally, the NFIP has been funded through three methods:

- receipts from the premiums of flood insurance policies, including fees and surcharges;
- direct annual appropriations for specific costs of the NFIP; and
- borrowing from the U.S. Treasury when the balance of the NFIF has been insufficient to pay the NFIP's obligations (e.g., insurance claims).

This section of the report briefly discusses each of these three methods of NFIP funding.

### Premium Fees and Surcharges

As of December 31, 2022, the written premium, fees, and surcharges on approximately 4.72 million policies in force was about $4.6 billion.[139] Included within the premiums are several fees and surcharges on flood insurance policies mandated by law. First, the Federal Policy Fee (FPF) was

---

Flood, by Diane P. Horn. For additional details on the effects of suspension, see FEMA's website at https://www.fema.gov/glossary/suspension.

[137] 42 U.S.C. §4012a(a).

[138] The NFIF is authorized by 42 U.S.C. §4017.

[139] FEMA, *Watermark, FY2022, Fourth Quarter*, https://www.fema.gov/sites/default/ files/documents/fema_watermark- q4-fy22.pdf.

authorized by Congress in 1990 and helps pay for the administrative expenses of the program, including floodplain mapping and some of the insurance operations.[140] The amount of the FPF is set by FEMA and can increase or decrease year to year. In April 2016, the FPF was set at a flat rate of $50 for SFIPs, and $25 for PRPs. In October 2017, the FPF was set at $25 for contents-only policies.[141] The FPF is now $47 for all NFIP policies other than residential condominiums with more than 20 units, for which the FPF is reduced according to the number of units.[142]

Second, a Reserve Fund assessment was authorized by Congress in BW-12 to establish and maintain a Reserve Fund to cover future claim and debt expenses, especially those from catastrophic disasters.[143] By law, FEMA is ultimately required to maintain a reserve ratio of 1% of the total loss exposure through the Reserve Fund assessment.[144] As of February 2023, the amount required for the reserve fund ratio was approximately $13 billion.[145] However, FEMA is allowed to phase in the reserve fund assessment to obtain the ratio over time, with an intended target of not less than 7.5% of the 1% reserve fund ratio in each fiscal year (so, using February 2023 figures, not less than approximately $975 million each year).

Since April 2016, using its discretion, FEMA has charged every NFIP policy a Reserve Fund assessment. The Reserve Fund assessment has increased from its original status, in October 2013, of 5% on all SFIPs and 0% on PRPs to 15% of the premium charged for all policies.[146] The reserve fund assessment was increased to 18% on April 1, 2020.[147]

In addition to the Reserve Fund assessment, all NFIP policies are also assessed a surcharge following the passage of HFIAA.[148] The amount of the surcharge is dependent on the type of property being insured. For primary

---

[140] 42 U.S.C. §4014(a)(1)(B)(iii).

[141] See FEMA, *Flood Insurance Manual, Appendix J: Rate Tables*, p. 3-49, revised April 2021, https://www.fema.gov/sites/default/files/documents/fema_nfip-flood-insurance-full-manual_102022.pdf.

[142] See FEMA, *Flood Insurance Manual: How To Write*, pp. 3-50 and 3-51, revised October 1, 2022, https://www.fema.gov/sites/default/files/documents/fema_nfip-flood-insurance-full-manual_102022.pdf.

[143] §100212 of P.L. 112-141, 126 Stat. 992, as codified at 42 U.S.C. §4017a.

[144] 42 U.S.C. §4017a(b).

[145] Calculated by CRS using data provided by FEMA Congressional Affairs staff February 8, 2023.

[146] See Federal Emergency Management Agency, *Flood Insurance Manual, Appendix J: Rate Tables*, p. J-16, revised October 2020, at https://www.fema.gov/sites/default/files/2020-09/fema_flood-insurance-manual-full-edition_april- oct2020.pdf.

[147] Ibid.

[148] §8(a) of P.L. 113-89, 128 Stat. 1023.

residences, the charge is $25; for all other properties, the charge is $250.[149] Revenues from these surcharges are deposited into the Reserve Fund.

## Appropriations and Offsetting Receipts

*Table 5* displays how Congress has appropriated and authorized offsetting receipts for the NFIP from FY2015 to FY2023. As provided for in law, all premiums from the sale of NFIP insurance are transferred to FEMA and deposited in the NFIF.[150] Congress then authorizes FEMA to withdraw funds from the NFIF, and use those funds for specified purposes needed to operate the NFIP. In addition to premiums, Congress has also provided annual appropriations to supplement floodplain mapping activities. In addition to the mix of discretionary and mandatory funding levels indicated in *Table 5*, which are set in appropriations legislation, fluctuating levels of mandatory spending occur in the NFIP in order to pay and adjust claims on affected NFIP policies.[151]

## Borrowing from the U.S. Treasury, NFIP Debt

Congress has authorized FEMA to borrow no more than $30.425 billion from the U.S. Treasury in order to operate the NFIP. The authorization for this borrowing would be reduced to $1 billion after September 30, 2024, were the NFIP to be allowed to lapse.[152] In January 2017, the NFIP borrowed $1.6 billion due to losses in 2016 (the August 2016 Louisiana floods and Hurricane Matthew). On September 22, 2017, the NFIP borrowed the remaining $5.825 billion from the Treasury to cover claims from Hurricane Harvey, Hurricane Irma, and Hurricane Maria, reaching the NFIP's authorized borrowing limit of $30.425 billion.[153] On October 26, 2017, Congress cancelled $16 billion of NFIP debt, making it possible for the program to pay claims for Hurricanes

---

[149] For a description of how the surcharge is applied to different policy types, see FEMA, *The HFIAA Surcharge Fact Sheet*, April 2015, https://dlnreng.hawaii.gov/nfip/wp-content/uploads/sites/11/2015/07/HFIAA-Surcharge-Fact- Sheet_Final-April-2015.pdf.

[150] 42 U.S.C. §4017(b).

[151] This mandatory spending is authorized by 42 U.S.C. §4017(d)(1). All other expenses using the NFIF must be authorized in appropriations acts, per 42 U.S.C. §4017(f).

[152] 42 U.S.C. §4016(a).

[153] FEMA, *The Watermark*, Fiscal Year 2018, First Quarter, vol. 1, March 21, 2018, at https://www.fema.gov/sites/default/files/2020-05/FIMA_Watermark_FY18_Q1.pdf.

Harvey, Irma, and Maria.[154] This represents the first time that NFIP debt has been cancelled, although Congress appropriated funds between 1980 and 1985 to repay NFIP debt.[155] FEMA borrowed another $6.1 billion on November 9, 2017, to fund estimated 2017 losses, including those incurred by Hurricanes Harvey, Irma, and Maria and anticipated programmatic activities, bringing the debt up to $20.525 billion. The NFIP has not borrowed since 2017 and currently has $9.9 billion of remaining borrowing authority.[156]

The NFIP's debt to the U.S. Treasury cannot be tied directly to any single incident, as any insurance claim paid by the NFIP is in some way responsible for the existing debt of the NFIP (i.e., a dollar paid in claims, and therefore expended by the NFIP, following a minor flooding incident is no different than a dollar paid following a major hurricane). However, the NFIP was forced to borrow heavily to pay claims in the aftermath of three catastrophic flood seasons, the 2005 hurricane season (particularly Hurricanes Katrina, Rita, and Wilma), Hurricane Sandy in 2012, and Hurricanes Harvey, Irma, and Maria in 2017.[157] For example, following Hurricane Sandy, Congress passed P.L. 113-1 to increase the borrowing limit of the NFIP from $20.775 billion to the current $30.425 billion. Prior to Hurricane Katrina in 2005, the NFIP had generally been able to cover its costs, borrowing relatively small amounts from the U.S. Treasury to pay claims, and then repaying the loans with interest.

The NFIP's debt is conceptually owed by current and future participants in the NFIP, as the insurance program itself owes the debt to the Treasury and pays for accruing interest on that debt through the premium revenues of policyholders. For example, from FY2006 to FY2022 (i.e., since the NFIP borrowed funds following Hurricane Katrina), the NFIP has paid $2.82 billion in principal repayments and $6.17 billion in interest to service the debt through the premiums collected on insurance policies.[158] Currently the NFIP is paying approximately $1.7 million in interest per day on the debt accrued from past

[154] P.L. 115-72, Title III, §308.

[155] Funds for "repayment under notes" were appropriated in P.L. 96-526, 94 Stat. 3053; P.L. 97-101, 95 Stat. 1425; P.L. 97-272, 96 Stat. 1169; P.L. 98-45, 97 Stat. 228; P.L. 98-371, 98 Stat. 1224; and P.L. 99-160, 99 Stat. 918.

[156] FEMA, *Watermark, FY2022, Fourth Quarter*, https://www.fema.gov/sites/default/files/documents/fema_watermark- q4-fy22.pdf.

[157] For accounting of the NFIP's premium revenues and claims/loss data, see *FEMA Watermark: National Flood Insurance Program Financial Statements*, at https://www.fema.gov/flood-insurance/work-with-nfip/watermark- financial-statements.

[158] Email from FEMA Congressional Affairs Staff, November 6, 2023.

**Table 5.** Budget authority for the NFIP, FY2015-FY2023

(millions of dollars of budget authority, available for the fiscal year unless otherwise indicated)

| Form of Budget Authority | Activity | FY2015 P.L. 114-4 | FY2016 P.L. 114-113 | FY2017 P.L. 115-31 | FY2018 P.L. 115-141 | FY2019 P.L. 116-6 | FY2020 P.L. 116-93 | FY2021 P.L. 116-260 | FY2022 P.L. 117-103 | FY2023 P.L. 118-47 |
|---|---|---|---|---|---|---|---|---|---|---|
| Discretionary appropriations | Flood hazard mapping and risk analysis programa (available until expended) | $100.0 | $190.0 | $177.5 | $262.6 | $262.5 | $263.0 | $263.0 | $275.5 | $281.475 |
| Spending authority from offsetting collections, discretionary | Salaries and expenses associated with flood management and flood insurance operations | $23.8 | $25.3 | $13.4b | $13.57b | $13.86b | $14.005b | $13.906b | $15.706b | $18.917b |
| | Floodplain management and flood mappingc | $155.5 | $155.9 | $168.4 | $189.9 | $188.3 | $192.777 | $190.506 | $199.0 | $221.066 |
| Spending authority from offsetting collections, mandatory (amount is shown as a limitation provided in appropriations legislation) | Operating expenses | $136.0 | $133.3 | $147.0b | $165.2b | $176.3b | $192.439b | $181.021b | $197.393b | $230.504b |
| | Commissions and taxes of agents | $1,139.0 | $1,123.0 | $1,123.0 | $1,123.0 | $1,123.0 | $1,151.0 | $1,164.0 | $876.743 | $1,300.0 |
| | Interest on Treasury borrowingsd | Such sums as necessary | Such sums as necessary | Such sums as necessary | Such sums as necessary | Such sums as necessary | Such sums as necessary | Such sums as necessary | Such sums as necessary | Such sums as necessary |
| | Flood mitigation assistance (available until expended) | $150.0 | $175.0 | $175.1 | $175.0 | $175.0 | $175.0 | $175.0 | $175.0 | $175.0 |
| | Flood Insurance Advocate | $5.0 | $5.0 | $5.0 | $5.0 | $5.0 | $5.0 | $5.0 | $5.0 | $5.0 |

Source: CRS analysis of P.L. 114-4, P.L. 114-113, P.L. 115-31, P.L. 115-141, P.L. 116-6, P.L. 116-93, P.L. 116-260,, P.L. 117-103, and P.L. 118-47.

Notes:

[a] Generally, for necessary expenses, including administrative costs, related to the Risk MAP program authorized by 42 U.S.C. §§4101, 4101a, 4101b, 4101c, 4101d, and 4101e.

[b] The budgets from FY2017 include the amount of offsetting collections for flood insurance operations within the "operating expenses" activity, instead of the broader "salaries and expenses associated with flood management and flood insurance operations" activity as was done previously in P.L. 114-4 and P.L. 114-113.

[c] Offsetting receipts for "floodplain management and flood mapping" can generally be viewed as supplementing the discretionary appropriation for "flood hazard mapping and risk analysis program."

[d] The amount of interest paid on borrowed amounts for the U.S. Treasury fluctuates annually based on a number of factors, including the interest rate of the borrowing; the available funds for interest and principal payments after claims payments; the amount borrowed; how the debt is being serviced in loans, and fiscal decisions by FEMA to build the Reserve Fund as opposed to paying off principal and interest on the debt. FEMA reported interest payments of approximately

[e] $318.59 million in FY2015, $345.32 million in FY2016, $393.76 million in FY2017, $367.64 million in FY2018, $415.34 in FY2019, $216.82 in FY2020, $356.81 in FY2021, and $143.3 in FY2022 quarters 1 and 2 (sources: FEMA, Watermark, FY2022, Second Quarter, https://www.fema.gov/sites/default/files/documents/fema_fy22- q2-watermark.pdf and FEMA, National Flood Insurance Program Debt Repayment Report, as of March 31, 2020, Report to Congress and the Secretary of the Treasury, May 17, 2021. Provided by FEMA Congressional Affairs staff. Not available online.

events.[159] FEMA predicts that over the next 10 years the NFIP will pay an additional $5.8 billion in interest expenses, and will have paid $10.6 billion in total interest expenses by the end of FY2029.[160]

As required by law, FEMA submits semiannual debt repayment reports to Congress on how the borrowed amount from the U.S. Treasury could be repaid within a 10-year period.[161] The most recent report concluded that, although the NFIP's financial position is expected to improve over the time period, it is not possible for the NFIP, as currently structured, to fully repay $20.525 billion in debt over the next 10 years.[162]

Whether or not FEMA will ultimately be able to pay off the debt is largely dependent on future insurance claims, namely if a catastrophic flooding incident such as Hurricanes Harvey, Sandy, or Katrina occurs again and with what frequency. FEMA noted that the latest private sector catastrophe modeling demonstrates that such events are not outside the expected range of NFIP losses. A single storm in the United States the size of Hurricane Katrina or larger ($21.2 billion in present dollars) has a 1%-2% chance of occurring in any given year. A coastal flood event at least as large as Hurricane Sandy ($9.8 billion in present dollars), or an inland flood event at least as large as the 2016 Louisiana flood ($2.6 billion in present dollars) each have a 2%-5% chance of occurring in any given year.[163]

FEMA's current policy is to prioritize building up the NFIP's cash reserves over paying down principal.[164] Under its current authorization, the only means the NFIP has to pay off the debt is through the accrual of premium revenues in excess of outgoing claims, and from payments made out of the growing Reserve Fund.

---

159 FEMA, "National Flood Insurance Program Continues to Pay Interest on its Treasury Debt," press release, October24, 2023, https://www.fema.gov/press-release/20231024/national-flood-insurance-program-continues-pay-interest-its- treasury-debt.

160 FEMA, *National Flood Insurance Program Debt Repayment Report, as of March 31, 2022*, Report to Congress and the Secretary of the Treasury, August 30, 2022, p. 11. Provided by FEMA Congressional Affairs staff.

161 See 42 U.S.C. §4016(d), as enacted by §100213(a) of P.L. 112-141 (BW-12).

162 FEMA, *National Flood Insurance Program Debt Repayment Report, as of March 31, 2022*, Report to Congress and the Secretary of the Treasury, August 30, 2022, p. 11. Provided by FEMA Congressional Affairs staff.

163 Ibid., pp. 3-4.

164 Ibid., p. 10.

## NFIP Purchase of Reinsurance

In HFIAA-14, Congress revised the authority of FEMA to secure reinsurance[165] for the NFIP from the private reinsurance and capital markets.[166] The purchase of private market reinsurance reduces the likelihood of FEMA needing to borrow from the Treasury to pay claims. However, since FEMA is withdrawing funds from the Reserve Fund to pay for this reinsurance, it subsequently increases the cost of insurance to policyholders. FEMA's modeling of the NFIP portfolio before the reinsurance purchase suggested that there was a 17.2% chance of losses from an event exceeding $4 billion in 2017.[167]

In September 2016, FEMA secured its first placement of reinsurance for the NFIP, contracting for reinsurance cover which ran from September 19, 2016, through March 19, 2017, structured into two coverage layers. Under the first layer, the reinsurers would indemnify FEMA $1 million for flood claims losses that exceed $5 million. Under the second layer, the reinsurers would indemnify FEMA $1 million when the total losses from a single flood event exceed $5.5 billion.[168]

In January 2017, FEMA purchased $1.042 billion of insurance, to cover the period from January 1, 2017, to January 1, 2018, for a reinsurance premium of $150 million. Under this agreement, the reinsurance covered 26% of losses between $4 billion and $8 billion arising from a single flooding event. Claims paid by FEMA for Hurricane Harvey exceeded the $8 billion threshold, triggering the full 2017 reinsurance.[169]

In January 2018, FEMA purchased $1.46 billion of reinsurance to cover the period from January 1, 2018, to January 1, 2019, for a premium of $235 million. The agreement was structured to cover losses above $4 billion for a single flooding event, covering 18.6% of losses between $4 billion and $6 billion, and 54.3% of losses between $6 billion and $8 billion.[170] In August

---

[165] Reinsurance is defined as a transaction between a primary insurer and another licensed (re)insurer where the reinsurer agrees to cover all or part of the losses and/or loss adjustment expenses of the primary insurer. See NAIC, *Glossary of Insurance Terms*, http://www.naic.org/consumer_glossary.htm#R.

[166] See §10 of P.L. 113-89, 128 Stat. 1025, as codified at 42 U.S.C. §4081(e).

[167] Ibid.

[168] See FEMA, *National Flood Insurance Program Reinsurance Program,* at https://www.fema.gov/flood-insurance/ work-with-nfip/reinsurance.

[169] Email correspondence from FEMA Congressional Affairs Staff, August 2, 2019.

[170] FEMA, *National Flood Insurance Program (NFIP) Reinsurance Program*, at https://www.fema.gov/flood- insurance/work-with-nfip/reinsurance.

2018, FEMA entered into its first transfer of NFIP risk to private risk markets through an insurance-linked securities transfer, in the form of a three-year agreement with Hannover Re, a reinsurance company. Hannover Re acted as a "transformer," transferring $500 million of the NFIP's financial risk to the capital markets by sponsoring issuance of an indemnity-triggered catastrophe bond. Hannover Re indemnified FEMA for a portion of claims for a single qualifying flooding event that occurs between August 1, 2018, and July 31, 2021. The agreement was structured into two tranches. The first provided reinsurance coverage for 3.5% of losses between $5 billion and $10 billion, and the second for 13% of losses between $7.5 billion and $10 billion. FEMA paid a premium of $62 million for each of the first year and second year of coverage.

Unlike the earlier reinsurance purchases, which covered all NFIP flood losses, the catastrophe bond applied only to flooding resulting directly or indirectly from a named storm and covers only the 50 states, the District of Columbia, Puerto Rico, and the U.S. Virgin Islands. Combined with the January 2018 reinsurance placement, FEMA transferred $1.96 billion of the NFIP's flood risk for the 2018 hurricane season to the private sector.[171]

In January 2019, FEMA purchased $1.32 billion of reinsurance to cover the period from January 1, 2019, to January 1, 2020, for a premium of $186 million. The agreement was structured to cover losses above $4 billion for a single flooding event, covering 14% of losses between $4 billion and $6 billion, and 25.6% of losses between $6 billion and $8 billion, and 26.6% of losses between $8 billion and $10 billion.[172] FEMA issued a second catastrophe bond on April 16, 2019, to transfer an additional $300 million of the NFIP's financial risk to the capital markets. The agreement is structured to cover 2.5% of losses between $6 billion and $8 billion, and 12.5% of losses between $8 billion and $10 billion. FEMA paid a premium of $32 million for the first year of coverage and $38 million for the second year of coverage.[173]

In January 2020, FEMA purchased $1.33 billion of reinsurance to cover the period from January 1, 2020, to January 1, 2021, for a premium of $205 million. The agreement was structured to cover losses above $4 billion for a single flooding event, covering 10.25% of losses between $4 billion and $6

---

[171] Ibid. For additional information on this, see CRS Insight IN10965, *The National Flood Insurance Program (NFIP), Reinsurance, and Catastrophe Bonds*, by Diane P. Horn and Baird Webel.

[172] FEMA, *National Flood Insurance Program (NFIP) Reinsurance Program*, at https://www.fema.gov/flood- insurance/work-with-nfip/reinsurance.

[173] Ibid.

billion, 34.68% of losses between $6 billion and $8 billion, and 21.8% of losses between $8 billion and $10 billion.[174] In February 2020, FEMA issued a third catastrophe bond to transfer an additional $400 million of the NFIP's financial risk to the capital markets. The agreement was structured to cover 3.33% of losses between $6 billion and $9 billion and 30% of losses between $9 billion and $10 billion. FEMA paid a premium of $50.28 million for the first year of coverage.[175]

In January 2021, FEMA purchased $1.153 billion of reinsurance to cover the period from January 1, 2021, to January 1, 2022, for a reinsurance premium of $195.8 million.[176] In February 2021, FEMA issued a fourth catastrophe bond to transfer an additional $575 million of the NFIP's financial risk to the capital markets for the period February 23, 2021, to February 22, 2024.

FEMA paid a premium of $79.44 billion for the first year. The agreement was structured to cover 12.5% of losses between $6 billion and $7 billion and 22.5% of losses between $7 billion and $9 billion.[177]

In January 2022, FEMA purchased $1.064 billion of reinsurance to cover the period from January 1, 2022, to January 1, 2023, for a reinsurance premium of $171.9 million.[178] The agreement was structured to cover 4.163% of losses between $4 billion and $6 billion, 26.565% of losses between $6 billion and $8 billion, and 22.453% of losses between $8 billion and $10 billion.[179] In February 2022, FEMA issued a fifth catastrophe bond to transfer an additional $450 million of the NFIP's financial risk to the capital markets to cover the period February 23, 2022, to February 22, 2025, with a premium of $61.23 for the first year.[180] The agreement was structured to cover 2.5% of losses between $6 billion and $7 billion, 5% of losses between $7 billion and $9 billion, and 32.5% of losses between $9 billion and $10 billion for a single flood event.[181]

In January 2023, the NFIP purchased $502.5 million of reinsurance to cover the period from January 1, 2023, to January 1, 2024, for a reinsurance premium of $90.2 million. The agreement was structured to cover 8.5625% of

---

[174] Ibid.

[175] Ibid.

[176] Ibid.

[177] Ibid.

[178] Ibid.

[179] FEMA, "FEMA Announces Reinsurance Program to Manage Future Flood Risk in 2022," press release, January 6, 2022, https://www.fema.gov/press-release/20220106/fema-announces-reinsurance-program-manage-future-flood-risk-2022.

[180] Ibid.

[181] FEMA, "FEMA Expands Its Reinsurance Program, Transfers $450 Million in Flood Risk to Capital Markets," press release, February 23, 2022, https://www.fema.gov/press-release/20220223/fema-expands-its-reinsurance-program-transfers-450-million-flood-risk.

losses between $7 billion and $9 billion and 16.5625% of losses between $9 billion and $11 billion.[182] In March 2023, FEMA issued a sixth catastrophe bond to transfer an additional $275 million of the NFIP's financial risk to the capital markets to cover the period March 7, 2023, to March 7, 2026, with a premium of $50.37 for the first year. The agreement was structured to cover 5% of losses between $7 billion and $8 billion and 11.25% of losses between $8 billion and $10 billion for a single flood event.[183]

In January 2024, the NFIP purchased $502.5 million of reinsurance to cover the period from January 1, 2024, to January 1, 2025, for a reinsurance premium of $121.1 million. The agreement was structured to cover 8.9125% of losses between $7 billion and $9 billion and 22.0625% of losses between $9 billion and $11 billion for a single flood event.[184] In March 2024, FEMA issued a seventh catastrophe bond to transfer an additional $575 million of the NFIP's financial risk to the capital markets to cover the period March 7, 2024, to March 7, 2027, with a premium of $85.7 for the first year. The agreement was structured to cover 10% of losses between $8 billion and $9 billion and 23.75% of losses between $9 billion and $11 billion for a single flood event.[185]

The NFIP has only claimed on reinsurance once, after Hurricane Harvey in 2017, receiving the full $1.042 billion of coverage. According to FEMA, as of March 2024, FEMA has paid $2.275 billion in reinsurance premiums.[186]

## Expiration of Certain NFIP Authorities

The statute for the NFIP does not contain a comprehensive expiration, termination, or sunset provision for the whole of the program. Rather, the

---

[182] FEMA, "FEMA Announces Reinsurance Program to Manage Future Flood Risk in 2023," press release, January 10, 2023, https://www.fema.gov/press-release/20230110/fema-announces-reinsurance-program-manage-future-flood-risk-2023.

[183] FEMA, *National Flood Insurance Program (NFIP) Reinsurance Program*, at https://www.fema.gov/flood-insurance/work-with-nfip/reinsurance and FEMA, "FEMA Expands Its Reinsurance Program by Transferring $275 Million in Flood Risk to Capital Markets," press release, March 8, 2023, https://www.fema.gov/press-release/ 20230308/ fema-expands-its-reinsurance-program-transferring-275-million-flood-risk.

[184] FEMA, "FEMA Announces Reinsurance Program to Manage Future Flood Risk in 2024," press release, January 4, 2024, https://www.fema.gov/press-release/20240103/fema-announces-reinsurance-program-manage-future-flood-risk-2024.

[185] FEMA, "FEMA Expands Its Reinsurance Program by Transferring $575 Million in Flood Risk to Capital Markets," press release, March 8, 2024, https://www.fema.gov/press-release/20240308/fema-expands-its-reinsurance-program- transferring-575-million-flood-risk.

[186] Email from FEMA Congressional Affairs Staff, March 13, 2024.

NFIP has multiple different legal provisions that generally tie to the expiration of key components of the program. Since the end of FY2017, 30 short-term NFIP reauthorizations have been enacted. These reauthorizations are listed in Table 6. The NFIP is currently authorized until September 30, 2024.

Unless reauthorized or amended by Congress, the following will occur after September 30, 2024:

- The authority to provide new flood insurance contracts will expire.[187] Flood insurance contracts entered into before the expiration would continue until the end of their policy term of one year.
- The authority for NFIP to borrow funds from the Treasury will be reduced from $30.425 billion to $1 billion.[188]

Other activities of the program would technically remain authorized following September 30, 2024, such as the issuance of FMA grants.[189] However, the expiration of the key authorities described above would have varied, generally serious effects on these remaining NFIP activities.

**Table 6.** Short-term extensions of the NFIP since end of FY2017

| Public Law | Date to Which Authorization Was Extended |
|---|---|
| P.L. 115-56 | December 8, 2017 |
| P.L. 115-90 | December 22, 2017 |
| P.L. 115-96 | January 19, 2018 |
| NFIP lapsed January 20 to January 22, 2018 | |
| P.L. 115-120 | February 8, 2018 |
| NFIP lapsed for 8 hours on February 9, 2018 | |
| P.L. 115-123 | March 23, 2018 |
| P.L. 115-141 | July 31, 2018 |
| P.L. 115-225 | November 30, 2018 |
| P.L. 115-281 | December 7, 2018 |
| P.L. 115-298 | December 21, 2018 |
| P.L. 115-396 | May 31, 2019 |
| P.L. 116-19 | June 14, 2019 |
| P.L. 116-20 | September 30, 2019 |
| P.L. 116-59 | November 21, 2019 |
| P.L. 116-69 | December 20, 2019 |

[187] 42 U.S.C. §4026.

[188] 42 U.S.C. §4016(a).

[189] See 42 U.S.C. §4104c and 42 U.S.C. §4104d.

**Table 6.** (Continued)

| Public Law | Date to Which Authorization Was Extended |
|---|---|
| NFIP lapsed for 8 hours on February 9, 2018 | |
| P.L. 116-94 | September 30, 2020 |
| P.L. 116-159 | September 30, 2021 |
| P.L. 117-43 | December 3, 2021 |
| P.L. 117-70 | February 18, 2022 |
| P.L. 117-86 | March 11, 2022 |
| P.L. 117-95 | March 15, 2022 |
| P.L. 117-103 | September 30, 2022 |
| P.L. 117-180 | December 16, 2022 |
| P.L. 117-229 | December 23, 2022 |
| P.L. 117-264 | December 30, 2022 |
| P.L. 117-328 | September 30, 2023 |
| P.L. 118-15 | November 17, 2023 |
| P.L. 118-22 | February 2, 2024 |
| P.L. 118-35 | March 8, 2024 |
| P.L. 118-40 | March 22, 2024 |
| NFIP lapsed for about 13 hours on March 23, 2024 | |
| P.L. 118-47 | September 30, 2024 |

Source: CRS analysis of legislation.

Chapter 2

# A Brief Introduction to the National Flood Insurance Program*

Diane P. Horn

The National Flood Insurance Program (NFIP) is the primary source of flood insurance coverage for residential properties in the United States. The NFIP has two main policy goals: (1) to provide access to primary flood insurance, thereby allowing for the transfer of some of the financial risk of property owners to the federal government; and (2) to mitigate and reduce the nation's comprehensive flood risk through the development and implementation of floodplain management standards. A longer-term objective of the NFIP is to reduce federal expenditure on disaster assistance after floods. As a public insurance program, the goals of the NFIP are different from the goals of private- sector insurance companies. It encompasses social goals to provide flood insurance in flood-prone areas to property owners who otherwise would not be able to obtain it and to reduce the government's cost after floods. The NFIP also engages in many "noninsurance" activities in the public interest: it identifies and maps flood hazards, disseminates flood-risk information through flood maps, requires community land-use and building-code standards, contributes to community resilience by providing a mechanism to fund rebuilding after a flood, and offers grants and incentive programs for household- and community-level investments in flood-risk reduction.

Over 22,000 communities in 56 states and jurisdictions participate in the NFIP, with over 4.7 million policies providing almost $1.28 trillion in coverage. The program collects about $4.3 billion in annual premium revenue. Floods are the most common and costly natural disaster in the U.S.

---

* This is an edited, reformatted and augmented version of Congressional Research Service Publication No. IF10988, updated March 29, 2024.

In: The National Flood Insurance Program (NFIP)
Editor: Jolene Rivera
ISBN: 979-8-89530-612-3

## Structure of the NFIP

The NFIP is managed by the Federal Emergency Management Agency (FEMA) through its subcomponent, the Federal Insurance and Mitigation Administration. A core design feature of the NFIP is that communities are not required to participate in the program by any law or regulation, but instead participate voluntarily in order to obtain access to NFIP flood insurance. Communities that choose to participate in the NFIP are required to adopt land use and control measures with effective enforcement provisions and to regulate development in the floodplain. FEMA has set forth in federal regulations the minimum standards required for participation in the NFIP; however, these standards have the force of law only because they are adopted and enforced by a state or local government. Legal enforcement of the floodplain management standards is the responsibility of the participating NFIP community, which can elect to adopt higher standards as a means of mitigating flood risk. In addition, FEMA operates a program, called the Community Rating System, to incentivize NFIP communities to adopt more rigorous floodplain management standards.

NFIP flood insurance policies are sold only in participating communities and are offered to both property owners and renters and to residential and nonresidential properties.

NFIP policies have relatively low coverage limits, particularly for nonresidential properties or properties in high-cost areas. The maximum coverage for single-family dwellings (which also includes single-family residential units within a 2-4 family building) is $100,000 for contents and up to $250,000 for building coverage. The maximum available coverage limit for other residential buildings is $500,000 for building coverage and $100,000 for contents coverage, and the maximum coverage limit for nonresidential business buildings is $500,000 for building coverage and $500,000 for contents coverage.

## Flood Mapping and Mitigation

The NFIP approaches the goal of reducing comprehensive flood risk primarily by requiring participating communities to collaborate with FEMA to develop and adopt flood maps called Flood Insurance Rate Maps (FIRMs). An area of specific focus of the FIRM is the Special Flood Hazard Area (SFHA). The

SFHA is defined by FEMA as an area with a 1% or greater risk of flooding every year. FIRMs provide the basis for identifying properties whose owners are required to purchase flood insurance and establishing floodplain management standards that communities must adopt and enforce as part of their participation in the NFIP. There is no consistent, definitive timetable for revising and updating FIRMs for a particular community. Generally, FIRMs may require updating after significant new building development in or near the flood zone, changes to flood- protection systems, or environmental changes in the community. Statutory guidelines set out the procedure for developing new FIRMs for a community. For example, FEMA is required to conduct extensive communication and outreach efforts with the community during the mapping process, which includes several review and comment periods of 30 to 90 days. Communities and individuals also have legal recourse to appeal the FIRM updating process. After a FIRM is finalized and adopted by a community, it can still be revised to correct for errors in map accuracy. To correct these inaccuracies, FEMA allows individuals and communities to request letters amending a FIRM.

FEMA also operates a Flood Mitigation Assistance (FMA) Grant Program that is funded through revenue collected by the NFIP. FMA grants are only available to communities that participate in the NFIP, to reduce or eliminate flood damage and structures insurable under the NFIP, particularly repetitive loss and severe repetitive loss structures. The Infrastructure Investment and Jobs Act appropriated $3.5 billion for the FMA program, with $700 million for each of FY2022 to FY2026.

## The Mandatory Purchase Requirement

In a community that participates or has participated in the NFIP, property owners in the mapped SFHA are required to purchase flood insurance as a condition of receiving a federally backed mortgage. Federal agencies, federally regulated lending institutions, and government-sponsored enterprises must require these property owners to purchase flood insurance as a condition of any mortgage that these entities make, guarantee, or purchase. To comply with this mandate, property owners may purchase flood insurance through the NFIP or through a private company, as long as the private flood insurance meets the condition set by statute that it "provides flood insurance coverage which is at least as broad as the coverage" of the NFIP, among other conditions. The mandatory purchase requirement is enforced by the lender, rather than FEMA. Property owners who do not obtain flood insurance when required may find they are not eligible for certain types of disaster assistance after a flood.

## Financial Standing of the NFIP

The NFIP is funded from premiums, fees, and surcharges paid by NFIP policyholders; direct annual appropriations for specific costs of the NFIP (currently only for the flood hazard mapping and risk analysis program); and borrowing from the Treasury when the balance of the National Flood Insurance Fund is insufficient to pay the NFIP's obligations (e.g., insurance claims). The NFIP was not designed to retain funding to cover claims for truly extreme events; instead, the statute allows the program to borrow money from the Treasury for such events. For most of the NFIP's history, the program was able to borrow relatively small amounts from the Treasury to pay claims and then repay the loans with interest. However, this changed when Congress increased the level of NFIP borrowing to $20.775 billion to pay claims in the aftermath of the 2005 hurricane season (particularly Hurricanes Katrina, Rita, and Wilma).

Congress increased the borrowing limit again following Hurricane Sandy to its current limit of $30.425 billion.

The 2017 hurricane season was the second-largest claims year in the NFIP's history—second only to the 2005 hurricane season. At the beginning of the 2017 hurricane season, the NFIP owed $24.6 billion. On September 22, 2017, the NFIP borrowed the remaining $5.825 billion from the Treasury to cover claims from Hurricane Harvey, reaching the NFIP's authorized borrowing limit of $30.425 billion. On October 26, 2017, Congress cancelled $16 billion of NFIP debt to pay claims for Hurricanes Harvey, Irma, and Maria. FEMA borrowed another $6.1 billion on November 9, 2017, to fund estimated 2017 losses, including those incurred by Hurricanes Harvey, Irma, and Maria, bringing the debt back up to $20.525 billion. The NFIP has not needed to borrow from the Treasury since 2017. As of March 2024, the NFIP has $9.9 billion of remaining borrowing authority, as well as possible reinsurance payments of over $1.9 billion.

The NFIP's debt is conceptually owed by current and future participants in the NFIP, as the insurance program itself owes the debt to the Treasury and pays for accruing interest on that debt through the premium revenues of policyholders. Under its current authorization, the only means the NFIP has to pay off the debt is through the accrual of premium revenues in excess of outgoing claims, and from payments made out of the reserve fund. For example, since 2005 the NFIP has paid $2.82 billion in principal repayments and $6.17 billion in interest to service the debt through the premiums collected on insurance policies. The cancellation of $16 billion of NFIP debt in October 2017 represents the first time that NFIP debt has been cancelled, although Congress appropriated funds between 1980 and 1985 to repay NFIP debt.

## Risk Rating 2.0

FEMA introduced a new pricing methodology, known as Risk Rating 2.0, which represents the biggest change to the way the NFIP calculates flood insurance premiums since the program began in 1968. The new rates went into effect on October 1, 2021, for new NFIP policies and went into effect on April 1, 2022, for existing NFIP policyholders.

Under the change, premiums for individual properties are tied to their actual flood risk and flood zones are no longer used in calculating a property's flood insurance premium, in contrast to the legacy rating system in which properties with the same NFIP flood risk were charged the same rates. Under Risk Rating 2.0 the premium is calculated based on the specific features of an individual property. Risk Rating 2.0 incorporates a broader range of flood frequencies and sources than the legacy rating system, including flooding from rivers, storm surge, and heavy rainfall. Flood zones will still be used for floodplain management purposes, and the boundary of the SFHA will still be required for the mandatory purchase requirement.

## Reauthorization of the NFIP

Since the end of FY2017, 30 short-term NFIP extensions have been enacted. The NFIP is currently authorized until September 30, 2024. The statute for the NFIP does not contain a comprehensive expiration, termination, or sunset provision for the whole of the program. Rather, the NFIP has multiple different legal provisions that generally tie to the expiration of key components of the program. Unless reauthorized or amended by Congress, the following will occur on September 30, 2024: (1) the authority to provide new flood insurance contracts will expire; however, insurance contracts entered into before the expiration would continue until the end of their policy term of one year; and (2) the authority for NFIP to borrow funds from the Treasury will be reduced from $30.425 billion to $1 billion.

## CRS Products About the NFIP

CRS Report R44593, *Introduction to the National Flood Insurance Program (NFIP)*.

CRS Insight IN10784, *National Flood Insurance Program Borrowing Authority*.

CRS Insight IN10835, *What Happens If the National Flood Insurance Program (NFIP) Lapses?*

CRS Insight IN11777, *National Flood Insurance Program Risk Rating 2.0: Frequently Asked Questions*.

CRS Report R45242, *Private Flood Insurance and the National Flood Insurance Program*.

# Chapter 3

# A Brief Introduction to the National Flood Insurance Program in the 118th Congress*

**Diane P. Horn**

## Introduction

The National Flood Insurance Program (NFIP) is authorized by the National Flood Insurance Act of 1968 (Title XIII of P.L. 90-448, as amended, 42 U.S.C. §§4001 et seq.) and is the primary source of flood insurance coverage for residential properties in the United States. The NFIP has more than 4.7 million flood insurance policies providing over $1.3 trillion in coverage, with 22,691 communities in 56 states and jurisdictions participating.

The NFIP has two main policy goals: (1) to provide access to primary flood insurance, thereby allowing for the transfer of some of the financial risk from property owners to the federal government, and (2) to mitigate and reduce the nation's comprehensive flood risk through the development and implementation of floodplain management standards. A longer-term objective of the NFIP is to reduce federal expenditure on disaster assistance after floods. The NFIP engages in many "noninsurance" activities in the public interest: it identifies and maps flood hazards, disseminates flood-risk information through flood maps, requires community land-use and building-code standards, contributes to community resilience by providing a mechanism to fund rebuilding after a flood, and offers grants and incentive programs for household- and community-level investments in flood-risk reduction.

* This is an edited, reformatted and augmented version of Congressional Research Service Publication No. IN11049, updated August 15, 2024.

In: The National Flood Insurance Program (NFIP)
Editor: Jolene Rivera
ISBN: 979-8-89530-612-3

The Federal Emergency Management Agency (FEMA) introduced a new pricing methodology in April 2022, known as Risk Rating 2.0, which represents the biggest change to the way the NFIP calculates premiums since the program began. Under the change, premiums for individual properties are based on their actual flood risk rather than flood zones.

## Structure of the NFIP

The NFIP is managed by FEMA through its subcomponent, the Federal Insurance Directorate (formerly the Federal Insurance and Mitigation Administration). Communities are not legally required to participate in the NFIP; they participate voluntarily to obtain access to NFIP flood insurance, and are required to adopt land-use and control measures with effective enforcement provisions and to regulate developmentin the floodplain. FEMA has set forth in federal regulations the minimum standards required for participation in the NFIP; however, these standards have the force of law only if they are adopted and enforced by a state or local government. Legal enforcement of floodplain management standards is the responsibility of participating NFIP communities, which also can elect to adopt higher standards to mitigate flood risk. The NFIP approaches the goal of reducing comprehensive flood risk primarily by requiring participating communities to collaborate with FEMA to develop and adopt flood maps called Flood Insurance Rate Maps (FIRMs). Property owners in the mapped Special Flood Hazard Area (SFHA), defined as an area with a 1% annual chance of flooding, are required to purchase flood insurance as a condition of receiving a federally backed mortgage. This mandatory purchase requirement is enforced by lenders rather than FEMA. Property owners who do not obtain flood insurance when required may find that they are not eligible for certain types of disaster assistance after a flood.

## Financial Standing of the NFIP

The NFIP is funded from (1) premiums, fees, and surcharges paid by NFIP policyholders; (2) annual appropriations for flood-hazard mapping and risk analysis; (3) borrowing from the Treasury when the balance of the National Flood Insurance Fund is insufficient to pay the NFIP's obligations (e.g., insurance claims); and (4) reinsurance if NFIP losses are sufficiently large. The NFIP was not designed to retain funding to cover claims for truly extreme events; instead, the statute allows the program to borrow money from the Treasury for such events. For most of the NFIP's history, the program was able to borrow relatively small amounts from the Treasury to pay claims and then repay the loans with interest. However, this changed when Congress increased the borrowing limit to $20.775 billion to pay claims in the aftermath of the 2005 hurricane season (particularly Hurricanes Katrina, Rita, and Wilma). Congress increased the borrowing limit again in 2013, after Hurricane Sandy, to the current limit of $30.425 billion.

The 2017 hurricane season was the second-largest claims year in the NFIP's history, with approximately $10.15 billion paid to date in response to Hurricanes Harvey, Irma, and Maria. At the beginning of the 2017 hurricane season, the NFIP owed $24.6 billion. On September 22, 2017, the NFIP borrowed the remaining $5.825 billion from the Treasury to cover claims from Hurricane Harvey, reaching the NFIP's borrowing limit. On October 26, 2017, Congress canceled $16 billion of NFIP debt in order to pay claims for Hurricanes Harvey, Irma, and Maria. FEMA borrowed another $6.1 billion on November 9, 2017, bringing the debt back up to $20.525 billion. As of August 2024, the NFIP has $9.9 billion of remaining borrowing authority. The NFIP transfers a portion of its risk to the private sector through the purchase of reinsurance and the issuance of catastrophe bonds.

The NFIP's debt is conceptually owed by current and future participants in the NFIP, as the insurance program itself owes the debt to the Treasury and pays for accruing interest on that debt through the premium revenues of policyholders. Since 2005, the NFIP has paid $2.82 billion in principal repayments and $6.17 billion in interest to service the debt through the premiums collected on insurance policies. The October 2017 cancellation of $16 billion of NFIP debt represents the first time NFIP debt has been cancelled.

## NFIP Reauthorization

Since the end of FY2017, Congress has enacted 30 short-term NFIP reauthorizations. The NFIP is currently authorized until September 30, 2024. The statute for the NFIP does not contain a comprehensive expiration, termination, or sunset provision for the whole of the program. Rather, the NFIP has multiple different legal provisions that generally tie to the expiration of key components of the program. Unless reauthorized or amended by Congress, the following will occur on September 30, 2024: (1) the authority to provide new flood insurance contracts will expire; however, insurance contracts entered into before the expiration would continue until the end of their policy term, and (2) the authority for the NFIP to borrow funds from the Treasury will be reduced from $30.425 billion to $1 billion.

# Chapter 4

# Private Flood Insurance and the National Flood Insurance Program*

**Diane P. Horn**
**and Baird Webel**

## Summary

The National Flood Insurance Program (NFIP) is the main source of primary flood insurance coverage in the United States, collecting over $4.6 billion in premiums, fees, and surcharges for over five million flood insurance policies. This is in contrast to the majority of other property and casualty risks, such as damage from fire or accidents, which are covered by a broad array of private insurance companies. One of the primary reasons behind the creation of the NFIP in 1968 was the withdrawal by private insurers from providing flood insurance coverage, leaving flood victims largely reliant on federal disaster assistance to recover after a flood. While private insurers have taken on relatively little flood risk, they have been involved in the administration of the NFIP through sales and servicing of policies and claims.

In recent years, private insurers have expressed increased interest in providing flood coverage. Advances in the analytics and data used to quantify flood risk along with increases in capital market capacities may allow private insurers to take on flood risks that they shunned in the past. Private flood insurance may offer some advantages over the NFIP, including more flexible flood polices, integrated coverage with homeowners insurance, or lower-cost coverage for some consumers. Private marketing might also increase the overall amount of flood

* This is an edited, reformatted and augmented version of Congressional Research Service, Publication No. R45242, updated January 9, 2023.

In: The National Flood Insurance Program (NFIP)
Editor: Jolene Rivera
ISBN: 979-8-89530-612-3

coverage purchased, reducing the amount of extraordinary disaster assistance necessary to be provided by the federal government. Increased private coverage could reduce the overall financial risk to the NFIP, reducing the amount of NFIP borrowing necessary after major disasters. Increasing private insurance, however, may have some downsides compared to the NFIP. Private coverage would not be guaranteed to be available to all floodplain residents, unlike the NFIP, and consumer protections could vary in different states. The role of the NFIP has historically been broader than just providing insurance. As currently authorized, the NFIP also encompasses social goals to provide flood insurance in flood-prone areas to property owners who otherwise would not be able to obtain it, and to reduce government's cost after floods. Through flood mapping and mitigation efforts, the NFIP has tried to reduce the future impact of floods, and it is unclear how effectively the NFIP could play this broader role if private insurance became a large part of the flood marketplace. Increased private insurance could also have an impact on the subsidies that are provided for some consumers through the NFIP.

The 2012 reauthorization of the NFIP (Division F, Title II of P.L. 112-141) included provisions encouraging private flood insurance; however, various barriers have remained. Legislation passed the House in the 114$^{th}$ Congress (H.R. 2901) and 115$^{th}$ Congress (H.R. 2874) which would have attempted to expand the role of private flood insurance; neither bill was taken up by the Senate. In the 116$^{th}$ Congress, no NFIP legislation advanced past introduction. Two bills were introduced in the 117$^{th}$ Congress for long-term reauthorization and reform of the NFIP.

The NFIP is currently operating under a short-term reauthorization until September 30, 2023.

## Introduction

Congress is currently considering long-term reauthorization of the National Flood Insurance Program (NFIP). Floods are the most common natural disaster in the United States, and all 50 states, plus DC, Puerto Rico, Guam, American Samoa, the U.S. Virgin Islands, and the Northern Mariana Islands have experienced flood events since May 2018.[190] The NFIP has paid a total of nearly \$19.03 billion in claims over the past five fiscal years.[191]

[190] Email correspondence from FEMA Congressional Affairs staff, August 5, 2019.

[191] Email correspondence from FEMA Congressional Affairs staff, December 30, 2020.

Expanding the role of private insurers, including reinsurers, has been seen by many as an answer to the variability of the financial position of the NFIP.[192] Increasing participation by private insurers could transfer more flood risk from policyholders to the private insurance sector, as opposed to transferring the risk to the federal government through the NFIP. In addition to the possible advantage to the NFIP, the increased availability of flood insurance as private companies enter the market may benefit households and businesses, as insured flood victims are likely to recover more quickly and more fully after a flood.

Private insurer interest in directly providing and underwriting flood risk has increased in recent years. Advances in the analytics and data used to quantify flood risk along with increases in capital market capacities may allow private insurers to take on flood risks that they shunned in the past. However, increasing the private sector role in providing flood insurance coverage directly to consumers may have implications for the operations and fiscal solvency of the NFIP as currently structured. Increased access to private flood insurance could provide individual policyholders with a wider choice of coverage and possibly cheaper premiums, but may also lead to variable consumer protections.

The extent to which private insurance companies participate in the U.S. flood insurance market represents an area of congressional concern. A number of bills have been introduced to address issues related to private flood insurance, but no legislation has yet been enacted. The NFIP is currently operating under its 25th short-term reauthorization, until September 30, 2023.[193]

This report describes the current role of private insurers in U.S. flood insurance, and discusses barriers to private sector involvement. The report considers potential effects of increased private sector involvement in the U.S. flood market, both for the NFIP and for consumers. Finally, the report outlines the provisions relevant to private flood insurance in House and Senate NFIP reauthorization bills from the 115th, 116th, and 117th Congresses.

---

[192] FEMA, National Flood Insurance Program Report to Congress on Reinsuring NFIP Insurance Risk and Options for Privatizing the NFIP, August 13, 2015, p. 41.

[193] P.L. 117-328. For further information on NFIP reauthorization, see CRS Insight IN10835, What Happens If the National Flood Insurance Program (NFIP) Lapses? by Diane P. Horn.

## Background[194]

The NFIP is the main provider of primary flood insurance coverage for residential properties in the United States, providing nearly $1.3 trillion in coverage for over five million residential flood insurance policies. In FY2018, the program collected about $3.51 billion in annual premium revenue, $1.09 billion in assessments, fees, and surcharges and $1.04 billion in payments from private reinsurers.[195] In FY2019, the program collected about $3.39 billion in annual premium revenue and $1.07 billion in assessments, fees, and surcharge, with no payments from private reinsurers.[196] In FY2020, the program collected about $3.51 billion in annual premium revenue and $1.11 billion in assessments, fees, and surcharge, with no payments from private reinsurers.

Nationally, over 22,000 communities participate in the NFIP.[197] The role of the federal government in flood insurance is in contrast to the majority of other property and casualty risks, such as damage from fire or accidents, which are covered by a broad array of private insurance companies. Total direct written premiums for private flood insurance in 2019 totaled $523 billion, compared to $420 million in 2018 and $390 million in 2017. Over 140 insurers wrote private flood insurance in 2019, up from 120 insurers in 2018, 90 insurers in 2017, and 50 insurers in 2016.[198] Total premiums for private property and casualty insurance in 2018 totaled $611 billion, with the policies backed by over $2 trillion in assets held by private insurers.[199]

---

[194] For more detail on the NFIP, see CRS Report R44593, *Introduction to the National Flood Insurance Program (NFIP)*, by Diane P. Horn and Baird Webel.

[195] Statistics on the National Flood Insurance Program (NFIP) policy and claims are available from the Federal Emergency Management Agency (FEMA) website "Policy and Claim Statistics for Flood Insurance," at https://www.fema.gov/policy-claim-statistics-flood-insurance; premium and fee data from *The Watermark Third Quarter 2021*, https://www.fema.gov/ sites/default/files/documents/fema_fima-watermark-FY2021-Q3.pdf.

[196] Fee data from *The Watermark Third Quarter 2021*, https://www.fema.gov/sites/default/files/documents/fema_fima-watermark-FY2021-Q3.pdf.

[197] Detailed information about which communities participate and where is available from the Community Status Book, found on FEMA's website at https://www.fema.gov/flood-insurance/work-with-nfip/community-status-book.

[198] National Association of Insurance Commissioners (NAIC), *Report on Private Flood Insurance Data*, April 28, 2020, provided by NAIC to CRS on October 24, 2020.

[199] Premium amounts used are net premiums written and asset amounts are admitted assets from A.M. Best, *2019 Best's Rankings: U.S. Property/Casualty - 2018 Financial Results*, March 25, 2019.

## Objectives of the NFIP

The NFIP has two main policy goals: (1) to provide access to primary flood insurance, thereby allowing for the transfer of some of the financial risk of property owners to the federal government; and (2) to mitigate and reduce the nation's comprehensive flood risk[200] through the development and implementation of floodplain management standards. A longer-term objective of the NFIP is to reduce federal expenditure on disaster assistance after floods.

As a public insurance program, the NFIP is designed differently from the way in which private- sector companies provide insurance. As currently authorized, the NFIP also encompasses social goals to provide flood insurance in flood-prone areas to property owners who otherwise would not be able to obtain it, and to reduce the government's cost after floods.[201] The NFIP also engages in many "non-insurance" activities in the public interest: it disseminates flood risk information through flood maps, requires communities to adopt land use and building code standards in order to participate in the program, potentially reduces the need for other post-flood disaster aid, contributes to community resilience by providing a mechanism to fund rebuilding after a flood, and may protect lending institutions against mortgage defaults due to uninsured losses. The benefits of such tasks are not directly measured in the NFIP's financial results from selling flood insurance.[202]

From the inception of the NFIP, the program has been expected to achieve multiple objectives, some of which may conflict with one another:

- to ensure reasonable insurance premiums for all;
- to have risk-based premiums that would make people aware of and bear the cost of their floodplain location choices;
- to secure widespread community participation in the NFIP and substantial numbers of insurance policy purchases by property owners; and

[200] In the context of this report, *comprehensive* flood risk means that the risk includes both financial risk (i.e., physical damage to property), and also the risk to human life.

[201] See 82 Stat. 573 for text in original statute (Section 1302(c) of P.L. 90-448). This language remains in statute (see 42U.S.C. §4001(c)).

[202] American Academy of Actuaries Flood Insurance Work Group, The National Flood Insurance Program: Challenges and Solutions, April 2017, p. 79, http://www.actuary.org/files/publications/FloodMonograph.04192017.pdf.

- to earn premium and fee income that, over time, covers claims paid and program expenses.[203]

## Primary Flood Insurance Through the NFIP

The NFIP offers flood insurance to anyone in a community that chooses to participate in the program. Flood insurance purchase generally is voluntary, except for property owners who are in a Special Flood Hazard Area (SFHA)[204] and whose mortgage is backed by the federal government.[205] Flood insurance policies through the NFIP are sold only in participating communities and are offered to both property owners and renters and to residential and nonresidential properties. NFIP policies have relatively low coverage limits, particularly for nonresidential properties or properties in high-cost areas. The maximum coverage for single-family dwellings (which also includes single-family residential units within a 2-4 family building) is $100,000 for contents and up to $250,000 for building coverage. The maximum available coverage limit for other residential buildings is $500,000 for building coverage and $100,000 for contents coverage, and the maximum coverage limit for nonresidential business buildings is $500,000 for building coverage and $500,000 for contents coverage.

### *The Mandatory Purchase Requirement*

By law and regulation, federal agencies, federally regulated lending institutions, and government- sponsored enterprises (GSEs)[206] must require the property owners in an SFHA to purchase flood insurance as a condition of any mortgage that these entities make, guarantee, or purchase.[207] In addition to this legal mandatory purchase requirement, lenders may also require

---

[203] National Research Council of the National Academies, *Affordability of National Flood Insurance Program Premiums: Report 1*, 2015, p. 3, http://www.nap.edu/catalog/21709/affordability-of-national-flood-insurance-program- premiums-report-1.

[204] A Special Flood Hazard Area (SFHA) is defined by FEMA as an area with a 1% or greater risk of flooding every year.

[205] This includes mortgages from banks insured by the Federal Deposit Insurance Corporation and mortgages backed by Fannie Mae or Freddie Mac, as well as federal entities such as the Federal Housing Administration and the Department of Veterans Affairs.

[206] Government-Sponsored Enterprises (GSEs) are private companies with congressional charters. Examples of GSEs providing mortgages that would be affected by the mandatory purchase requirement include the Federal Home Loan Mortgage Corporation (Freddie Mac) and the Federal National Mortgage Association (Fannie Mae).

[207] 42 U.S.C. §4012a.

borrowers outside of an SFHA to maintain flood insurance as a means of financially securing the property.

In order to comply with this mandate, property owners may purchase flood insurance through the NFIP, or through a private company, so long as the private flood insurance "provides flood insurance coverage which is at least as broad as the coverage" of the NFIP, among other conditions.[208] The mandatory purchase requirement is enforced by the lender, rather than FEMA, and lenders can be fined up to $2,000 by banking regulators for each failure to require flood insurance or provide notice.[209] Property owners who do not obtain flood insurance when required may find that they are not eligible for certain types of disaster assistance after a flood.[210]

### *Premium Subsidies and Cross-Subsidies*

Flood insurance rates in the NFIP generally are directed by statute to be "based on consideration of the risk involved and accepted actuarial principles,"[211] meaning that the rate is reflective of the true flood risk to the property. However, Congress has directed FEMA not to charge actuarial rates for certain categories of properties and to offer discounts to other classes of properties.[212] FEMA is not, however, provided funds to offset these subsidies and discounts,[213] which has contributed to FEMA's need to borrow from the U.S. Treasury to pay NFIP claims. There are three main categories of properties that pay less than full risk-based rates:

---

[208] 42 U.S.C §4012a(b). For additional information on private flood insurance, see CRS Insight IN10450, *Private Flood Insurance and the National Flood Insurance Program (NFIP)*, by Baird Webel and Diane P. Horn. The "at least as broad as" requirement is discussed in more detail in the section titled "Flood Insurance Coverage "at Least as Broad as" the NFIP" in this report.

[209] 42 U.S.C §4012a(f).

[210] For additional information, see CRS Report R44808, *Federal Disaster Assistance: The National Flood Insurance Program and Other Federal Disaster Assistance Programs Available to Individuals and Households After a Flood*, by Diane P. Horn.

[211] 42 U.S.C. §4014(a)(1).

[212] For a full discussion of NFIP subsidies and cross-subsidies, see the section on Pricing and Premium Rate Structure in CRS Report R44593, *Introduction to the National Flood Insurance Program (NFIP)*, by Diane P. Horn and Baird Webel, the section on Premiums Subsidies and Cross-Subsidies in CRS Report R46095, *The National Flood Insurance Program: Selected Issues and Legislation in the 116th Congress*, by Diane P. Horn and Baird Webel, and the section on Premium Subsidies and Cross-Subsidies in CRS Report R45999, *National Flood Insurance Program: The Current Rating Structure and Risk Rating 2.0*, by Diane P. Horn.

[213] Government Accountability Office (GAO), *Flood Insurance: Comprehensive Reform Could Improve Solvency and Enhance Resilience*, GAO-17-425, April 2017, p. 17, https://www.gao.gov/products/GAO-17-425.

- *Pre-FIRM*: properties that were built or substantially improved before December 31, 1974, or before FEMA published the first Flood Insurance Rate Map (FIRM) for their community, whichever was later;[214]
- *Newly mapped*: properties that are newly mapped into a SFHA on or after April 1, 2015, if the applicant obtains coverage that is effective within 12 months of the map revision date;[215] and
- *Grandfathered*: properties that were built in compliance with the FIRM in effect at the time of construction and are allowed to maintain their old flood insurance rate class if their property is remapped into a new flood rate class.[216]

## NFIP Reauthorization and Legislation

### *117th Congress*

The NFIP is currently authorized until September 30, 2023.[217] Since the end of FY2017, 25 short- term NFIP reauthorizations have been enacted. Two companion bills were introduced in the 117th Congress for reform and reauthorization of the NFIP: S. 3128 and H.R. 5802, the National Flood Insurance Program Reauthorization and Reform Act of 2021. These bills were not considered by the committees of jurisdiction.

### *Prior Congresses*

The House passed standalone legislation to encourage private insurance in the 114th Congress (H.R. 2901); however, the Senate did not take up H.R. 2901 in the 114th Congress.

---

[214] 42 U.S.C. §4015(c).

[215] §6 of P.L. 113-89, 128 Stat.1028, as codified at 42 U.S.C. §4015(i).

[216] For a full description, see FEMA, *Grandfathering*, March 2020, https://www.fema.gov/node/404682.

[217] The statute for the NFIP does not contain a comprehensive expiration, termination, or sunset provision for the whole of the program. Rather, the NFIP has multiple different legal provisions that generally tie to the expiration of key components of the program. Unless reauthorized or amended by Congress, the following will occur on September 30, 2023: (1) The authority to provide new flood insurance contracts will expire. Flood insurance contracts entered into before the expiration would continue until the end of their policy term of one year; and (2) The authority for NFIP to borrow funds from the Treasury will be reduced from $30.425 billion to $1 billion (42 U.S.C. §4016(a)). The most recent reauthorization of the NFIP is in P.L. 117-328.

In the 115th Congress, a number of bills were introduced to provide a longer-term reauthorization of the NFIP as well as make numerous other changes to the program. The House of Representatives passed H.R. 2874 (The 21st Century Flood Reform Act) by a vote of 237-189 on November 14, 2017. Among its numerous provisions, H.R. 2874 would have authorized the NFIP until September 30, 2022.

Three bills were introduced in the Senate that would have reauthorized the expiring provisions of the NFIP:

- S. 1313 (Flood Insurance Affordability and Sustainability Act of 2017);
- S. 1368 (Sustainable, Affordable, Fair, and Efficient [SAFE] National Flood Insurance Program Reauthorization Act of 2017);[218] and
- S. 1571 (National Flood Insurance Program Reauthorization Act of 2017).

None of these bills were considered by the full Senate in the 115th Congress. Among their other provisions, S. 1313 would have authorized the NFIP until September 30, 2027; S. 1368 would have authorized the NFIP until September 30, 2023; and S. 1571 would have authorized the NFIP until September 30, 2023.

The four reauthorization bills in the 115th Congress differed significantly in the degree to which they would have encouraged private participation in flood insurance, particularly flood insurance sold by private companies in competition with the NFIP. In general, legislation passed by the House was more encouraging of private flood insurance than Senate legislation. In the 115th Congress, the House included the same provisions in H.R. 2874 and in an unrelated bill to reauthorize the Federal Aviation Administration (H.R. 3823). The Senate removed the flood insurance language from H.R. 3823 before passing it. Reportedly, the provisions relating to private flood insurance were a particular issue of concern.[219] The Senate ultimately did not take up

---

[218] A similar bill was introduced in the House, H.R. 3285.

[219] See, for example, Shaun Courtney, "'Hard to Envision' Senate Democrats Blocking FAA Extension, Thune Says," *Bloomberg BNA*, September 27, 2017, Daily Report for Executives, Thune wants to see the Senate pass the House bill under unanimous consent, but committee ranking member Bill Nelson (D-Fla.) made that sound unlikely. "That will not get passed here," Nelson said Sept. 26 in response to Bloomberg BNA's inquiry about the House's flood insurance provision.... Senator Sherrod Brown (D-Ohio), ranking member on the Banking, Housing, and Urban Affairs Committee, which has jurisdiction over flood insurance proposals, said the House provision was unacceptable. "We're not

H.R. 2874 during the 115th Congress. S. 1313 included some similar provisions to H.R. 2874 on private flood insurance, but S. 1368 and S. 1571 did not.

In the 116th Congress, the House Financial Services Committee completed markup of a bill for the long-term reauthorization of the NFIP, the National Flood Insurance Program Reauthorization Act of 2019 (H.R. 3167), and ordered it reported on June 12, 2019.[220] H.R. 3167 would have reauthorized the NFIP until September 30, 2024. One bill was introduced in the Senate, on July 18, 2019, to reauthorize the expiring provisions of the NFIP: the National Flood Insurance Program Reauthorization and Reform Act of 2019 (S. 2187), with a companion bill in the House, H.R. 3872.[221] The latter two bills were not considered by the committees of jurisdiction. S. 2187 and H.R. 3872 would also have reauthorized the NFIP until September 30, 2024. Details of the provisions relating to private insurance in the House and Senate bills in the 116th Congress are described in the Appendix, and Table A-1 relates the provisions in the bills in the 116th Congress to the issues discussed in this report.

## The Current Role of Private Insurers in the NFIP

Private insurers can be involved in the flood insurance market in a number of ways, including (1) by helping to administer the NFIP; (2) by sharing risk with the NFIP as a reinsurer; or (3) by taking on risk themselves as a primary insurer, where the insurer contracts directly with a consumer. Since 1983, private insurers have played a major role in administering the NFIP, including selling and servicing policies and adjusting claims, but they largely have not been underwriting flood risk themselves.[222] Instead, the NFIP retains the direct financial risk of paying claims for these policies. The NFIP has purchased reinsurance since 2016, thus transferring some of the flood risk to the private sector.

---

going to do it," Brown said. "This would undermine all of our flood insurance efforts. It will cause all kinds of cherry-picking by private insurance."

220 See H.Rept. 116-262, Part 1, https://www.congress.gov/116/crpt/hrpt262/CRPT-116hrpt262.pdf.

221 H.R. 3872 was introduced on July 22, 2019.

222 Underwriting risk refers to the potential loss to an insurer or reinsurer. An insurer takes on this risk in return for a premium, and promises to pay an agreed amount in the event of a loss. See NAIC, *Glossary of Insurance Terms*, http://www.naic.org/consumer_glossary.htm#U.

## Servicing of Policies and Claims Management

While FEMA provides the overarching management and oversight of the NFIP, the majority of the day-to-day operation of the NFIP is handled by private companies. This includes marketing, selling and writing policies, and all aspects of claims management.[223] FEMA has established two different arrangements with private industry. The first is the Direct Servicing Agent, or DSA, which operates as a private contractor, selling NFIP policies on behalf of FEMA for individuals seeking to purchase flood insurance policies directly from the NFIP.[224] The DSA also handles the policies of severe repetitive loss properties.[225] The second arrangement is the Write-Your-Own (WYO) program, where private insurance companies are paid to issue and service NFIP policies. With either the DSA or WYO program, the NFIP retains the actual financial risk of paying claims for the policy, and the policy terms and premiums are the same. Approximately 13% of the total NFIP policy portfolio is managed through the DSA and 87% of NFIP policies are sold by the 57 companies participating in the WYO program.[226]

Companies participating in the WYO program are compensated through a variety of methods, but this compensation is not directly based on the costs incurred by the WYOs. In the Biggert-Waters Flood Insurance Reform Act of 2012 (Division F, Title II of P.L. 112-141, hereinafter BW-12), Congress required FEMA to develop and issue a rulemaking on a "methodology for determining the appropriate amounts that property and casualty insurance companies participating in the WYO program should be reimbursed for selling, writing, and servicing flood insurance policies and adjusting flood insurance claims on behalf of the National Flood Insurance Program."[227] This rulemaking was required within a year of enactment of BW-12. FEMA published an Advanced Notice of Proposed Rulemaking to revise the

[223] See primarily 42 U.S.C. §4081 and §4018, and 44 C.F.R. Part 62.

[224] The current Direct Servicing Agent is a company called National Flood Services., who was awarded the contract in October 2020. See https://nationalfloodservices.com/press/nfs-awarded-nfip-direct-service-provider-contract/https:// content.govdelivery.com/accounts/USDHSFEMA/bulletins/1c9da05.

[225] Severe repetitive loss properties are those that have incurred four or more claim payments exceeding $5,000 each, with a cumulative amount of such payments over $20,000; or at least two claims with a cumulative total exceeding the value of the property. See 42 U.S.C. §4014(h) and 44 C.F.R. §79.2(h).

[226] Email correspondence from FEMA Congressional Affairs staff, March 1, 2019. A list of companies participating in the WYO program is available at https://nfipservices.floodsmart.gov/wyo-program-list.

[227] §100224 of P.L. 112-141, 126 Stat. 936.

compensation structure of the WYOs on July 8, 2019.[228] The comment period closed on September 6, 2019. Until the analysis is complete, it is difficult to ascertain how much it actually costs WYO companies to administer the NFIP policies, or the WYO's profit margins (if any).

In the 115th Congress, H.R. 2874 would have capped the allowance paid to the WYOs at 27.9% of premiums, while S. 1368 would have capped the allowance at 22.46%.

In the 116th Congress, Section 302 of S. 2187 would have established that the total amount of reimbursement paid to WYO companies could not be greater than 22.46% of the aggregate amount of premiums charged by the company. This section would also have required FEMA to ensure that the commission paid by a WYO company to agents of the company would not be less than 15%. Section 304 of S. 2187 would require FEMA, within 12 months of enactment, to develop a schedule to determine the actual costs of WYO companies and reimburse the WYO companies only for the actual costs of the service or products. It would have required that all reimbursements made to WYO companies be made public, including a description of the product or service provided to which the reimbursement pertains. Section 405 of S. 2187 would have required FEMA to establish penalties for underpayment of claims by WYO companies that are not less than the penalty for overpayment of a claim. Both H.R. 3872 and S. 2187 contained provisions giving FEMA the authority to terminate a WYO contract under certain conditions, such as fraud or other conduct detrimental to the NFIP.

### *Reinsurance*

In the Homeowner Flood Insurance Affordability Act of 2014 (P.L. 113-89, HFIAA), Congress revised the authority of FEMA to secure reinsurance[229] for the NFIP from the private reinsurance and capital markets.[230] The purchase of private market reinsurance reduces the likelihood of FEMA needing to borrow

---

[228] Federal Emergency Management Agency, "National Flood Insurance Program (NFIP); Revisions to Methodology for Payments to Write Your Own (WYO) Companies," 84(130) *Federal Register* 32,371-32,379, July 8, 2019, and Federal Emergency Management Agency, "National Flood Insurance Program (NFIP); Revisions to Methodology for Payments to Write Your Own (WYO) Companies; Correction," 84(170) *Federal Register* 45,933-45,934, September 3, 2019.

[229] Reinsurance is defined as a transaction between a primary insurer and another licensed (re)insurer where the reinsurer agrees to cover all or part of the losses and/or loss adjustment expenses of the primary insurer. See NAIC, *Glossary of Insurance Terms*, http://www.naic.org/consumer_glossary.htm#R.

[230] See §10 of P.L. 113-89, 128 Stat. 1025, as codified at 42 U.S.C. §4081(e).

from the Treasury to pay claims. In addition, as the U.S. Government Accountability Office (GAO) noted, reinsurance could be beneficial because it allows FEMA to price some of its flood risk up front through the premiums it pays to the reinsurers rather than borrowing from Treasury after a flood.[231] From a risk management perspective, using reinsurance to cover losses in only the more extreme years could help the government to manage and reduce the volatility of its losses over time.

Transfer of risk to the private sector through reinsurance, however, is unlikely to lower the overall cost of the NFIP because reinsurers understandably charge FEMA premiums to compensate for the risk they assume. The primary benefit of reinsurance is to transfer and manage risk rather than to reduce the NFIP's long-term fiscal exposure.[232] For example, a reinsurance scenario which would provide the NFIP with $16.8 billion coverage (sufficient for Katrina-level losses) could cost an estimated $2.2 billion per year.[233] Such a reinsurance premium, however, would be a large portion of the total premiums paid into the NFIP, approximately two-thirds of the current premium amounts. Devoting such a large portion of premiums to reinsurance could leave insufficient funds for paying claims outside of large disasters,[234] or for covering the other purposes for NFIP funds, such as flood mitigation, mapping, and improving NFIP rating structures.

Reinsurance has been purchased by FEMA through two different mechanisms, "traditional" reinsurance and reinsurance backed by catastrophe bonds.[235] The traditional reinsurance has been purchased from a varied group of reinsurance companies with each reinsurer bearing part of the risk. The catastrophe bond reinsurance is facilitated by a single company, with the risk then transferred to capital market investors who purchase the bonds. The specifics of each reinsurance purchase has varied, but in general, the reinsurance has been designed to pay a certain percentage of the losses from a

---

231 GAO, *Flood Insurance: Comprehensive Reform Could Improve Solvency and Enhance Resilience*, GAO-17-425, April 2017, p. 19, https://www.gao.gov/products/GAO-17-425.

232 Ibid.

233 FEMA, *National Flood Insurance Program Report to Congress on Reinsuring NFIP Insurance Risk and Options for Privatizing the NFIP*, August 13, 2015, p. 171.

234 The NFIP reinsurance purchases have been designed to cover claims for only one large flood, and smaller flood claims will continue to be paid from NFIP premiums.

235 For more details see FEMA, *National Flood Insurance Program (NFIP) Reinsurance Program*, https://www.fema.gov/flood-insurance/work-with-nfip/reinsurance and CRS Insight IN10965, *The National Flood Insurance Program (NFIP), Reinsurance, and Catastrophe Bonds*, by Diane P. Horn and Baird Webel.

single, large scale event, with a higher percentage if losses are higher.[236] Coverage has typically started after $4 billion in losses, a loss level that has only been reached by the NFIP in three events—Hurricane Katrina, Superstorm Sandy, and Hurricane Harvey. Table 1 outlines the various reinsurance purchases, including the dates in force, type of reinsurance, amount of coverage, premiums paid by FEMA, and claims paid to FEMA.

**Table 1.** NFIP reinsurance purchases

($ billions)

| Date | Type | Coverage Amount | Coverage Levels | Premiums Paid by FEMA | To Date Claims Paid to FEMA |
|---|---|---|---|---|---|
| CY2017 | Traditional | $1.042 | $4-8 | $0.150 | $1.042 |
| CY2018 | Traditional | $1.46 | $4-8 | $0.235 | $0 |
| August 2018-July 2021 | Catastrophe Bond | $0.5 | $5-10 | $0.188a | $0 |
| CY2019 | Traditional | $1.32 | $4-10 | $0.186 | $0 |
| April 2019-April 2022 | Catastrophe Bond | $0.3 | $6-8 | $0.107b | |
| CY2020 | Traditional | $1.33 | $4-10 | $0.205 | $0 |
| February 2020-February 2023 | Catastrophe Bond | $0.4 | $6-10 | $0.101c | $0 |
| CY2021 | Traditional | $1.46 | $4-10 | $0.195 | $0 |
| February 2021-February 2024 | Catastrophe Bond | $0.575 | $6-9 | $0.079d | $0 |

Source: FEMA websites at https://www.fema.gov/flood-insurance/work-with-nfip/reinsurance and information provided by FEMA Congressional Affairs staff, November 15, 2021.

[a] Premiums of $62 million in each of first and second years, $63.75 million in third year.

[b] Premiums of $32 million in first year, $38 million in second year, $37.2 million in third year.

[c] Premiums of $50.28 million in first year and $50.88 million in second year.

[d] Premium of $79.44 million in the first year.

---

236 For example, the 2020 traditional reinsurance purchase covered 10.25% of NFIP losses from $4 billion to $6 billion, 34.68% of losses from $6 billion to $8 billion, and $21.80% of losses from $8 billion to $10 billion.

In the 115th Congress, H.R. 2874, S. 1313, and S. 1571 all contained provisions that would have required or encouraged the NFIP to transfer a portion of its risk to the private reinsurance market. In the 116th Congress, H.R. 3167, Section 406, would have required FEMA annually to evaluate ceding a portion of the risk of the NFIP to the private reinsurance or capital markets, if the Administrator determines that the rates and terms are reasonable and doing so would further the development and maintenance of a sound financial framework for the NFIP. The Senate bill in the 116th Congress, S. 2187, did not contain any provisions related to reinsurance. In the 117th Congress, companion bills S. 3128 and H.R. 5802 did not contain any provisions related to reinsurance.

The NFIP has claimed on reinsurance once, after the losses experienced after Hurricane Harvey, which resulted in over $9 billion paid by the NFIP to policyholders and triggered the full claim of $1.042 billion on the 2017 reinsurance. To date, FEMA has not claimed on any of the catastrophe bonds.

## Private Flood Insurance Outside the NFIP: Issues and Barriers

One of the reasons that Congress created the NFIP in 1968 was the general unavailability of flood insurance from private insurers. Private flood insurance was offered between 1895 and 1927, but losses incurred from the 1927 Mississippi River floods and additional flood losses in 1928 led most insurers to stop offering flood policies.[237] Private flood insurance companies largely concluded that flood peril was uninsurable because of the catastrophic nature of flooding, the difficulty of determining accurate rates, the risk of adverse selection,[238] and the concern that they could not profitably provide risk-based flood coverage at a price that consumers felt they could afford.[239]

---

[237] National Research Council of the National Academies, *Affordability of National Flood Insurance Program Premiums: Report 1*, 2015, p. 23, http://www.nap.edu/catalog/21709/affordability-of-national-flood-insurance- program-premiums-report-1.

[238] Adverse selection is the phenomenon whereby persons with a higher than average probability of loss seek greater insurance coverage than those with less risk. See National Association of Insurance Commissioners (NAIC), *Glossary of Insurance Terms*, http://www.naic.org/consumer_glossary.htm.

[239] See GAO, *Flood Insurance: Strategies for Increasing Private Sector Involvement*, GAO-47-127, January 2014, p. 6, https://www.gao.gov/products/GAO-14-127, and Caroline Kousky and Howard Kunreuther, *The National Flood Insurance Program: Yesterday, Today and Tomorrow*, NAIC, Center for Insurance Policy and Research Study Series 2017-1: Flood Risk and Insurance, Kansas City, MO, April 2017, pp. 23-45, http://www.naic.org/documents/cipr_study_1704_flood_risk.pdf.

Currently, the private flood insurance market most commonly provides commercial coverage, secondary coverage above the NFIP maximums, or coverage in the lender-placed market.[240] The 2018 premiums for private flood insurance as reported to the National Association of Insurance Commissioners (NAIC)[241] totaled $644 million, up from $589 million in 2017 and $376 million in 2016,[242] compared to the $3.5 billion total amount of NFIP premiums. In general, the private flood market tends to focus on high-value properties, which command higher premiums and therefore the extra expense of flood underwriting can be more readily justified.[243]

Currently few private insurers compete with the NFIP in the primary residential flood insurance market. One illustration of this is that the NAIC only began systematically collecting separate data on private flood insurance in 2016.

As discussed in the following sections, private insurers have identified a number of potential barriers to more widespread private sector involvement in providing flood insurance. Increasing private insurance may present a number of issues for the NFIP and for consumers.

## Flood Insurance Coverage "at Least as Broad as" the NFIP

In BW-12, Congress explicitly provided for private flood insurance to fulfill the mandatory purchase mortgage requirement as long as the private flood insurance "provides flood insurance coverage which is at least as broad as the coverage" of the NFIP, among other conditions.[244]

Implementation of this requirement has proved challenging. The crux of the implementation issue is in answering the question of who would evaluate whether specific policies met the "at least as broad as" standard and what criteria would be used in making this evaluation. Some lending institutions feel that they lack the necessary technical expertise to evaluate whether a flood

---

[240] The lender-placed or forced-place market is where lenders can force-place flood insurance on properties that are out of compliance with the mandatory purchase requirement.

[241] The NAIC is an organization of the state regulators of insurance and, among other things, collects the data that the regulators require to be reported by insurance companies.

[242] Statistics provided by the National Association of Insurance Commissioners to CRS. They do not include coverage written in the surplus lines marketplace by non-U.S. insurers.

[243] FEMA, National Flood Insurance Program Report to Congress on Reinsuring NFIP Insurance Risk and Options for Privatizing the NFIP, August 13, 2015, p. 32.

[244] 42 U.S.C §4012a(b).

insurance policy meets the definition of private flood insurance set forth in BW-12.[245]

The responsible federal agencies[246] issued two separate Notices of Proposed Rulemaking (NPRM) on the question, the first in October 2013,[247] and the second in November 2016.[248] On February 12, 2019, the agencies announced a final rule implementing this BW-12 requirement.[249] Of particular note, the agencies indicate the rule

- "allows institutions to rely on an insurer's written assurances in a private flood insurance policy stating the criteria are met; [and]
- clarifies that institutions may, under certain conditions, accept private flood insurance policies that do not meet the Biggert-Waters Act criteria."[250]

This second point may seem unusual, because BW-12 included a specific definition of private flood insurance, while the agencies indicate that the rule allows acceptance of private flood insurance that does not meet this statutory definition. In creating the exception that allows private flood insurance that does not follow the statutory definition of "private flood insurance," the agencies relied on the usage of the more general term "flood insurance" in 42

---

[245] Department of the Treasury, Federal Reserve System, Federal Deposit Insurance Corporation, Farm Credit Administration, National Credit Union Administration, "Loans in Areas Having Special Flood Hazards, Proposed Rule." vol. 78, no. 201 *Federal Register* 65113, October 30, 2013.

[246] Office of the Comptroller of the Currency, Board of Governors of the Federal Reserve System, Federal Deposit Insurance Corporation, Farm Credit Administration, and National Credit Union Administration.

[247] Department of the Treasury, Federal Reserve System, Federal Deposit Insurance Corporation, Farm Credit Administration, National Credit Union Administration, "Loans in Areas Having Special Flood Hazards, Proposed Rule," vol. 78, no. 201, *Federal Register* 65108-65144, October 30, 2013.

[248] Department of the Treasury, Federal Reserve System, Federal Deposit Insurance Corporation, Farm Credit Administration, National Credit Union Administration, "Loans in Areas Having Special Flood Hazards—Private Flood Insurance," vol. 81, no. 215, *Federal Register* 78063-78080, November 7, 2016.

[249] Department of the Treasury, Federal Reserve System, Federal Deposit Insurance Corporation, Farm Credit Administration, National Credit Union Administration, "Loans in Areas Having Special Flood Hazards—Private Flood Insurance," vol. 84, no. 34, *Federal Register* 4953-4975, February 20, 2019.

[250] Federal Reserve System, Farm Credit Administration, Federal Deposit Insurance Corporation, National Credit Union Administration, and Office of the Comptroller of the Currency, "New Rule Covers Private Flood Insurance," press release, February 12, 2019, at https://www.occ.gov/news-issuances/news-releases/2019/nr-ia-2019-15.html.

U.S.C. 4012a(b)(1)(A) combined with the perceived congressional intent to promote private insurance in BW-12.[251]

The rule took effect on July 1, 2019. Press reports described it as generally welcomed by the banking industry,[252] but it is unclear to what extent this new rule will encourage private flood insurance or whether additional legislative changes might be needed if Congress seeks to further encourage development of the private flood insurance market.

In the 115th Congress, H.R. 2874 and S. 1313 included provisions that would have revised the definition of private flood insurance, striking existing statutory language requiring private flood insurance to provide coverage "at least as broad as the coverage" provided by the NFIP in order to meet the mandatory purchase requirements. Instead, the new definition would have relied on whether the insurance policy and insurance company were in compliance with the laws and regulations in the state where the insurance was purchased. S. 1368 and S. 1571 had no similar provisions. Neither of the bills in the 116th Congress included any provisions related to the definition of private flood insurance.

## Continuous Coverage

An associated issue is that of continuous coverage, which is required for property owners to retain any subsidies or cross-subsidies in their NFIP premium rates. Under existing law, if an NFIP policyholder allows their policy to lapse, any subsidy that they currently receive would be eliminated immediately.[253] Unless legislation specifically allows private flood insurance to count for continuous coverage, a borrower may be reluctant to purchase private insurance if doing so means they would lose their subsidy should they later decide to return to NFIP coverage.

In the 115th Congress, H.R. 2874 included a provision that would have specified that if a property owner purchases private flood insurance and

---

[251] For the complete agency rationale, see the section entitled "Discretionary Acceptance" in Department of the Treasury, Federal Reserve System, Federal Deposit Insurance Corporation, Farm Credit Administration, National Credit Union Administration, "Loans in Areas Having Special Flood Hazards—Private Flood Insurance," vol. 84, no. 34, *Federal Register* 4959-4960, February 20, 2019.

[252] See, for example, Sinnock, Bonnie, "Banks Claim Victory in New Private Flood Insurance Rule," *American Banker*, February 11, 2019.

[253] As required by §100205(a)(1)(B) of BW-12 (P.L. 112-141, 126 Stat. 917), only for NFIP policies that lapsed in coverage as a result of the deliberate choice of the policyholder.

decides then to return to the NFIP, they would be considered to have maintained continuous coverage. S. 1313 included a provision to allow private flood insurance to count as continuous coverage. S. 1368 and S. 1571 had no similar provisions. In the 116th Congress, Section 401 of H.R. 3167 would have considered any period during which a property is covered by a flood insurance policy, either through the NFIP or a private company, to be a period of continuous coverage. S. 2187 did not contain any provisions related to continuous coverage.

## The "Non-Compete" Clause

Before FY2019, the Write Your Own carriers, private insurers who sell and service NFIP policies, were restricted in their ability to sell flood insurance policies on their own behalf while also participating as a WYO, due to a "non-compete" clause contained in the standard NFIP contracts.[254] These contracts governing the WYO companies' participation in the NFIP restricted the WYO carriers from selling their own standalone private flood products.[255] A non-compete clause would require WYO companies to decide whether to offer private flood insurance policies in their own right or to act as WYO carriers, thus potentially limiting the size of the private flood market. In the 115th Congress, H.R. 2874 would have eliminated the non-compete clause in place at the time, while S. 1313 would have provided temporary authorization for WYOs to sell private flood insurance for certain types of properties,[256] with a follow-up study by FEMA to determine if the authorization should be made permanent.

The CBO cost estimate of H.R. 2874[257] considered the impact of eliminating the WYO companies' non-compete agreement. CBO estimated that, over the 2017-2027 period, holders of about 690,000 properties that, under existing law, would have been purchased under the NFIP would instead

---

[254] Details of the FY2021 WYO company arrangements are available at https://www.fema.gov/sites/default/files/2020-10/fema_fy-21-wyo-financial-subsidy-arrangement_october-2020.pdf.

[255] GAO, *Flood Insurance: Potential Barriers Cited to Increased Use of Private Insurance*, GAO-16-611, July 14, 2016, p. 31, https://www.gao.gov/assets/680/678414.pdf.

[256] Nonresidential properties, severe repetitive loss properties, business properties, or any property that has incurred flood-related damage in which the cumulative amount of payments equaled or exceeded the fair market value of the property.

[257] Congressional Budget Office, *Cost Estimate. H.R. 2874, 21st Century Flood Reform Act*, Washington, DC, September 8, 2017, pp. 1-13, https://www.cbo.gov/publication/53088.

choose to buy private flood insurance to cover those properties if H.R. 2874 were enacted.

CBO did not expect any property owners who are subsidized by the NFIP to be among those leaving the program.[258] CBO estimated that eliminating the non-compete clause and making NFIP data publically available would lead to an increase in spending of $39 million for the 2018-2022 period and $393 million for the 2018-2017 period.[259]

FEMA implemented changes in the standard WYO contracts for FY2019 removing the restrictions on WYO companies offering private flood insurance, while maintaining requirements that such private insurance lines remain entirely separate from a WYO company's NFIP insurance business.[260] The non-compete clause has again been excluded from the WYO agreements for FY2020[261] and FY2021.[262] This action removes the non-compete clause without legislation, although FEMA in the future would retain the authority to reinstate the non-compete clause.

## NFIP Subsidized Rates

FEMA's subsidized rates are often seen as one of the primary barriers to private sector involvement in flood insurance.[263] However, even without the subsidies mandated by law, the NFIP's definition of full-risk rates differs from that of private insurers. Whereas the NFIP's full- risk rates must incorporate expected losses and operating costs, a private insurer's full-risk rates must also incorporate a profitable return on capital. As a result, even those NFIP policies which are considered to be actuarially sound from the perspective of the NFIP

---

[258] Ibid., p. 9.

[259] Ibid., p. 5.

[260] FEMA, "National Flood Insurance Program (NFIP); Assistance to Private Sector Property Insurers, Notice of FY 2019 Arrangement," 83(52) *Federal Register* 11772-11778, March 16, 2018.

[261] FEMA, Federal Insurance and Mitigation Administration, *FY2020 Financial Assistance/ Subsidy Arrangement*, October 1, 2019, https://www.fema.gov/sites/default/files/2020-05/FY2020-WYO-Financial-Assistance-Subsidy-Arrangement.pdfhttps://www.fema.gov/media-library-data/1572968146685-72df1f4c423446afef8104ba79ee81c3/FY2020-WYO-Financial-Assistance-Subsidy-Arrangement.pdf.

[262] FEMA, Federal Insurance and Mitigation Administration, *FY2021 Financial Assistance/ Subsidy Arrangement*, October 1, 2020, https://www.fema.gov/sites/default/files/2020-10/fema_fy-21-wyo-financial-subsidy-arrangement_october-2020.pdf.

[263] GAO, *Flood Insurance: Comprehensive Reform Could Improve Solvency and Enhance Resilience*, GAO-17-425, April 2017, p. 34, https://www.gao.gov/products/GAO-17-425.

may still be underpriced from the perspective of private insurers.[264] In order to make the flood insurance market attractive, private insurers would want to be able to charge premium rates that reflect the full estimated risk of potential flood losses while still allowing the companies to make a profit. A reformed NFIP rate structure could have the effect of encouraging more private insurers to enter the primary flood market because NFIP full-risk based rates would be closer to the rates that private insurers would likely charge; however, this could lead to higher rates for households.

In the 115th Congress, H.R. 2874 would have phased out the pre-FIRM subsidy for primary residences at a rate of 6.5%-15% (compared to the current rate of 5%-18%),[265] in a staged manner. In the first year after enactment, the minimum rate increase would have been 5%; in the second year after enactment, the minimum rate increase would have been 5.5%; and in the third year of enactment, the minimum rate increase would have been 6%. The phaseout of the pre-FIRM subsidy for other categories of properties[266] would have remained at 25%. The Senate bills in the 115th Congress did not contain any provisions related to premium rate subsidies. In the 116th Congress, H.R. 3167 would not have changed the rates at which subsidies can be phased out. S. 2187, Section 102, would have prohibited FEMA from increasing the amount of covered costs above 9% per year on any policyholder during the five-year period beginning on the date of enactment. Covered costs include premiums, surcharges (including the surcharge for ICC coverage and the HFIAA surcharge), and the Federal Policy Fee. This would have limited the rate of increase of covered costs for all categories of policies, not just policies for primary residences, and would be particularly significant for those policies where the pre-FIRM subsidy is currently being phased out at 25% per year.

FEMA introduced a redesigned risk rating system for the NFIP, known as Risk Rating 2.0.[267] The new premium rates went into effect for new NFIP policies on October 1, 2021, and took effect for current policyholders on April 1, 2022. Premiums under Risk Rating 2.0 reflect an individual property's risk

---

[264] FEMA, *National Flood Insurance Program Report to Congress on Reinsuring NFIP Insurance Risk and Options for Privatizing the NFIP*, August 13, 2015, p. 58.

[265] For a discussion of the rates at which NFIP subsidies can be phased out, see the section on Pricing and Premium Rate Structure in CRS Report R44593, *Introduction to the National Flood Insurance Program (NFIP)*, by Diane P. Horn and Baird Webel.

[266] Non-primary residences, nonresidential properties, severe repetitive loss properties, properties with substantial cumulative damage, and properties with substantial damage or improvement after July 6, 2012.

[267] For additional information on Risk Rating 2.0, see CRS Report R45999, *National Flood Insurance Program: The Current Rating Structure and Risk Rating 2.0*, by Diane P. Horn.

and reflect more types of flood risk in rates. Premiums are calculated based on the specific features of an individual property, including structural variables such as the foundation type of the structure, the height of the lowest floor of the structure relative to base flood elevation, and the replacement cost value of the structure. Risk Rating 2.0 incorporates a broader range of flood frequencies and sources than the current rating system, as well as geographical variables such as the distance to water, the type and size of nearest bodies of water, and the elevation of the property relative to the flooding source. Risk Rating 2.0 continues the overall policy of phasing out NFIP subsidies, but will not be able to increase rates annually beyond the limitations on annual premium increases which are set in statute.[268] Risk Rating 2.0 will not eliminate the three categories of properties which pay less than the full risk-based rates, nor the process of phasing out subsidies which began with BW-12. In general, Risk Rating 2.0 is expected to lead to the reduction of cross-subsidies between NFIP policyholders, and the eventual elimination of premium subsidies and cross-subsidies once all properties are paying the full risk-based rate. This should bring NFIP premiums closer to the premiums of private insurers and could potentially increase competition.

## Regulatory Uncertainty

As addressed above, the rules on the acceptance of private insurance for the mandatory purchase requirement, and whether or not private flood insurance would count for continuous coverage, have had a significant impact on the market potential for private insurers.[269] Another driver of private sector concern is regulatory uncertainty at the state level. The role of state regulators would increase in a flood insurance market with increased private sector involvement, which could increase the burden of oversight. The involvement of 56 state and territorial insurance regulators is likely to add complexity and additional costs for insurers, lenders, or property owners.[270] For example, some private insurers cited the intervention of state regulators in controlling rates for wind insurance in Florida as a reason for withdrawing from that

---

[268] 42 U.S.C. §4015(e).

[269] See FEMA, National Flood Insurance Program Report to Congress on Reinsuring NFIP Insurance Risk and Options for Privatizing the NFIP, August 13, 2015, p. 62; and GAO, Flood Insurance: Potential Barriers Cited to Increased Use of Private Insurance, GAO-16-611, July 14, 2016, pp. 26-29, https://www.gao.gov/assets/680/678414.pdf.

[270] Ibid., p. 63.

market.[271] However, this could also lead to the development of state-specific insurance solutions, which might better suit local social and economic conditions.[272] In the 115th Congress, H.R. 2874 and S. 1313 referenced state laws and regulations in their definition of private flood insurance that could meet the mandatory purchase requirements. Neither of the bills in the 116th Congress included any provisions related to state laws or regulation of private flood insurance.

## Ability to Assess Flood Risk Accurately

Many insurers view the lack of access to NFIP data on flood losses and claims as a barrier to more private companies offering flood insurance. It is argued that increasing access to past NFIP claims data would allow private insurance companies to better estimate future losses and price flood insurance premiums, and ultimately to determine which properties they might be willing to insure.[273] However, FEMA's view is that the agency would need to address privacy concerns in order to provide property level information to insurers, because the Privacy Act of 1974[274] prohibits FEMA from releasing policy and claims data which contain personally identifiable information. Private insurers have also suggested that better flood risk assessment tools such as improved flood maps and inland and storm surge models are needed in order to price risks at the individual and portfolio level.[275] In the 115th Congress, H.R. 2874 would have required FEMA to make all NFIP claims data publicly available in a form that does not reveal personally identifiable information, while S. 1313 would have authorized FEMA to sell or license individual claims data while requiring FEMA to make aggregate claims data available. In the 116th Congress, H.R. 3167, Section 404, would have allowed FEMA to provide

---

[271] Ibid., p. 105.

[272] Ibid., p. 41.

[273] American Academy of Actuaries Flood Insurance Work Group, *The National Flood Insurance Program: Challenges and Solutions*, April 2017, p. 60, http://www.actuary.org/files/publications/FloodMonograph.04192017.pdf.

[274] P.L. 93-579, 5 U.S.C. §552a, as amended.

[275] See, for example, GAO, *Flood Insurance: Strategies for Increasing Private Sector Involvement*, 14-127, January 2, 2014, pp. 10-11, https://www.gao.gov/products/GAO-14-127; FEMA, *National Flood Insurance Program Report to Congress on Reinsuring NFIP Insurance Risk and Options for Privatizing the NFIP*, August 13, 2015, p. 61; and Albert Kuller and Eleanor Gibson, *After the Storms: Harvey, Irma and Maria: Lessons Learned*, Lloyds, Market Insight Report 2018, May 24, 2018, pp. 1-30, https://www.lloyds.com/news-and-risk-insight/risk-reports/library/natural-environ ment/afterthestorms.

current and historical property-specific information on flood insurance program coverage, flood damage assessments, and payment of claims to private insurers, on the condition that private insurers provide the same information to FEMA, homeowners and home buyers. S. 2187, Section 305, would have required FEMA to report on the feasibility of selling or licensing the use of historical structure-specific NFIP claims data to non-governmental entities, while reasonably protecting policyholder privacy.

## Adequate Consumer Participation

Insurers need sufficient consumer participation to manage and diversify their risk exposure. Many private insurers have expressed the view that broader participation in the flood insurance market would be necessary to address adverse selection and maintain a sufficiently large risk pool.[276] A long-standing objective of the NFIP has been to increase purchases of flood insurance policies, and this objective was the motivation for introducing the mandatory purchase requirement.

Despite the mandatory purchase requirement, not all covered mortgages carry the insurance as dictated, and no up-to-date data on national compliance rates with the mandatory purchase requirement are available. A 2006 study commissioned by FEMA found that compliance with this mandatory purchase requirement may be as low as 43% in some areas of the country (the Midwest), and as high as 88% in others (the West).[277] A 2017 study of flood insurance in New York City found that compliance with the mandatory purchase requirement by properties in the SFHA with mortgages increased from 61% in 2012 to 73% in 2016.[278] The escrowing of NFIP insurance premiums, which began in January 2016, may increase compliance with the mandatory purchase requirement more widely, but no data are yet available.

---

[276] GAO, *Flood Insurance: Strategies for Increasing Private Sector Involvement*, 14-127, January 2, 2014, p. 14, https://www.gao.gov/products/GAO-14-127.

[277] Lloyd Dixon, Noreen Clancy, and Seth A. Seabury, et al., *The National Flood Insurance Program's Market Penetration Rate: Estimates and Policy Implications*, RAND Corporation, prepared as part of the Evaluation of the National Flood Insurance Program, February 2006, p. 23, https://www.rand.org/content/dam/rand/pubs/technical_reports/2006/RAND_TR300.pdf.

[278] Lloyd Dixon, Noreen Clancy, and Benjamin M. Miller, et al., The Cost and Affordability of Flood Insurance in New York City: Economic Impacts of Rising Premiums and Policy Options for One- to Four- Family Homes, Rand Corporation, RAND RR1776, Santa Monica, CA, April 2017, pp. 15-18, https://www.rand.org/pubs/research_reports/RR1776.html.

The mandatory purchase requirement could potentially be expanded to more (or all) mortgage loans made by federally regulated lending institutions for properties in communities participating in the NFIP.[279] Another possible option would be to require all properties within the SFHA to have flood insurance, not just those with federally backed mortgages.[280] Consumer participation could also be increased if the federal government were to mandate that homeowners' insurance policies include flood coverage or require all homeowners to purchase flood insurance.[281] All four 115th Congress bills contained provisions for some form of study to assess the compliance with the mandatory purchase requirement. H.R. 2874 would also have increased civil penalties on lenders for failing to enforce the mandatory purchase requirement. In the 116th Congress, both H.R. 3167, Section 408, and S. 2187, Section 108, would have required GAO to determine the percentages of properties with federally backed mortgages located in SFHAs that satisfy the mandatory purchase requirement, and the percentage of properties with federally backed mortgages located in the 500- year floodplain[282] that would satisfy the mandatory purchase requirement if the mandatory purchase requirement applied to such properties. Both bills would also have required GAO to conduct a study to address how to increase participation rates through programmatic and regulatory changes.

## Potential Effects of Increased Private Sector Involvement in the Flood Market

### Increased Consumer Choice

Current NFIP policies offer a relatively limited array of coverages, particularly compared to what is available in private markets for similar insurance against perils other than floods. Private insurance companies could potentially

---

[279] NFIP, *Report to Congress on Reinsuring NFIP Insurance Risk and Options for Privatizing the NFIP*, Appendix C: Flood Insurance Risk Study: Options for Privatizing the NFIP, August 13, 2015, p. 86.

[280] Association of State Floodplain Managers, Inc., *Rethinking the NFIP*, ASFPM Comments on NFIP Reform, January 11, 2011, p. 5, https://www.floods.org/whats-new/rethinking-the-nfip-comments-from-asfpm/.

[281] GAO, *Flood Insurance: Strategies for Increasing Private Sector Involvement*, 14-127, January 2, 2014, p. 22, https://www.gao.gov/products/GAO-14-127.

[282] The 500-year floodplain is defined by FEMA as an area with a 0.2% or greater risk of flooding every year.

compete with the NFIP by offering coverage not available under the NFIP, such as business interruption insurance, living expenses while a property is being repaired, basement coverage, coverage of other structures on a property, and/or by offering policies with coverage limits higher than the NFIP. The NFIP currently also has a 30-day waiting period in almost all cases before the insurance coverage goes into effect,[283] whereas private insurance companies may have a shorter waiting period. Private companies could also offer flood coverage as an add-on to a standard homeowners' policy, which could eliminate the current problem of distinguishing between flood damage (which is covered by the NFIP) and wind damage (which is often covered by standard homeowners' insurance). Unlike the NFIP, private flood insurance companies may also issue a policy without necessarily requiring elevation certificates, perhaps by using new technology to measure the elevation of individual structures.

## Cheaper Flood Insurance

Since some properties receive lower NFIP rates due to cross subsidies from other NFIP policyholders, it seems likely that some of the non-subsidized NFIP policyholders would be able to obtain less expensive flood insurance from private insurers. Private insurers may also be able to offer premiums more closely tied to individual risks than the NFIP currently does, which would provide lower premiums for some policyholders. Quantifying the potential savings for some policyholders from private insurance is, however, difficult, as the amount and extent of cross- subsidization within the NFIP is not fully known. One example of an attempt to provide estimates of NFIP versus private insurance is a modeling exercise carried out by two private companies, Milliman and KatRisk, which looked at premiums for single-family homes in Louisiana, Florida, and Texas. Their modeling suggested that 77% of single-family homes in Florida, 69% in Louisiana, and 92% in Texas would pay less with a private policy than with the NFIP; however, 14% in Florida, 21% in Louisiana, and 5% in Texas would pay over twice as much.[284]

---

[283] See FEMA, *Flood Insurance Manual, Before You Start*, Revised April 2021, pp. 2-11 to 2-14, https://www.fema.gov/sites/default/files/documents/fema_nfip-all-flood-insurance-manual-apr-2021.pdf.

[284] Nancy P. Watkins, *Could Private Flood Insurance Be Cheaper Than the NFIP?* Milliman, Milliman Briefing Paper, San Francisco, CA, July 10, 2017, pp. 1-2, http://www.milliman.com/insight/2017/Could-private-flood-insurance-be- cheaper-than-the-NFIP/.

Milliman did not provide any details of the coverage offered by these private policies, nor the basis on which their figures were estimated.

## Variable Consumer Protections

The consumer protections associated with private policies are likely to be enforced at a state level and will therefore be variable; some states may offer a higher level of protection than others.

Because private insurers are free to accept or reject potential policyholders as necessary in order to manage their risk portfolio, private insurers may not necessarily renew a policy. A private flood insurance policy might be less expensive than an NFIP policy, but it might also offer less extensive coverage, which a policyholder may not realize until they make a claim following a flood. Unlike the NFIP, the language in private flood insurance policies is not standardized and has not yet been tested in court in the same way as, for example, homeowners' insurance. Thus there may be greater variability in claims outcomes for consumers in the early years of private flood insurance penetration.

## Adverse Selection

Private sector competition might increase the financial exposure and volatility of the NFIP, as private markets will likely seek out policies that offer the greatest likelihood of profit. In the most extreme case, the private market may "cherry-pick" (i.e., adversely select against the NFIP) the profitable, lower-risk NFIP policies that are "overpriced" either due to cross-subsidization or imprecise flood insurance rate structures, particularly when there is pricing inefficiency in favor of the customer.[285] This could leave the NFIP with a higher density of actuarially unsound policies that are being directly subsidized or benefiting from cross-subsidization. Because the NFIPcannot refuse to write a policy, those properties that are considered "undesirable" by private insurers are likely to remain in the NFIP portfolio—private insurers will not compete against the NFIP for policies that are inadequately priced

[285] David Altmaier, Andy Case, and Mike Chaney, et al., *Flood Risk and Insurance*, NAIC Center for Insurance Policy and Research, CIPR Study Series 2017-1, April 2017, p. 47, http://www.naic.org/documents/ cipr_study_1704_flood_risk.pdf.

from their perspective.[286] Private insurers, as profit- seeking entities, are unlikely independently to price flood insurance policies in a way that ensures affordable premiums as a purposeful goal, although some private policies could be less expensive than NFIP policies. It is likely that the NFIP would be left with a higher proportion of subsidized policies, which may become less viable in a competitive market.[287]

The extent of such "cherry picking" is uncertain with some arguing that it would have little effect.[288] However, evidence from the UK flood insurance market suggests that even in an entirely private market "cherry picking" can be difficult to avoid. Interviews of private insurers indicate that one of the key drivers for the introduction of Flood Re, the UK private flood insurance scheme which was introduced in 2016, was the emergence of new entrants in the flood insurance market after 2000. These new entrants had little or no existing high-flood-risk business and no commitment to continue to insure this business under the terms of the then-existing informal agreement with the government. This gave them a competitive advantage, as they could choose to select the more profitable lower-risk business. One driver for change therefore was that Flood Re would include these new entrants and force them to contribute by charging their clients for the cross-subsidy for Flood Re, leveling the playing field between the private insurers.[289]

A significant increase in private flood insurance policies that "depopulates" the NFIP may also undermine the NFIP's ability to generate revenue, reducing the amount of past borrowing that can be repaid or extending the time required to repay the debt. If the number of NFIP policies decreases, it would likely become increasingly difficult for the remaining NFIP policyholders to subsidize policies, raising prices for the non-subsidized policyholders and thus accelerating the move to private insurance. In the long term the program could be left as a "residual market" for subsidized or high-risk properties. Residual market mechanisms are used in areas such as auto insurance, where consumers may be required to purchase insurance, but higher

---

[286] FEMA, National Flood Insurance Program Report to Congress on Reinsuring NFIP Insurance Risk and Options for Privatizing the NFIP, August 13, 2015, p. 85.

[287] American Academy of Actuaries Flood Insurance Work Group, *The National Flood Insurance Program: Challenges and Solutions*, April 2017, p. 66, http://www.actuary.org/files/publications/FloodMonograph.04192017.pdf.

[288] See, for example, R.J. Lehman, "Private Flood Insurance Market Is Getting Bigger, More Competitive, Less Profitable," *Insurance Journal*, March 18, 2018, at https://www.insurancejournal.com/blogs/right-street/2018/03/18/ 483689.htm.

[289] Edmund C. Penning-Rowsell, Sally Priest, and Clare Johnson, "The Evolution of UK Flood Insurance: Incremental Change Over Six Decades," *International Journal of Water Resources Development*, vol. 30, no. 4 (2014), pp. 694-713.

risk individuals may be unable to purchase it from regular insurers. The exact form of residual market mechanisms varies in different states and for different types of insurance, but they typically require some form of outside support either from the government or from insurers themselves.

In the 115th Congress, S. 1313 would have required FEMA, within two years of enactment, to report on the extent to which the properties for which private flood insurance is purchased tend to be at a lower risk than properties for which NFIP policies are purchased (i.e., the extent of adverse selection), by detailing the risk classifications of the private flood insurance policies. S. 1313 would also have provided the FEMA Administrator the power to limit the participation of WYO companies in the broader flood insurance marketplace if the Administrator determined that private insurance adversely impacts the NFIP. Neither of the bills in the 116th Congress included any provisions related to adverse selection.

## Issues for NFIP Flood Mapping and Floodplain Management

If the number of NFIP policyholders were to decrease significantly, it might also be difficult to support the NFIP's functions of reducing flood risk through flood mapping and floodplain management.[290] NFIP flood mapping is currently funded in two ways, through (1) annual discretionary appropriations; and (2) discretionary spending authority from offsetting money collected from the Federal Policy Fee (FPF).[291] The FPF is paid to FEMA and deposited in the National Flood Insurance Fund (NFIF). The income from the FPF is designated to pay for floodplain mapping activities, floodplain management programs, and certain administrative expenses.[292] About 66% of the resources from the FPF are allocated to flood mapping, with floodplain management receiving about 19% of the overall income from the FPF.[293] To the extent that the private flood insurance market grows and policies move from the NFIP to private insurers, FEMA will no longer collect the FPF on those policies and less revenue will be available for floodplain mapping and management.

---

[290] For a further discussion of the NFIP's floodplain management and mapping functions, see CRS Report R46095, *The National Flood Insurance Program: Selected Issues and Legislation in the 116th Congress*, by Diane P. Horn and Baird Webel.

[291] For an additional explanation of NFIP funding, including the funding for mapping, see CRS Report R44593, *Introduction to the National Flood Insurance Program (NFIP)*, by Diane P. Horn and Baird Webel.

[292] 42 U.S.C. §4014(a)(1)(B)(iii).

[293] Email correspondence from FEMA Congressional Affairs staff, December 6, 2016.

Concerns have been raised about maintaining the activities funded by the FPF, with some stakeholders arguing that a form of FPF equivalency, or some form of user fee, should be applied to private flood insurance.[294] In the 115th Congress, both S. 1313 and S. 1368 contained mechanisms by which private insurance companies could have contributed to the costs of floodplain mapping in lieu of paying the FPF. In the 116th Congress, S. 2187, Section 303, would have required FEMA to develop a fee schedule based on recovering the actual costs of providing FIRMs and charge any private entity an appropriate fee for use of such maps.

Enforcement of floodplain management standards could be more challenging within a private flood insurance system, as the current system makes the availability of NFIP insurance in a community contingent on the implementation of floodplain management standards. For example, the Association of State Floodplain Managers (ASFPM) has expressed concerns that the widespread availability of private flood insurance could lead some communities to drop out of the NFIP and rescind some of the floodplain management standards and codes they had adopted, leading to more at-risk development in flood hazard areas.[295] ASFPM suggested that this issue could be addressed by allowing private policies to meet the mandatory purchase requirement only if they were sold in participating NFIP communities.[296] FEMA suggested that access to federal disaster assistance could be made partially contingent on the adoption of appropriate mitigation policies, but noted that this approach could be politically challenging.[297] However, a positive consequence is that government investment in mitigation could increase private market participation by reducing the flood exposure of high-risk properties and thereby increasing the number of properties that private insurers would be willing to cover.[298]

---

[294] Association of State Floodplain Managers, *ASFPM Detailed Priorities for NFIP Reauthorization and Reform*, April 1, 2019, p. 1, https://cdn.ymaws.com/floodplain.org/resource/resmgr/ASFPM_2019_NFIP_Reauthorizat.pdf.

[295] Association of State Floodplain Managers, *ASFPM's Comments on Loans in Areas Having Special Flood Hazards - Private Flood Insurance Joint Notice of Proposed Rulemaking*, January 6, 2017, pp. 1-4, https://asfpm-library.s3-us- west-2.amazonaws.com/ASFPM_Pubs/ASFPM_Comemnts_SFHA_Loans_Private_Flood_Insurance_2017.pdf.

[296] Ibid.

[297] FEMA, *National Flood Insurance Program Report to Congress on Reinsuring NFIP Insurance Risk and Options for Privatizing the NFIP*, August 13, 2015, p. 92.

[298] Ibid., p. 108.

## Concluding Comments

The policy debate surrounding NFIP and private insurance has evolved over time. The discussion in 2012 was framed in the context of privatization of the NFIP and actions that might be taken to create conditions for private sector involvement. One of the primary interests of Congress at the time was to reduce the federal government's role in flood insurance by transferring its exposure to the private sector,[299] with an expectation that a realignment of roles would allow the federal government to focus on flood risk mitigation while private markets focused on providing flood insurance.[300] One argument for increasing private sector participation in the U.S. flood market was that competition should lead to innovation in flood risk analytics and modeling and produce new flood insurance products that would better meet customer needs and lead to greater levels of insurance market penetration.[301] In fact, private sector flood risk analytics and modeling have improved significantly before any sizable entry of private insurers into the market. Another argument was that, in contrast to the NFIP, which cannot diversify its portfolio of flood risk by insuring unrelated risks, the insurance industry can diversify catastrophic risks with uncorrelated or less correlated risks from other perils, other geographic regions, non-catastrophic risks, or risks from unrelated lines of business.[302]

FEMA considered a range of concrete steps by which the barriers to private sector involvement could be addressed.[303] Two of these have been introduced: the purchase of reinsurance and reporting to make premium subsidies and cross-subsidies more transparent.[304] The reduction of premium subsidies for some properties will occur with the introduction of Rating 2.0.[305]

---

[299] Ibid., p. 2.

[300] Ibid., p. 52.

[301] FEMA, National Flood Insurance Program Report to Congress on Reinsuring NFIP Insurance Risk and Options for Privatizing the NFIP, August 13, 2015, p. 50.

[302] Ibid., p. 51.

[303] Ibid., pp. 82-84.

[304] The requirement in §28 of HFIAA (P.L. 113-89, 128 Stat. 1033) that the Administrator "clearly communicate full flood risk determinations to individual property owners regardless of whether their premium rates are full actuarial rates."

[305] For a full discussion of NFIP subsidies and cross-subsidies, see the section on Pricing and Premium Rate Structure in CRS Report R44593, *Introduction to the National Flood Insurance Program (NFIP)*, by Diane P. Horn and Baird Webel; the section on Premiums Subsidies and Cross-Subsidies in CRS Report R46095, *The National Flood Insurance Program: Selected Issues and Legislation in the 116th Congress*, by Diane P. Horn and Baird Webel; and the section on Premium Subsidies and Cross-Subsidies in CRS Report

Although BW-12 directed FEMA to make a recommendation about the best manner in which to accomplish the privatization of the NFIP, FEMA presented the report without a recommendation, arguing that any privatization strategy is complex and involves significant policy decisions that would require input from a variety of stakeholders. They concluded that there is no single, clear solution; it is heavily politicized; and harsh criticism of any change is inevitable.[306]

Currently the discussion is more focused on sharing risk and increasing penetration rates, with the recognition that neither the NFIP nor the private sector is likely to be able to write all of the policies needed to cover all of the flood risk in the United States. FEMA has identified the need to increase flood insurance coverage across the nation as a major priority for NFIP reauthorization, and this also forms a key element of their 2018-2022 strategic plan.[307] FEMA has developed a "moonshot" with the goal of doubling flood insurance coverage by 2023 through the increased sale of both NFIP and private policies.

FEMA's view is that both the NFIP and an expanded private market will be needed to increase flood insurance coverage for the nation and reduce uninsured flood losses.[308] However, the private market is unlikely to expand significantly without congressional action. The concerns of private companies related to the mandatory purchase requirement and continuous coverage and the concerns of some Members of Congress about adverse selection are among the most pressing issues likely to be addressed in any long-term NFIP reauthorization.

---

R45999, *National Flood Insurance Program: The Current Rating Structure and Risk Rating 2.0*, by Diane P. Horn.

[306] FEMA, National Flood Insurance Program Report to Congress on Reinsuring NFIP Insurance Risk and Options for Privatizing the NFIP, August 13, 2015, p. 84.

[307] FEMA, 2018-2022 Strategic Plan, https://www.fema.gov/media-library/assets/documents/160940.

[308] U.S. Congress, Senate Committee on Banking, Housing, and Urban Affairs, Statement of Roy E. Wright, Hearing on Reauthorization of the National Flood Insurance Program, Part I, 115th Cong., 1st sess., March 14, 2017, pp. https://www.fema.gov/sites/default/files/2020-07/roy-e-wright_reauthorization-nfip_statement_3-14-2017.pdf.

# Appendix. Provisions Related to Private Flood Insurance in Legislation in the 116th Congress

The provisions in the 116th Congress legislation that relate to private flood insurance, and the issues raised as barriers to private sector involvement, are summarized below and compared side- by-side in Table A-1. S. 2187 also includes provisions related to administrative reforms of the NFIP, some of which may be relevant to private insurance companies, which are not described in this report. Comparable administrative reforms are included in H.R. 3111, the National Flood Insurance Program Administrative Reform Act of 2019, rather than H.R. 3167.

## H.R. 3167, National Flood Insurance Program Reauthorization Act of 2019

- H.R. 3167, Section 107, would direct FEMA, if an NFIP policyholder switches to private flood insurance but has already paid the NFIP premiums for the whole year up front, to provide a prorated refund of the NFIP premium. This section would also direct that Increased Cost of Compliance (ICC) premiums[309] wouldnot be refunded if measures had been implemented using ICC coverage, and that premiums would not be refunded if a claim has been paid or is pending under the policy term for which the refund is sought.
- H.R. 3167, Section 401, would direct FEMA to consider private flood insurance that satisfies the mandatory purchase requirement as also satisfying the continuous coverage requirement to keep NFIP premium subsidies in place.
- H.R. 3167, Section 404, would allow FEMA to provide current and historical property-specific information on flood insurance program coverage, flood damage assessments, and payment of claims to private insurers, on the condition that private insurers provide the same information to FEMA, homeowners, and home buyers. Section

[309] The NFIP requires most policyholders, excluding condominium units and contents-only policies, to purchase Increased Cost of Compliance (ICC) coverage, which is in effect a separate insurance policy to offset the expense of complying with more rigorous building code standards when local ordinances require them to do so. ICC coverage provides an amount up to $30,000 in payments for certain eligible expenses.

404 could potentially create conflicts with the Privacy Act of 1974, which prohibits federal agencies from releasing data which contains Personally Identifiable Information. In addition, although these data could beused to better inform the participation of private insurers in offering private flood insurance, the availability of NFIP data could make it easier for private insurers to identify the NFIP policies that are "overpriced" due to explicit cross-subsidization or imprecise flood insurance rate structures. Private insurers may adversely select such properties, while the government would likely retain the policies that benefit from those subsidies and imprecisions, potentially increasing the deficit of the NFIP.[310]

- H.R. 3167, Section 406, would require FEMA annually to evaluate ceding a portion of the risk of the NFIP to the private reinsurance or capital markets.
- H.R. 3167, Section 407, would give FEMA the authority to terminate any WYO arrangement in its entirety upon 30 days written notice for (1) fraud or misrepresentation; (2) nonpayment to FEMA of any amount due; or (3) material failure to comply with the requirements of the arrangement or with the written standards, procedures, or guidance by FEMA.
- H.R. 3167, Section 408, would require GAO to determine the percentages of properties with federally backed mortgages located in SFHAs that satisfy the mandatory purchase requirement, and the percentage of properties with federally backed mortgages located in the 500-year floodplain[311] that would satisfy the mandatory purchase requirement if the mandatory purchase requirement applied to such properties.

---

[310] American Academy of Actuaries Flood Insurance Work Group, The National Flood Insurance Program: Challenges and Solutions, April 2017, p. 79, http://www.actuary.org/files/publications/FloodMonograph.04192017.pdf.

[311] American Academy of Actuaries Flood Insurance Work Group, The National Flood Insurance Program: Challenges and Solutions, April 2017, p. 79, http://www.actuary.org/files/publications/FloodMonograph.04192017.pdf.

## S. 2187, National Flood Insurance Program Reauthorization and Reform Act of 2019

- S. 2187, Section 102, would prohibit FEMA from increasing the amount of covered costs above 9% per year on any policyholder during the five-year period beginning on the date of enactment. Covered costs include premiums, surcharges (including the surcharge for ICC coverage and the HFIAA surcharge), and the Federal Policy Fee. This would limit the rate of increase of covered costs for all categories of policies, not just policies for primary residences, and would be particularly significant for those policies where the pre-FIRM subsidy is currently being phased out at 25% per year. This cap on premium increases could potentially limit FEMA's ability to implement rate increases under Risk Rating 2.0. Section 102 would also amend the basis on which premiums are determined so that the calculation of an average historical loss year[312] would exclude catastrophic loss years. This would probably lower premiums for all policyholders.
- S. 2187, Section 108, would require GAO to determine the percentages of properties with federally backed mortgages located in SFHAs that satisfy the mandatory purchase requirement, and the percentage of properties with federally backed mortgages located in the 500-year floodplain that would satisfy the mandatory purchase requirement if the mandatory purchase requirement applied to such properties.
- S. 2187, Section 302, would establish that the total amount of reimbursement paid to WYO companies could not be greater than

[312] The average historical loss year is the minimum target amount that the NFIP needs to collect from all premiums to cover at least average annual losses, as determined by historical data. FEMA uses this estimate to calculate the premium that would be sufficient to pay for the average level of losses that occurred in past years and help set the rate level for subsidized flood insurance policies. When the NFIP was originally established, the average historical loss year did not include catastrophic loss years. BW-12 directed FEMA to review the basis on which it was setting NFIP rates, with specific attention to ensuring that catastrophic loss years would be fully incorporated into the NFIP calculation of average historical loss year. See GAO, Financial Challenges Underscore Need for Improved Oversight of Mitigation Programs and Key Contracts, GAO-08-457, June 16, 2008, p. 19, https://www.gao.gov/products/gao-08-437; and National Research Council of the National Academies, Affordability of National Flood Insurance Program Premiums: Report 1, 2015, p. 42, http://www.nap.edu/catalog/21709/affordability-of-national-flood-insurance-program-premiums- report-1.

22.46% of the aggregate amount of premiums charged by the company. It would also require FEMA to ensure that the commission paid by a WYO company to agents of the company would not be less than 15%.

- S. 2187, Section 303, would require FEMA to develop a fee schedule based on recovering the actual costs of providing FIRMs and charge any private entity an appropriate fee for use of such maps. This requirement could provide a mechanism by which private insurance companies could contribute to the costs of floodplain mapping in lieu of paying the FPF.
- S. 2187, Section 304, would require FEMA, within 12 months of enactment, to develop a schedule to determine the actual costs of WYO companies and reimburse the WYO companies only for the actual costs of the service or products. It would require that all reimbursements made to WYO companies be made public, including a description of the product or service provided to which the reimbursement pertains.
- S. 2187, Section 305, would require FEMA to report on the feasibility of selling or licensing the use of historical structure-specific NFIP claims data to non- governmental entities, while reasonably protecting policyholder privacy.
- S. 2187, Section 405, would require FEMA to establish penalties for underpayment of claims by WYO companies that are not less than the penalty for overpayment of a claim.
- S. 2187, Section 408, would give FEMA the authority to direct a WYO company, on 14 days' notice, to terminate a contract or other agreement with any covered entity[313] that provides services to the WYO company, if FEMA determines that the covered entity has engaged in conduct that is detrimental to the NFIP.
- S. 2187, Section 415, would authorize FEMA to create a pilot program under which WYO companies and NFIP direct servicers would be required to investigate pre-existing structural conditions that might result in the denial of an NFIP claim, at the request of a policyholder or potential policyholder, before providing or renewing flood insurance coverage.

[313] A covered entity is defined in S. 2187, §408, as any attorney, law firm, consultant, or third-party company that provides services to a WYO company.

**Table A-1.** Provisions related to private flood insurance in legislation in the 116th congress

| Provision | H.R. 3167 | S. 2187 |
|---|---|---|
| Continuous coverage | §401. Would direct FEMA to consider private flood insurance that satisfies the mandatory purchase requirement as also satisfying the continuous coverage requirement to keep NFIP premium subsidies in place. | No comparable provisions |
| Cap on premium increases | No comparable provisions | §102. Would prohibit FEMA from increasing the amount of covered costs[a] above 9% per year on any policyholder during the five-year period beginning on the date of enactment. |
| Risk transfer | §406. Would require FEMA annually to evaluate ceding a portion of the risk of the NFIP to the private reinsurance or capital markets, if the Administrator determines that the rates and terms are reasonable and doing so would further the development and maintenance of a sound financial framework for the NFIP. | No comparable provisions |
| WYO allowance | No comparable provisions | §302. Would establish that the total amount of reimbursement paid to WYO companies could not be greater than 22.46% of the aggregate amount of premiums charged by the company. |
| WYO costs | No comparable provisions | §302. Would require FEMA to ensure that the commission paid by a WYO company to agents of the company would not be less than 15%.<br>§304. Would require FEMA, within 12 months of enactment, to develop a schedule to determine the actual costs of WYO companies and reimburse the WYO companies only for the actual costs of the service or products. Would also require that all reimbursements made to WYO companies be made public, including a description of the product or service provided to which the reimbursement pertains. |

**Table A-1.** (Continued)

| Provision | H.R. 3167 | S. 2187 |
|---|---|---|
| WYO pilot program | No comparable provisions | §415. Would authorize FEMA to create a pilot program under which WYO companies and NFIP direct servicers would be required to investigate pre-existing structural conditions that might result in the denial of an NFIP claim, at the request of a policyholder or potential policyholder, before providing or renewing flood insurance coverage. |
| WYO penalties | No comparable provisions | §405. Would require FEMA to establish penalties for underpayment of claims by WYO companies that are not less than the penalty for overpayment of a claim. |
| | §407. Would give FEMA the authority to terminate any WYO arrangement in its entirety upon 30 days written notice for (1) fraud or misrepresentation; (2) nonpayment to FEMA of any amount due; or (3) material failure to comply with the requirements of the arrangement or with the written standards, procedures, or guidance by FEMA. | §408. Would give FEMA the authority to direct a WYO company, on 14 days' notice, to terminate a contract or other agreement with any covered entity[b] that provides services to the WYO company, if FEMA determines that the covered entity has engaged in conduct that is detrimental to the NFIP. |
| NFIP claims data | §404. Would allow FEMA to provide current and historical property-specific information on flood insurance program coverage, flood damage assessments, and payment of claims to private insurers, on the condition that private insurers provide the same information to FEMA, homeowners, and home buyers. | §305. Would require FEMA to report on the feasibility of selling or licensing the use of historical structure-specific NFIP claims data to non-governmental entities, while reasonably protecting policyholder privacy. |
| Funding for flood mapping | No comparable provisions | §303. Would require FEMA to develop a fee schedule based on recovering the actual costs of providing FIRMs and charge any private entity an appropriate fee for use of such maps. |

| Provision | H.R. 3167 | S. 2187 |
| --- | --- | --- |
| Study of compliance with mandatory purchase requirement | §408. Would require GAO to determine the percentages of properties with federally backed mortgages located in SFHAs that satisfy the mandatory purchase requirement, and the percentage of properties with federally backed mortgages located in the 500-year floodplain that would satisfy the mandatory purchase requirement if the mandatory purchase requirement applied to such properties. | §108. Would require GAO to determine the percentages of properties with federally backed mortgages located in SFHAs that satisfy the mandatory purchase requirement, and the percentage of properties with federally backed mortgages located in the 500-year floodplain that would satisfy the mandatory purchase requirement if the mandatory purchase requirement applied to such properties. |

Source: CRS analysis of legislation from http://www.congress.gov.

Notes: H.R. 3167, as reported by the House Financial Services Committee (H.Rept. 116-262, Part I).

[a] Covered costs include premiums, surcharges (including the surcharge for ICC coverage and the HFIAA surcharge), and the Federal Policy Fee.

[b] A covered entity is defined as any attorney, law firm, consultant, or third-party company that provides services to a WYO company.

## Chapter 5

# Private Flood Insurance and the National Flood Insurance Program (NFIP)*

**Baird Webel**
**and Diane P. Horn**

### The National Flood Insurance Program

The NFIP was first authorized by the National Flood Insurance Act of 1968 (42 U.S.C. §4001 et seq.) and was reauthorized until the end of FY2017 by the Biggert-Waters Flood Insurance Reform Act of 2012 (BW-12; Title II of P.L. 112-141). After 30 short-term reauthorizations, the NFIP is currently authorized until September 30, 2024 (P.L. 118-35). In statute, Congress has found that

1. many factors have made it uneconomic for the private insurance industry alone to make flood insurance available to those in need of such protection on reasonable terms and conditions; but
2. a program of flood insurance with large-scale participation of the Federal Government and carried out to the maximum extent practicable by the private insurance industry is feasible and can be initiated. (42 U.S.C. §4001(b)).

By law or regulation, federal agencies, federally regulated lending institutions, and government-sponsored enterprises (GSEs) must require

* This is an edited, reformatted and augmented version of Congressional Research Service Publication No. IN10450, updated March 29, 2024.

In: The National Flood Insurance Program (NFIP)
Editor: Jolene Rivera
ISBN: 979-8-89530-612-3

certain property owners to purchase flood insurance as a condition of any mortgage that these entities make, guarantee, or purchase. Property owners are required to purchase flood insurance if their property is identified as being in a Special Flood Hazard Area (SFHA, defined as having a 1% or greater risk of flooding every year) and is in a community that participates in the NFIP.

Historically, this generally has meant such property owners were required to purchase a Standard Flood Insurance Policy (SFIP) from the NFIP. In BW-12, Congress explicitly provided for private flood insurance to fulfill this mortgage requirement instead of the SFIP, if the private flood insurance met the conditions defined further in statute at 42 U.S.C. §4012a(b)(7).

## Rulemaking on Accepting Private Flood Insurance

To fulfill the mortgage requirement, a private insurance policy must provide, among other conditions, "flood insurance coverage which is at least as broad as the coverage provided under a [SFIP] ... including when considering deductibles, exclusions, and conditions offered by the insurer." Implementation of this requirement has proved challenging. The responsible federal regulators (the Federal Reserve, Farm Credit Administration, Federal Deposit Insurance Corporation, National Credit Union Administration, and Comptroller of the Currency) issued two separate Notices of Proposed Rulemaking (NPRM) addressing the issue in October 2013 and November 2016. The crux of the implementation issue can be seen as answering the question of who would judge whether specific policies met the "at least as broad as" standard and what criteria would be used in making this judgment. The uncertainty as to whether particular private policies would meet the standard has been seen as "at odds with" greater private participation in the flood insurance marketplace.

On February 12, 2019, the regulators announced a final rule implementing the BW-12 "requirement that regulated lending institutions accept private flood insurance policies." Of particular note, the rule

- "allows institutions to rely on an insurer's written assurances in a private flood insurance policy stating the criteria are met; [and]
- clarifies that institutions may, under certain conditions, accept private flood insurance policies that do not meet the Biggert-Waters Act criteria."

Issues for Congress The rule took effect on July 1, 2019. Press reports described it as generally welcomed by the banking industry. It does not apply directly to other federal agencies or to GSEs, which would be subject to separate rulemaking.

A number of bills have been introduced to ensure that if a property owner purchases private flood insurance and then decides to return to the NFIP, the owner would be considered to have maintained continuous coverage. Continuous coverage is required for property owners to retain any subsidies or cross-subsidies in their NFIP premium rates. A borrower may be reluctant to purchase private insurance if doing so means they would lose their subsidy should they later decide to return to NFIP coverage. In the 118th Congress, H.R. 900 and S. 2110 would consider any period during which a property is covered by a flood insurance policy, either through the NFIP or through a private company, to be a period of continuous coverage. The availability of such continuous coverage may become more important with the introduction of Risk Rating 2.0, as 77% of NFIP policyholders saw an increase in their premiums in the first year and may consider private flood insurance as an alternative.

Section 100232(a) of BW-12 required FEMA and the Government Accountability Office (GAO) to produce separate studies that "assess a broad range of options, methods, and strategies for privatizing the [NFIP]." In the GAO study on privatization, GAO reviewed a wide range of strategies to encourage private flood insurance. The strategies included (1) eliminating subsidies of NFIP premium rates entirely or providing the subsidies in an explicit form not hidden in the premium; (2) authorizing the NFIP to issue catastrophe bonds to transfer some of the insured risk; (3) shifting the federal role to reinsuring primary flood insurance instead of directly providing it; and (4) mandating flood coverage in homeowners insurance policies. The first two of these strategies have been addressed. FEMA has issued catastrophe bonds since 2018 and is phasing out subsidies under Risk Rating 2.0.

FEMA's 2015 study on options for privatizing the NFIP discussed several key challenges that may be presented by privatizing a larger segment of NFIP policy base, including how to

- maintain the funding of federal flood mapping and flood mitigation programs largely paid for through flood insurance premiums, fees, and surcharges;
- reduce and pay off the billions of dollars of debt NFIP owes to the U.S. Treasury; and

- ensure the affordability and continued availability of flood insurance to property owners in flood zones.

These continue to be issues of concern, and FEMA has identified the need to increase flood insurance coverage across the nation as a major priority, with the recognition that neither the NFIP nor the private sector alone is likely to be able to write all of the policies needed to cover all of the flood risk in the United States.

For further discussion of private insurance and the NFIP, see CRS Report R45242, Private Flood Insurance and the National Flood Insurance Program.

# Chapter 6

# What Happens If the National Flood Insurance Program (NFIP) Lapses?*

Diane P. Horn

This Insight provides a short overview of what would happen if the National Flood Insurance Program (NFIP) were not to be reauthorized by September 30, 2024, and allowed to lapse.

## Expiration of Certain NFIP Authorities

The NFIP is authorized by the National Flood Insurance Act of 1968 (Title XIII of P.L. 90-448, as amended, 42 U.S.C. §§4001 et seq.). The NFIP does not contain a single comprehensive expiration, termination, or sunset provision for the whole of the program. Rather, the NFIP has multiple different legal provisions that tie to the expiration of key components of the program.

Since the end of FY2017, 30 short-term NFIP reauthorizations have been enacted (Table 1). The NFIP is currently authorized until September 30, 2024.

Unless reauthorized or amended by Congress, the following will occur on September 30, 2024:

- The authority to provide *new* flood insurance contracts will expire. Flood insurance contracts entered into before the expiration would continue until the end of their policy term of one year.

---

* This is an edited, reformatted and augmented version of Congressional Research Service Publication No. IN10835, dated Updated April 1, 2024.

In: The National Flood Insurance Program (NFIP)
Editor: Jolene Rivera
ISBN: 979-8-89530-612-3

- The authority for NFIP to borrow funds from the Treasury will be reduced from $30.425 billion to $1 billion.

Other activities of the program would technically remain authorized, such as the issuance of Flood Mitigation Assistance Grants. However, the expiration of the key authorities listed above would have potentially significant impacts on the remaining NFIP activities.

**Table 1.** Short-term extensions of the NFIP since end of FY2017

| Public Law | Date to Which Authorization Was Extended |
|---|---|
| P.L. 115-56 | December 8, 2017 |
| P.L. 115-90 | December 22, 2017 |
| P.L. 115-96 | January 19, 2018 |
| NFIP lapsed January 20 to January 22, 2018 | |
| P.L. 115-120 | February 8, 2018 |
| NFIP lapsed for 8 hours on February 9, 2018 | |
| P.L. 115-123 | March 23, 2018 |
| P.L. 115-141 | July 31, 2018 |
| P.L. 115-225 | November 30, 2018 |
| P.L. 115-281 | December 7, 2018 |
| P.L. 115-298 | December 21, 2018 |
| P.L. 115-396 | May 31, 2019 |
| P.L. 116-19 | June 14, 2019 |
| P.L. 116-20 | September 30, 2019 |
| P.L. 116-59 | November 21, 2019 |
| P.L. 116-69 | December 20, 2019 |
| P.L. 116-94 | September 30, 2020 |
| P.L. 116-159 | September 30, 2021 |
| P.L. 117-43 | December 3, 2021 |
| P.L. 117-70 | February 18, 2022 |
| P.L. 117-86 | March 11, 2022 |
| P.L. 117-95 | March 15, 2022 |
| P.L. 117-103 | September 30, 2022 |
| P.L. 117-180 | December 16, 2022 |
| P.L. 117-229 | December 23, 2022 |
| P.L. 117-264 | December 30, 2022 |
| P.L. 117-328 | September 30, 2023 |
| P.L. 118-15 | November 17, 2023 |
| P.L. 118-22 | February 2, 2024 |
| P.L. 118-35 | March 8, 2024 |
| P.L. 118-40 | March 22, 2024 |
| NFIP lapsed for approximately 13 hours on March 23, 2024 | |
| P.L. 118-47 | September 30, 2024 |

Source: CRS analysis.

If there were to be a lapse in authorization on or after September 30, 2024, with borrowing authority reduced to $1 billion, FEMA would continue to adjust and pay claims as premium dollars come into the National Flood Insurance Fund (NFIF) and reserve fund. As of March 13, 2024, there was $760 million in the NFIF and $2.979 billion in the reserve fund. If the funds available to pay claims were to be depleted, claims would have to wait until sufficient premiums were received to pay them unless Congress were to appropriate supplemental funds to the NFIP to pay claims or increase the borrowing limit.

The NFIP is the primary source of flood insurance coverage for residential properties in the United States.

The NFIP has 4.7 million flood insurance policies providing $1.28 trillion in coverage, with 22,678 communities in 56 states and jurisdictions participating. The program collects about $4.6 billion in annual premium revenue and fees.

## The Mandatory Purchase Requirement

The expiration of the NFIP's authority to provide new flood insurance contracts has potentially significant implications due to the mandatory purchase requirement (MPR). By law or regulation, federal agencies, federally regulated lending institutions, and government-sponsored enterprises must require certain property owners to purchase flood insurance as a condition of any mortgage that these entities make, guarantee, or purchase. Property owners, both residential and commercial, are required to purchase flood insurance if their property is identified as being in a Special Flood Hazard Area (SFHA, which is equivalent to having an estimated 1% or greater risk of flooding every year) and is in a community that participates in the NFIP. Without available flood insurance, real estate transactions in an SFHA potentially would be significantly hampered.

Federal agencies may accept private flood insurance to fulfill the MPR if the private flood insurance meets the conditions defined in statute. Although the private flood insurance market is growing, the MPR is still generally met through NFIP coverage. FEMA does not enforce the MPR, but lenders must continue their regulatory requirements during a lapse, including MPR enforcement.

## Past Lapses of the NFIP

The NFIP was extended 17 times between 2008 and 2012, and lapsed 4 times: March 1 to March 2, 2010; March 29 to April 15, 2010; June 1 to July 2, 2010; and October 1 to October 5, 2011. In most cases when the NFIP lapsed, Congress reauthorized the NFIP retroactively. In 2018, P.L. 115-120 also authorized FEMA to honor all policy-related transactions accepted during the NFIP lapse. During these NFIP lapses, the FDIC issued guidance to lending institutions, and the Federal Reserve also issued informal guidance to lenders. In addition, FEMA provided guidance for the Write-Your-Own (WYO) Program, where private insurance companies are paid to write and service NFIP policies.

In past NFIP lapses, borrowers were not able to obtain flood insurance to close, renew, or increase loans secured by property in an SFHA until the NFIP was reauthorized. During the lapse in June 2010, estimates suggest over 1,400 home sale closings were canceled or delayed each day, representing over 40,000 sales per month. These figures applied to residential properties, but commercial properties were also affected by the NFIP lapse. In addition, the largest WYO insurer left the NFIP in 2011, reportedly because of the administrative burden associated with very short-term reauthorizations and lapses in authorization. Although no detailed analysis of the NFIP lapses in 2010-2011 has been undertaken, the economic impact could have been broader than the reported effects on the domestic real estate market.

## Chapter 7

# The Reauthorization of the National Flood Insurance Program: FEMA's Perspective*

## Committee on Financial Services

Friday, April 28, 2023

U.S. House of Representatives, Subcommittee on Housing
and Insurance, Committee on Financial Services,
Washington, D.C.

The subcommittee met, pursuant to notice, at 9 a.m., in room 2128, Rayburn House Office Building, Hon. Warren Davidson [chairman of the subcommittee] presiding.

Members present: Representatives Davidson, Posey, Luetkemeyer, Fitzgerald, Garbarino, Lawler, De La Cruz, Houchin; Cleaver, Velazquez, Tlaib, Torres, Garcia, Williams of Georgia, Horsford, and Pettersen.

Ex officio present: Representatives McHenry and Waters.

Chairman DAVIDSON. The Subcommittee on Housing and Insurance will come to order. Without objection, the Chair is authorized to declare a recess of the subcommittee at any time.

Today's hearing is entitled, "The Reauthorization of the National Flood Insurance Program: FEMA's Perspective."

I now recognize myself for 5 minutes for an opening statement. Mr. Maurstad, thank you for appearing today for the second hearing of the Housing and Insurance Subcommittee in the 118th Congress. The Federal Emergency

---

* This is an edited, reformatted and augmented version of Hearing Before the Subcommittee on Housing and Insurance of the Committee on Financial Services U.S. House of Representatives, Serial No. 118–18, dated April 28, 2023.

In: The National Flood Insurance Program (NFIP)
Editor: Jolene Rivera
ISBN: 979-8-89530-612-3

Management Agency (FEMA) plays a vital role through its disaster recovery efforts, and today, we will explore its management of the National Flood Insurance Program (NFIP), which has existed for over 50 years, and until recently has operated in the same manner and relied on the same outdated tools since its creation. And I just applaud the progress you are making as flooding in the United States is a significant, costly problem for both coastal and inland residents.

Unfortunately, there is only one provider for nearly all residential flood insurance, the government-backed NFIP, which sells 93 to 95 percent of all residential flood insurance in the country. That is not just a bad idea from the perspective of creating a workable insurance model; it has also proven to be costly for taxpayers. To date, the program finds itself $20.5 billion in debt, even after Congress outright forgave $16 billion just a few years ago.

It seems clear to me that the program is in desparate need of reform, and I am glad that FEMA is bringing that reform. The process needs to start with this hearing, and with a reauthorization, and we hope this hearing will help us achieve the consensus to pass legislation.

Lately, the committee has not been too involved in the oversight of ongoing operations and programs. Today is the first time we have heard from FEMA on the NFIP in over 6 years. That is something we need to get more serious about, if we are going to modernize the program that was created before the Moon landing in the 1960s.

This committee has an important role to play in its oversight of the NFIP. And through hearings like this, Congress can identify whether the program is operating in an effective and transparent manner. Congress, however, has been missing in action from that job, as the previous Majority left the program on autopilot for a series of short-term extensions and appropriations bills.

And frankly, the previous Republican Majority didn't finish a major reform. That has not only removed us from the process; it has made the program vulnerable to uncertainty for its 4.7 million policyholders. We can and we must do better.

To ensure stability while Congress does this important work of reforming the program on a longer-term basis, I have introduced H.R. 1392, the National Flood Insurance Program Extension Act of 2023, which would reauthorize the program through at least December of 2024. This bill would not only avoid a lapse in coverage, but it would also give this committee the time and the deadline freedom it needs to do a deeper dive into flood insurance reforms and to conduct additional hearings on NFIP-engaged stakeholders and craft a longer-term reauthorization.

This work is crucial and will ensure that the program is moving in the right direction for both taxpayers and policyholders, particularly given FEMA's recent internal work to incorporate industry best practices and technology into its management of the program. That includes, most notably, the work regarding the adoption of Risk Rating 2.0 methodology, which is a transformative initiative to modernize how accurately it measures flood risk.

Risk Rating 2.0 is a good first step in moving towards long-term financial visibility for the NFIP, and one that certainly deserves our attention to ensure this program can serve communities most at risk of flood events, and remain viable for years to come. I look forward to exploring it and FEMA's other recent modernization acts with you today. And we may have a set of policy recommendations for Congress on reforms that get this program on a sustainable path.

With that, I thank the witness for his testimony today, and I look forward to the conversation.

I yield back. And I now recognize the ranking member of the subcommittee, Mr. Cleaver from Missouri, for 4 minutes for an opening statement.

Mr. CLEAVER. Thank you very much, Mr. Chairman. And let me preface my comments by saying that I look forward to working with you. I think this is a serious and significant issue to which we have to give a great deal of our time and interest and creativity to resolve.

Floods are the most frequent and severe weather threat and the costliest natural disaster facing the United States of America.

Flooding events have occurred in all 50 States and 98 percent of U.S. counties. According to the Department of Homeland Security, 90 percent of natural disasters in the United States involve flooding. Supercharged by climate change, these natural disasters are increasing in both frequency and severity.

Shortly after I was elected, Hurricane Katrina hit. And at that time, our ranking member, Ms. Waters, and Representative Biggert led a delegation down to Mississippi and Louisiana. We saw first- hand what devastation had occurred in that area. And since Katrina, we have had significant events even on the East Coast, even in New Jersey and New York. We need to address this issue. Hurricane Katrina was destructive and it cost a great deal of money, the costliest flood in U.S. history, which means that the National Flood Insurance Program was hit with major losses and is still struggling. This includes $16.2 billion for Hurricane Katrina, $1.3 billion for Hurricane Irene, $8.8 billion for

Hurricane Sandy, $1.1 billion for Hurricane Irma, and $1.5 billion for Hurricane Ida and others.

The NFIP is indispensable to the resiliency of American communities and more than 5 million policyholders. Many of these families are low- and moderate-income families or are forced to live in flood-prone areas due to the affordable housing crisis that this committee has not yet held a hearing on this Congress.

However, the growing strength of floods and the storms that cause them are increasingly straining the financial health of the NFIP. The NFIP is now over $20 billion in debt, and the program pays well over $1 million a day in U.S. Treasury interest. This is the third-largest NFIP activity by cost. In no uncertain terms, the current program is fiscally unsustainable.

I said all 50 States earlier, but that should also include the U.S. Territories. In many ways, they have been dealt with almost as if they were stepchildren to the United States of America. In no uncertain terms, the current program is fiscally unsustainable. NFIP reauthorization, what should be a long-term reauthorization, is an opportunity to put the program on sound financial footing, increase risk analysis and communication, improve community resilience, and make technical and operational enhancements to the program. This committee has an opportunity to make our families, businesses, and communities safer and more resilient, and to build and rebuild in a way that meets the challenges of the reality of climate change.

I am interested to see the Republican plan on flood reform, as I just mentioned to the Chair. And I intend to make myself available to work with him.

Thank you very much. I yield back.

Chairman DAVIDSON. The ranking member yields back.

The Chair now recognizes the Chair of the full Financial Services Committee, Chairman McHenry, for 1 minute.

Chairman MCHENRY. I want to thank the chairman and the ranking member. And I want to thank the members of this committee for working in a bipartisan way to reauthorize the National Flood Insurance Program. This is a continuation of the work that then-Chairwoman Waters, and myself as then-Ranking Member, worked on 4 years ago, to authorize the program in a balanced way.

We reported that bill out of committee without an ascending vote, and dealt with a lot of challenging issues there. So, we want to reauthorize the program in a balanced and bipartisan way.

We thank the Administrator for being here, for his testimony, and for his leadership and his team's leadership to make sure that we take into account the changing climate, and make sure that we take care of those in our society who are challenged to pay these bills.

We want to make sure that we have a program that is current with the risks and balanced for the American people. So, I want to thank this subcommittee for dealing with this in a thoughtful way.

For a point of personal privilege, I want to acknowledge a long-time Financial Services staffer, Ed Skala, who has worked on this committee for longer than I have been a Member of Congress. And for the first time, his mother, Beatrice, is here, and his sister, Bonnie, as well as his niece, Alexa. Thank you for being here. Thank you for keeping tabs on Ed. He has sharpened up today, because you're here, and we are grateful for that. But I am very grateful for his advice and his counsel. He is a long-time key member of the Financial Services Committee staff, and works with both Democrat staff and Republican staff very well. And I count on Ed's counsel every day, so thank you.

With that, I yield back.

Chairman DAVIDSON. The Chair recognizes the ranking member of the Full Committee, Ms. Waters, for 1 minute.

Ms. WATERS. Thank you very much, Mr. Davidson, and I appreciate this hearing today.

Congress designed the NFIP to be self-funded through annual insurance premiums collected from policyholders. Currently, the NFIP is drowning in $20.5 billion of debt, with $1 million in interest accruing every single day. And I just wonder what effect it would have if Congress simply enacted a clean reauthorization of the NFIP and maintained the status quo for the program instead? I am not going to raise that question now, but I am anxious to hear what is going to be said today. I want Mr. Maurstad to explain to us how he is going to carry out the functions of the NFIP. I want him to talk about money. I want him to talk about debt.

And I want to get down to some real answers today. With that, I yield back the balance of my time.

Chairman DAVIDSON. The ranking member yields back.

Today, we welcome the testimony of Mr. David Maurstad. Mr. Maurstad is FEMA's Assistant Administrator of the Federal Insurance Directorate and Senior Executive of the National Flood Insurance Program. He has over 25 years of experience in both public service and insurance. Mr. Maurstad received his Masters of Business Administration from the University of Nebraska.

We thank you for taking the time to be here. You will be recognized for 5 minutes to give an oral presentation of your testimony. And without objection, your written statement will be made a part of the record.

Mr. Maurstad, you are now recognized for 5 minutes to give your oral remarks.

## Statement of David Maurstad, Assistant Administrator, Federal Insurance Directorate, Federal Emergency Management Agency (FEMA)

Mr. MAURSTAD. Good morning, Subcommittee Chairman Davidson, Subcommittee Ranking Member Cleaver, Full Committee Chairman McHenry, Full Committee Ranking Member Waters, and members of the subcommittee. Thank you for the opportunity to testify today regarding FEMA's perspective for the reauthorization and reform of the National Flood Insurance Program. For more than 50 years, the NFIP has been critical to the nation's resilience policy.

Today, as our changing climate poses a serious threat to our nation, and as the number and severity of disasters continues to grow, the NFIP requires meaningful structural change. Since the NFIP's last multi-year reauthorization in 2017, the NFIP has experienced 25 short-term extensions and 3 brief lapses. The short-term extensions are disruptive and cause existing and potential policy- holders to lose confidence in the NFIP. We believe that a 10-year reauthorization, with comprehensive program reforms, is vital. We propose 17 recommendations to reform the NFIP that are guided by four key principles.

First, ensuring that more Americans are covered by flood insurance by making insurance more affordable to low- and moderate income policyholders. Flood insurance is unaffordable for some policyholders. Under current law, FEMA does not have the authority to establish and charge premiums based on a policyholder's ability to pay. Although the NFIP offers mandatory discounts and cost subsidies, these discounts and subsidies do not take into consideration the policyholder's financial need, and in fact can make risk communication difficult because people may equate lower costs with lower risk.

Reforms that address affordability, such as the use of a targeted assistance program, can offer current and prospective low- and moderate-income NFIP policyholders a graduated risk premium discount, while providing them with the knowledge of the full risk to communicate a property's true flood risk.

Second, communicated risk in real-time, providing Americans with the tools to manage flood risk. Reforms that increase the scale and frequency of flood mapping and incorporate emerging priorities and technologies into the flood hazard and flood risk identification process will expand the ways in which the NFIP communicates risk. Raising awareness of true flood risk enables people to make informed decisions about their family and property. Home buyers and renters may lack awareness about flood risk when they complete real estate transactions.

Reforms that would require States to establish minimum flood risk reporting requirements for sellers and lessors before residential transactions close would address this challenge. Additionally, we need to reform how we measure and communicate flood risk. The nation's evolving risks require flood hazard information that is more robust than Special Flood Hazard Area, and 1 percent annual chance to flood elevation.

Third, reducing risk by addressing extreme repetitive-loss properties. Previous losses are a significant indicator of risk, meaning that if a property has flooded before, there is a high likelihood it will flood again. Since 1978, 350,000 structures have had 2 or more paid losses, and nearly 3,000 have suffered 10 or more losses. The NFIP must have better tools to address insured structures that experience multiple flood claims. Almost 3 percent of insured properties are considered unmitigated repetitive-loss properties.

Reforming the NFIP to institute an objective threshold to deny coverage to the most flood-prone structures would discourage unmitigated rebuilding in areas with a history of flooding, and reduce financial risk to the NFIP, while ensuring coverage is still widely available to individuals, families, and businesses who might not be eligible for private-market coverage.

Fourth, instituting a sound and transparent financial framework that allows the NFIP to balance affordability and fiscal soundness. Without this in place, longevity and sustainability of the program is at risk. The NFIP currently carries $20.5 billion in debt to the U.S. Treasury and anticipates paying approximately $619 million in interest in Fiscal Year 2023. As currently structured, the program is burdened with interest expense and is unable to pay this debt back in full.

Canceling the NFIP's debt provides the program with a solid foundation that can support financial reforms around borrowing, future interests, enhanced liquidity, and an upper limit for the size of an NFIP event. These reforms address fundamental structural challenges and are essential to building the viable, sustainable NFIP that the nation needs and deserves.

It is critical that Congress provides urgently-needed multi-year reauthorization and currently reform the NFIP. We look forward to working with Congress to develop a long-term solution that addresses the needs of the NFIP, its policyholders, and the nation.

I am pleased to answer any questions.

[The prepared statement of Assistant Administrator Maurstad can be found on page 32 of the appendix.]

Chairman DAVIDSON. Thank you, Mr. Maurstad. We will now turn to Member questions, and I will recognize myself for 5 minutes.

Thanks for addressing the need for reform. For 15 years now, the Government Accountability Office (GAO) has consistently labeled NFIP as a, "high-risk program," calling it out for several things, including premium rates that do not reflect the full risk loss, transferring some of the financial burden of flood risk from individuals to taxpayers. And a lack of transparency that leads some to, "mistakingly perceive that they are not at risk of flood loss."

Unresolved affordability issues, which are addressed for many policyholders—all of that seems like a pretty grim picture with the job that you have walked into. Can you paint for us a picture of what the program's future looks like if we don't reform NFIP? And how critical is it that we bring this 50-year-old program into the 21st Century with modern tools and techniques?

Mr. MAURSTAD. Yes, sir. Thank you very much.

First of all, it starts with the financial structure of the program. As already been mentioned a number of times, being saddled with interest costs that provide no real benefit to the program is harmful. If we do nothing, there is a 2-percent chance that at the end of 10 years, the National Flood Insurance Fund will have more dollars than when they started. But if we enact all of the proposals that we have put forward, there is an 81-percent chance, not 2 percent, an 81-percent chance that the fund will have more resources at the end of that 10 years.

So structurally, as we look at the NFIP as a multipronged program of floodplain management, of flood risk grants and flood risk identification, the insurance having that sound financial framework is critical for the sustainability of the program.

Chairman DAVIDSON. Thank you for that. I applaud you, frankly, for the progress you have made on IT infrastructure for the program as well. One of the things that comes up often is mapping. So, how can a homeowner appeal or challenge a zoning determination?

I know that under Risk Writing 2.0, flood zones are no longer a rating element for NFIP rates, but they are important for the application of mandatory purchase requirements for properties under the Flood Disaster Protection Act of 1973, as well as to determine eligibility for policyholder discounts like the Newly Mapped status, et cetera.

Can you describe what the NFIP's current mapping appeals process is for homeowners under Risk Writing 2.0? And how that interacts with the appeals process? And I guess maybe how that is distinct from the mandatory purchase requirement?

Mr. MAURSTAD. The investment of probably over $5 billion in the 22,400 community flood maps across the country is vital as we continue to look at how we can best identify flood risk.

There are two primary purposes, as you indicated. The first outlined the Special Flood Hazard Area, the high-risk area where communities then agree on participating with the program to regulate construction in that area. And the second is the mandatory purchase requirement.

Dealing with the first, it is a local ordinance, so to start with, you can look to the local government to make sure that your property is accurately reflected in the local community's Flood Insurance Rate Map. Beyond that, we have two ways, you can go directly to FEMA for a flood map amendment, and then, there is also a second way. So, we encourage policyholders to work with their agents, and to work with their community leaders and regional staff who are there to be helpful. Also, if there is a question about their flood zoning, to come to FEMA, and we will help address that.

Chairman DAVIDSON. Thank you. When it relates to a mandatory purchase, I think in particular it would be good to have a path where if the lender for a property doesn't necessarily agree that it is in a flood zone, if you can establish with surveys and whatnot that this is clearly not in a flood zone, that we let the underwriter take the risk and then say, okay, those are astute folks you have chosen, and proven that it is not in a flood zone, you can decide. I think just for the record, and you might not note this off the top of your head, but let's look to repeat losses. What is the record for the number of times we have repaid or paid for the same property? I have heard reports as high as 30 or 35 times. Do you know the record off the top of your head?

Mr. MAURSTAD. I do not. I know that it is way too high.

Chairman DAVIDSON. Could you get back to us with that, the record holder?

Mr. MAURSTAD. Yes, I will.

Chairman DAVIDSON. Thank you. My time has expired.

I now recognize the ranking member of the subcommittee, Mr. Cleaver from Missouri, for his questions.

Mr. CLEAVER. Thank you very much, Mr. Chairman.

With Hurricane Katrina, some of the things we saw were Senator Trent Lott's house was wiped away, with nothing left. Congressman Gene Taylor's house was wiped away; only the front stoop was still there. Even though we had some initial problems, eventually they were taken care of, but the majority of the victims were poor, in Mississippi, in and around Biloxi, and also in New Orleans. And while renters do qualify to purchase NFIP coverage, and are often affected by flood disasters, they are less likely to have flood insurance. The people in New Orleans—we had public housing decimated in New Orleans. And at the time, we only had one—we still do, one replacement. So, we could only replace the units that were just awful. The poorest people in the country suffer the most when these disasters hit.

Mr. Maurstad, can you discuss what we know about the renters' relationships with private flood insurance and what may be some answers to this issue?

Mr. MAURSTAD. Yes, sir. Thank you for that question. I recall the devastation associated with Katrina very well, as I was leading the National Flood Insurance Program at that time also. And it really exposed a number of the faults associated with the program that we need to continue to work on and address.

And certainly, there is no question that with the discriminatory land practices of the past, many less-fortunate Americans live in the high-risk areas for flood in communities across the country, which is really why the affordability proposal that we have included in our recommendations is important for the committee to consider. Being able to help those individuals get the financial resources they need after a flooding event is critical, because they are the ones who have the most difficulty in recovery. We have seen that time and time again.

Mr. CLEAVER. Thank you very much.

We know that a defining characteristic between the NFIP and the private market is that the Federal Government cannot deny consumers who apply for coverage, including from the NFIP. Yet, the private market often can, unless it is based on some kind of discrimination. In fact, we have heard from homeowners in Houston, Texas, that when the water came out of the bayou after Hurricane Harvey, they were dropped by their private insurers. While some had the means and desire to still purchase new flood coverage after being dropped, many share that they were denied coverage by the private market. Can you expand on the market trends and what role NFIP might play here?

Mr. MAURSTAD. There are a couple of points I would like to make, sir. One is we need more property owners, renters, and small businesses to have flood insurance coverage. There is a huge flood insurance gap that needs to be filled. The NFIP is working to do that, but we also need the private sector to increase their efforts to try to make sure that property owners have the coverage that they need. As you pointed out, especially renters, because we know very few renters recognize the flood risk they have.

So, we are working with our agents to make sure that we also have a focus on not just the dwelling but also those who rent. It is a very serious problem.

One of the provisions in our recommendation is to let a policy-holder who leaves the National Flood Insurance Program and tests the private market, and then decides they they want to come back to the NFIP, that we bring them back into the program in the same position that they were in when they left the program. So, if they were on a glide path to their full risk rate, they would enter the program back in the same place on that glide path as when they left.

Mr. CLEAVER. Thank you. My time has run out. I am really interested in the whole issue of reinsurance and how it impacts the industry. You and I have had some conversations about this already.

I yield back, Mr. Chairman.

Chairman DAVIDSON. Thank you.

The gentleman from Wisconsin, Mr. Fitzgerald, is now recognized for 5 minutes.

Mr. FITZPATRICK. Thank you, Mr. Chairman. In late July 2022, FEMA released a concerning draft proposal called, "Direct to Customer." In its release, FEMA noted that it is imperative that FEMA enable the digital sale and servicing of flood insurance to increase the number of people covered. FEMA noted that this is a long-term project and stressed that they are in early stages of looking at the concept. In this digital age, there is often a rush to cut corners under the erroneous notion that an automated process can replace human interaction and expertise.

Any kind of proposal that undercuts the valuable and trusted role of the independent insurance agents and brokers in their role in how this plays out could have a negative impact on increasing flood insurance participation rates. We talked a little bit that about earlier this morning.

We saw a similar dynamic play out in Economic Injury Disaster Loans (EIDLs) offered directly by the Small Business Administration (SBA) during the pandemic, a perfect example, which had a much higher incidence of fraud than the Paycheck Protection Program (PPP) loans which were issued through financial institutions. We have had a lot of concerns about the Direct to Customer approach to distribute flood insurance, which ultimately would not reach customers that the NFIP or agents are not already reaching. And the agents, whom we heard from last month, continue to play a role in the servicing plans. It is unlikely a call center would offer the same kind of perspective. To me, it sounds like a mess. So my question to you is, what is your take on the status of FEMA's exploration of offering Direct to Customer flood insurance plans?

Mr. MAURSTAD. Thank you very much for that question. My first response would be that we are being very careful and very deliberate about our exploration of whether it makes sense for the National Flood Insurance Program to entertain the thought of developing a Direct to Customer program. As an agent for 2 decades, I fully understand the value associated with agents. And at this point in time, and as we continue our exploration, there is no intent to not have agents involved in our Direct to Customer program.

We rely on the insurance agents to be able to accurately and helpfully provide the information that their customers need to analyze their flood risk, and then have the insurance coverage that they need so much after a flood event.

Mr. FITZPATRICK. Bear with me, too, on this question, but just kind of following up on a proposed Direct to Customer online sales—I just wanted to prove that point. But the data that is required, simple stuff, the foundation type, the presence and number of flood openings, depending on the foundation type, data on construction, existence and identification of any substantial improvements, construction type, flood-proofing status, eligibility for machinery and equipment elevation discount, square footage, number of floors, and building replacement costs are all of the things that a hands-on agent would take a look at, am I correct? This is not just a simple formula in which you say, plug in this number, plug in this number, and here is how much you are going to get.

Mr. MAURSTAD. Absolutely. You are not going to get any argument from me on the importance of the agent in the process. And again, I would emphasize that we are in the exploration phase of looking at this, but we do feel it is our responsibility today to look at every way in which we can potentially close the insurance gap that the country faces. If we are going to have a modern NFIP that meets the needs of the customers where we are, we at least have to have the answer as to why we do or do not have Direct to Customer.

Mr. FITZPATRICK. Thank you very much.

One of my concerns is that this can definitely be oversimplified, especially in some of the hearings that we have had here in Congress.

I yield back.

Chairman DAVIDSON. The gentleman yields back. The Chair now recognizes the ranking member of the full Financial Services Committee, the gentlewoman from California, Ms. Waters.

Ms. WATERS. Thank you very much.

I am from California and we have been suffering recently with both fires and flood. And for a couple of years, we had a drought. And then, because of climate change, which is denied by some people, it rained for, I think, 3 weeks or more every day, so we have some real problems.

And now, we really have to figure out what to do. Not only are we having these problems in California, but I was recently in Florida and I saw people who had gotten a little bit of money from FEMA that won't even begin to restore their homes, et cetera, et cetera.

Congress has designed the NFIP to be self-funded through annual insurance premiums collected from policyholders. Currently, the NFIP is drowning in $25.5 billion in debt. To who do you owe the debt?

Mr. MAURSTAD. We owe the debt to the Federal Treasury, ma'am.

Ms. WATERS. To the government.

Mr. MAURSTAD. Yes, to the government.

Ms. WATERS. Are you part of the government?

Mr. MAURSTAD. We are.

Ms. WATERS. So, the government wants you to repay the government this debt. Is that right?

Mr. MAURSTAD. That is our obligation.

Ms. WATERS. Oh, that doesn't make good sense.

The NFIP is drowning in $20.5 billion in debt with a million dollars in interest accruing every single day. Again, what effect would it have if Congress simply enacts a clean reauthorization of the NFIP and maintains the status quo for the program and its debt?

Mr. MAURSTAD. Thank you. The cancelation of the debt is one of the 17 recommendations that we put forward, and is the basis from which we can start to begin a sound financial framework for the program that is understandable, transparent, and predictable. So, it is vitally important that we have the debt canceled, that we don't have the burden of the interest costs that you mentioned that are only going up in this high-interest environment. It is a key part of the recommendations that we have put forward.

Ms. WATERS. So in addition to your basic responsibilities, you can't even get to mitigation and helping locals with mitigation measures and other kinds of things that would help when these floods come? Have you made it known to everybody on both sides of the aisle that we need debt cancelation?

Mr. MAURSTAD. Yes. We have been very clear on how important that is. And we also do want to thank Congress and the Administration for the unprecedented amount of dollars that have been provided to FEMA for our mitigation programs, whether that be for building infrastructure and community programs, or for our Flood Mitigation Assistance Grant Program.

We do have more mitigation dollars available than we had before. We still are a long way from meeting the entire need, but it is definitely progress. And we are looking at making sure that all communities, including socially-disadvantaged, vulnerable communities, are also a part of these new grant proposals that are unfolding.

Ms. WATERS. Since I have worked on flood insurance for a long time, would you describe the competition in the United States from various areas putting pressure on you to say, my area is more important than their area, I need more up here than they need? Would you describe the kind of competition that you are confronted with, where people are desparate for help that you cannot provide?

Mr. MAURSTAD. There isn't any question that Members are most concerned about their own constituents, and that is who we hear from a lot. But I would say that all across the country, we work through our regions with the States to identify the risky areas in their communities that would be able to have access to our mitigation funding. So, we run a national program. We are sensitive to all parts of the country. And I think we are doing a good job of making sure that we don't leave anybody behind.

Ms. WATERS. You are doing the best job that you can possibly do, but today, I want you to let these people know they can leave us fighting with each other about what is needed on the East Coast as opposed to what is needed in the south and on and on and on, or we can cancel this debt and do something about flood insurance. That is all I want you to do.

Mr. MAURSTAD. There is no question that the competition for mitigation funds is steep. We generally are 3 to 4 times over-subscribed when we have our grant process, so there is a great need for mitigation across the country.

Mr. FITZGERALD. [presiding]. The gentlewoman yields back. Next, we have the gentlewoman from Texas, Ms. De La Cruz, for 5 minutes.

Ms. DE LA CRUZ. Thank you, Mr. Chairman, for holding this important hearing today. And thank you, Mr. Maurstad, for taking the time to appear before Congress.

As the chairman mentioned, this is the first time that a FEMA official has appeared before this committee in over 6 years. It is time for Congress to assert its role in reforming the National Flood Insurance Program in order to ensure its long-term solvency after years of short-term funding extensions and minimal oversight from this body.

As the vice chairwoman of this subcommittee, I look forward to working with Chairman Davidson, along with my colleagues here, to ensure that the NFIP is best serving the American taxpayers and is sustainable for the long-term. With that in mind, what steps has FEMA taken to improve the efficiency and effectiveness of the NFIP's administration? And how can the program be reformed to better serve its policyholders and taxpayers?

Mr. MAURSTAD. I would say that the answer to that is in the 17 recommendations that we have provided. There were nearly 100 subject matter experts who worked on the development of the recommendations, and thousands of hours were put into what the program experts believe needs to happen to make sure that we have an NFIP that is sustainable into the future. We are looking at what we need to do from a pricing perspective to make sure that we are fairly and accurately identifying the risk and charging the right premium for it. We are in the process of developing new policy forms, our products, so to speak, so that we can better serve our policyholders and improve our distribution of the program through a simpler method by which agents can do business with the NFIP.

Ms. DE LA CRUZ. And with that being said, I have had insurance experience for over 20 years; I owned my own agency for over 20 years. And the NFIP is something very near and dear to my heart. I have one of the poorest counties in the entire nation in my district, Hidalgo County, that is really dependent on NFIP and the benefits that it provides to the customers. So when we talk about reform to better serve the policyholders, I think about how we can distribute this product to get more consumers involved. As an agent myself, I can tell you it is burdensome.

What is burdensome is that we have to use our agency platform in order to sell homeowners coverage, and then we have to go to a completely different platform in order to actually sell the flood insurance product. And that takes time, and it takes more education in learning a whole new platform. How can we solve the efficiency in the agency program to make it easier for an agent to be able to sell the product?

Mr. MAURSTAD. As I mentioned earlier, I was an agent for a couple of decades also, and I certainly understand the concerns that you raise, which was one of the drivers behind why we developed a new rating engine, and have replaced the old manual, which was twice the size of the binder that I have in front of me, and it took many hours to be able to write a policy.

With our new rating engine, you can answer roughly a dozen questions and get the premium for a particular property. So, we have really streamlined the application process and the ability for agents to more effectively market and sell our product.

Ms. DE LA CRUZ. With that, I yield back.

Mr. FITZGERALD. The gentlewoman yields back.

Next, we will go to the gentlewoman from New York, Ms. Velazquez, for her questions.

Ms. VELAZQUEZ. Administrator Maurstad, I have long called for a 10-year reauthorization of NFIP. And I believe that it is important so that it provides sufficient time for Congress and FEMA to evaluate the programs and consider the types of reforms that are needed to make it more stable.

But wouldn't you also agree that it is hard to consider reforms or have hearings like this when you are working under short-term reauthorization windows? I am constantly worried about the program lapsing.

Mr. MAURSTAD. The short answer is yes, which is why one of our recommendations is in fact to reauthorize the program for 10 years, to provide the stability that the program needs and that the communities and our policyholders deserve.

Ms. VELAZQUEZ. I represent New York, and in New York, multi-family housing is central to the housing stock. To date, FEMA data on Risk Rating 2.0 has focused exclusively on its impact on the single-family residential market. Where multifamily and commercial properties are included, they are combined with single-family and do not shed full light on the risk these buildings my face. Is FEMA planning to separate data on multifamily and commercial properties from data on single-family structures so that the owners of these properties might fully understand their risk?

Mr. MAURSTAD. I think you certainly raise an interesting concern, and it's one that I will take back. We of course are looking at ways that we can best understand the impact our program has, whether it is on renters, single-family homeowners, or multifamily dwellings.

We are looking at ways that we can now capture the data with our improved information technology system. And we will definitely take that back and have more conversations with you on—

Ms. VELAZQUEZ. Please, do so. This is an issue that I have been raising every time we have held hearings on flood insurance.

While it seems small compared to single-family homes in the NFIP risk pool, commercial and multipolicies must pay significant amounts into the NFIP overall. Can you give us a sense of how much those properties are receiving on the claims side in an average year? Are they on financial traffic or a benefit on the program?

Mr. MAURSTAD. I don't have that information with me, but we can certainly get that information for you and provide it to you.

Ms. VELAZQUEZ. Thank you.

Mr. MAURSTAD. Yes, ma'am.

Ms. VELAZQUEZ. According to the Puerto Rico Planning Board— and we are talking about a U.S. Territory—200,000 residences on the island are located in flood-prone areas. Yet, according to FEMA's data, as of February 2023, only 4,368 units have active NFIP policies. What actions is FEMA taking to ensure that more homeowners and renters in Puerto Rico are covered by NFIP policies in light of what we witnessed after Hurricane Maria?

Mr. MAURSTAD. Yes. That is very much an issue of concern to the program. I have actually met with the insurance commissioner of Puerto Rico when I was down there working with him on what we can do to increase the number of property owners who have flood insurance protection.

And we will keep working on that, because as I said, seeing homeowners and renters who don't have coverage in neighborhoods that I visited after events is tragic; their lives are completely disrupted and turned over. So, we need to do what we can to make sure they have their coverage. I believe the affordability proposal that we have included in our recommendation would be helpful.

Ms. VELAZQUEZ. You need to be more proactive in that sense; a lack of awareness and information is an issue here. Thank you.

Mr. FITZGERALD. The gentlewoman yields back.

Next, we will turn to the gentleman from Florida, Mr. Posey.

Mr. POSEY. Thank you, Mr. Chairman.

Mr. Maurstad, how much has the flood insurance program spent on maps?

Mr. MAURSTAD. I will get you the exact figure, but it is upwards of a $5-billion investment.

Mr. POSEY. A $5-billion investment?

Mr. MAURSTAD. Yes, sir.

Mr. POSEY. Does that include recent years?

Mr. MAURSTAD. I will get you the exact figure and the amount by year, but that is cumulative. In the last few years, roughly speaking, it is been about $600 million.

Mr. POSEY. What is the most times the flood insurance program has paid for a total loss or maximum policy limits on one single insured property?

Mr. MAURSTAD. The number of times?

Mr. POSEY. Yes.

Mr. MAURSTAD. I don't have the exact number. That question came up earlier. I will certainly get it. I know that as I indicated in my opening remarks, there are hundreds of properties that have more than 10 losses.

Mr. POSEY. We have heard numbers as high as 16 times paid for a single total loss. I even heard one time that they paid 30 times for a total loss of a property, which is absolute, complete insanity, in my opinion.

Mr. MAURSTAD. Sir, right now we don't have the authority or the ability to not provide coverage to someone who is in a participating community. That is why we put forward in our recommendations a multiloss provision that would address the problem that you—

Mr. POSEY. I would think once you paid for total loss, you say, okay this is off the map, we are not going to insure this property again, much less more than 10 times, thousands of properties, perhaps. Last fall, one news source said that Administrator Criswell called the FEMA flood maps, "useless." Could you briefly explain what she meant by that?

Mr. MAURSTAD. I am not familiar with that remark. I know in my conversations with Administrator Criswell, she is supportive of the mapping program that we have, recognizing as we put forward in our recommendations that we can do more than we are doing now to identify risk outside the high-risk areas through non-regulatory products. And I believe that the Administrator, without doubt, sees the value associated with the Flood Insurance Rate Maps in the 22,400 communities across the country.

Mr. POSEY. When I was first elected 14 years ago, they said that to properly evaluate risk, they needed new maps, which would cost $500 million, and then, it would take 3 to 5 years to evaluate the maps. I passed amendments here a couple of times saying, why don't you just use DOD, Homeland Security or NOAA maps; they have a current topo in every inch of this country. There is no need to go outside to pay for more maps to be developed.

The Association of State Floodplain Managers estimated that the price to consistently update floodmaps would range from $107 million to $480 million annually. Director Criswell has said that the current policy fee for mapping would have to be raised to a level that would threaten affordability and discourage insurance. Would you care to comment on that?

Mr. MAURSTAD. Again, I think that the investment in our flood maps, whether it is from the policyholder fee or whether it is from the appropriation from Congress, is important to make sure that our maps accurately reflect the 1 in 100 percent chance event in the communities across the country.

Mr. POSEY. Why does FEMA continue to resist making all of the data and methods models that they use, the calculations and how they calculate it under Risk Rate 2.0, completely and fully transparent?

Mr. MAURSTAD. Sir, I believe we have provided all the information that we have been requested to provide. We have been very transparent; we provided the entire methodology for the development of the actuarial sound pricing model that we now use. If there is additional information that would be helpful to you, we will certainly do our best to provide it for you.

Mr. POSEY. How can policyholders appeal their premiums under 2.0?

Mr. MAURSTAD. They can work with their agent the same way that they work with premiums on the other insurance that they have with the agent. If they think the information that has gone into developing their premium for their particular property is inaccurate, then they can work with their insurance agent to correct that and make sure that the premium that they are being charged reflects the risk of their property.

Chairman DAVIDSON. The gentleman's time has expired.

Next, we will go to the gentlewoman from Michigan, Ms. Tlaib.

Ms. TLAIB. Thank you so much, Mr. Chairman.

If I may, I would like to submit a New York Times article, "A Broke, and Broken, Flood Insurance Program," into the record.

Chairman DAVIDSON. Without objection, it is so ordered.

Ms. TLAIB. Thank you so much.

Mr. Maurstad, thank you so much for being here.

As you know, I come from an incredibly strong community, the City of Detroit, where we have birthed movements on a number of things that I think kind of change the trajectory for our whole country, not just in the automotive industry, but in music, and everything.

But even now, I talked to our Chair of our committee about the fact that many of our families farther away from bodies of water are now impacted in a very significant way from flooding. We are seeing that more and more.

In my district, I was shocked that 4 times within one summer, I think between June and July, the City of Dearborn had huge amounts of flooding. In Inkster, I met a senior citizen whose basement didn't get coverage or anything. She is still dealing with mold, and she is in her 70s.

So, I started looking and researching, what is the process of getting flood insurance? Of course, mapping continues to come up. But, say, for instance, Mrs. Smith from Inkster, or from Aviation Sub in Detroit, or from Dearborn, picks up the phone and says, "I want to get flood insurance."

By the way, the average home insurance in Detroit specifically is about $3,700. And the majority of homes in my communities that I mentioned are valued at less than $100,000. These are working-class families.

But she picks up the phone, and she wants insurance. You go to the list or whatever, and it comes back incredibly unaffordable, right? We talked about this. What is she supposed to do at that point? Because whether she went to the FEMA site, they said, sorry. First, they don't clean out basements—I don't understand that—unless there is, like, a room or somebody sleeps down there. It is this whole process they go through.

And then, even though she brought her pictures, she showed me her receipts of all of the things, there was no sense of how she could even get covered. I don't know what we are supposed to do when the national program, to me, doesn't include all of the Americans who are impacted by flooding right now.

And even when I talk to Full Committee Chair McHenry—we talked about this. I don't know. You tell me, Administrator. Out of the close to 5 million who can afford this, what is their income? What is the value of their homes? Is it the million-dollar homes that get access to the flood insurance? I want to know, because the families in my community are not able to access this in an equitable way. And I don't know how we change this, because I know we are just going to renew this and not make any changes. That is exactly what is going to happen. I have seen it happen over and over again.

Mr. MAURSTAD. The affordability problem is one that has been around for a while. And, in fact, Congress recognized in the 2012 reauthorization that, as discounts and subsidies were going to move away, that affordability was going to be more of an issue.

So, you charged FEMA with developing an affordability framework, which we provided to Congress in 2018, which is the basis for the proposal that we have put forward to develop a means-tested, premium-assistance affordability program. But the report tells us that about 25 percent of the individual policyholders in the high-risk area are low-income. It also tells us that 50 percent of the property owners in the high-risk area are low-income.

So, it is abundantly clear—and I understand how difficult it is to have those kind of conversations with people who need the coverage so badly and have had losses. But it has the information that we need to provide assistance through our affordability proposal.

And I appreciate the committee's attention to that recommendation.

Ms. TLAIB. I will end with this. One of the things—and I agree with Congresswoman Velazquez about the lack of access of information in regards to accessing the flood insurance. What I do notice is, even when my folks do have some sort of insurance, I have to call. And I personally call, and I would recommend my colleagues to pick up the phone and use the power of your office to call these insurance companies that deny the claims.

It infuriates me when I have to pick up the phone or use my letterhead to say, hey, here is all of the things that my resident submitted. Is there is nothing you can do in regards to some of what is happening there? My residents are paying into a system and they are not getting—

Mr. MAURSTAD. There absolutely is something that we can do. And, in fact, Congress also took steps to do something when we created the Office of the Flood Insurance Advocate for those who are having a difficult time working their way through the program, so they have that means.

So, in addition to your having to do what you indicated you do with your letterhead, you can also send them to the Office of the Flood Insurance Advocate at FEMA to help them.

But back to some of the earlier conversations—

Chairman DAVIDSON. The gentlewoman's time has expired.

Maybe you could get that in writing.

I will now turn to the gentleman from New York, Mr. Garbarino.

Mr. GARBARINO. Thank you, Mr. Chairman.

Superstorm Sandy was one of the biggest natural disasters in U.S. history. While it was technically no longer a hurricane by the time it reached the shores of Long Island, Sandy caused massive coastal flooding that reached the heights of 5 and 6 feet in places across my district.

Given the risk of flooding along the South Shore of Long Island, my constituents are keenly aware of the need for affordable flood insurance. However, since Risk Rating 2.0's implementation, just under 4 million

Americans have seen their premiums increase. In many instances, individual household rates have more than doubled since the launch of the new Risk Rating 2.0.

Mr. Maurstad, you have gone on the record as saying it is both equitable and adaptable. You have also gone on to say that it corrects pricing inequities for close to a million policyholders living in low- and moderate-income communities. However, these comments seem to be in direct contrast with recent comments made by Secretary Mayorkas during his most recent appearance before the House Homeland Security Committee.

To quote Secretary Mayorkas, "DHS is reviewing and needs to continue to review the Risk Rating 2.0, given the concerns that have been expressed."

To me, it sounds as if the methodology for setting flood insurance premiums needs more tweaking than initially expected. From the outside, looking in, there seems to be a clear disconnect between you and the Secretary on the effectiveness of Risk Rating 2.0. Is FEMA and/or DHS currently reviewing the methodology behind Risk Rating 2.0's determination of risk? And, if so, can you provide an explanation of what is exactly is being reevaluated?

Mr. MAURSTAD. Yes, sir. Thank you.

I actually have been in conversation with the Secretary's office, and they continue to be as supportive of Risk Rating 2.0 as when he issued a statement on April 1, 2022, in support of the changes. The only report that I am aware of is that the GAO is currently reviewing the Risk Rating 2.0, and we are cooperating fully with them. And I think that report will be coming out in the next couple of months.

Mr. GARBARINO. Okay. I think you should check with the Secretary, because last week in front of the committee, he said that DHS is reviewing and needs to continue to review Risk Rating 2.0. With what I have seen happen with a lot of constituents and their policies under Risk Rating 2.0, I think it needs to be reviewed and possibly changed. So, I think I understand what he said last year in support of it, but what he said last week is different.

One comment I will make before I move on to my next question is that this is a topic I have been following closely since arriving to Congress, and I have been working closely with Leader Scalise on it. I appreciate his leadership on the issue, and I hope that we all can work together that ensure that the U.S. flood insurance market is stable and affordable for all Americans, particularly those on a fixed income.

And I want to ask this as a follow-up to my colleague, Mr. Posey's, question. He asked about—and I think in your answer you talked about how, if something is wrong with the premiums or if a homeowner thinks their premiums are too high, they can go to their agent and possibly get it fixed. I believe 93 percent of insurance policies, flood insurance policies, are written under NFIP and set.

And I also heard from my constituents. One thing I keep hearing from them is that on Long Island, they have taken steps to mitigate flooding, whether it is by raising their house or by other structural changes. But those changes are not reflected in their monthly premium. I asked one of the witnesses at our last hearing about whether there are clear financial benefits for policyholders who have implemented these mitigation features, and the answer that I received really just created more uncertainty.

We were told that the challenges that agents have under Risk Rating 2.0 is that the black box rating engine is making it nearly impossible for agents and floodplain officials to provide specific guidance to consumers who want to both implement mitigation and know what their return on investment or monthly premium is going to be.

So, Mr. Maurstad, I will pose the same question to you that I did at the last hearing. Under Risk Rating 2.0, are there clear financial benefits for policyholders who have implemented these mitigation features, as it uniquely pertains to the person's monthly premiums? If so, what do those benefits look like?

Mr. MAURSTAD. Yes, certainly, there is no question that if policyholders take measures to mitigate their risk, either by elevation of their structure or by moving air conditioning equipment up off the floor, there is a credit for that. And it is very clear, and we can provide you some examples of that.

Back to the rating engine that I mentioned before, there have been over 100 million quotes provided through that rating engine. So, people are clearly looking at what the options are within Risk Rating 2.0.

Mr. GARBARINO. I am out of time.

Chairman DAVIDSON. The gentleman's time has expired.

The Chair now recognizes the gentlewoman from Colorado, Ms. Pettersen.

Ms. PETTERSEN. Thank you, Mr. Chairman.

I am grateful that this committee is focused on a pathway forward to reauthorize the National Flood Insurance Program because this is absolutely critical in Colorado. My communities throughout my district experience heavy snow melts or serious storms which can potentially lead to damaging and dangerous floods.

In recent years, the ongoing risk of catastrophic wildfires has only compounded the challenges that Coloradans are facing. We now see communities narrowly avoid immediate danger of a wildfire, only to find their homes susceptible to flood damage.

As Coloradans recover from fires, we also are seeing communities where the ability to purchase wildfire insurance is not even an option. Similar to flood insurance, though, many homeowners don't even realize that their typical insurance policy does not cover these catastrophic events until disaster strikes.

Improved transparency and clear disclosures of flood and fire danger are necessary to better educate people about their potential risks when they are purchasing homes, and I do hope this committee also works on providing tangible support for homeowners who live in communities like mine, which are susceptible to wildfires.

Post-fire flooding can damage and harm communities for months and even years following a wildfire. How does FEMA's Flood After Fire Campaign seek to work to educate homeowners about the potential threat of flooding in the aftermath of a wildfire? And are additional resources necessary to ensure that more people actually follow through and purchase flood insurance after a wildfire?

Mr. MAURSTAD. There are many sources of flooding, and you have articulated a couple that a lot of folks don't think about. Certainly, flood after fire is a huge issue. The circumstances can actually—it sometimes takes more than 6 years for the ground to be able to be like it was before. So, that flood risk is not only just for that next season, but for about 5 or 6 seasons afterwards.

And yes, we did a Flood After Fire Campaign in Colorado to try to help people understand what their flood risk is, and we are doing similar things in other parts of the country. And we are going to continue, because it is vital, as one of the themes, of course, is we need to close the flood insurance gap. Only 4 percent of property owners in the country have flood insurance and we need to do better than that.

So, any help that we can provide you in that regard, we certainly want to provide.

Ms. PETTERSEN. Great. And do you actually target it specifically to communities for your awareness campaign around potential flooding and the options for flood insurance to those communities that have been affected specifically? And do you do it after every wildfire? Or how does that work?

Mr. MAURSTAD. Yes. We don't do it after every wildfire. But we do work with State insurance commissioners and different State insurance organizations in situations where we have flood after fire. We do some targeted outreach, as we did in Colorado. We don't do it after every wildfire.

Ms. PETTERSEN. It seems like our offices could help support our constituents with information like that when, unfortunately, things like this are inevitable in communities like Colorado.

Another question that I have is, currently, the flood-related disclosure requirements are set at the State level, and neither renters nor homeowners may be aware of the flood risks of a particular property. What are the requirements to obtain and maintain flood insurance following a disaster assistance for previous floods? Do you think federally-required flood disclosures would be a helpful tool for consumers, especially for renters, to understand their risks and the availability of fair and affordable flood insurance cover through NFIP?

Mr. MAURSTAD. I absolutely do. And one of our 17 recommendations, in fact, would create such a uniform standard throughout the States and Territories.

Ms. PETTERSEN. Great. Thank you so much. I yield back.

Chairman DAVIDSON. The gentlewoman yields back.

We are jumping around here. We have Members who are voting, but Mr. Horsford from Nevada will be next.

Mr. HORSFORD. Thank you, Mr. Chairman.

While I appreciate that we are continuing the important discussion around the National Flood Insurance Program and the importance of its reauthorization with a long-term reauthorization, I do have to say that I wish we were better using the time of this subcommittee to really focus on the pressing issues that our constituents really need us to address, including the housing affordability crisis that is crippling our country. At a time when sales volumes remain depressed, pending listings are down 23 percent from last year, and the average household spends 31 percent of their income on mortgage or rent, Congress needs to act.

My constituents are struggling to find a way to put and maintain a roof over their heads, and that should be the first concern for this subcommittee. I know under the leadership of the Democratic Majority, that was the priority, so I want to know, where is the housing on our agenda? When are we going have a hearing on housing affordability?

We entered this Congress 4 month ago in the midst of a housing shortage, and it has only deepened since then. While I understand that we have to cover a whole host of issues and topics, today's housing crisis is just simply too consequential for me to remain silent. We are nearly 14 million homes short of the aggregate demand, and this lack of supply is driving housing costs through the roof.

I am told stories, painful stories, by constituents in my district who are struggling to be able to afford rent or to buy a home. However, from what I have seen, there is only one approach coming from the other side and that is to slash the Federal housing budget, putting millions more of our people, our constituents at risk of losing their homes, and doing nothing to incentivize new constructions.

This is a nationwide crisis and, again, I ask the Majority on the other side of the aisle: Where is the plan on housing? When will we have a hearing? This is the Subcommittee on Housing. So, I would ask the Majority: When will we have a hearing?

I also want to ask the Majority whether you will work with me on the bill that I have introduced, H.R. 702, the Housing Oversight and Mitigating Exploitation Act (HOME Act), to protect the limited supply of housing that we have and to protect everyday Nevadans from being exploited by out-of-State corporate speculators who are driving up the cost of housing.

These massive corporations and investors have been outbidding my constituents everywhere we look, and far too often the homes these non-occupant investors purchase will never resurface on the housing market. That is unconscionable. These homes should be going to the individuals who live in our communities, and, instead, they are taken off the market to pad the pockets of wealthy Wall Street hedge funds.

While reports continue to come in that these corporate speculators predominantly target neighborhoods of color and single moms, my bill, the HOME Act, will give HUD the tools necessary to investigate these allegations. Not only will HUD be able to collect the necessary data on who these speculators are targeting, but it also gives HUD the tools necessary to ensure that we have a level playing field in the housing market.

So, I would encourage my colleagues on this committee to look at this bill, H.R. 702, so that we can advance serious policy on a serious issue.

I would also encourage everyone to come to my district and to hear from my constituents about the pain associated with the lack of affordable housing options. Actually, this issue is so pressing in my district, I am bringing together the Tri-Caucus, the Black, His panic, and Asian Pacific American Caucuses for a housing summit in my district on May 8th.

We are working hard every day to address the issues that matter most to our communities. And if anyone wants to deliver real results for our communities, then I welcome you to join us in this work.

This is the priority that this Subcommittee and the Full Committee should be focused on. I would ask the Majority to please make housing affordability the priority that it deserves to be. That is what this subcommittee should be charged with while we reauthorize flood insurance for the next 10 years.

With that, I yield back.

Chairman DAVIDSON. The gentleman's time has expired.

We are going to make a change in the Chair, and then we are going to go vote.

We are going to have the committee recess, and then we will reconvene immediately once we have Members in place.

[Brief recess.]

Mrs. HOUCHIN. [presiding]. The committee will come to order.

I would now like to recognize myself for 5 minutes. Thank you. Thank you, Mr. Maurstad, for being here today.

Flood insurance is an issue that has an important impact on my district in Indiana. While we are firmly in America's heartland and have no risk of flooding from hurricanes, much of Indiana's Ninth District sits along the Ohio River, running from Aurora in Dearborn County, to New Albany in Floyd County, and along the river in Harrison County.

Indiana's Ninth District is also home to many creeks, ponds, and lakes, each of which can have a flooding impact on properties, businesses, and homes during times of heavy rainfall, causing property damage and sometimes death.

Just last September, I was on the ground with the Indiana Department of Homeland Security for flooding that occurred in Switzerland, Jefferson, and Ohio counties in my district. Several years ago, I worked for U.S. Senator Dan Coats and we worked with stakeholders during the last map update.

I want to say, first, I really appreciate the work of FEMA. Also, when I was working for Senator Coats, I was on the ground for the tornado that hit Henryville, Indiana, and I worked with FEMA for about 6 months and they provided excellent service during that time. So, thank you.

Many Hoosiers face the threat of flooding. The vast majority of properties in Indiana lack flood insurance coverage. Approximately 2.5 million properties currently don't have NFIP coverage. The number of homes and businesses covered has also dropped in recent years. In March 2021, there were 20,100 NFIP policies in place in Indiana. As of last October, there were less than 17,400 policies, a drop of more than 13 percent, or over 2,700 policies, from just a year-and-a-half prior.

One reason why Indiana has been dropping NFIP policies is due to cost. Between 1978 and 2017, Hoosiers paid over $440 million in NFIP premiums, while they received less than $290 million back. So they paid $150 million more than they received. With inflation forcing Americans to tighten their belts, many can't afford to pay these high premiums, which in Indiana, as of 2018, averaged $993.

It is not an unique issue to Indiana, and I have recently said that I appreciate that we are looking at a modernization of the flood insurance program because, if it is not working in Louisiana, and it is not working in Indiana, we probably need to find a way to fix some of the issues.

My question is: While the implementation of Risk Rating 2.0 reflects an attempt to more-accurately measure risk within the NFIP, Congress will still need to work further on NFIP reforms to maximize the efficiency and the potential of the program. It is likely that NFIP will never be able to provide protection against all floods and flood risks nationwide by itself.

Do you support efforts to encourage more private insurers to enter the flood market to help lighten the flood risk for NFIP?

Mr. MAURSTAD. First of all, the area in Indiana you describe sounds a lot like my home in southeast Nebraska. So, I certainly understand what you are talking about.

When the National Flood Insurance Program began, the first government reinsurance program, part of the thinking there was that it would allow the private insurance industry to better understand flood risks so that more companies on the private side would come in and help us close the flood insurance gap.

And one of the provisions, as I mentioned earlier, of our recommendations is to let concurrent coverage come back, so that somebody who leaves can come back. We think that will certainly be helpful. I think the other reforms that we are making also are beneficial for the private sector, which many times mirrors how the NFIP handles flood.

Mrs. HOUCHIN. I know Indiana isn't unique to this issue. Americans across the country face a risk of flooding. I look forward to working on meaningful solutions to address this. Thank you.

I yield back.

The gentlewoman from Georgia, Ms. Williams, is now recognized for 5 minutes.

Ms. WILLIAMS OF GEORGIA. Thank you.

We are in the middle of a housing crisis, and I have constituents who can't afford their mortgage or rent payments. But today, we are going to have another hearing on flood insurance, for the second time in 2 months, instead of discussing how we can lower housing costs in our districts and across the country.

In the fourth quarter of 2022, rent in the Atlanta metro area increased by 6.4 percent, compared to the fourth quarter of 2021. Since we have yet to focus any of our time in the subcommittee on housing, community development, and insurance, figuring out how to increase the supply of affordable housing, or drive down home prices for our constituents, I am happy to have this conversation again today about the needed reforms to the National Flood Insurance Program that would help those who manage to buy a house or rent an apartment keep their home, should it flood.

Atlanta is a city with the largest racial wealth gap in the country. And as I mentioned, Atlantans face skyrocketing housing costs. In Georgia's Fifth Congressional District, people who need flood insurance might not be able to afford it. But if their home floods, like so many did in the catastrophic flooding in 2009, which caused $500 million worth of damage, they simply can't afford to not have it.

Mr. Maurstad, I am very supportive of the Administration's recommendation to create a means-tested assistance program that will help low- and moderate-income families afford flood insurance by offering them a graduated discount benefit.

Has FEMA fleshed out what the particulars of this program could be, for example, what the discount percentages or the amounts would look like and how much money people could save?

Mr. MAURSTAD. Thank you for your support and for the question. To date, we have not actually developed the program. What we have outlined is a framework for the direction that we believe the program should be instructed to go by Congress in developing this affordability framework. So the details, we have not—

Ms. WILLIAMS OF GEORGIA. Still working on it.

Mr. MAURSTAD. Still working on it.

Ms. WILLIAMS OF GEORGIA. In our March 10th hearing, I asked once of our witnesses about legislative solutions for addressing racial disparities that people of color face. Communities of color are more likely to be susceptible to flooding but are not designated as Special Flood Hazard Areas. Additionally, the Urban Institute found that people of color are less likely to have flood insurance, and if they do have insurance, they experience a higher rate of unpaid claims.

Is the NFIP aware of and proactively collecting data on these disparities?

Mr. MAURSTAD. There is no question that what you describe should not occur. We are working on making sure that all of our programs are based in equity. It is a priority of the Administration. As I had mentioned, answering an earlier question, as we look at how we can provide the data that is necessary for you to make policy decisions, if you have any suggestions for us, we will take those. And we will try to do a better job of providing the data that would be helpful.

So, I would like to get back to you and work on exactly what information that you are looking for to see if we can deliver that.

Ms. WILLIAMS OF GEORGIA. I would love to hear more on the data collection.

Also, are there any additional steps that NFIP can take to reduce these disparities? And do you have any thoughts on what they are?

Mr. MAURSTAD. We are working with our adjustors to make sure that they understand unconscious bias and that they make sure they treat every policyholder fairly. That is critical. When I talk with adjustors, I suggest to them that they should handle that claim as though it was my mother's claim, because if it is not handled well and comes onto my desk, we are going to have a discussion about it. And that also goes for making sure we treat everyone fairly.

So if there are circumstances where that is not happening, I want to know about it, because we will correct it.

Ms. WILLIAMS OF GEORGIA. Thank you.

Last Congress, we took steps to improve stormwater infrastructure, a vital step in protecting our most-marginalized communities, and addressing the threat posed by more-frequent extreme weather events caused by climate change. While much more needs to be done, this is an important step in the mitigation.

Since mitigation efforts are included in risk assessment, have these efforts affected rates?

Mr. MAURSTAD. They are affected in a couple of different ways. One, as they are reflected in the communities' Flood Insurance Rate Maps, they are reflected there. As they are picked up in the CAT Modeling, in the experience of the catastrophe modelers, when mitigation activity occurs, those benefits are a part of the catastrophe models.

So, we are looking at making sure that mitigation efforts are and continue to be recognized in the program, because when we talk about what property owners need, we talk about the need for insurance and we talk about the need for mitigation. It is a two-pronged approach that we need to take.

Ms. WILLIAMS OF GEORGIA. Thank you.

My time has expired, and I yield back.

Mrs. HOUCHIN. Thank you, Ms. Williams.

The gentleman from New York, Mr. Lawler, is now recognized for 5 minutes.

Mr. LAWLER. Thank you, Madam Chairwoman.

And thank you, Mr. Maurstad, for being here today and addressing our questions and concerns.

As you mentioned in your opening statement, my district, like many across the nation, has seen more frequent and intense flood events occurring in recent years. And this is likely to continue. These are threats that will cost American homeowners, renters, and businesses billions of dollars in the near future.

And it is an important topic. Despite that fact, this hearing will mark the first appearance by FEMA before this committee in over 6 years, going back to March of 2017. So, I want to commend Chairman Davidson for having this hearing and making an effort to restore the committee's oversight of the NFIP program and see that these important issues are being examined.

Mr. Maurstad, the Government Accountability Office has observed that the NFIP has two competing goals: keeping flood insurance affordable; and keeping the program fiscally solvent. The balance between these two goals would appear to be especially difficult at the moment. While inflation is at a 41-year high and Americans are dealing with an affordability crisis, the implementation of Risk Rating 2.0 has led to increases in premiums for millions of Americans. We have heard reports of premiums in New York nearly doubling, increasing from $1,184 to $2,197, on average. When contemplating those two objectives, how does FEMA attempt to strike a balance between them?

Mr. MAURSTAD. First of all, thank you for the question.

And certainly, there are competing interests within the program that we are working hard to make sure we balance. Making premiums reasonable and making premiums be risk-based and actuarially sound can happen. And that is what our program has done. There is some misconception out there that the new pricing methodology increased the amount of premium dollars the program needs, and that is not the case. First, we would have needed to collect the same amount from all of our policyholders in the old legacy system that we now collect under the new rating methodology. Now, we base that premium on actual risk characteristics of the property instead of the zone in which that property happens to be located.

Second, another piece of the new methodology that is not well- recognized is that new policyholders come into the program at full risk rates. They no longer come into the program with a discount or a subsidy. So, the doubling of the insurance costs that you mentioned is not for a current policyholder. A current policyholder's premium can only go up the statutorily-required 18 percent. But new property owners have to pay the full risk rate.

The third point that I would make is that for the first time, the program is actually able to tell policyholders and property owners what their full risk is; we couldn't do that before. So now, folks understand that at some point, their rates are going to go from $1,500 to $3,000, but they are going to go there on an 18-percent glide path. But that number of knowing what it is has people concerned, rightfully, because now they know what their full risk is and they can take steps to mitigate.

Mr. LAWLER. Can you speak to what reforms would help grow awareness of the need for flood insurance and would encourage more Americans to be covered either through the NFIP or through the private market? We have seen over in Europe, certain programs and advertisements to try and encourage that. But what are we doing here in the United States to encourage people?

Mr. MAURSTAD. Yes, there's no question that flood risk is under-appreciated across the country. We can all do a better job of making sure people understand the peril associated with floods and the reason why that financial security of a flood insurance policy is so important.

But we don't work on this alone. It is not just FEMA. We work with the 48 write-your-own insurance companies that administer the program on behalf of us. We rely on them to do their part to make sure people understand flood risks. We work with community members, the 22,400 communities that participate in the program. We try to provide them the information, and many of them do their own campaigns. Many State insurance commissioners do their own campaigns, trying to raise flood awareness.

So, there is no question that we need to do a better job of making sure people appreciate the true flood risk the nation faces.

Mrs. HOUCHIN. The gentleman's time has expired. Thank you, Mr. Lawler.

The gentlewoman from Texas, Ms. Garcia, is now recognized for 5 minutes.

Ms. GARCIA. Thank you, Madam Chairwoman.

And thank you to Mr. Maurstad for being here with us today to bring us an update on the flood insurance program.

I represent the Houston area. And as our ranking member has mentioned, we have a lot of flood-prone areas and have had numerous 500-year events, both flooding and just rainy events. And the biggest priority for me is, of course, accessibility and affordability. The area itself was hit by Hurricane Harvey in 2017, which caused about $125 billion in damages and over 100 deaths. That is, what, about 4 times your authorization of $30 billion. In the greater Houston area alone, there are over 332,000 residential properties in FEMA-designated floodplains, and one out of seven projects has sustained substantial risk of flooding, or will by 2050. Research also shows that low-income and non-White communities are more at risk for flooding in the Houston area as a result of longstanding discriminatory housing policies.

For many people in my district, they really cannot afford the insurance. That is really the biggest, biggest barrier. And that is also true for most minority communities. In fact, some of the distribution of our dollars has been challenged as unfair and with a disparate impact on our minorities.

Because my district is 77-percent Latino and largely working- class, we have found that the biggest challenge we have is lots of rentals, and a lot of older populations who own their homes and can't afford the insurance.

I heard you respond to my colleague, Ms. Williams, that you are still working on it. And I just want to implore; I heard the same answer last time. It has been over a year at least since I have been here to ask some of these questions.

What is it that is keeping you going from using this new modeling to make it more affordable and accessible? I just don't understand why we keep getting the same answers.

Mr. MAURSTAD. We do not have the statutory authority to develop a program that bases the premium on one's income, which is why it is one of our 17 recommendations and is so important with not only making sure people who need the coverage in the areas that you describe but that we can develop a program that works for all Americans.

So, it is simply that we don't have the authority right now to develop that program.

Ms. GARCIA. But if you could, what would it look like? I think that was—

Mr. MAURSTAD. If we could—

Ms. GARCIA. —the question, and your answer was, "We are still looking at it."

Mr. MAURSTAD. If I said we are still looking at it, then I misspoke.

What we don't have is the details. We haven't written the regulation. We don't have all of the I's dotted and the T's crossed. So, what we have said is we are proposing to develop an affordability program that, if you are at 120 percent of the average mean income in your area, you would start to receive premium assistance, not your whole premium paid but premium assistance. And then, as your income goes down to 60 percent of the average mean income in your area, you would receive more of a discount than the moderate-income individual at the beginning of our program.

Ms. GARCIA. It would be—you are looking at a means-based, but will it be based on household? For example, we are flood-prone, but Montana may not be. So, will you look at regional considerations and considerations for—as the ranking member mentioned, California gets hit by fires and floods. For us, it is mostly floods and rain.

Mr. MAURSTAD. Sure.

Ms. GARCIA. And hurricanes.

Mr. MAURSTAD. The flood risk in every State is certainly different, and we recognize that now. But 98 percent of counties across the country have had a flood event. So, flooding can happen anywhere that it can rain.

And so, we want to work with you to make sure that we have the awareness needed to make sure that renters, and low-income people, understand they need the protection, but then also work with you to get our proposal in place so that we can design the program that is going do so much good.

Ms. GARCIA. I would hope, sir, with all due respect, that the next time we have you here, we don't hear again that you're looking at—

Chairman DAVIDSON. The gentlewoman's time has expired.

Ms. GARCIA. Thank you.

And I yield back.

Chairman DAVIDSON. The gentleman from New York, Mr. Torres, is now recognized for 5 minutes.

Mr. TORRES. Thank you, Mr. Chairman.

I represent the lowest-income congressional district in America. The lowest-income Americans are hit the hardest by the crippling costs of the National Flood Insurance Program. Under Rating 2.0, FEMA is intent on raising premiums by as much as 18 percent a year for as long as 10 years. And FEMA would be raising premiums even higher than 18 percent, were it not for the statutory cap that Congress put in place several years ago. And an even stronger cap is needed to protect the lowest-income families from rapidly-rising flood insurance payments.

You brought up earlier the notion of calculating premiums in light of income. And when it comes to housing, the threshold for affordability is 30 percent, right? No one should pay more than 30 percent of their income toward their rent. What would be the threshold when it comes to a flood insurance policy?

Mr. MAURSTAD. The program that we designed, and the Administration supports, that we recommended, looks at it from the average mean income of the property owner.

The affordability framework that we developed actually outlined a number of ways that you could develop an affordability program. So, we are certainly willing to look and have a conversation with you if there is a different manner in which we could provide this much-needed—

Mr. TORRES. Is that something you would study, what would constitute an affordable percentage of one's income with respect to flood insurance?

Mr. MAURSTAD. My sense would be—I am not an expert in that—

Mr. TORRES. Because that is the approach we take with student debt, and with affordable housing. So, why approach it differently with respect to flood insurance?

Mr. MAURSTAD. We looked at the most-effective way, in our opinion, and that is what we have proposed. We certainly will look at different ideas if you have them.

Mr. TORRES. I want to move on. If you live in a Special Flood Hazard Area and have a federally-backed mortgage, you are required to have flood insurance. But not every person who lives in a Special Flood Hazard Area with a federally-backed mortgage has flood insurance. Do you track noncompliance? And if so, what is the number of people who fall into that category?

Mr. MAURSTAD. We do not. That is actually a lender requirement, not an NFIP requirement, so we don't track those numbers. I think there has been some study done on it. We could provide you the information that we have, but the lenders would have that information.

Mr. TORRES. I am assuming the more participants in the program, the more financially-sustainable the program?

Mr. MAURSTAD. Actually, from an insurance perspective, it depends where those policyholders are. So, it is not as simple—

Mr. TORRES. Do you have a sense of where the enforcement is breaking down as far as the—

Mr. MAURSTAD. I don't know that the enhancement has broken down. So, I can't comment on that.

Mr. TORRES. Just judging by the noncompliance, that would seem to suggest that there is a breakdown in enhancement.

FEMA has a new methodology, Rating 2.0. I have heard complaints that the new methodology for calculating premiums is largely known only to insiders, and it is opaque to the rest of us, particularly State and local governments.

Does FEMA have any plans to make its methodology for calculating premiums more accessible and available to the public and pertinent stakeholders?

Mr. MAURSTAD. The rating methodology that we developed, that for the first time reduced a million policyholders' premiums an average $60 a month—we have provided that methodology publicly already. We have also provided premium calculation worksheets and a number of other tools on our website that agents and companies have.

Mr. TORRES. Do you feel like there is sufficient transparency?

Mr. MAURSTAD. I believe we have been very, very transparent.

Mr. TORRES. We have heard otherwise from New York State. Do you know why people are under the impression that your method is insufficiently transparent?

Mr. MAURSTAD. Sir, I think that we have done a good job of providing all of the information someone needs—

Mr. TORRES. So, where is the misunderstanding?

Mr. MAURSTAD. —to assess the program, and GAO will be issuing their—

Mr. TORRES. Do you have a sense of where the misunderstanding is?

Mr. MAURSTAD. —report. Excuse me?

Mr. TORRES. Where is the misunderstanding? Because there seems to be—there is a common complaint I have heard that there is a lack of transparency around your methodology. You seem to be claiming otherwise. So, I want to understand, where is the breakdown in communication? Where is the misunderstanding?

Mr. MAURSTAD. I don't know the answer to that.

Mr. TORRES. It is something I would want to explore.

Would the program be solvent if the Federal Government paid the debt associated with FEMA—with Katrina?

Mr. MAURSTAD. The program is backed by the full faith of the U.S. Treasury, so, solvency—

Mr. TORRES. But apart from the full faith, the program historically has been self-sustaining, and self-financing. Would you be—

Mr. MAURSTAD. Actually, it has not been self-sustaining. And the very nature of a catastrophic insurance program indicates that it would be very challenging, if not impossible, for it to ever be self-sufficient.

Mrs. HOUCHIN. The gentleman's time has expired.

I would like to thank the witness for his testimony today.

The Chair notes that some Members may have additional questions for this witness, which they may wish to submit in writing. Without objection, the hearing record will remain open for 5 legislative days for Members to submit written questions to this witness and to place his responses in the record. Also, without objection, Members will have 5 legislative days to submit extraneous materials to the Chair for inclusion in the record.

This hearing is adjourned.

[Whereupon, at 10:49 a.m., the hearing was adjourned.]

## Appendix

## Statement of David Maurstad, Assistant Administrator, Federal Insurance Directorate Federal Emergency Management Agency U.S. Department of Homeland Security Before the Committee on Financial Services Subcommittee On Housing And Insurance United States House of Representatives

### "The Reauthorization of the National Flood Insurance Program: FEMA's Perspective"

Washington, D.C. April 28, 2023

Good morning, Chairman Davidson, Ranking Member Cleaver, and other members of the Subcommittee. My name is David Maurstad, and I am the

Assistant Administrator for the Federal Insurance Directorate and Senior Executive of the National Flood Insurance Program (NFIP) at the Federal Emergency Management Agency (FEMA). I thank you for the opportunity to testify today in support of reauthorization and reform of FEMA's NFIP.

Flooding is the most common and costly natural hazard in the United States, and has occurred in more than 98% of counties and territories in the country over time. Although just one inch of flood water can cause up to $25,000 of damage in a home, flooding is not covered under most homeowners' standard insurance policies. With more frequent and intense flood events occurring, flood risk is becoming more severe across the nation. In Calendar Year 2022, the NFIP paid over $3.8 billion to policyholders for flood damage. Flooding also results from many disasters, and we continue to see not just riverine and coastal flooding, but flooding in burn areas that have recently experienced wildland fires and from torrential rainfall as well.

Every year, thousands of families across the country are affected by these incidents. Families that live at the margins struggle with recovery the most and are usually the last to recover if ever.

Flood insurance is an essential part of that recovery. I respectfully request that Congress expeditiously reauthorize and reform the NFIP to ensure the long-term viability of this essential program, along the lines that I will describe.

Congress established the NFIP in 1968 to encourage communities to make wise land-use decisions, and, in return for the community enacting floodplain management ordinances consistent with federal standards, the NFIP makes available flood insurance that allows people to protect homes in flood-prone areas.

For more than 50 years, the NFIP has been critical to the nation's resilience, however, much of the NFIP continues to operate on a construct developed over 50 years ago. Today, as our changing climate poses a serious threat to our nation and as the number and severity of disasters continue to grow, the NFIP requires structural changes.

On September 30, 2023, the NFIP's statutory authority to sell and renew flood insurance policies will expire. Since the NFIP's last multi-year reauthorization expired on September 30, 2017, the NFIP has experienced 25 short-term extensions and 3 brief lapses. The short-term extensions are disruptive and cause existing and potential policyholders to lose confidence in the NFIP.

To maintain this vital program and to rebuild and retain the trust of millions of Americans who rely on the NFIP, a multi-year reauthorization with comprehensive program reforms is imperative.

Last year, the Administration submitted 17 reform proposals embodying certain foundational principles that we believe should drive NFIP reform. And we will be submitting the proposals again this Congress. Today, I will speak to four of these key principles: ensure more Americans are covered by flood insurance, build the nation's climate resilience, reduce disaster suffering, and establish a sound and transparent financial framework for the NFIP.

*First, ensure that more Americans are covered by flood insurance by making insurance more affordable to low-and moderate-income policyholders.* Flood insurance is unaffordable for some low- and moderate-income policyholders. Under the current law, FEMA does not have the authority to establish and charge premiums based on a policyholder's ability to pay.

Although the NFIP currently offers mandatory discounts and cross-subsidies based on factors unrelated to risk, those discounts and subsidies do not take into consideration the policyholder's financial need and, in fact, can make risk communication difficult; people may equate lower cost with lower risk. Reforms that address affordability, such as the use of a targeted assistance program, can offer low- and moderate-income, current and prospective NFIP policyholders a graduated risk premium discount while providing them with knowledge of the full-risk price to communicate a property's true flood risk.

*Second, build the nation's climate resilience by communicating risk in real time and providing Americans with tools to manage flood risk.* NFIP can expand the ways it communicates risk to current and prospective policyholders through reforms that increase the scale and frequency of flood mapping and incorporate emerging priorities and technologies into the flood hazard and flood risk identification. Anywhere it rains, it can flood, and raising awareness of true flood risk enables people to make informed decisions about their family and property. Home buyers and renters may lack awareness about flood risk when they complete real estate transactions. Reforms that would require states to establish minimum flood-risk reporting obligations for sellers and lessors before residential transactions close would address this challenge. As climate change continues to make disasters more frequent and intense, it is vital that we provide people with the tools they need to protect themselves financially as well as physically.

Additionally, we need to reform how we measure and communicate flood risk. The nation's evolving risks require flood hazard information that is more robust than the special flood hazard area (SFHA) and 1-percent annual chance flood elevation.

*Third, reduce disaster suffering and mitigate risk by addressing extreme repetitive loss properties.* Previous losses are a significant indicator of risk, meaning that if a property flooded before, there is a high likelihood that it will flood again. Since 1978, over 350,000 structures have had two or more paid losses and more than 3,000 structures have suffered 10 or more losses. The NFIP must have better tools to address insured structures that have experienced multiple flood claims. These repetitive loss and severe repetitive loss properties are responsible for a disproportionate share of overall losses and have a high risk of future flooding. About 2.6% of insured properties are considered unmitigated repetitive loss properties. Continuing to cover these types of structures without question contributes to the NFIP's financial challenges and can increase the risk that families living in those structures will face threats to their lives, health, and safety. Reforming the NFIP to institute an objective threshold to deny coverage to the most egregiously flood-prone structures would discourage unmitigated rebuilding in areas with a history of flooding and reduce financial risk to the NFIP, while ensuring that coverage is still widely available to individuals, families, and businesses who might not be eligible for private market coverage.

*Fourth, institute a sound financial framework that allows the NFIP to balance affordability and fiscal soundness.* Without this in place, the longevity and sustainability of the program is at risk. Congress authorized FEMA to borrow from the U.S. Treasury up to $30 billion to pay claims. The NFIP currently carries $20.5 billion in debt to the U.S. Treasury and anticipates paying $619 million in interest expenses in Fiscal Year 2023 – this means we are using current premiums to pay for past claims. As currently structured, the program is unable to pay this debt back in full. Canceling the NFIP's debt provides the program with a solid foundation that can support financial reforms around borrowing authorities, future interest, enhanced liquidity, and an "upper limit" for the size of an NFIP event. These types of reforms address fundamental structural challenges and are essential to building a viable NFIP.

It is critical that Congress provide urgently needed multi-year reauthorization and <u>concurrently</u> reform the NFIP. Comprehensive and transformative reform is necessary to transition the NFIP to a sustainable program that balances affordability and fiscal soundness, builds climate resilience, and reduces risk, loss, and disaster suffering.

On behalf of the Administration, FEMA looks forward to working with Congress to develop a long-term solution that addresses the needs of the NFIP, its policyholders, and the nation.

Thank you again for the opportunity to discuss this important issue, and I would be pleased to answer any questions that you may have.

R Street

1212 New York Ave. NW
Suite 900
Washington, D.C. 20005
202-525-5717

*Free Markets. Real Solutions.*
*www.rstreet.org*

April 25, 2023

The Honorable Warren Davidson
Chairman
Subcommittee on Housing and Insurance
Committee on Financial Services
U.S. House of Representatives
Washington, D.C. 20515

The Honorable Emanuel Cleaver
Ranking Member
Subcommittee on Housing and Insurance
Committee on Financial Services
U.S. House of Representatives
Washington, D.C. 20515

Dear Chairman Davidson, Ranking Member Cleaver and members of the subcommittee:

Thank you for your decision to hold a hearing on April 28, 2023, titled "The Reauthorization of the National Flood Insurance Program: FEMA's Perspective." My name is Jerry Theodorou. I am the director of the R Street Institute's (R Street) Finance, Insurance and Trade Program. R Street is a nonprofit, nonpartisan, public policy research organization based in Washington, D.C. Our mission is to engage in policy research and outreach to promote free markets and limited, effective government in many areas, including insurance. My expertise and background is in property and casualty insurance, with over 30 years employment as an insurance analyst and manager in the insurance industry. Flood insurance is an issue I follow closely. I have testified to U.S. Senate committees three times on insurance issues, including to the Banking, Housing and Urban Affairs committee hearing focused on reauthorization of the National Flood Insurance Program (NFIP), Part II, on June 16, 2022.[1]

Flooding is the most common natural disaster in the United States, and is responsible for more economic loss than any other catastrophe, according to the National Oceanic and Atmospheric Administration (NOAA).[2] The NOAA estimates that 44 percent of the country is at risk of flooding this spring.[3] The NFIP is the primary source of flood insurance, responsible for over 90 percent of the flood insurance market.[4] It is therefore important for the health of the economy and the well-being of Americans that the NFIP be structured and managed prudently. We support long-term reauthorization of the NFIP. We also strongly support the six reforms and action items described below for the program to perform its role more effectively to develop a flood insurance market that provides protection from flood losses for more Americans.

**Risk-Based Rating**. The introduction and implementation of Risk Rating 2.0 in 2022/23 was a step in the right direction to bring fairness to the flood insurance marketplace. The rating methodology prior to Risk Rating 2.0 was binary—if a home was in a floodplain the premium would be much higher than if the home was not in a floodplain.[5] This approach did not recognize the reality of the degree of flood exposure ranging widely along a scale. Risk Rating 2.0 takes into account numerous factors contributing to a home's exposure to flood.

**Private Market for Flood Insurance**. The private market for flood insurance is small, estimated at approximately $300 million in premium/year, compared to the NFIP's $3.5 billion.[6] This is largely because the NFIP has been underpricing or providing premium subsidies to many homes, a practice which has led to the NFIP being $20.5 billion in debt, not counting the $16 billion of debt forgiveness in 2017.[7] As risk-adjusted rates earn into the portfolio, private insurers will be more willing to allocate capital to flood insurance.

**Public/Private Partnerships and Risk Sharing.** The NFIP already avails itself of private market reinsurance. An example of how private market reinsurance has helped to reduce the burden on the NFIP's balance sheet was the $1 billion reinsurance recovery following Hurricane Harvey in 2017.[8] The cost of the reinsurance was $150 million. We believe the NFIP should continue to structure its reinsurance tower with private market reinsurance, as well as insurance-linked securities (catastrophe bonds).

**Promote Mitigation Measures**. Mitigation is significantly preferable to *ad hoc* post-disaster government aid. What is more, mitigation sends appropriate price signals. Loss mitigation measures contribute to lower repair costs, which lead to lower insurance premiums. Many insurers give premium credits to homeowners who take measures to mitigate loss potential from flooding.

**Repeatedly Flooded Properties.** A disproportionately large percentage of flood losses are to homes that have been repeatedly flooded.[9] We support measures to limit loss payouts to homeowners whose properties have been repeatedly flooded and rebuilt without adopting protective measures to reduce loss potential from future flooding events. We support sanctions on homeowners and communities that fail to comply with recommended flood-mitigation measures.

**Expand the Risk Pool**. There are only approximately 5 million homes with flood insurance coverage out of the nation's 70 million homes.[10] Ownership/buyership of flood insurance needs to be increased to help create a healthy risk pool that does not suffer from adverse selection. Adverse selection occurs when only those who pose more risk buy insurance.

Thank you again for holding this important hearing and for your consideration of my views. Should you have any questions or wish to have further discussion, please do not hesitate to contact me.

Sincerely,

Jerry Theodorou
/s/
Director, Finance, Insurance & Trade Program
R Street Institute
jtheodorou@rstreet.org

---

[1] "Reauthorization of the National Flood Insurance Program: Protecting Communities from Flood Risk," U.S. Senate Committee on Banking, Housing, and Urban Affairs, June 16, 2022. https://www.banking.senate.gov/hearings/reauthorization-of-the-national-flood-insurance-program-protecting-communities-from-flood-risk.

[2] Brittney Meredith-Miller, "The 10 most costly U.S. floods," ALM Property Casualty 360, May 18, 2022. https://www.propertycasualty360.com/2022/05/18/the-10-most-costly-u-s-floods.

[3] Elana Ashanti Jefferson, "NOAA: Nearly half of U.S. at risk of spring flooding," ALM Property Casualty 360, March 17, 2023. https://www.propertycasualty360.com/2023/03/17/noaa-nearly-half-of-u-s-at-risk-of-spring-flooding.

[4] "Spotlight on: Flood Insurance," Insurance Information Institute, Dec. 6, 2022. https://www.iii.org/article/spotlight-on-flood-insurance#:~:text=Private%20Flood%20Insurance,-According%20to%20NAIC&text=Restated%20net%20premiums%20written%20for%202020%20are%20%24302.4%20million%20and,from%20%24522.6%20million%20in%202019; Federal Insurance and Mitigation Administration, *The Watermark* 16, Federal Emergency Management Agency, 2021. https://www.fema.gov/sites/default/files/documents/fema_fy-2021-q4-watermark.pdf.

[5] Federal Emergency Management Agency, "Risk Rating 2.0: Equity in Action," U.S. Department of Homeland Security, April 19, 2023. https://www.fema.gov/flood-insurance/risk-rating.

[6] Insurance Information Institute. https://www.iii.org/article/spotlight-on-flood-insurance#:~:text=Private%20Flood%20Insurance,-According%20to%20NAIC&text=Restated%20net%20premiums%20written%20for%202020%20are%20%24302.4%20million%20and,from%20%24522.6%20million%20in%202019; Federal Insurance and Mitigation Administration. https://www.fema.gov/sites/default/files/documents/fema_fy-2021-q4-watermark.pdf.

[7] Diane P. Horn et al., "Introduction to the National Flood Insurance Program (NFIP)," Congressional Research Service, Jan. 6, 2023. https://sgp.fas.org/crs/homesec/R44593.pdf.

[8] "U.S. Flood Program to Collect $1 Billion in Reinsurance for Hurricane Harvey Claims," *Insurance Journal*, Dec 6, 2017. https://www.insurancejournal.com/news/national/2017/12/06/473261.htm.

[9] Laura Lightbody and Brian Watts, "Repeatedly Flooded Properties Will Continue to Cost Taxpayers Billions of Dollars," The Pew Charitable Trusts, Oct. 1, 2020. https://www.pewtrusts.org/en/research-and-analysis/articles/2020/10/01/repeatedly-flooded-properties-will-continue-to-cost-taxpayers-billions-of-dollars.

[10] Diane P. Horn, "National Flood Insurance Program: The Current Rating Structure and Risk Rating 2.0," Congressional Research Service, April 4, 2022. https://sgp.fas.org/crs/homesec/R45999.pdf.

Chapter 8

# Flood Insurance: FEMA's New Rate- Setting Methodology Improves Actuarial Soundness but Highlights Need for Broader Program Reform*

United States Government Accountability Office

## Abbreviations

| | |
|---|---|
| AMI | area median income |
| BISG | Bayesian Improved Surname Geocoding |
| CRS | Community Rating System |
| FEMA | Federal Emergency Management Agency |
| FIRM | Flood Insurance Rate Map |
| HFIAA | Homeowner Flood Insurance Affordability Act of 2014 |
| HHI | household income |
| MBA | means-based assistance |
| NAIC | National Association of Insurance Commissioners |
| NFIP | National Flood Insurance Program |
| SFHA | special flood hazard area |
| WYO | Write Your Own |

* This is an edited, reformatted and augmented version of the United States Government Accountability Office Report to Congressional Addressees, Publication No. GAO-23-105977, dated July 2023.

In: The National Flood Insurance Program (NFIP)
Editor: Jolene Rivera
ISBN: 979-8-89530-612-3

## Why GAO Did This Study

NFIP was created with competing policy goals—keeping flood insurance affordable and the program fiscally solvent. A historical focus on affordability has led to premiums that do not fully reflect flood risk, insufficient revenue to pay claims, and, ultimately, $36.5 billion in borrowing from Treasury since 2005.

FEMA's new Risk Rating 2.0 methodology is intended to better align premiums with underlying flood risk at the individual property level.

This report examines several objectives, including (1) the actuarial soundness of Risk Rating 2.0, (2) how premiums are changing, (3) efforts to address affordability for policyholders, (4) options for addressing the debt, and (5) implications for the private market.

GAO reviewed FEMA documentation and analyzed NFIP, Census Bureau, and private flood insurance data. GAO also interviewed FEMA officials, actuarial organizations, private flood insurers, and insurance agent associations.

## What GAO Recommends

GAO recommends six matters for congressional consideration.

Specifically, Congress should consider the following:

- Authorizing and requiring FEMA to replace two policyholder charges with risk-based premium charges
- Replacing discounted premiums with a means-based assistance program that is reflected in the federal budget
- Addressing NFIP's current debt— for example, by canceling it or modifying repayment terms—and potential for future debt
- Authorizing and requiring FEMA to revise NFIP rules hindering the private market related to (1) continuous coverage and (2) partial refunds for midterm cancellations

GAO is also making five recommendatons to FEMA, including that it publishes an annual report on NFIP's actuarial soundness and fiscal outlook. The Department of Homeland Security agreed with the recommendations.

## What GAO Found

In October 2021, the Federal Emergency Management Agency (FEMA) began implementing Risk Rating 2.0, a new methodology for setting premiums for the National Flood Insurance Program (NFIP). The new methodology substantially improves ratemaking by aligning premiums with the flood risk of individual properties, but some other aspects of NFIP still limit actuarial soundness. For example, in addition to the premium, policyholders pay two charges that are not risk based. Unless Congress authorizes FEMA to align these charges with a property's risk, the total amounts paid by policyholders may not be actuarially justified, and some policyholders could be over- or underpaying. Further, Congress does not have certain information on the actuarial soundness of NFIP, such as the risk that the new premiums are designed to cover and projections of fiscal outlook under a variety of scenarios. By producing an annual actuarial report that includes these items, FEMA could improve understanding of Risk Rating 2.0 and facilitate congressional oversight of NFIP.

Risk Rating 2.0 is aligning premiums with risk, but affordability concerns accompany the premium increases. FEMA had been increasing premiums for a number of years prior to implementing Risk Rating 2.0. By December 2022, the median annual premium was $689, but this will need to increase to $1,288 to reach full risk. Under Risk Rating 2.0, about one-third of policyholders are already paying full-risk premiums. Many of these policyholders had their premiums reduced upon implementation of Risk Rating 2.0. All others will require higher premiums, including 9 percent who will eventually require increases of more than 300 percent. Further, Gulf Coast states are among those experiencing the largest premium increases Policies in these states have been among the most underpriced, despite having some of the highest flood risks.

Estimated Premium Changes under Risk Rating 2.0, as of December 2022

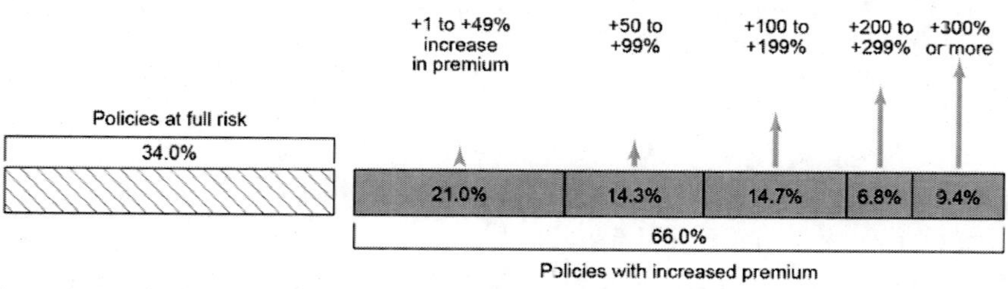


Source: GAO analysos of Federal Emergency Management Agency data. | GAO-23-105977.

Annual premium increases for most policyholders are limited to 18 percent by statute. These caps help address some affordability concerns in the near term, but have several limitations.

- First, the caps perpetuate an unfunded premium shortfall. GAO estimated it would take until 2037 for 95 percent of current policies to reach full-risk premiums, resulting in a $27 billion premium shortfall (see figure below). The costs of shortfalls are not transparent to Congress or the public because they are not recognized in the federal budget and become evident only when NFIP must borrow from the Department of the Treasury after a catastrophic flood event.
- Second, the caps address affordability poorly. For example, they are not cost-effective because some policyholders who do not need assistance likely are still receiving it. Concurrently, some policyholders needing assistance likely are not receiving it, and the discounts will gradually disappear as premiums transition to full risk.
- Third, the caps keep NFIP premiums artificially low, which undercuts private-market premiums and hinders private-market growth.

Estimated Premium Shortfall and Percentage of National Flood Insurance Program Policies at Full-Risk Premiums, by Calendar Year

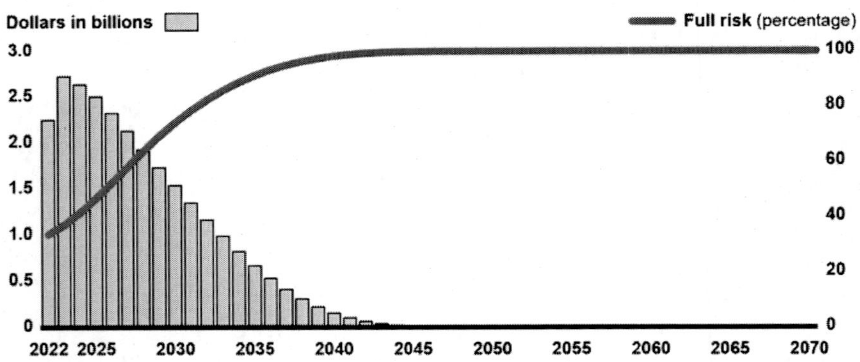


Source: GAO analysos of Federal Emergency Management Agency data. | GAO-23-105977.

An alternative to caps on annual premium increases is a means-based assistance program that would provide financial assistance to policyholders based on their ability to pay and be reflected in the federal budget. Such a program would make NFIP's costs transparent and avoid undercutting the private market. If affordability needs are not addressed effectively, more policyholders could drop coverage, leaving them unprotected from flood risk and more reliant on federal disaster assistance. Addressing affordability needs is especially important as actions to better align premiums with a property's risk could result in additional premium increases.

FEMA has had to borrow from Treasury to pay claims in previous years and would have to use revenue from current and future policyholders to repay the debt. NFIP's debt largely is a result of discounted premiums that FEMA has been statutorily required to provide. In addition, a statutorily-required assessment has the effect of charging current and future policyholders for previously incurred losses, which violates actuarial principles and exacerbates affordability concerns. Even with this assessment, it is unlikely that FEMA will ever be able to repay the debt as currently structured. For example, with the estimated premium shortfalls, repaying the debt in 30 years at 2.5 percent interest would require an annual payment of about $1.9 billion, equivalent to a 60 percent surcharge for each policyholder in the first year. Such a surcharge could cause some policyholders to drop coverage, leaving them unprotected from flood risk and leaving NFIP with fewer policyholders to repay the debt. Unless Congress addresses this debt—for example, by canceling it or modifying repayment terms—and the potential for future debt, NFIP's debt will continue to grow, actuarial soundness will be delayed, and affordability concerns will increase.

Risk Rating 2.0 does not yet appear to have significantly changed conditions in the private flood insurance market because NFIP premiums generally remain lower than what a private insurer would need to charge to be profitable. Further, certain program rules continue to impede private-market growth. Specifically, NFIP policyholders are discouraged from seeking private coverage because statute requires them to maintain continuous coverage with NFIP to have access to discounted premiums, and they do not receive refunds for early cancellations if they switch to a private policy. By authorizing FEMA to allow private coverage to satisfy NFIP's continuous coverage requirements and to offer risk-based partial refunds for midterm cancellations replaced by private policies, Congress could promote private-market growth and help to expand consumer options.

July 31, 2023

The Honorable Sherrod Brown
Chairman

The Honorable Tim Scott
Ranking Member
Committee on Banking, Housing, and Urban Affairs
United States Senate

The Honorable Patrick McHenry
Chairman

The Honorable Maxine Waters
Ranking Member
Committee on Financial Services
House of Representatives

The Honorable Bennie G. Thompson Ranking Member
Committee on Homeland Security
House of Representatives

The Honorable Troy Carter
Ranking Member
Subcommittee on Emergency Management and Technology
Committee on Homeland Security
House of Representatives

The National Flood Insurance Program (NFIP) has competing policy objectives: being fiscally solvent while keeping flood insurance affordable for policyholders. Balancing these objectives has been challenging over the years, and a historical focus on affordability has come at the expense of solvency. In particular, Congress has required the Federal Emergency Management Agency (FEMA) to allow many policyholders to pay discounted premiums that do not fully reflect their properties' flood risk.

This approach has contributed to a shortfall in revenue and insufficient funds to pay claims, causing FEMA to borrow about $36.5 billion from the

Department of the Treasury since 2005. For these reasons, we placed NFIP on our High-Risk List in 2006.[1]

The ratemaking methodology used until recently by FEMA has contributed to these challenges.[2] This legacy methodology had become outdated, as it had remained largely unchanged since NFIP was created in 1968. To modernize its ratemaking methodology and better align premiums with underlying flood risk at the individual property level, FEMA developed a new methodology called Risk Rating 2.0 and began implementing it in October 2021. Under Risk Rating 2.0, most policyholders will continue to experience premium increases.[3] While these increases will help move NFIP toward fiscal solvency and more accurately signal to homeowners the flood risk of their property, they will also amplify affordability concerns.

In April 2017, we outlined a road map for comprehensive reform that, among other things, addresses the trade-offs between solvency and affordability.[4] Since September 2017, NFIP has been operating under a series of short-term reauthorizations without comprehensive reform. In September 2023, NFIP's current authorization will expire.

We performed our work under the authority of the Comptroller General in light of congressional interest in FEMA's new ratemaking methodology and NFIP's impending reauthorization. This report examines (1) the actuarial soundness of the new methodology, (2) how premiums are changing for policyholders, (3) efforts to make flood insurance affordable for policyholders, (4) options for addressing program debt, (5) the potential implications of Risk Rating 2.0 for the private flood insurance market, and (6) FEMA's efforts to promote policyholder understanding of Risk Rating 2.0.

To examine the actuarial soundness of Risk Rating 2.0, we reviewed FEMA documentation and actuarial assumptions and methods used to develop premiums. We also reviewed the premiums, assessments, surcharges, and fees that policyholders pay and the costs these charges are designed to cover. Finally, we interviewed FEMA officials and an actuarial association and compared the methodology and results against actuarial standards and principles.

---

[1] GAO, *High Risk: Efforts Made to Achieve Progress Need to Be Maintained and Expanded to Fully Address All Areas*, GAO-23-106203 (Washington, D.C.: Apr. 20, 2023).

[2] Ratemaking is the process used to determine what prices (premiums) an insurer charges.

[3] Under the previous methodology, policyholders did not experience premium decreases. However, under Risk Rating 2.0, about 19 percent of policyholders experienced an immediate decrease in premiums.

[4] GAO, *Flood Insurance: Comprehensive Reform Could Improve Solvency and Enhance Resilience*, GAO-17-425 (Washington, D.C.: Apr. 27, 2017).

To examine how premiums are changing for policyholders, we analyzed NFIP policy data and Census Bureau data by geography and household income.[5] We also used a statistical technique to estimate the probability that NFIP policyholders identify as a particular race or ethnicity and analyzed premium changes by these factors.[6]

To examine efforts to make insurance affordable for policyholders, we reviewed legislative proposals as well as policy goals established in our prior work.[7] We analyzed NFIP policy data to estimate the time it might take for FEMA to transition current policyholders to full-risk premiums and the continued federal cost until the transition is completed. We accounted for annual premium increase caps, inflation rates, flood risk, and NFIP policy renewal, and we analyzed alternate scenarios for each of these assumptions to determine how our estimates might change. We also analyzed NFIP policy data and census data to estimate the potential costs associated with providing means-based affordability assistance for flood insurance.

To examine options for addressing program debt, we analyzed NFIP policy data and reviewed our previous work on NFIP, as well as reports from the Congressional Budget Office, Congressional Research Service, FEMA, and others. We assessed the options against actuarial standards as well as policy goals we established in prior work.

To examine the potential implications of Risk Rating 2.0 for the private flood insurance market, we analyzed NFIP policy data and data from the National Association of Insurance Commissioners (NAIC) on private flood insurance.[8] We also interviewed private insurers and reviewed laws and regulations that affect private insurers' ability to provide flood insurance. We assessed these laws and regulations against policy goals we established in prior work.

---

[5] We assessed the reliability of NFIP data we analyzed by reviewing relevant documentation; testing the data to identify missing data, outliers, and any obvious errors; and comparing our results to published data. We also interviewed FEMA officials and reviewed relevant documentation. We determined that the NFIP data we analyzed were sufficiently reliable for the purposes of our report.

[6] We assessed the reliability of these estimates by conducting a literature review on the accuracy of the technique and by examining the completeness and distributions of the estimates for NFIP policyholders. We determined that the data were sufficiently reliable for estimating the race or ethnicity of NFIP policyholders.

[7] See GAO-17-425.

[8] We assessed the reliability of these data by comparing data elements to totals from other sources. We also interviewed NAIC officials about the accuracy and limitations of the data and their process for ensuring reliability. We determined that the data were sufficiently reliable to describe trends in the private flood insurance market.

To examine FEMA's efforts to promote policyholder understanding of Risk Rating 2.0, we reviewed NFIP policy documents, FEMA's web materials, and training materials for agents and Write Your Own (WYO) insurers.[9] We also interviewed FEMA officials and insurance agent associations.

We compared this information against FEMA's strategic plan. A more detailed description of our scope and methodology is included in appendix I.

We conducted this performance audit from March 2022 to July 2023 in accordance with generally accepted government auditing standards.

Those standards require that we plan and perform the audit to obtain sufficient, appropriate evidence to provide a reasonable basis for our findings and conclusions based on our audit objectives. We believe that the evidence obtained provides a reasonable basis for our findings and conclusions based on our audit objectives.

## Background

Congress first proposed providing flood insurance in the 1950s, after it became clear that private insurance companies could not profitably provide flood coverage. Specifically, limited knowledge of flood risk at the time made it difficult for insurers to determine accurate premiums. This uncertainty, combined with the catastrophic nature of flooding, would have required premiums that many consumers might not have been able to afford. In 1968, Congress created NFIP to help reduce the escalating costs of providing federal flood assistance to repair damaged homes and businesses.[10] NFIP was also intended to address the policy objectives of identifying flood risk, offering reasonable insurance premiums to encourage program participation, and promoting community-based floodplain management.[11]

---

[9] FEMA's WYO program allows private insurers to sell and service policies and adjust claims for NFIP.

[10] Pub. L. No. 90-448, Tit. XIII, 82 Stat. 476, 572 (1968).

[11] On June 1, 2023, 10 states and multiple local jurisdictions filed a lawsuit in the Eastern District of Louisiana against FEMA alleging, among other claims, that Risk Rating 2.0 is inconsistent with the objective of making flood insurance available when necessary at reasonable rates and that the agency's actions violated legal requirements of notice and comment rulemaking. *Louisiana, et. al. v. Mayorkas*, Case No. 2:23-cv-01839 (E.D. La. June 1, 2023). We do not address this lawsuit or any legal authorities discussed in the lawsuit in this report.

## Community Participation, WYO Program, and Purchase Requirements

Community participation in NFIP is voluntary. For a community's residents to purchase flood insurance through the program, the community must participate in NFIP.[12] Participation requires communities to meet certain requirements, including enforcing regulations for land use, building standards, and new construction in special flood hazard areas (SFHA).[13] FEMA uses community assistance visits and community assistance contacts to oversee community enforcement of NFIP requirements. Community assistance visits are on-site assessments of a community's floodplain management program and its knowledge and understanding of NFIP's floodplain management requirements.

In 1990, FEMA implemented a voluntary incentive program for communities participating in NFIP called the Community Rating System (CRS) to recognize and encourage community floodplain management activities that exceed the minimum NFIP requirements. According to FEMA, CRS's goals are to reduce and avoid flood damage to insurable property, strengthen and support the insurance aspects of NFIP, and foster comprehensive floodplain management. Communities may apply to join CRS if they are in full compliance with the minimum NFIP floodplain management requirements. FEMA groups CRS communities into classes based on their ratings. Communities can improve their ratings by earning CRS credits for activities such as increasing public information about flood risks, preserving open space, taking steps to mitigate flood damage, and preparing residents for floods. Policyholders in these communities receive a discount on their flood insurance premiums ranging from 5 to 45 percent, depending on the community's rating.

Consumers can purchase NFIP policies from a licensed property and casualty agent. Most agents sell policies underwritten through FEMA's WYO program, which allows private insurers to sell and service policies and adjust claims for NFIP. To become a WYO insurer, private insurers enter into an arrangement with FEMA to issue flood policies in their own name. The insurers must have experience in property and casualty insurance lines, be in good standing with state insurance departments, and be capable of selling and

---

[12] As of May 2023, FEMA had identified 24,767 communities across the United States. Of these, 22,621 (91 percent) participated in NFIP.

[13] SFHAs are land areas that would be submerged by the floodwaters of the "base flood"— a flood that has a 1 percent chance of being equaled or exceeded in any given year.

servicing the policies. WYO insurers do not assume any risk, and they receive an expense allowance for their services (currently about 30 percent of the premium a policyholder pays). Agents can also contract directly with FEMA to sell NFIP policies under the agency's NFIP Direct program.[14] Consumers pay the same premium, regardless of how they purchase their policy.

Generally, homeowners with federally backed mortgages in SFHAs have been required by law to purchase flood insurance since 1973.[15] As part of its role in administering NFIP, FEMA develops floodplain maps— historically known as Flood Insurance Rate Maps (FIRM)—that provide the basis for identifying which properties are required to purchase flood insurance by delineating the boundaries of SFHAs.[16] Properties located in these areas that have certain federally backed mortgages are subject to the mandatory purchase requirement for flood insurance.

## Risk Rating 2.0 and Authority for Premium Increases

In October 2021, FEMA began implementing a new methodology for calculating flood insurance premiums, known as Risk Rating 2.0.

Beginning on October 1, 2021, all new NFIP policyholders were required to pay the full-risk premium determined using Risk Rating 2.0, and all renewing policyholders were able to opt into Risk Rating 2.0 if it lowered their premium.[17] Beginning on April 1, 2022, all NFIP policyholders became subject to the new methodology as their policies were renewed, so that as of April 1, 2023, all NFIP policies were subject to Risk Rating 2.0.[18]

Under the legacy methodology, some properties (also known as "pre-FIRM" properties) paid discounted "subsidized" premiums if they were built before floodplain maps for their area were published and flood risk in those

---

[14] As of January 2020, approximately 88 percent of NFIP policies were sold by companies participating in the WYO program, and 12 percent of policies were sold through the NFIP Direct Servicing Agent.

[15] 42 U.S.C § 4012a. Federally backed mortgages are those made, insured, or guaranteed by federally regulated lenders or federal agencies, or purchased by the government- sponsored enterprises for housing—Fannie Mae and Freddie Mac.

[16] FEMA floodplain maps also serve as the basis for local floodplain management standards that communities must adopt and enforce as part of their NFIP participation. Prior to Risk Rating 2.0, FEMA also used its floodplain maps to set premiums.

[17] FEMA refers to its premiums that encompass all of the elements of the individual risk transfer as full-risk premiums.

[18] NFIP policies generally have a 1-year term. We refer to annual premium amounts that reflect the policy term.

locations was properly understood. Other policies paid discounted "grandfathered" premiums when a new flood map placed them into a flood zone that would have increased their premiums; these properties' premiums continued to be based on the previous, lower-risk flood zone.

Premium increases for renewing NFIP policies are generally limited by statute.[19] For most policies, FEMA is prohibited from increasing premiums by more than 18 percent per year.[20] FEMA is also required by law to increase premiums by 25 percent per year for certain other policies until they reach full risk, such as those covering pre-FIRM secondary residences, businesses, and severe repetitive loss properties.[21] FEMA is to increase premiums from 5 to 15 percent per year for certain other policies, including those covering properties that were built before flood maps were available for their area.

## NFIP Funding Structure and Flow of Funds

FEMA generally pays claims and funds its operations from premium revenue from policyholders. In addition to paying for flood claims and adjustment expenses, FEMA uses premium revenue to pay other costs, including WYO expense allowances, interest on debt, operating expenses, and mitigation grants.

FEMA offers coverage to homeowners, renters, and businesses for buildings and their contents.[22] In addition to premiums for building and

---

[19] 42 U.S.C. § 4015(e).

[20] FEMA also is prohibited from increasing premiums for certain groups of policies with the same flood risk classification by more than 15 percent per year on average. Such groups include properties that were built before flood maps were available for their area and properties that pay discounted premiums because they were newly mapped into an SFHA on or after April 1, 2015, if the applicant gets flood insurance coverage within a year of the mapping.

[21] A severe repetitive loss property is an NFIP-insured structure that has incurred flood- related damage for which (a) four or more separate claims have been paid that exceeded $5,000 each and cumulatively exceeded $20,000, or (b) at least two separate claim payments have been made under such coverage, with the cumulative amount of such claims exceeding the fair market value of the insured structure. 42 U.S.C. § 4104c(h); 42U.S.C. § 4014(h).

[22] NFIP's maximum coverage limit for one-to-four-family residential policies is $250,000 for buildings and $100,000 for contents. For nonresidential policies, the maximum coverage limit is $500,000 per building and $500,000 for the building owner's contents. NFIP policies offer a variety of deductible options. Renters can purchase contents-only coverage. FEMA also offers Increased Cost of Compliance coverage, which provides up to $30,000 to help cover the cost of mitigation measures following a flood loss when a property is declared to be substantially or repetitively damaged.

contents coverage, NFIP policyholders pay separate assessments, surcharges, and fees (see table 1).

**Table 1.** National Flood Insurance Program (NFIP) policyholder assessm

| Charge | Authority | Purpose | Amount | FEMA authority |
|---|---|---|---|---|
| Reserve fund assessment | Biggert-Waters Flood Insurance Reform Act of 2012 (codified as amended at 42 U.S.C. § 4017a) | Establish and maintain a reserve fund to cover future claim and debt expenses, especially those from catastrophic disasters | 18% of current premium per policy starting on April 1, 2020 (previously 15% since April 2016) | The Federal Emergency Management Agency (FEMA) has limited authority to determine the amount (statute specifies a reserve fund target and minimum annual payments into the fund until the target is reached). |
| Homeowner Flood Insurance Affordability Act surcharge | Homeowner Flood Insurance Affordability Act of 2014 (codified at 42 U.S.C. § 4015a) | Offset the cost of discounted premiums | $25 for primary residences; $250 for all other properties | FEMA has no authority to determine the amount or eliminate the surcharge before statutory requirements for full-risk premiums are generally universally met—that is nearly all NFIP policies must be at full-risk, with some exceptions. |
| Federal Policy Fee | Omnibus Budget Reconciliation Act of 1990 (codified as amended at 42 U.S.C. §4014 (a)(1)(B)(iii)) | Pay for administrative expenses incurred in carrying out flood insurance and floodplain mapping activities | $47 for all policies under Risk Rating 2.0 (previously $50 and $25, depending on policy type, since October 2017) | FEMA has certain authority to determine the amount. |

Source: GAO. | GAO-23-105977.

Note: In addition to premiums, which are based on risk, NFIP policyholders pay separate assessments, surcharges, and fees.

For example, a hypothetical single-family primary residence had been paying an annual premium of $1,017 prior to Risk Rating 2.0. Under Risk Rating 2.0, FEMA determined that this hypothetical policyholder should be paying $2,200 to reflect the full risk of loss of the insured property.

Because this policy is subject to an 18 percent statutory cap on annual premium increases, in the first year FEMA can only raise the premium by 18 percent, from $1,017 to $1,200. Therefore, in the first year of Risk Rating 2.0, the policyholder receives a $1,000 discount relative to the full- risk premium of $2,200. The policyholder then pays $288 in additional assessments, surcharges, and fees, bringing the total payment to $1,488. The premium will increase each year, subject to the statutory caps, until the full-risk premium is reached. Figure 1 illustrates the costs for this hypothetical policyholder in the first year under Risk Rating 2.0.

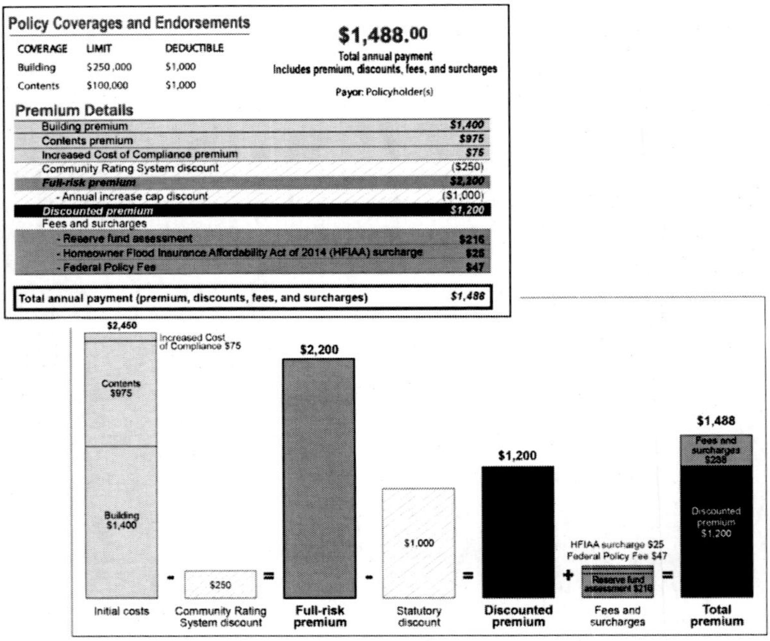


Source: GAO analysis of Federal Emergency Management Agency data. | GAO-23-105977.

**Figure 1**. Policyholder Costs for a Hypothetical National Flood Insurance Program Policy.

FEMA also has reinsurance agreements and borrowing authority from Treasury to fulfill its obligations. Collections are deposited into an insurance fund, and some are transferred to a reserve fund (see Figure 2).[23] In most years,

[23] The National Flood Insurance Fund was established in the U.S. Treasury by the National Flood Insurance Act of 1968. The National Flood Insurance Reserve Fund was established

NFIP premium revenue is sufficient to pay claims and generate a cash surplus. In years when losses exceed premium revenue, FEMA uses any amounts in these funds to pay claims, first from the insurance fund and then, if necessary, from the reserve fund. When individual or accumulated losses in a year exceed a certain threshold, FEMA can receive payouts from its reinsurance agreements. When revenue, reinsurance, and any accumulated surplus are insufficient, FEMA has authority to borrow from the Treasury.[24]

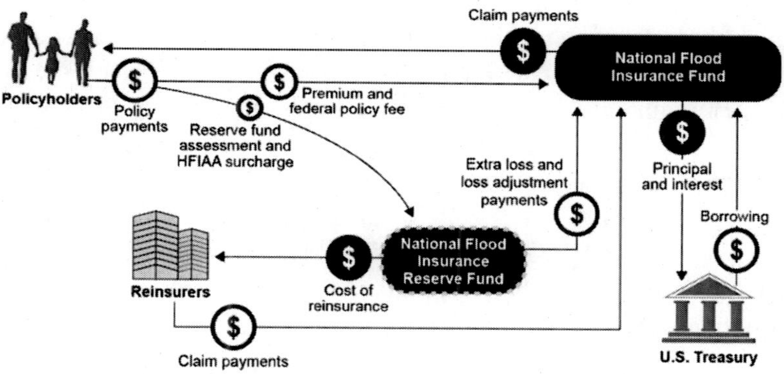


Source: GAO. | GAO-23-105977.

Note: All policyholder payments are deposited into the National Flood Insurance Fund, but the reserve fund assessment and Homeowner Flood Insurance Affordability Act (HFIAA) surcharge are transferred into the National Flood Insurance Reserve Fund.

**Figure 2.** National Flood Insurance Program (NFIP) Flow of Funds.

---

by the Biggert-Waters Flood Insurance Reform Act of 2012 to help meet future NFIP obligations and principal and interest payments on any outstanding Treasury loans (42 U.S.C. § 4017a). Specifically, FEMA is required to establish a reserve fund with a balance equal to 1 percent of the sum of the total potential loss exposure of all outstanding flood insurance policies in force in the prior fiscal year. FEMA's total exposure in fiscal year 2022 was $1.28 trillion, which equates to a target reserve fund balance of $12.8 billion for fiscal year 2022. FEMA is required to contribute at least 7.5 percent of its target balance each year until it achieves the target reserve fund balance. This equates to a reserve fund contribution of $960 million for fiscal year 2022.

[24] 42 U.S.C. § 4016. Congress authorized FEMA to borrow from the Treasury when needed, up to a preset statutory limit. Originally, Congress authorized a borrowing limit of $1 billion and increased it significantly in 2005 and 2013. The limit currently stands at $30.425 billion.

## Risk Rating 2.0 Significantly Improves Ratemaking, but Certain Aspects of NFIP Limit Actuarial Soundness

### With Risk Rating 2.0, FEMA Improved Ratemaking by Applying Actuarial Principles

In developing Risk Rating 2.0, FEMA applied actuarial principles to better align premiums with flood risk, representing a substantial improvement from its legacy ratemaking methodology. The methodology and process FEMA used to develop full-risk premiums in Risk Rating 2.0 generally reflect statutory premium requirements and relevant actuarial principles and standards.[25]

According to FEMA, Risk Rating 2.0 was the first change in its ratemaking methodology since the 1970s. The legacy methodology had become out of date for several key reasons, including that it largely based premiums on a property's height relative to the base flood elevation and broadly defined flood zone and charged the same premium nationwide based on these characteristics.[26] The legacy rating methodology also did not capture many potential flood sources or reflect flood risk from catastrophic events. We previously identified a number of challenges with this ratemaking process.[27]

Under Risk Rating 2.0, FEMA better aligns premiums with flood risk and takes advantage of new technology and advances in the insurance industry's understanding of flood risk. For instance, Risk Rating 2.0 does the following:

---

[25] 42 U.S.C. § 4014(a). Casualty Actuarial Society, *Statement of Principles Regarding Property and Casualty Ratemaking* (Arlington, Va.: May 7, 2021). The Actuarial Standards Board's relevant Actuarial Standards of Practice include 12 (Risk Classification for All Practice Areas); 23 (Data Quality); 25 (Credibility Procedures); 29 (Expense Provisions in Property/Casualty Insurance Ratemaking); 30 (Treatment of Profit and Contingency Provisions and the Cost of Capital in Property/Casualty Insurance Ratemaking); 38 (Catastrophe Modeling); 39 (Treatment of Catastrophe Losses in Property/Casualty Insurance Ratemaking); 53 (Estimating Future Costs for Prospective Property/Casualty Risk Transfer and Risk Retention); and 56 (Modeling).

[26] Under the legacy methodology, SFHAs included two categories of flood zones: A (high- risk noncoastal) and V (high-risk coastal). Non-SFHAs generally included three categories: B, C, and X (low to moderate risk).

[27] See GAO, *National Flood Insurance Program: Continued Progress Needed to Fully Address Prior GAO Recommendations on Rate-Setting Methods*, GAO-16-59 (Washington, D.C.: Mar. 17, 2016) and *Flood Insurance: FEMA's Rate-Setting Process Warrants Attention*, GAO-09-12 (Washington, D.C.: Oct. 31, 2008).

- *Ties premiums to individual property flood risk rather than to broadly defined flood zones.* Premiums under the legacy methodology relied heavily on a structure's flood zone as depicted on FEMA's floodplain maps.[28] Structures within each flood zone generally were rated similarly, meaning that while properties may have had different premiums because of other variables (e.g., occupancy type and elevation), the premium did not vary based on the property's particular geographic location within the zone. Risk Rating 2.0 calculates premiums based on the characteristics of each individual insured structure and no longer uses the flood zone.
- *Integrates input from commercial catastrophe models.* Catastrophe models are computerized processes that simulate potential losses due to catastrophic events, such as floods.[29] Their use has become standard practice in the insurance industry since they were first developed in the 1980s. The models have evolved significantly as technology has advanced and exposure data have improved. Under Risk Rating 2.0, FEMA uses catastrophe models to estimate the annual losses from potential flood events.
- *Accounts for more sources of flooding.* The previous methodology accounted only for coastal and riverine flooding, but Risk Rating 2.0 also includes pluvial (rainfall), Great Lakes, coastal erosion, and tsunami flooding.
- *Accounts for the replacement cost value of the property.* NFIP residential coverage is generally limited to $250,000. Although the legacy methodology did not adjust premiums based on the value of the insured property, insured homes with values above the $250,000 limit still affected NFIP's risk exposure. For example, $250,000 in coverage was priced the same for a $250,000 home as for a $5 million home. However, this approach was inequitable because the same flooding event is likely to cause more damage to a higher-value structure. For example, $250,000 in damage to a $250,000 home—a total destruction of home value—would occur only with an infrequent severe flood event. In contrast, $250,000 of damage to a $5 million home—a destruction of just 5 percent of home value—could occur

[28] FEMA floodplain maps are the official maps of communities on which FEMA has delineated the SFHA and base flood elevations applicable to the community.

[29] Actuarial standards of practice define a catastrophe model as a model of low-frequency events with high-severity or widespread potential effects. Catastrophe models may be used to explain a system, to study effects of different components, or to derive estimates.

> with far less severe and more frequent flood events. As a result, the $5 million home has a much higher probability of incurring $250,000 in damage than does a $250,000 home, and should have a higher premium. By not accounting for this difference in probabilities, the legacy rating methodology tended to undercharge homes that are more expensive and overcharge homes that are more modest. By incorporating replacement cost value into its ratemaking, Risk Rating 2.0 more accurately accounts for differences in flood risk from properties of different values.

In its Risk Rating 2.0 ratemaking process, FEMA incorporates the damage or loss estimates of multiple catastrophe models, which include commercial models as well as FEMA models that use data from other government agencies, including the U.S. Army Corps of Engineers.

These models do not produce suggested premium rates, but FEMA uses the output of these models in its ratemaking process. According to FEMA, the agency makes use of multiple catastrophe models because, although each model has its own strengths, no single model adequately covers all circumstances. For example, FEMA uses data from the U.S. Army Corps of Engineers to model damage and losses in areas behind levees, and it uses data from the National Oceanic and Atmospheric Administration and other agencies to model coastal flooding. Catastrophe models, including those used by FEMA, are generally based on simulations and thus involve some amount of uncertainty.

NFIP is statutorily required to develop premiums that are actuarially sound.[30] According to actuarial principles, an actuarially sound premium is an estimate of the expected value of future costs of the individual risk transfer.[31] These expected costs include insurance claims, claims-related expenses, commissions, operational expenses, reinsurance costs, and a provision for

---

[30] 42 U.S.C. § 4014(a).

[31] Casualty Actuarial Society, *Statement of Principles*. Further, the Actuarial Standards Board sets standards for appropriate actuarial practice in the United States through the development and promulgation of Actuarial Standards of Practice, which describe the procedures an actuary should follow when performing actuarial services and identify what the actuary should disclose when communicating the results of those services. According to Actuarial Standard of Practice 1, "actuarial soundness" has different meanings in different contexts and might be dictated or imposed by an outside entity. In rendering actuarial services, if the actuary identifies a process or result as "actuarially sound," the actuary should define the meaning of "actuarially sound" in that context.

retained risk.[32] Actuarial principles also state that an actuarially sound premium should be reasonable and should not be excessive, inadequate, or unfairly discriminatory. In developing Risk Rating 2.0, FEMA followed the statutory definition of actuarial rates and followed recognized actuarial principles and actuarial standards of practice.[33] FEMA refers to its premiums that encompass all of the elements of the individual risk transfer as full-risk premiums.

The process of ratemaking under Risk Rating 2.0 included three core components: creating market baskets representative of single-family homes, estimating NFIP's aggregate target premium, and allocating individual premiums to policyholders. Creating market baskets involved grouping U.S. single-family homes with several of the same risk factors using geographic information system data and commercially available data.[34] FEMA incorporated the market baskets into catastrophe models from several vendors and modeled NFIP's flood risk using policy data as of May 31, 2018. According to FEMA officials, they updated their assumptions using data as of May 31, 2020.

FEMA then developed NFIP's aggregate target premium—the total premium for the entire program—using the average annual losses generated from the catastrophe models, as well as provisions for WYO expense allowances, loss adjustment expenses, and the net cost of reinsurance and retained risk.

FEMA then used the aggregate target premium to determine individual policyholder premiums based on the risk factors of their insured properties and the potential flood sources. FEMA used rating variables, which are characteristics that have been shown through analysis to correlate with the likelihood of losses. When developing rating factors, FEMA compared the

---

[32] Reinsurance is insurance for insurers. The net cost of reinsurance includes the excess of reinsurance premiums paid to the reinsurer over recoveries for claims from the reinsurer. Retained risk is the exposure that an insurer chooses to cover itself rather than transferring it to a third party, such as a reinsurer, and includes the risk of random variation from expected costs plus the risk of systematic underestimation of expected costs. In private-sector contexts, a provision for risk is also referred to as a cost of capital.

[33] The statutory definition of an actuarial rate is one that covers all costs, as prescribed by principles and standards of practice in ratemaking adopted by the American Academy of Actuaries and the Casualty Actuarial Society, including an estimate of the expected value of future costs, all costs associated with the transfer of risk, and the costs associated with an individual risk transfer with respect to risk classes, as defined by FEMA. 42 U.S.C. § 4014 (a)(1)(B)(iv).

[34] Data sources included the U.S. Geological Survey, the National Oceanic and Atmospheric Administration, and the U.S. Army Corps of Engineers.

annual expected losses derived from the catastrophe models to NFIP's historical losses from January 1, 1992, to June 30, 2018, and adjusted accordingly. Specifically, FEMA compared a range of modeled losses for each market basket of properties to the historical losses experienced by actual policies within that market basket to verify whether the historical losses fell into the model's estimated range.

FEMA performed a rating factor analysis by peril separately for single-family homes not protected by a levee, single-family homes protected by a levee, and non-single-family homes.[35] FEMA's analyses identified a set of rating factors that reflect several characteristics:

- location (including distance to flooding sources and elevation relative to flooding sources);
- structural characteristics (including occupancy type, foundation type, first floor height, number of floors, construction type, existence of flood openings, and location of machinery and equipment); and
- replacement cost value, coverage, and deductible amounts.

All of these rating factors combined allow FEMA to group policyholders with similar risks together to help determine the full-risk premium. FEMA officials told us they plan to review and update premiums to continue using the best available data, science, and models. They also plan to account for changes in other factors, such as flood risk and their understanding of it, as well as changes in inflation, expenses, fees, and policyholder population.

## Some Additional Policyholder Charges Limit Actuarial Soundness

In addition to premiums, NFIP policyholders pay separate charges that are determined outside of the actuarial ratemaking process. These additional charges are not proportional to the individual risk of the insured property and result in some policyholders being charged more than the actuarial cost of the risk transfer.

---

[35] Risk Rating 2.0 accounts for the level of risk reduction that levees provide to the buildings located behind them. Levees reduce flood risk but do not eliminate it. According to FEMA, limitations of levees include their capacity to reduce flooding in leveed areas (from overtopping) and their ability to perform adequately during flood events, and this information is fundamental in assessing the risk.

- *Reserve fund assessment.* FEMA is statutorily required to establish and maintain a reserve fund to provide additional funds to cover future claims and debt expenses, especially those from catastrophic disasters. Specifically, FEMA must move toward a target balance of 1 percent of insurance-in-force by making minimum annual contributions of 7.5 percent of the target balance until the fund reaches the target.[36] FEMA does so by implementing a reserve fund assessment, which FEMA has set at 18 percent of the premium since 2020.[37] FEMA applies the reserve fund assessment to the discounted premium rather than the full-risk premium. As a result, the assessment is not proportional to the actual risk of the property.[38] FEMA officials told us that they view the reserve fund assessment as a capitalization charge that is separate from the full-risk premium. However, FEMA also includes in its full-risk premium a risk load for the risk of future catastrophic losses, in accordance with actuarial principles. As a result, the statutorily required reserve fund assessment results in policyholders paying a charge for catastrophic losses in two places, and being at risk of overpaying the cost of risk transfer, especially policyholders paying full-risk premiums.[39]
- *Homeowner Flood Insurance Affordability Act (HFIAA) surcharge.* The HFIAA surcharge, which was statutorily established and offsets the cost of discounted premiums, is set at $25 for primary residences and $250 for other properties. Because the HFIAA surcharge is a flat amount, it is not tied to the risk of the individual property, and while

---

[36] 42 U.S.C. § 4017a(b)(1),(d)(1).

[37] FEMA initially set the reserve fund assessment at 5 percent but increased it to 15 percent in April 2016 and 18 percent in April 2020.

[38] For example, a policyholder who pays a full-risk premium would pay a higher reserve fund assessment than a policyholder with the same risk who pays a discounted premium.

[39] FEMA is required to develop rates based on actuarial principles and in consideration of risk to include operating and administrative expenses. 42 U.S.C. § 4014. This includes a risk load for catastrophic losses, according to FEMA officials. Further, FEMA officials stated that Risk Rating 2.0 includes this catastrophic load in the premium and that this premium must be deposited into the National Flood Insurance Fund. Additionally, FEMA is generally required by statute to increase premiums to fund the reserve fund to meet the target or reserve ratio for the year. 42 U.S.C. § 4017a. FEMA officials stated that the reserve fund assessment should not be viewed as an actuarial charge, but as a congressional mandate. Additionally, FEMA officials stated that the reserve fund assessment is subject to the aggregate annual premium increase cap of 18 percent a year. According to FEMA, due to this constraint, policyholders who are paying their full- risk rate will be charged the full reserve fund assessment, while those policyholders receiving a premium increase discount will not pay the full reserve fund assessment. Additionally, all premium increases to build up the reserve fund must be deposited into the reserve fund. 42 U.S.C. § 4017a.

> the $25 surcharge for primary residences is relatively small, the $250 surcharge for other properties is not. In addition, while the HFIAA surcharge offsets the cost of discounted premiums, it is charged to all policyholders, including those already paying the full-risk premium, so that these policyholders are partially subsidizing policyholders paying discounted premiums. The amount of the HFIAA surcharge is set in statute, so FEMA lacks the authority to eliminate or reduce it until statutory requirements for full-risk premiums are generally universally met—that is, nearly all NFIP policies must be at full-risk, with some exceptions.

Because the full-risk premium covers the full cost of the risk transfer, including a risk load, policyholders paying the full-risk premium plus the reserve fund assessment and the additional HFIAA surcharge are paying more than the actuarially determined cost of insurance. Moreover, the size and duration of the reserve fund assessment will vary with claims experience. For example, if the reserve fund is used to help pay claims in a catastrophic loss year, the reserve fund assessment might need to be increased, extended, or reinstated to reach the target balance. This would result in current or future policyholders paying for past losses, in violation of actuarial principles.

To the extent that the reserve fund assessment and HFIAA surcharge are not proportional to the individual risk of the insured property or result in policyholders paying more than an actuarially justified cost of the risk transfer, the total costs a policyholder pays will not be actuarially sound. Specifically, FEMA cannot ensure that the amounts charged align with the flood risk of specific properties, which limits the ability of these charges to accurately signal flood risk and results in some policyholders overpaying and others potentially underpaying. Were Congress to authorize and require FEMA to incorporate the reserve fund assessment, to the extent necessary based on actuarial principles, into the risk charge within the full-risk premium, it would enhance the actuarial soundness of the total costs policyholders pay. Further, were Congress to repeal the HFIAA surcharge and authorize and require FEMA to replace forgone revenue with actuarially determined premium adjustments, it would enhance the actuarial soundness of the total costs policyholders pay.

## CRS Discounts Are Not Actuarially Justified

Premium discounts provided under the CRS program are not actuarially justified and are paid for, in large part, through a cross-subsidization by policyholders not receiving the discount. As previously discussed, FEMA uses premium discounts ranging from 5 to 45 percent to promote CRS program goals: to reduce and avoid flood damage to insurable property, to strengthen and support the insurance aspects of NFIP, and to foster comprehensive floodplain management.[40] As a community engages in additional eligible activities, its residents become eligible for larger premium discounts.

FEMA officials told us they set full-risk premiums so that after applying the CRS discounts, the total premium revenue within each state represents the full aggregate risk of all policies in that state. This approach results in a cross-subsidy because policyholders outside of CRS communities are paying higher premiums than are actuarially justified to subsidize the discounts that policyholders in participating CRS communities receive.

Further, it is likely that policyholders receiving the CRS discount are paying lower premiums that do not fully reflect their flood risk. The amounts of CRS discounts—both to individual properties and program- wide—are not closely linked to potential loss reduction of currently insured properties. While the activities that FEMA promotes through CRS are important, few of them directly mitigate flood risk in the policy period.[41] FEMA officials told us that CRS helps improve future resilience to flood risk but does little to reduce the estimated flood losses of the properties NFIP currently insures.[42] For example, four eligible activities reduce potential flood damage: floodplain management planning, acquisition and relocation, flood protection, and drainage system maintenance.[43] However, CRS provides discounts for 15 other activities

---

[40] As of May 2023, 22,621 communities participated in NFIP. As of April 2023, 1,504 NFIP communities received a CRS discount, and 454 received a discount of at least 20 percent.

[41] Until October 2021, discounts were available only to properties in SFHAs, but under Risk Rating 2.0, FEMA provides discounts to all policies in a participating community.

[42] Broadly speaking, resilience is the ability to prepare and plan for, absorb, recover from, and more successfully adapt to actual or potential adverse events.

[43] FEMA defines floodplain management planning as the adoption of flood hazard mitigation or natural functions plans using the CRS planning process, or conducting repetitive loss area analyses. Acquisition and relocation refer to acquiring insurable buildings and relocating them out of the floodplain and leaving the property as open space. Flood protection of the insured building includes activities such as floodproofing, elevation, or minor structural projects. Drainage system maintenance includes annual inspections of channels and retention basins and maintenance of the drainage system's flood-carrying and storage capacity.

related to public information, mapping and regulations, and warning and response that do not reduce the potential for flood damage to currently insured properties.[44] While we recognize the value of such activities, it is not actuarially justifiable to incentivize them through premium discounts or through overcharging policyholders outside of CRS communities. FEMA has not evaluated the actuarial benefits of these other activities in terms of loss mitigation or other means of incentivizing them.

In addition, FEMA officials stated that some of the rating variables used in Risk Rating 2.0 already account for the reduced flood risk that results from certain CRS activities in calculating full-risk premiums. For example, one rating variable is a property's elevation height in relation to flood sources. Elevating properties is one activity a community could undertake to receive a CRS discount. As a result, some properties could receive lower premiums because they are elevated and also receive a CRS discount for being located in a community that is working to elevate properties. At the same time, nonelevated properties in the community would still receive the CRS discount without having received any risk- reduction benefit from the community's activities.

Actuarial principles suggest that the amount of premium discount should align with the amount of loss reduction for each individual property.

Further, while statute requires FEMA to apply CRS discounts, it does not prescribe the amount of the discounts or the specific community activities FEMA should use to determine them.[45] Rather, it says that FEMA should provide CRS discounts based on the estimated reduction in flood risk from the measures adopted by the community.

If FEMA does not adjust CRS ratings so that only community activities that can be actuarially justified to reduce flood risk contribute toward a community's rating and does not incorporate discounts into the full-risk premium based on the actuarial evaluation of risk reduction, then premiums will not be actuarially sound, and policyholders will continue over- or underpaying premiums. Further, by evaluating other means of incentivizing desirable community-wide activities that cannot be actuarially justified,

---

[44] Public information activity categories include elevation certificates, map information service, outreach projects, hazard disclosure, flood protection information, flood protection assistance, and flood insurance promotion. Mapping and regulations activity categories include floodplain mapping, open space preservation, higher regulatory standards, flood data maintenance, and stormwater management. Warning and response activity categories include flood warning and response, levees, and dams.

[45] 42 U.S.C. § 4022(b).

FEMA could help ensure such activities continue if they are no longer incentivized through CRS discounts.

## FEMA Has Not Fully Reported on Risk Rating 2.0's Actuarial Soundness and Its Effect on NFIP's Fiscal Exposure

Implementing Risk Rating 2.0 is helping FEMA to address NFIP's historical premium inadequacy and overall actuarial soundness, but Congress and the public do not have certain information on the new methodology and NFIP's long-term fiscal outlook.

FEMA has communicated Risk Rating 2.0's actuarial soundness and NFIP's fiscal outlook to Congress through three primary means:

- Legislative reform proposals. In May 2022, the Department of Homeland Security submitted to Congress 17 legislative proposals that included establishing a "Sound Financial Framework."[46] According to FEMA, the framework would call for NFIP to pay all claims for a flood event that has a 5 percent chance of being exceeded in any given year—about $10.5 billion, similar to claims from Hurricane Harvey in 2017. Congressional action on an emergency supplemental appropriation would be needed only if claims exceeded this amount. FEMA said this framework would require the implementation of several reforms.[47] FEMA estimated the framework would result in a 75 percent likelihood that NFIP could manage flood events up to the established ceiling and have a positive balance in its available funds at the end of a 10-year period.
- Budget request. In its 2024 budget request, FEMA estimated the budgetary effects of its proposed reforms for establishing the

---

[46] Department of Homeland Security, *Legislative Reform Package* (Washington, D.C.: May 11, 2022).

[47] To achieve the Sound Financial Framework, FEMA proposed (1) canceling the existing debt, (2) eliminating interest on future debt, (3) decreasing NFIP's borrowing authority from $30.425 billion to two-thirds of total expected premiums in force in the following fiscal year, (4) directing annual equalization payments to cover premium shortfalls from discounted premiums, (5) allowing the ability to transfer funds between the insurance and reserve funds, (6) eliminating the Reserve Fund Ratio, and (7) eliminating the HFIAA surcharge.

framework.[48] FEMA also requested an equalization payment to cover what it estimated to be the cost of premium discounts in fiscal year 2024.

- Debt report to Congress. In August 2022, FEMA submitted to Congress a report on NFIP's debt as of March 2022.[49] The report communicated the uncertainty of flood losses, NFIP's estimated annual losses for a 10-year period, and projections of NFIP's debt and financial position over this period.

In addition to these reports, FEMA posted on its website a report from its actuarial contractor that describes the actuarial modeling and data sources used in developing Risk Rating 2.0 premium rates.

These communications provide important information on NFIP, but Congress and the public lack some information because these communications are fragmented and incomplete. For example, FEMA's Sound Financial Framework communicates NFIP's estimated capacity if it were to receive annual equalization payments for the cost of premium discounts and if its other requested reforms were implemented. However, FEMA did not estimate NFIP's current capacity (absent these reforms) or estimate its future capacity for either scenario. The framework also does not include a plan to regularly update these estimates. Further, FEMA has designed full-risk premiums under Risk Rating 2.0 based on an estimated average annual loss target but has not incorporated this estimate into these communications. Moreover, while FEMA estimated premium revenue and shortfalls for a 10-year period when preparing its budget request, the actual budget request only included the estimates for 2024.

In addition, the 10-year projections in FEMA's budget request and debt report included a single baseline scenario rather than a range of scenarios that would illustrate the uncertainty of NFIP's future financial condition.

One of FEMA's strategic objectives is empowering risk-informed decision- making, and FEMA's strategic plan states that the availability of, access to, and understanding of future conditions data and modeling within FEMA must be expanded.[50] In this regard, a comprehensive annual actuarial

---

[48] Office of Management and Budget, Budget of the U.S. Government, Fiscal Year 2024—Department of Homeland Security (Washington, D.C.: Mar. 9, 2023).

[49] Department of Homeland Security, National Flood Insurance Program Semi-Annual Debt Repayment Report, March 31, 2022 (Washington, D.C.: Aug. 30, 2022).

[50] Federal Emergency Management Agency, 2022–2026 FEMA Strategic Plan: Building the FEMA Our Nation Needs and Deserves (Washington, D.C.: 2021).

report could help better inform Congress and the public about Risk Rating 2.0's actuarial soundness and NFIP's fiscal outlook.[51] Ensuring that such a report is informed by relevant actuarial standards would enhance its usefulness and credibility.[52]

Elements of a comprehensive annual actuarial report could include communicating the accuracy and adequacy of NFIP's premiums in managing the program's fiscal exposure. The report could also communicate the target loss level that full-risk premiums are designed to cover, the uncertainty associated with the full-risk premium, and the likelihood that the estimated premium revenue will cover the target loss for the policy year. Further, the report could evaluate and communicate estimated premium revenue and shortfall, the likelihood of additional Treasury borrowing, and NFIP's short- and long-term fiscal outlook under a variety of scenarios for future claims experience and policy renewals, lapses, and new policies. Without a comprehensive annual actuarial report on Risk Rating 2.0's soundness and NFIP's fiscal outlook, available information for overseeing the program will continue to be fragmented and incomplete.

## Risk Rating 2.0 Is Aligning Premiums with Risks, but Some Policyholders Face Increasing Affordability Concerns

### Premiums Are Increasing for Many Policies but Will Better Reflect Flood Risk

As noted earlier, a key goal of Risk Rating 2.0 is to more closely align premiums with individual property flood risk. Because legacy premiums on many policies do not fully reflect the underlying flood risk, aligning premiums with risks will require premium increases on most policies.[53] As of December

---

[51] Examples of comprehensive annual reports for other programs that involve actuarial assessments of risk include the annual trustees' reports for Social Security and Medicare and the annual projections report produced by the Pension Benefit Guaranty Corporation.

[52] For more information, see, for example, Actuarial Standards of Practice 41 (Actuarial Communications), 46 (Risk Evaluation in Enterprise Risk Management), 47 (Risk Treatment in Enterprise Risk Management), and 56 (Modeling).

[53] As discussed previously, NFIP policyholders pay premiums, which are based on risk, as well as separate assessments, surcharges, and fees. In this section, we analyzed the entire amount a policyholder pays, including building premium, contents premium, Increased Cost of Compliance premium, severe repetitive loss premium, reserve fund assessment, HFIAA surcharge, Federal Policy Fee, and probation surcharge. CRS discounts, when applicable,

2022, NFIP policyholders paid a median annual premium of $689.[54] However, the median annual full-risk premium was $1,288.[55] As a result, the median premium will need to increase by almost 90 percent to reach full risk.[56]

However, different policies will require different premium changes to align them with actual risk and reach full-risk premiums. For example, 35 percent of policies will require an increase of less than 100 percent, while about 9 percent will require an increase of 300 percent or more (see Figure 3). Overall, about 66 percent of policies still required premium increases as of December 2022. In September 2021, under the legacy methodology, FEMA considered about 22 percent of its policies to be paying premiums that were less than full risk.[57] In contrast, the fact that 66 percent of policies are paying less than full-risk premiums under Risk Rating 2.0 indicates that the legacy system significantly underestimated flood risk and that Risk Rating 2.0 is correcting this underpricing.

While FEMA is increasing premiums for most policies, it has reduced premiums on about 19 percent of policies, which indicates that FEMA has determined that the anticipated cost of insuring these properties is lower than it had previously determined. According to FEMA, many of these properties have lower replacement cost value, and by accounting for it, Risk Rating 2.0 is able to offer a lower premium. FEMA is implementing the full amount of

---

are also reflected. For simplicity and clarity, in this section we refer to the total policyholder payments as "premiums."

[54] For condominiums, NFIP offers a Residential Condominium Building Association Policy, which covers all units within a condominium. As a result, it is necessary to adjust for the number of condominium units to determine the number of policies. We account for the number of condominium units when reporting the aggregate number of NFIP policies, but otherwise we treat these condominium policies as single policies.

[55] FEMA determined full-risk premiums for policies subject to Risk Rating 2.0, which includes new policies beginning October 1, 2021, and renewed policies beginning April 1, 2022. We analyzed NFIP data for policies in effect on December 31, 2022, which included full-risk premiums that were valid as of that date for 89 percent of NFIP policies. Our analysis excludes the remaining policies, which were due for renewal from January 1, 2023, to March 31, 2023, because FEMA had not yet determined their full-risk premiums. Full-risk premiums are FEMA's best estimates of the premium that would need to be charged to cover the estimated cost of the risk transfer and associated expenses for the year FEMA determined them. As noted earlier, FEMA officials told us they will modify premiums as input factors change (such as housing values and flood risk) and as they continue to improve their understanding of flood risk.

[56] FEMA's estimates of full-risk rates reflect current WYO expense allowances (about 30 percent of the premium a policyholder pays). As premiums increase with implementation of Risk Rating 2.0, the amount of expense allowance per policy will increase. Any changes to the compensation structure would affect the calculation of full-risk rates.

[57] Under the legacy methodology, subsidized and grandfathered premiums were considered less than full risk.

these premium decreases immediately upon policy renewal, whereas it must phase in premium increases, often over many years, as required by law.

FEMA had been increasing premiums for a number of years prior to implementing Risk Rating 2.0. In implementing previous reforms, FEMA increased premiums by an average of 6 to 11 percent in each year from 2015 to 2021. Under the previous methodology, FEMA was unable to calculate full-risk premiums for many of its policies.[58] Even if FEMA had not implemented Risk Rating 2.0, it would still have had the authority to increase most premiums by 18 percent annually until it determined it had collected enough to pay for expected losses in the aggregate. However, FEMA would not have known if it was charging a full-risk premium for any individual property. Because Risk Rating 2.0 allows FEMA to calculate full-risk premiums for all policies, FEMA can determine when each policy no longer requires an annual increase to reach full risk. By better aligning premiums with flood risks, Risk Rating 2.0 provides an actuarial justification for these premium increases and helps reduce NFIP's net cost to the federal government—that is, the government's fiscal exposure.

## Gulf Coast States Are among Those Most Underpriced and Requiring the Largest Premium Increases

To align premiums with flood risk, premium increases, on average, will be greater in some states than in others. Policies requiring the highest premium increases under Risk Rating 2.0 are also those that were previously the most heavily underpriced. For example, all five Gulf Coast states—Alabama, Florida, Louisiana, Mississippi, and Texas—are in the highest premium increase group (see Figure 4). With high premium increases skewed toward Gulf Coast states where flood risk is higher and most (61 percent) of NFIP's policies are concentrated, Risk Rating 2.0 is correcting a geographical pricing imbalance and addressing a historical source of fiscal exposure.

---

[58] Under the legacy methodology, FEMA required elevation certificates to determine premiums for full-risk policies. However, it generally did not require elevation certificates for subsidized policies because it did not use elevation information for determining subsidized premiums. Because FEMA lacked elevation for these policies, it was not able to calculate their full-risk rates. See GAO, *Flood Insurance: More Information Needed on Subsidized Properties*, GAO-13-607 (Washington, D.C.: July 3, 2013).

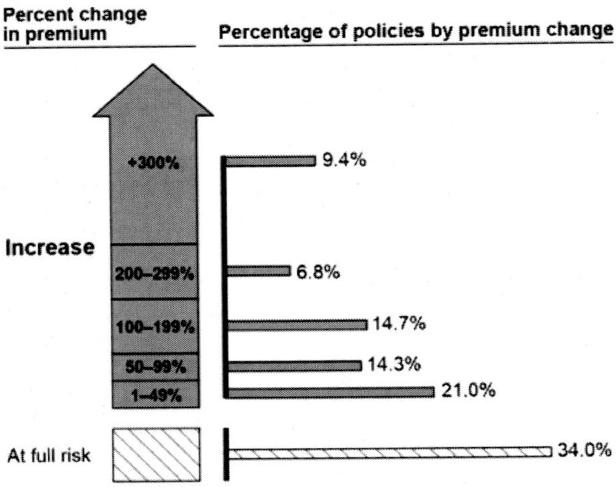


Source: GAO analysis of Federal Emergency Management Agency data. | GAO-23-105977.

Note: This analysis includes the 89 percent of policies subject to Risk Rating 2.0 and in effect on December 31, 2022. The remaining 11 percent of policies were due for renewal from January 1, 2023, to March 31, 2023, at which point FEMA determined their full-risk premiums. About 19 percent of policies in effect on September 30, 2021, received premium decreases under Risk Rating 2.0. The "at full risk" category includes these policies; new policies, most of which were subject to full-risk premiums; and policies that reached full-risk premiums upon renewal because the required increase was less than the statutory cap on annual premium increases for those policies.

**Figure 3.** Estimated Future Premium Changes under Risk Rating 2.0, as of December 2022.

The five non-Gulf Coast states experiencing high premium increases—Connecticut, Hawaii, New Hampshire, New Jersey, and West Virginia—account for 5 percent of NFIP policies. For more detailed information on premiums as of December 31, 2022, and full-risk premiums, percent change, and affordability, see the interactive graphic available at http://www.gao.gov/products/gao-23-105977.

Further, many of the states with the lowest premiums as of December 31, 2022, are those with higher flood risk, further indicating historical underpricing and explaining the premium increases under Risk Rating 2.0. As discussed previously, many policies have not yet reached their full-risk premiums under Risk Rating 2.0. For example, nearly every southeastern coastal state is in the group of states with the lowest median premiums as of

December 31, 2022 (see Figure 5). However, these are also among the states with the highest risk of hurricane and coastal flooding combined, and they have historically accounted for a majority of NFIP claims.

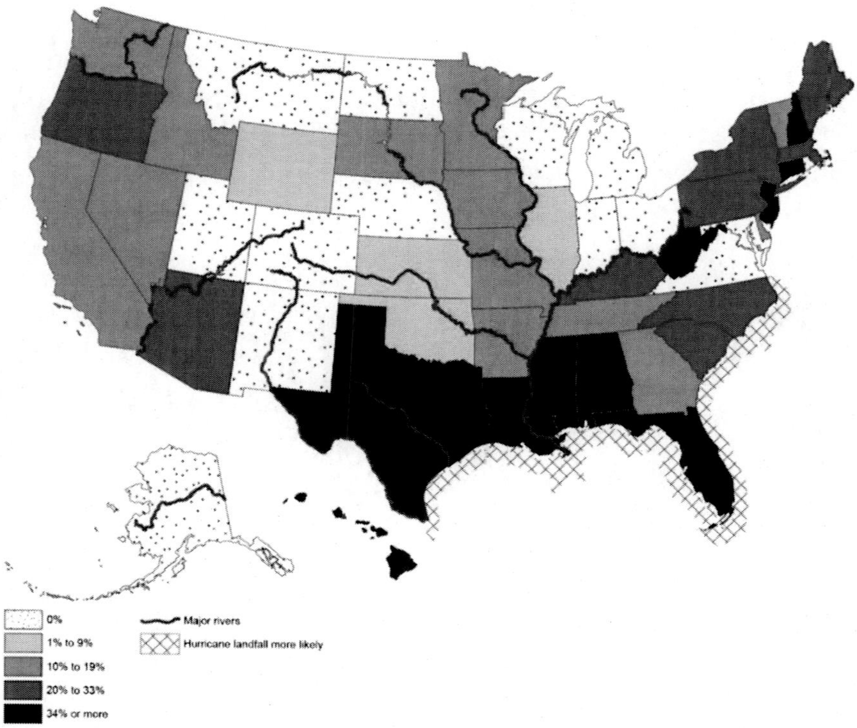


Source: GAO analysis of Federal Emergency Management Agency data. | GAO-23-105977.

Legend: NFIP = National Flood Insurance Program.

**Figure 4.** Median Percent Change from Legacy NFIP Premium to Full-Risk Premium under Risk Rating 2.0, by State, as of December 31, 2022.

Affordability concerns are growing as NFIP premiums continue to increase over time until reaching full-risk premiums. We estimated the affordability of each NFIP policy by expressing the full-risk premium as a percentage of the median household income of the census tract in which the insured property is located.[59] We then calculated the median percentage in

[59] To estimate the household income of each policyholder, we used the median household income of the census tract in which the insured property is located, according to the Census Bureau's American Community Survey. We calculated affordability for all primary

each state. Under Risk Rating 2.0, the median percentage of household income represented by the full-risk premium will exceed 1 percent in 45 states and will equal or exceed 2 percent in 10 states (see Figure 6). Some proposals for means-based assistance for flood insurance use a certain percentage of household income or area median income as thresholds for determining policyholder eligibility for assistance. Most policyholders in a number of states—particularly along the Gulf of Mexico, throughout Appalachia, and into the Northeast—likely will exceed these thresholds as FEMA continues transitioning to full-risk premiums.

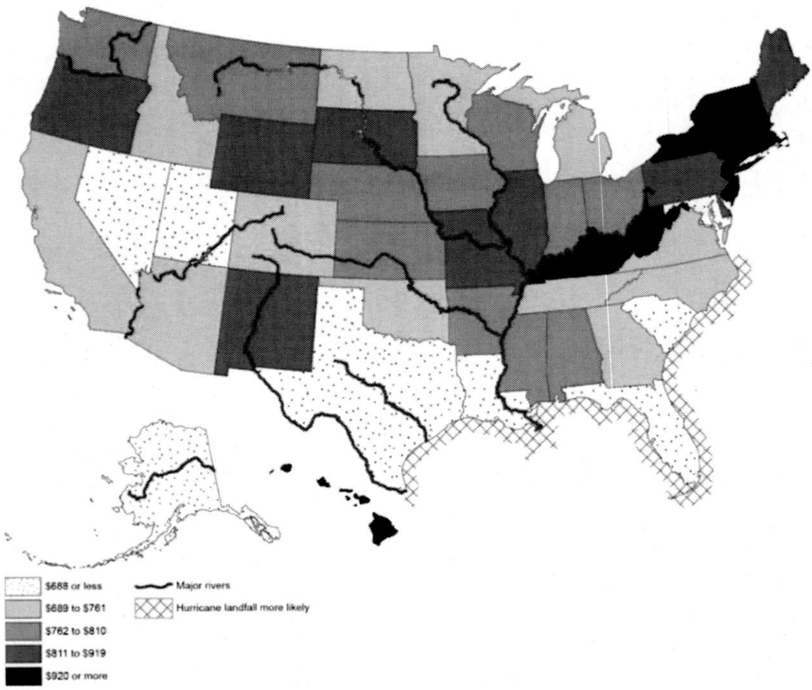


Source: GAO analysis of Federal Emergency Management Agency data. | GAO-23-105977.

Legend: NFIP = National Flood Insurance Program.

**Figure 5.** Median NFIP Premium, by State, as of December 31, 2022.

---

residential, noncondominium policies for which full-risk rates were available. FEMA research indicates that policyholder incomes are higher than nonpolicyholder incomes, which means that current policies may be more affordable than we report here. Federal Emergency Management Agency, *An Affordability Framework for the National Flood Insurance Program* (Washington, D.C.: Apr. 17, 2018), 11.

In addition to creating affordability concerns, increasing premiums also have the potential to negatively affect property values and the associated property tax revenues. For example, for properties located in areas where homeowners must purchase flood insurance, an increase in required annual expenses could decrease the purchase price potential buyers could afford. Lower property values could then lead to lower property tax revenues. However, flood insurance is not required on a majority of properties, and not all property owners will be affected similarly by an increase in a single cost component of owning a home. As a result, our analysis focuses on affordability as a whole rather than changes in property value.

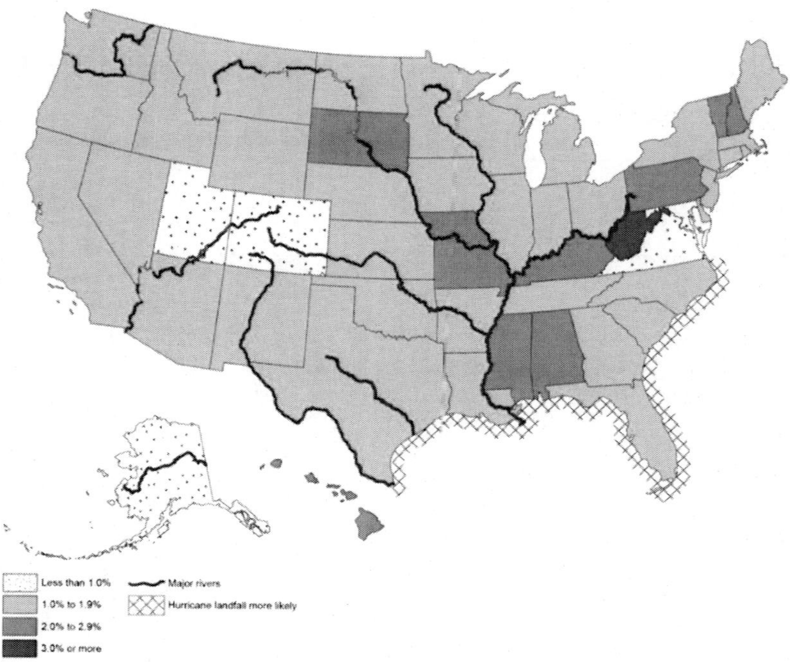


Source: GAO analysis of Federal Emergency Management Agency and Census Bureau data. | GAO-23-105977.

Legend: NFIP = National Flood Insurance Program.

Note: This analysis assumes the household income of NFIP policyholders is equal to the median income of the census tract where the insured property is located, according to the Census Bureau's American Community Survey. It includes all primary residential, noncondominium policies for which full-risk premiums were available as of December 31, 2022.

**Figure 6.** Median Full-Risk NFIP Premiums as a Percentage of Household Income, by State, as of December 31, 2022.

## Premium Increases Are Similar by Race and Ethnicity, but Less Affordable for Black Policyholders

Under Risk Rating 2.0, premiums and changes in premiums are relatively similar by race and ethnicity, but affordability varies.[60] Full-risk premiums generally will increase for all races and ethnicities we analyzed (see table 2).[61]

**Table 2.** Estimated Median National Flood Insurance Program (NFIP) premiums, by race and ethnicity

| Racial/ethnic group | Premium as of December 31, 2022 | Full-risk premium | Percent difference in medians |
|---|---|---|---|
| All policies | $688 | $1,282 | 86% |
| Black or African American | $687 | $1,281 | 86% |
| White | $689 | $1,281 | 86% |
| Hispanic or Latino | $664 | $1,288 | 94% |
| Asian | $688 | $1,295 | 88% |

Source: GAO analysis of Federal Emergency Management Agency and Census Bureau data. | GAO-23-105977.

Note: This analysis estimates the race and ethnicity of NFIP policyholders using the Bayesian Improved Surname Geocoding method. Full-risk premiums are for policies that have renewed under Risk Rating 2.0 as of December 31, 2022.

For Black policyholders, however, the premium paid as of December 31, 2022, constitutes a higher percentage of their estimated household income than all other racial and ethnic groups, and their full-risk premiums are expected to do so once fully implemented (see Figure 7). This is because the

[60] In this report, we use the term "Black" to refer to "Black or African American" and "Hispanic" to refer to "Hispanic or Latino."

[61] We used the Bayesian Improved Surname Geocoding (BISG) method to predict the race and ethnicity for policyholders of residential, noncondominium NFIP policies, based on their surname and residential location. Several studies have validated BISG estimates against self-reported racial data collected through administrative or survey sources in the health care and financial sectors. BISG makes estimates by calculating the probability that a person with a given surname and residential location will identify with selected racial and ethnic groups based on data from the Census Bureau. For other reports in which we have used this methodology, see GAO, *Tax Equity: Enhanced Evaluation Could Improve Outreach to Small Business Owners,* GAO-22-104582 (Washington, D.C.: Aug. 3, 2022) and *Social Security Administration: Remote Service Delivery Increased during COVID-19, but More Could Be Done to Assist Vulnerable Populations*, GAO-23-104650 (Washington, D.C.: Nov. 17, 2022). For more details on our methodology, see app. I.

median household income of Black policyholders is estimated to be lower than that of policyholders of other races and ethnicities.[62] Asian and Hispanic policyholders, on average, will pay slightly lower percentages of their incomes for flood insurance than White and Black policyholders as FEMA transitions to full-risk premiums.

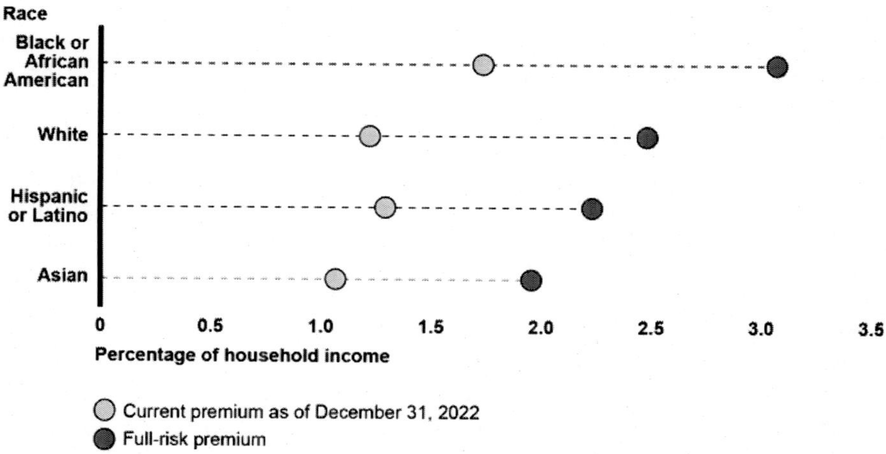


Source: GAO analysis of Federal Emergency Management Agency data. | GAO-23-105977.

Note: This analysis assumes that the household income of NFIP policyholders is equal to the median income of the census tract where the insured property is located, according to the Census Bureau's American Community Survey. It estimates race and ethnicity of policyholders using the Bayesian Improved Surname Geocoding method.

**Figure 7.** Affordability of National Flood Insurance Program (NFIP) Premiums, by Race and Ethnicity.

[62] We estimated the household income of policyholders using the median household income of the policyholder's census tract, according to the 2019 5-year estimate of the Census Bureau's American Community Survey. Using this method, we estimate that Black NFIP policyholders have a median income of $54,676, compared with $81,605 for all policyholders.

## Means-Based Assistance Could Address Affordability More Transparently and Efficiently Than Discounted Premiums

### Statutory Caps Address Affordability by Slowing the Transition to Full-Risk Premiums, but Allow Significant Revenue Shortfalls to Continue

To address affordability concerns, Congress has capped annual premium increases on NFIP policies, requiring FEMA to transition from discounted to full-risk premiums gradually.[63] We refer to the period of a policy's transition to its full-risk premium as a "glidepath." Because policies on a glidepath pay discounted rather than full-risk premiums, they cause a shortfall in NFIP premium revenue, which is equal to the difference between the full-risk premium and the premium actually paid. For example, a hypothetical NFIP policy currently paying a $500 premium with an estimated full-risk premium of $1,000 and subject to an 18 percent annual premium increase cap would have a premium shortfall of $351 (net of WYO expenses) in the first year and would reach its full-risk premium in 2028 (see Figure 8). This policy would have incurred a total shortfall of $1,477 in its 6 years on the glidepath.[64]

As of December 31, 2022, 66 percent of NFIP policies that had renewed since April 1, 2022, were on the glidepath. We estimated the following:[65]

---

[63] 42 U.S.C. § 4015(e). Policies are subject to annual rate increase caps ranging from 5 to 25 percent until they reach their full-risk rates. About 85 percent of policies, including those for most primary residences, are subject to an 18 percent cap. The transition will take multiple years for policyholders whose increase necessary to reach full risk exceeds the statutorily allowed 1-year increase. We use "discounted" to refer to premiums that are not yet full risk and therefore result in a premium shortfall. As discussed previously, other statutory discounts exist, such as CRS discounts. FEMA plans to review full-risk premiums annually, and these premiums include many rating factors. As these factors change, the full-risk premium is likely to change to reflect FEMA's most current understanding of flood risk. It also is possible that events may occur that change the models' loss estimates more significantly.

[64] The total premium shortfall is net of WYO expenses. The total premium shortfall before WYO expenses is $2,121.

[65] Our estimates include several assumptions. Our shortfall calculations do not account for assessments, surcharges, and fees. We increased full-risk premiums for inflation and changes in flood risk and increased premiums actually paid by applicable annual premium increase caps. We also assumed that all policies on the glidepath would renew NFIP coverage and that policies would keep the same coverage and deductible amounts until reaching full-risk premiums. Further, we assumed that policies that had not yet renewed under Risk Rating 2.0 would follow a glidepath similar to those of policies that had renewed. By 2049, 99.99 percent of policies would have reached full risk. Finally, we calculated the total premium shortfall net of WYO expenses. In fiscal year 2023, FEMA

- Policies on the glidepath will result in a total premium shortfall of $2.7 billion in 2023.
- By 2037, 95 percent of policies will reach full-risk premiums.
- By 2049, virtually all policies will reach full-risk premiums.
- The total premium shortfall will be $26.7 billion (see figure 9).

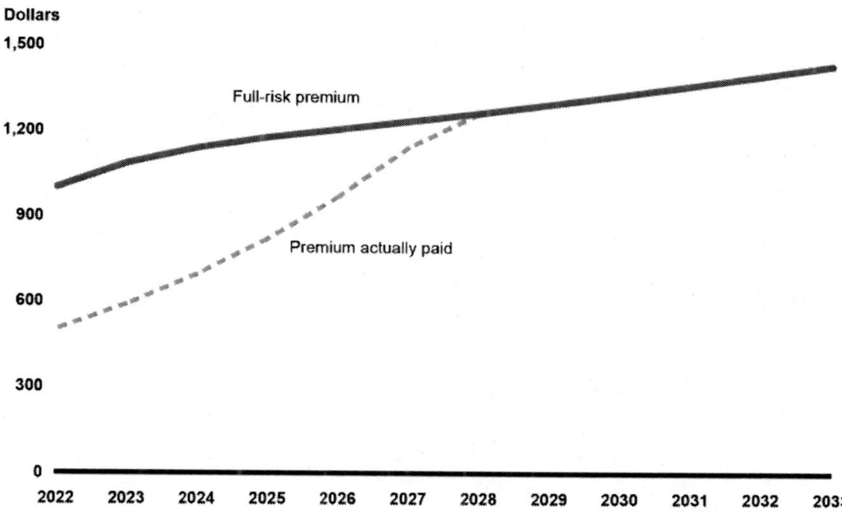


Source: GAO analysis of Federal Emergency Management Agency data. | GAO-23-105977.

Note: These calculations assume that the premium actually paid increases 18 percent annually and that the full-risk premium increases annually to account for inflation and increases in flood risk.

**Figure 8**. Illustration of the Premium Shortfall and Transition to Full-Risk Premium for a Hypothetical National Flood Insurance Program Policy.

Our model for estimating the duration and cost of policies on the glidepath included four key inputs—annual premium increase caps, inflation rates, flood risk, and NFIP policy renewal.[66] Changing each input resulted in different estimates. For example, we found that lowering the annual premium increase cap (currently 18 percent for most policies) to 9 percent for all policies would

agreed to pay WYO insurers 29.7 percent of premiums. The present value of the total shortfall is $23 billion (using a discount rate of 2.82 percent as of December 31, 2022). Full results of our analysis are included in app. II.

[66] In our sensitivity analysis, we incorporated alternative inflation, flood risk, annual rate increase caps, and NFIP renewal rates and changed these assumptions individually while holding the others at the baseline level.

significantly extend the glidepath (for 95 percent of policies) from 15 to 34 years. It would also increase the total premium shortfall from $26.7 billion to $69 billion (see Figure 10). By comparison, increasing the annual premium increase cap to 25 percent for all policies would shorten the glidepath to 11 years and reduce the shortfall to $18 billion.[67]

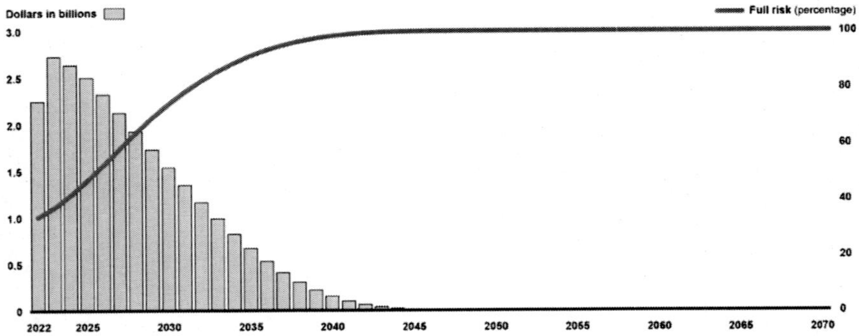


Source: GAO analysis of Federal Emergency Management Agency data. | GAO-23-105977.

Note: Shortfall calculations start in April 2022 when renewing policies became subject to Risk Rating 2.0. The total estimated glidepath shortfall is $26.7 billion (present value of $23 billion as of December 31, 2022).

**Figure 9.** Estimated Premium Shortfall and Percentage of National Flood Insurance Program Policies at Full-Risk Premiums, by Calendar Year.

We also found that higher inflation would slightly increase the shortfall amount. For the alternative scenarios, we assumed inflation would be 1 percentage point higher or lower in the first year and converge to the baseline over 5 years. Higher inflation would increase the total shortfall from $26.7 billion to $27 billion. By comparison, lower inflation would reduce the shortfall to $26 billion.[68]

Changing flood risk has little effect on our model's estimates because the projected increases in flood risk are smaller when annualized and are projected

---

[67] For this sensitivity analysis, we chose a lower premium increase cap of 9 percent to reflect a level that has been specifically proposed in legislation and a higher rate cap of 25 percent to reflect the highest current premium increase cap for certain properties. The present values of the total shortfalls are $48 billion and $16 billion, respectively, for the 9 and 25 percent rate cap scenarios.

[68] For the baseline inflation estimate, we used projections from the Congressional Budget Office, *The Budget and Economic Outlook: 2023 to 2033* (Washington, D.C.: February 2023). The present values of total shortfalls are $23 billion and $22 billion under the higher and lower inflation scenarios, respectively.

to increase in severity by 2100.[69] Under both alternative scenarios, the glidepath would remain at 15 years (for 95 percent of policies), and the total shortfall would change by less than $1 billion.

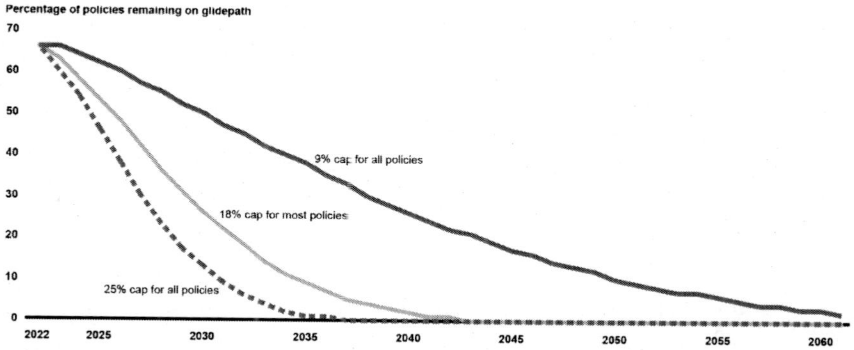


Source: GAO analysis of Federal Emergency Management Agency data. | GAO-23-105977.

Note: The baseline scenario (gray line) assumes current annual premium increase caps, which are 18 percent for most policies but range from 5 to 25 percent.

**Figure 10**. National Flood Insurance Program Policies Remaining on the Glidepath under Alternative Annual Premium Increase Caps, by Year.

Premium shortfalls would be reduced if policyholders on the glidepath dropped their insurance. For example, if 6 percent of policies on the glidepath choose not to renew each year, this would reduce the total estimated shortfall from $26.7 billion to $19 billion.[70] However, to the extent that policyholders drop coverage in a way that significantly changes NFIP's distribution of risk among all policies, FEMA would have to change premiums to reflect the new distribution of risk.[71] Further, to the extent that these policyholders do not replace their NFIP coverage with private flood coverage, resilience would

---

[69] For the flood risk estimates, we used projections from the Office of Management and Budget, *Analytical Perspectives: Budget of the United States Government, Fiscal Year 2023* (Washington, D.C.: Mar. 28, 2022). These projections estimated that NFIP's gross average annual losses would increase by 7 to 13 percent by 2050 and 40 to 84 percent by 2100. Using the 2050 projections, we calculated a baseline annual flood risk increase of 0.31 percent, the midpoint between the alternative scenarios of 0.22 and 0.40 percent.

[70] We assumed that nonrenewals would be randomly distributed among the policies on the glidepath. The present value of the total premium shortfall is $17 billion as of December 31, 2022.

[71] The ability to spread risk across a portfolio depends on the diversification of the risks covered by those policies. An insurer can diversify its risks by insuring risks that are more independent of each other—that is, that are less likely to cause losses at the same time.

decline and fiscal exposure could increase as former policyholders increase their reliance on disaster assistance.

## Discounted Premiums Hide Fiscal Exposure, Address Affordability Poorly, and Hinder Private- Market Growth

Current policy addresses affordability through discounted premiums by capping annual premium increases, but this approach has several limitations.

- *Hides fiscal exposure.* The discounted premiums and the resulting premium shortfalls generate fiscal exposure that is not transparent to Congress and the public. Specifically, the premium shortfalls have contributed to the $36.5 billion in borrowing from Treasury since 2005. While these costs were incurred when the discounted premiums were charged, they were not evident until years later when FEMA had to borrow from Treasury. In other words, the policy decision to address affordability by charging discounted premiums prevented NFIP from building a surplus in lower-loss years that it could have used to pay some of the claims in higher-loss years. As mentioned previously, prior to Risk Rating 2.0, FEMA was unable to reliably calculate NFIP's total annual premium shortfall because it lacked full-risk premium information for many of its policies. However, Risk Rating 2.0 allows FEMA to calculate full-risk premiums for all policies.
- *Addresses affordability poorly.* Discounted premiums are not tied to a policyholder's ability to pay, in terms of both the amount of the discounts and who receives them. As a result, some policyholders who do not need assistance are likely still receiving it (or are receiving more than they need), thus unnecessarily increasing fiscal exposure. Concurrently, some policyholders are likely not receiving enough assistance to make their flood insurance affordable, which may reduce consumer participation if policyholders drop coverage because they cannot afford it. Policyholders subject to the mandatory purchase requirement, however, do not have the option of dropping coverage if premiums become unaffordable. In addition, because full-risk premiums are being implemented through gradual but steady premium increases, the affordability assistance is temporary. As the

discounts are phased out, fiscal exposure will decrease, but affordability concerns will increase, potentially further reducing consumer participation and resilience. Moreover, reaching the end of the glidepath does not mean premiums will not increase further. Premiums can increase for a number of reasons, including increased repair costs or higher estimates of the frequency and severity of flooding events.

- *Hinders private-market growth.* Discounts also make NFIP premiums lower than are actuarially justified. Private insurers told us this undercuts the premiums they are able to charge and places them at a competitive disadvantage. This impedes private-market growth and limits insurance options for homeowners. It also increases fiscal exposure to the extent that NFIP continues to cover risk exposure that the private sector could otherwise assume.

We previously identified several policy goals for flood insurance reform.[72] These include requiring transparency of the federal fiscal exposure, encouraging consumer participation, promoting flood risk resilience, and minimizing federal fiscal exposure (including by encouraging private- sector involvement). However, the current approach to addressing affordability does not achieve these goals because Congress provides assistance by capping annual premium increases rather than through a means-based program that is reflected in the federal budget. Addressing affordability through a means-based assistance program that is recognized in the federal budget, rather than through discounted premiums, could make the premium shortfall costs transparent and could lessen the need for large program borrowing in the future.[73] It could also improve Congress's ability to oversee the program and the public's ability to scrutinize it. A means-based assistance program would also be a long- term solution to address affordability that could target assistance more effectively and encourage consumer participation and private sector involvement.

---

[72] See GAO-17-425.

[73] We have reported that setting up and administering an assistance program would incur some administrative costs. See GAO, *National Flood Insurance Program: Options for Providing Affordability Assistance*, GAO-16-190 (Washington, D.C.: Feb. 10, 2016).

## Key Considerations for Means-Based Assistance Include Cost, Consumer Participation, and Effects on the Private Market

A policy decision to design a means-based assistance program would require additional decisions about eligibility, including income-level requirements, the amount of assistance desired for each level of income, and the types of policyholders who would be eligible. Each of these decisions ultimately involves balancing costs with encouraging consumer participation. For example, costs could be limited by providing assistance only to certain categories of current NFIP policyholders. However, providing assistance to future NFIP policyholders could encourage greater consumer participation. Further, providing assistance to private- market policyholders could further encourage consumer participation while treating NFIP and the private market equitably.

We estimated the cost and number of recipients of a means-based assistance program for which only current NFIP policyholders of primary single-family residences would be eligible.[74] We assumed a means-based assistance program would replace the glidepath, so any policy receiving assistance would immediately convert to the full-risk premium. We considered two alternatives for determining the assistance amount: (1) covering the amount of the premium that exceeded a certain percentage of household income and (2) covering a certain percentage of the premium.[75]

The first alternative also would restrict eligibility to policyholders whose household income was below a certain percentage of the area median income (AMI). For instance, a policyholder with household income of $40,000 where the AMI is $80,000 would be at 50 percent of AMI. This policyholder would

---

[74] All costs of flood insurance—full-risk premiums as well as any assessments, surcharges, or fees—would be considered in determining eligibility for assistance and how much assistance to offer. As such, we refer to the total policyholder payments as "premiums" in this section. We based our estimates on elements of several recent proposals. Most proposals limit assistance to policyholders with low or moderate household income. Some proposals also feature other eligibility criteria, including accounting for wealth in the means test and further limitations based on federal poverty guidelines. Because we cannot include these criteria, we may overestimate cost. All assessments, surcharges, and fees levied by NFIP on policies are included in the premium amount that is used to determine eligibility for and level of assistance. Full results of our analysis are included in app. II.

[75] The Department of Homeland Security proposed a means-tested assistance program for flood insurance that would offer a graduated premium discount to current and new NFIP policyholders with household income at or below 120 percent of AMI. This proposal is similar to the second alternative we discuss. See Department of Homeland Security, *Legislative Reform Package.*

be eligible as long as the AMI threshold was set at or above 50 percent. If the policyholder's premium was $900 and assistance covered the portion of the premium that exceeded 1 percent of household income, the policyholder would be responsible for paying 1 percent of household income ($400) and the assistance would cover the remaining $500.

The first alternative would cost the federal government roughly $585 million to $2.0 billion in the first year and cover roughly 470,000 to 1.6 million policyholders (see Figure 11).[76] The estimates vary depending on the level at which the assistance begins (either 1 or 2 percent of household income) and the policyholders who are determined to be eligible (those with household incomes below either 80, 100, or 120 percent of AMI).[77]

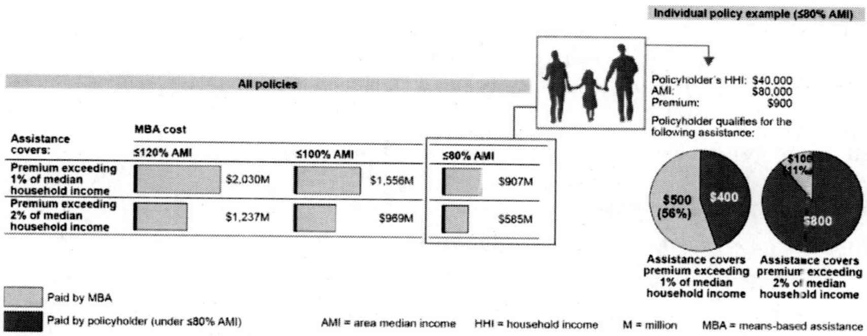


Source: GAO analysis of Federal Emergency Management Agency, Census Bureau, and Department of Housing and Urban development; GAO (icon). | GAO-23-105977.

**Figure 11**. Cost Estimates of a Means-Based Assistance Program—Alternative 1.

The second alternative would provide premium discounts on a sliding scale, whereby the discount would increase as a policyholder's household income decreased relative to AMI. These estimates assume discounts of 40, 60, and 80 percent for AMI thresholds at 100, 80, and 50 percent, respectively. The same policyholder cited above, with a $900 premium and household income of $40,000 in a county with an AMI of $80,000, would receive assistance covering 80 percent of the premium ($720), leaving the

[76] The cost of a means-based assistance program depends on a number of parameters, including policyholder eligibility and level of support. We discuss our methodology in more detail in app. I.

[77] We estimated policyholder incomes using the median household income of the census tract in which the insured property is located. As previously mentioned, this may understate policyholder incomes, and therefore overstate the cost of affordability programs.

policyholder to pay the remaining $180 (see Figure 12). This second alternative would cost the federal government roughly $1.3 billion in the first year and cover roughly 1.5 million policyholders.

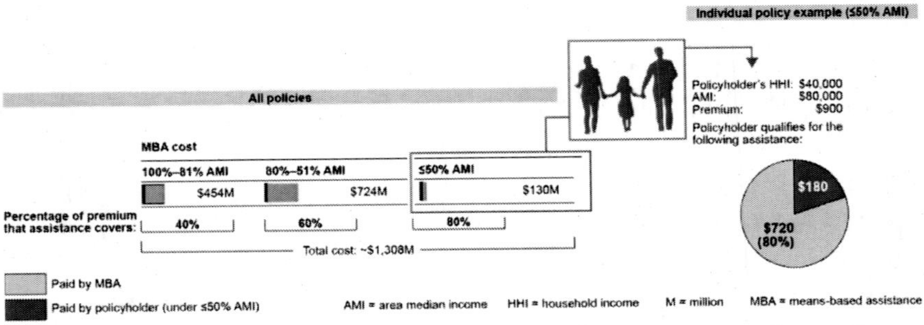


Source: GAO analysis of Federal Emergency Management Agency, Census Bureau, and Department of Housing and Urban development; GAO (icon). | GAO-23-105977.

**Figure 12**. Cost Estimates of a Means-Based Assistance Program—Alternative 2.

Providing means-based assistance to current NFIP policyholders likely would be more cost-effective than providing assistance through discounted rates because it would be targeted to policyholders who need it. As previously mentioned, we estimated that providing assistance through discounted rates will cost about $3.9 billion in 2023. In contrast, we estimated that the cost of means-based assistance would be significantly less, ranging from $585 million to $2.0 billion in the first year.

Additional modifications to eligibility could help further limit the cost of a means-based assistance program or encourage the participation of more or different consumers. For instance, to decrease costs, FEMA could restrict eligibility to properties with high flood risk, exclude repetitive loss properties from receiving assistance, or require mitigation to receive assistance. To increase coverage, FEMA could make new NFIP policyholders, private-market policyholders, or both eligible for assistance.

Restricting eligibility based on property flood risk or purchase requirements. Restricting assistance would reduce program costs. For example, assistance could be restricted to policyholders required to purchase insurance (because they generally do not have the option of dropping coverage if they cannot afford it) or to those with properties exceeding a certain threshold of flood risk (because they generally have more need for protection). FEMA does not track which policies are subject to the mandatory purchase requirement, but properties in SFHAs can serve as an upper bound approximation.[78] We estimated that restricting assistance to policyholders in SFHAs would reduce program costs to between roughly $380 million and $1.3 billion for the first alternative, depending on the eligibility thresholds chosen. However, we and others have reported that some of FEMA's floodplain maps designating high-risk areas are outdated.[79] We have also reported that expanding the mandatory purchase requirement could increase consumer participation and enhance resilience.[80] As a result, flood risk metrics other than the SFHA boundary line could be useful in determining eligibility.

*Excluding repetitive loss properties.* According to the Department of Homeland Security, unmitigated repetitive loss properties make up about 2.5 percent of NFIP policies, but such policies have accounted for a disproportionate share of claims. For example, as of December 2021, 48 percent of NFIP claims by dollar value had been paid to properties with two or more losses. This high risk of flood loss makes their premiums— and thus their potential assistance cost—high. Excluding these properties from assistance could limit costs and discourage development in high-risk areas.

*Incorporating mitigation into affordability assistance.* Premiums help to signal flood risk, and with higher premiums, policyholders have a greater incentive to undertake mitigation efforts to reduce their flood risk and premiums. Conversely, premium assistance can reduce incentives for mitigation, so incorporating mitigation into assistance could help preserve and increase resilience while addressing affordability. For example, the program could provide up-front assistance for mitigation measures. This approach would entail larger initial costs, but in the long term it would reduce the risk of loss and the amount of premium assistance needed, as well as the need for federal disaster assistance. Further, several studies have proposed pairing

---

[78] Generally, the mandatory purchase requirement applies to properties in SFHAs with federally backed mortgages (those made, insured, or guaranteed by federally regulated lenders or federal agencies, or purchased by the government-sponsored enterprises for housing—Fannie Mae and Freddie Mac).

[79] See GAO, *FEMA Flood Maps: Better Planning and Analysis Needed to Address Current and Future Flood Hazards*, GAO-22-104079 (Washington, D.C.: Oct. 25, 2021); Elyssa L. Collins et al., "Predicting Flood Damage Probability across the Conterminous United States," *Environmental Research Letters*, vol. 17 (2022); and Natural Resources Defense Council and Association of State Floodplain Managers, Inc., *Petition Requesting That The Federal Emergency Management Agency Amend Its Regulations Implementing the National Flood Insurance Program* (Jan. 5, 2021). As discussed previously, FEMA no longer uses these maps for setting premiums under Risk Rating 2.0. However, FEMA still uses them for determining mandatory purchase requirements and setting local floodplain management standards.

[80] See GAO-17-425.

mitigation assistance with premium assistance by requiring mitigation financed through a low- interest loan and providing a means-tested voucher.[81]

*Expanding eligibility to new NFIP policyholders*. Making assistance available to property owners who do not yet have NFIP coverage could increase consumer participation and enhance resilience. However, it is difficult to estimate the number of new policyholders that affordability assistance might attract to NFIP, and consequently the level of assistance necessary to meet that demand. Studies have found that NFIP policyholders were price-sensitive to premium changes, indicating that affordability assistance likely would increase NFIP take-up.[82] The number of NFIP policies has also been steadily decreasing in recent years. At the beginning of 2019, NFIP had 5.11 million policies.[83] As of December 2022, NFIP had 4.77 million policies, which includes a reduction of 175,000 policies (3.5 percent) since Risk Rating 2.0 implementation began in October 2021 (see Figure 13). Premiums increased every year during this period, and some former policyholders might want to reenroll if affordability assistance were available.

Further, we estimated that only about 3.9 percent of occupied housing units had NFIP flood insurance, indicating the potential for significant growth in flood insurance take-up, especially with assistance increasing affordability. To limit demand from new policyholders, expanding eligibility to new NFIP policyholders could be combined with restricting eligibility based on purchase requirements or flood risk. Because most homeowners subject to the mandatory purchase requirement already have an NFIP policy (exceptions

---

[81] Carolyn Kousky and Howard Kunreuther, "Addressing Affordability in the National Flood Insurance Program," *Journal of Extreme Events*, vol. 1 (2014); Wendy Zhao, Howard Kunreuther, and Jeffrey Czajkowski, "Affordability of the National Flood Insurance Program: Application to Charleston County, South Carolina," *Natural Hazards Review*, vol. 17, no. 1 (February 2016); and National Research Council of the National Academies, *Affordability of National Flood Insurance Program Premiums—Report 1* (Washington, D.C.: March 2015). The National Academies issued its second report in 2016, which proposed procedures with which FEMA might analyze policy options. See National Academies of Sciences, Engineering, and Medicine, *Affordability of National Flood Insurance Program Premiums—Report 2* (Washington, D.C.: 2016).

[82] See Larry Baeder and David Evans, *Insights into Consumer Demand for Flood Insurance: Trends in Take-Up* (San Francisco, Calif.: Milliman, September 2021) and Jacob Bradt, Carolyn Kousky and Oliver Wing, "Voluntary Purchases and Adverse Selection in the Market for Flood Insurance," *Journal of Environmental Economics and Management*, vol. 110 (2021).

[83] Policy numbers in this section account for each unit within a Residential Condominium Building Association Policy as a separate policy.

include those with a private-market policy or not in compliance), such restrictions could help limit cost increases.[84]

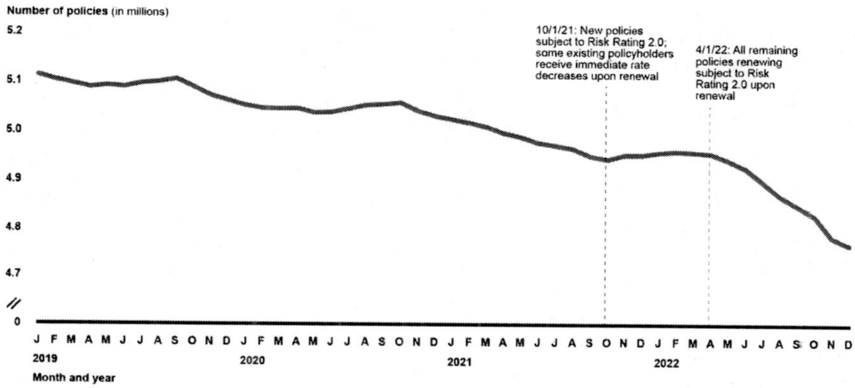


Source: GAO analysis of Federal Emergency Management Agency data. | GAO-23-105977.

Note: Policy numbers account for each unit within a Residential Condominium Building Association Policy as a separate policy.

**Figure 13.** Number of National Flood Insurance Program Policies, 2019–2022.

*Expanding eligibility to private-market policyholders.* Providing assistance for private flood insurance policyholders could allow private flood insurance premiums to compete fairly with NFIP premiums and therefore promote the private market. Specifically, private flood insurers told us that providing assistance only for NFIP policies would put them at a competitive disadvantage because many NFIP customers would pay lower premiums. They said they generally supported an assistance program if private-market policyholders were eligible. They also said that because of privacy concerns, private flood insurers would not want to be responsible for examining policyholders' tax-related documents and determining eligibility. As with expanding eligibility to new NFIP policyholders, this modification could increase consumer participation and enhance resilience, but it could also be combined with eligibility restrictions to limit demand and costs.[85]

[84] For more information on the mandatory purchase requirement, see GAO, *National Flood Insurance Program: Congress Should Consider Updating the Mandatory Purchase Requirement*, GAO-21-578 (Washington, D.C.: July 30, 2021).

[85] The private residential flood market made up 7 percent of the total residential flood market as of December 2021.

# Options Exist to Address NFIP's Legacy Debt and the Potential for Future Debt

## NFIP's Current Debt Delays Actuarial Soundness and Exacerbates Affordability Concerns

NFIP owed $20.5 billion to Treasury as of April 2023, and not addressing this legacy debt—and the structural issues that caused it—will likely result in increased debt.[86] It will also delay NFIP's actuarial soundness, worsen policyholder affordability concerns, and reduce consumer participation.

FEMA covers NFIP flood claims and program expenses primarily by using insurance premiums, assessments, surcharges, and fees paid by policyholders. When revenue, reinsurance, and any accumulated surplus are insufficient, FEMA has authority to borrow from Treasury. Before 2005, NFIP was mostly self-sustaining, but since then, NFIP has had to borrow $36.5 billion to pay claims.[87] NFIP's borrowing has followed catastrophic flood events, most notably Hurricane Katrina in 2005, Hurricane Sandy in 2012, and Hurricane Harvey in 2017 (see Figure 14).

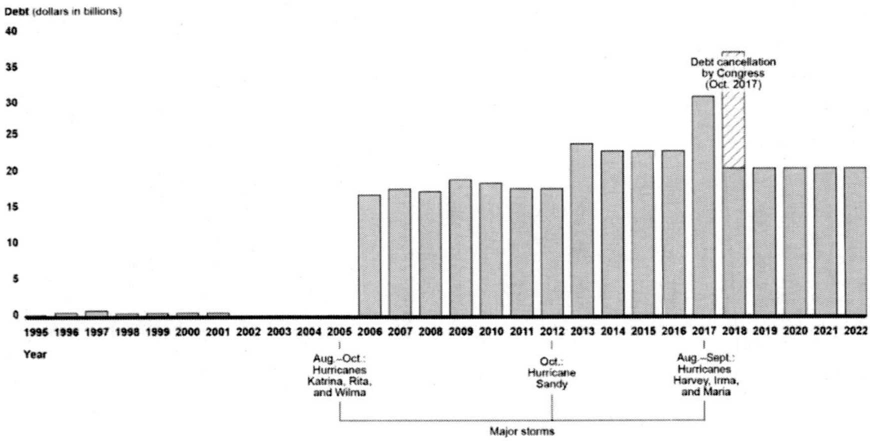


Source: GAO analysis of Department of the Treasury data. | GAO-23105977.

**Figure 14.** National Flood Insurance Program Annual Year-End Outstanding Debt to the Department of the Treasury, Fiscal Years 1995–2022.

---

[86] We refer to the debt that has built up to date as the legacy debt, as distinct from additional debt that might accrue in the future.

[87] Congress appropriated funds to retire NFIP's approximately $200 million debt to Treasury in 1985. NFIP also had intermittent debt in the 1990s, reaching nearly $1 billion in 1997, but it paid off the debt in subsequent years. Congress forgave $16 billion of NFIP debt in October 2017.

Absent congressional action, the program's debt likely will continue to grow as the caps on annual premium increases are slowing the transition to full-risk premiums.

NFIP's debt largely is a result of premium inadequacy, due to the policy decision to prioritize affordability over solvency. This is because requiring FEMA to charge discounted premiums that did not reflect the full risk of loss left NFIP with inadequate funds to pay claims in some years.

Specifically, FEMA has been statutorily required to offer discounted premiums for certain properties since the program's inception. While NFIP had relatively little debt for nearly 40 years, the subsidized premiums prevented NFIP from building a surplus that could have helped cover some of the higher-loss years and reduced or avoided some of the borrowing that began in 2005. In other words, while the cost of the subsidized premiums did not become evident until 2005 when it began materializing in debt, the costs began accruing when FEMA charged the discounted premiums. If FEMA had been able to charge full-risk premiums, it might have built up more funds that would have enabled it to pay a greater portion of those larger losses in 2005 and after and given it additional revenue in those years.

NFIP's debt raises concerns about the actuarial soundness of the program, the program's affordability for policyholders, and consumer participation.

*Actuarial soundness concerns.* Although FEMA was prevented from collecting full-risk premiums from previous policyholders, it is statutorily required to repay the debt and any accrued interest using revenue from current and future policyholders.[88] From fiscal years 2006 through 2022, FEMA paid an annual average of $336 million in interest on the debt, but it has not made any repayments of principal since 2014, and Congress forgave $16 billion of principal in October 2017.[89] Debt arising from the experience of previous policyholders is not a cost associated with the risk of current policyholders. Therefore, requiring FEMA to repay this debt and the resulting interest

---

[88] 42 U.S.C. § 2414(e). NFIP debt normally has a 3-year maturity unless Treasury grants an exception for a longer maturity. Principal and interest payments are permitted at any time, and the debt may be repaid or refinanced at maturity.

[89] FEMA is required to repay the debt, but it can refinance the debt as long as the total debt is less than the borrowing limit. FEMA has not paid principal on the debt since 2014 because it has prioritized building NFIP's reserve fund. FEMA is statutorily required to maintain a reserve fund, with a target balance of at least 1 percent of insurance-in-force (42 U.S.C. § 4017a(b)(1)), and to make a minimum annual payment into the fund of 7.5 percent of the target balance until the fund balance reaches the target amount. According to FEMA, interest payments will continue to consume a significant amount of revenue that would otherwise serve to grow the reserve fund for future catastrophic events, particularly when interest rates rise.

expenses obliges FEMA to charge current and future policyholders, which is not actuarially justified.[90]

*Affordability concerns*. Charging current or future policyholders to service the debt also exacerbates affordability concerns. From fiscal years 2017 through 2022, FEMA made annual interest payments ranging from $300 million to $438 million—or the equivalent of $63 to $92 per policyholder per year.

Moreover, FEMA has no realistic prospect of repaying the debt as currently structured. FEMA also has reported that repayment of the legacy debt is beyond NFIP's current capability.[91] Further, the statutory annual premium increase caps result in premium shortfalls that make additional future debt more likely. For example, repaying the legacy debt—plus future debt we estimated could accrue due to glidepath shortfalls—in 30 years at 2.5 percent interest would require an annual payment of about $1.9 billion.[92] NFIP collected $3.24 billion in premiums in fiscal year 2022. Therefore, this payment would have required a 60 percent surcharge per policyholder in the first year.[93]

*Consumer participation concerns.* NFIP policyholder decreases have accompanied premium increases, and such a surcharge likely would cause many more policyholders to drop their NFIP coverage. Some of these

---

[90] Statutory requirements to repay program debt and build a reserve fund preceded Risk Rating 2.0 and operate outside of the Risk Rating 2.0 ratemaking process. FEMA created full-risk premiums to be prospective and therefore does not include provisions for interest expenses on its debt, nor for repayment of its debt, when calculating them. However, FEMA uses revenue from current policyholders to make these interest payments. Generally, revenue from premiums and the Federal Policy Fee goes into the insurance fund, and revenue from the reserve fund assessment and HFIAA surcharge goes into the reserve fund. FEMA makes interest payments using the insurance fund first, and if necessary, the reserve fund. The requirement to pay interest on legacy debt effectively slows FEMA's ability to achieve the target reserve fund balance, and in turn, requires FEMA to charge current and future policyholders a higher reserve fund assessment, or to charge a reserve fund assessment for a longer period of time, than would otherwise be necessary.

[91] According to FEMA, even with the implementation of Risk Rating 2.0, NFIP would be unable to make consistent principal repayments sufficient to improve overall fiscal solvency. FEMA estimated that NFIP could reasonably be expected to accrue an additional $15 billion of debt in 10 years. See Department of Homeland Security, *Legislative Reform Package*, and *National Flood Insurance Program Semi-Annual Debt Repayment Progress Report, March 31, 2022, Report to Congress and the Secretary of the Treasury* (Washington, D.C.: Aug. 30, 2022).

[92] We assumed a 2.5 percent interest rate for FEMA debt based on the interest rate for the current FEMA debt, trending slightly higher. We estimated that premium shortfalls would contribute $24.5 billion in additional debt during this 30-year repayment period.

[93] The surcharge percentage would need to change in future years as NFIP premium collections and debt levels change.

policyholders might replace their coverage with a private-market policy—especially those policyholders subject to the mandatory purchase requirement. However, some policyholders would choose to drop coverage altogether, leaving them unprotected from flood risk, reducing resilience, and increasing reliance on federal disaster assistance. Further, having fewer NFIP policyholders to repay the debt would necessitate higher surcharges and likely cause more policyholders to leave NFIP.

## Options for Addressing the Legacy Debt Include Canceling the Debt or Modifying Repayment

Addressing the legacy debt would require action by Congress. Two options for doing so are canceling the debt and modifying the repayment terms.

*Canceling the debt.* One option for addressing the $20.5 billion legacy debt would involve canceling it (or alternatively, eliminating the requirement that FEMA repay it).[94] This would free current and future policyholders from paying for obligations they were not responsible for incurring and address the existing inequity by allowing current and future policyholders to pay only for their own flood risk. Further, it would make insurance more affordable, thus encouraging consumer participation and resilience. Congress has used this option before when it canceled $16 billion in NFIP debt in October 2017.[95]

In one sense, canceling the debt transfers costs to taxpayers because current and future policyholders would no longer be paying interest on the debt. However, because it is not likely that current and future policyholders will be able repay the debt under current rules, the cost has essentially already been transferred to taxpayers. This transfer largely occurred each time FEMA sold a policy at statutorily required discounted premiums. Further, the 2017 debt cancellation did not require an appropriation.

---

[94] In May 2022, FEMA submitted to Congress a 104-page list of 17 legislative proposals that, among other things, proposed canceling the debt, decreasing NFIP's borrowing authority to two-thirds of expected premiums in force in the following year, implementing a plan to manage the program to a 1-in-20 occurrence loss level (about $10.5 billion, similar to claims from Hurricane Harvey in 2017), eliminating interest on future debt, and requiring any need for future debt to be funded through emergency supplemental appropriations. See Department of Homeland Security, *Legislative Reform Package*.

[95] On September 22, 2017, FEMA borrowed $5.825 billion from the Treasury and reached NFIP's authorized borrowing limit of $30.425 billion. On October 26, 2017, Congress canceled $16 billion of NFIP debt to enable FEMA to pay claims for Hurricanes Harvey, Irma, and Maria. On November 9, 2017, FEMA borrowed an additional $6.1 billion, increasing the debt to $20.525 billion.

*Modifying debt repayment.* Alternatively, addressing the debt could involve defining a plan to repay the legacy debt and any future debt that is estimated to accrue through an additional surcharge on policyholders.

Such a plan could include modified terms of repayment, such as forgiving some or all interest charges. Such a plan also could include immediately charging full-risk premiums to all policyholders—thereby eliminating the premium shortfall and reducing the likelihood of future debt.[96] However, all of these options would involve substantial costs to future policyholders, which would both exacerbate affordability concerns and charge policyholders premiums significantly greater than are actuarially justified.

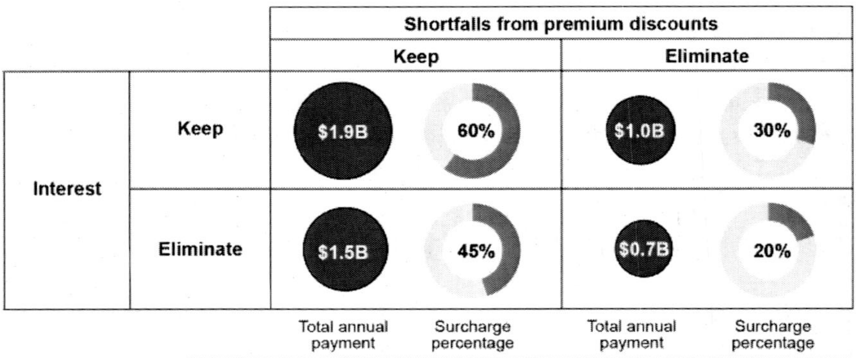


Source: GAO analysis of Federal Emergency Management agency (FEMA)data. | GAO-23-105977.

Note: Under the scenarios that keep premium shortfalls in place, we assume the debt will increase each year by the amount of the premium shortfall. As a result, FEMA would be paying off both the legacy debt and this estimated future debt. The surcharge percentage is the total annual payment as a percentage of NFIP's $3.24 billion in premium collections in fiscal year 2022. The surcharge percentage would need to change in future years as NFIP premium collections and debt levels change.

**Figure 15.** Estimated Effects of Various Requirements for Repaying National Flood Insurance Program (NFIP) Debt over 30 Years.

If interest was eliminated and all policyholders were charged full-risk premiums, repaying the debt in 30 years would require an annual payment of

[96] Immediately charging full-risk rates would reduce the annual payment required to repay the debt because doing so would eliminate premium shortfalls, and therefore the likelihood of increases in future debt. As discussed previously, replacing the glidepath with means- based assistance could help address affordability concerns arising from immediately charging full-risk rates.

about $663 million. At NFIP's fiscal year 2022 premium revenue, the annual payment would require a 20 percent surcharge per policyholder. This $663 million annual payment is significantly less than repaying the debt with interest while allowing discounted premiums to continue, which would increase the likelihood of future debt requiring repayment and require an annual payment of about $1.9 billion, or a 60 percent surcharge per policyholder (see Figure 15). Taken independently, immediately charging full-risk premiums to all policyholders would do more to reduce the annual repayment costs (which would come to approximately $963 million) than would eliminating interest (which would bring costs to approximately $1.5 billion).

This approach of eliminating interest on the debt and allowing FEMA to charge full-risk premiums to all policyholders would recoup some costs for taxpayers. It would also create a plan to repay the debt, rather than allowing it to continue in perpetuity. However, it would worsen the inequity for current and future policyholders by requiring them to pay for the loss experience of previous policyholders. Further, a 20 percent surcharge could exacerbate affordability concerns and cause some policyholders to drop coverage, thus reducing consumer participation and harming resilience. The surcharge could also increase costs for any future means- based assistance program or reduce the net amount of help individuals receive because the program would have to provide more assistance to make flood insurance costs affordable.

## Options for Addressing Future Debt Include Purchasing Additional Reinsurance and Changing Financing of Catastrophic Losses

The rollout of more actuarially sound premiums does not mean that additional borrowing will not be needed in the future. The cap on annual premium increases means that most policyholders will continue to pay discounted premiums for years to come. Congress could eliminate this source of future borrowing risk by removing the cap on annual premium increases so that actuarial, full-risk premiums can be charged, or by appropriating funds to make up for the discounted premiums. Congress could also provide means-based premium assistance in combination with either of these options.

These actions would reduce NFIP's need to borrow in the future, but not eliminate it. The program would still be subject to both "modeling risk" and "sequencing risk." Modeling risk is the inherent risk that even the best up- to-date flood models, using reasonable assumptions and methods, are not guaranteed to be accurate and could underestimate certain aspects of flood risk. Sequencing risk is the risk that even if the models accurately forecast average flood risk over time, there will be both good and bad flood years around that average. If the bad flood years happen first, the program will need to borrow. Sequencing risk is especially acute with catastrophic floods.

Even if NFIP were to collect revenue sufficient to meet long-term expected losses, the magnitude, volatility, and geographic concentration of flood risk means that catastrophic events will happen and might exceed what NFIP can financially manage without relying on additional funding.

As a result, it is important to consider options that could help NFIP reduce the likelihood of future borrowing and establish clear expectations for the program's capabilities. Two of these options are purchasing additional reinsurance and changing the financing of catastrophic losses.

*Purchasing additional reinsurance.* One option for addressing potential future debt is for FEMA to secure more reinsurance coverage for catastrophic losses from the private reinsurance and capital markets.[97] Doing so would allow FEMA to price some of its flood risk up front through the premiums it pays to reinsurers rather than borrowing from Treasury after a flood, thus reducing the volatility of future catastrophic losses.

A key benefit of reinsurance is to transfer and manage risk rather than to reduce NFIP's long-term fiscal exposure. However, even if FEMA were to collect sufficient revenue to meet long-term estimated losses, FEMA might not be able to fully address its future debt through reinsurance.

Specifically, the amount of reinsurance FEMA can purchase depends on the amount of coverage reinsurers are willing to sell, the price they are willing to charge, and the coverage provided. In fact, reinsurance costs have increased in recent years, and FEMA has purchased less coverage. Reinsurance likely will not lower the average cost of NFIP policies because reinsurers charge premiums to compensate for the risk they assume.

In addition, since NFIP must pay fair market premiums for private reinsurance coverage, reinsurance cannot fully address future debt as long as NFIP revenues remain actuarially inadequate. With inadequate NFIP revenue,

---

[97] FEMA has entered into two types of reinsurance agreements with private entities: traditional reinsurance and capital markets reinsurance. Traditional reinsurance agreements reimburse FEMA directly if losses from an event covered by the reinsurance agreement exceed a certain threshold. Since 2017, FEMA has entered into 1-year traditional reinsurance agreements each calendar year. Capital markets reinsurance consists of catastrophe bonds issued to a large number of bondholders who agree to release a portion of their bond principal to FEMA if losses from a covered event exceed the threshold. FEMA's current catastrophe bonds have a 3-year maturity.

reinsurance recoveries from occasional catastrophic events can help delay the accumulation of future debt in the short-term, but cannot fully address it.

*Changing financing of catastrophic losses.* Another option is to define NFIP's program capacity and require FEMA to manage the program to this capacity before requiring additional funding. This would include establishing an annual risk threshold for the maximum amount of losses that NFIP would be expected to cover based on its premium revenue. For example, FEMA estimated in November 2021 that a risk threshold of a 1- in-20 occurrence flood for NFIP currently is about a $10.5 billion event, approximately the size of Hurricane Harvey.[98] Under this option, FEMA would use the risk threshold as one of its ratemaking objectives when developing full-risk premiums.

In the occasional cases when the annual losses exceed the threshold, Treasury could fund claims through the Disaster Relief Fund and, if needed, through an emergency supplemental appropriation.[99] Financing future shortfalls as needed would avoid recreating debt and the potential for charging future policyholders to repay it, which would improve equity, affordability, consumer participation, and resilience. Further, Treasury would effectively serve as a reinsurer to NFIP, so this option likely would be less costly than FEMA purchasing private-sector reinsurance if Treasury were to choose not to charge FEMA premiums for the cost of the risk transfer. Alternatively, Treasury could choose to charge estimated fair market rates for the risk transfer, but could provide a more reliable source of capital than might be available at certain times in the private markets.[100]

Policy decisions regarding how to address legacy debt and potential future debt have implications for current and future policyholders. Debt arising from the loss experience of prior generations of policyholders is not a cost associated with the risk of current and future policyholders, and therefore charging a policyholder to pay it is not actuarially justified.

---

[98] See Department of Homeland Security, *Legislative Reform Package*. A "1-in-20 occurrence flood" is a flood event with losses having a 5 percent probability of being equaled or exceeded in any given year.

[99] FEMA's Disaster Relief Fund is the primary source of federal disaster assistance for state and local governments when a disaster is declared. The Disaster Relief Fund is appropriated no-year funding, which allows FEMA to fund, direct, coordinate, and manage response and recovery efforts—including certain efforts by other federal agencies and state and local governments, among others—associated with domestic disasters and emergencies. No-year funding refers to appropriations that remain available for obligation for an indefinite period of time.

[100] Treasury likely would need to estimate fair market rates because the private reinsurance market might not always offer coverage at levels sought by NFIP.

Further, we previously identified policy goals for flood insurance reform, including encouraging consumer participation, promoting flood risk resilience, and minimizing federal fiscal exposure.[101] Without statutory changes to address the legacy debt and determine an approach for addressing potential future debt, NFIP's debt likely will continue to grow without any prospect of repaying it. As a result, NFIP's fiscal solvency will be delayed and issues of policyholder equity and affordability will persist. There will also be increased risk to consumer participation in flood insurance and resilience to flood risk.

## Risk Rating 2.0 Has Not Yet Significantly Affected the Private Insurance Market, but Some NFIP Rules Hinder Market Growth

Selected private insurers told us that current NFIP premiums generally were lower than what they would need to charge to profitably underwrite flood risk. We have also reported that discounted NFIP premiums undercut private-sector premiums, place private insurers at a competitive disadvantage, impede private-market growth, and ultimately limit insurance options for policyholders.[102] While Risk Rating 2.0 may help to address these concerns by implementing full-risk premiums, it does not yet appear to have significantly affected the private flood insurance market because the transition to full-risk premiums will take many years. The private insurers told us they had not experienced a discernable change in their flood insurance portfolios since Risk Rating 2.0 was implemented, although some said other factors, such as inflation and the housing market, could also be affecting their growth.[103]

The private flood insurance market has grown, both in absolute terms and relative to NFIP, according to data NAIC began collecting in 2018. From 2018 to 2022, the private market grew from 372,000 policies and $404 million in direct written premium to 641,000 policies and almost $1.3 billion in direct

---

[101] See GAO-17-425.

[102] See GAO, *Flood Insurance: Potential Barriers Cited to Increased Use of Private Insurance*, GAO-16-611 (Washington, D.C.: July 14, 2016).

[103] We interviewed six private insurers in September and October 2022, approximately 12 months after FEMA began implementing Risk Rating 2.0 for new policies and 6 months after implementation for renewals. Private insurers said much of their business comes from new home purchases, so a slowing housing market would slow their growth.

written premium.[104] Relative to NFIP, the private market share grew from 7 to 12 percent of policies and from 8 to 22 percent of direct written premium during this period (see Figure 16).

Commercial flood insurance accounted for much of this increase, with the private market share growing from 25 to 47 percent of all commercial flood insurance policies. Private insurers told us their commercial policies were particularly competitive because private insurers can offer a commercial policy that covers multiple buildings and locations, while NFIP requires separate policies for each insured building, which incurs additional expenses. Other industry officials told us that the growth in the private market share of commercial policies might be due to greater awareness of flood risk among risk managers of commercial real estate. Private insurers also told us that a key factor contributing to the growth of the residential private flood insurance market was a 2019 interagency rule from federal financial regulators requiring lenders to accept private insurance for compliance with the mandatory purchase requirement.[105] The private insurers also said they are able to offer higher coverage limits and broader coverage options than NFIP, which has helped them compete.[106]

---

[104] From 2018 to 2022, the number of NFIP policies decreased by about 356,000 policies. During this same period the private market grew by about 269,000 policies. It is likely that some policyholders that dropped NFIP coverage replaced their flood coverage with a private insurer. Written premium is the contractually determined amount charged on new and renewing policies by the insurer to the policyholder based on the expectation of risk, policy benefits, and expenses associated with the coverage provided by the policy.

[105] Specifically, the Biggert-Waters Act requires federal regulators to direct lenders to accept private-market policies that meet the statutory definition of private flood insurance, and the regulators implemented this requirement, effective in July 2019. *Loans in Areas Having Special Flood Hazards*, 84 Fed. Reg. 4953 (Feb 20, 2019).

[106] NFIP's maximum coverage limit for one-to-four-family residential policies is $250,000 for buildings and $100,000 for contents. For nonresidential policies, the maximum coverage limit is $500,000 per building and $500,000 for the building owner's contents. Many private flood insurers offer higher coverage limits and broader coverage, such as coverage of basement contents and living expenses.

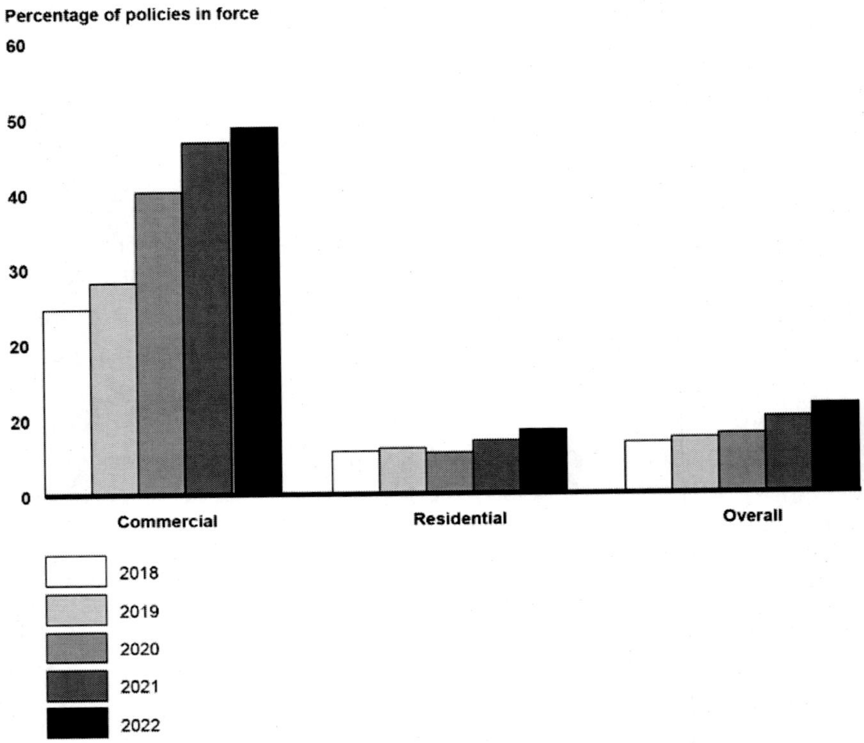


Source: GAO analysis of Federal Emergency Management Agency and the National Association of Insurance Commissioners. | GAO-23-105977.

Note: Policy counts are as of December 31 of each year and account for each unit within a Residential Condominium Building Association Policy as a separate policy.

**Figure 16.** Private Flood Insurance Share of Flood Insurance Policies, by Number of Policies.

Although the private market has grown in recent years, we have previously reported on several barriers to private-sector involvement in flood insurance.[107] Private insurers told us that two of these barriers, in addition to discounted NFIP premiums, continue to impede private-market growth.

- *Continuous coverage rules.* NFIP policyholders who receive discounted premiums must maintain continuous flood insurance coverage through NFIP to continue receiving the discounts.

[107] See GAO-17-425; GAO-16-611; and GAO, *Flood Insurance: Strategies for Increasing Private Sector Involvement*, GAO-14-127 (Washington, D.C.: Jan. 22, 2014).

Specifically, if a former NFIP policyholder who changed flood coverage to a private insurer wants to repurchase NFIP coverage, the policyholder must do so at full-risk premiums rather than rejoining the glidepath. As a result, many NFIP policyholders may be reluctant to consider private flood insurance policies out of concern that they would be unable to return to NFIP at the discounted premium if the private insurer were to significantly increase its premium or decide to stop providing coverage. However, according to FEMA, the agency lacks the legal authority to recognize private flood insurance policies as continuous coverage.

- *Lack of NFIP partial refunds.* NFIP policyholders also are unable to obtain partial refunds if they cancel their policy before the end of their term (typically 1 year) and replace it with a private policy. To avoid losing money, an NFIP policyholder must therefore consider private coverage only near the end of the policy term. However, private insurers told us this window is often too short, so many NFIP policyholders are effectively unable to convert to private coverage. FEMA previously began allowing partial refunds for midterm cancellations in October 2018 but ceased doing so in March 2019 because it determined it lacked legal authority to do so. FEMA officials said there is a seasonal component to flood risk, meaning that flood losses tend to occur during certain periods each year in some areas. For example, in the Southeast, most flooding occurs during hurricane season in the summer and fall. As a result, if FEMA were to provide refunds for midterm cancellations on a strict pro-rata basis, they would not be actuarially sound. For example, to be actuarially sound, a 1-year policy canceled after 6 months likely would receive more or less than a 50 percent refund, depending on when the cancellation occurred in relation to the timing of the policy term relative to the seasonality of flood risk. If most of the risk occurred in the first 6 months, less than a 50 percent refund would be given.

We previously identified several policy goals for flood insurance reform, including promoting flood risk resilience, minimizing federal fiscal exposure (including by encouraging private-sector involvement), and encouraging consumer participation.[108] However, because FEMA's interpretation of the law finds that FEMA lacks the legal authority to allow private coverage to

[108] See GAO-17-425.

satisfy the continuous coverage requirement or to allow partial refunds for midterm cancellations, NFIP policy rules discourage NFIP policyholders from seeking private coverage. This slows the growth of the private flood insurance market and limits options for consumers, both of which could result in less consumer participation in flood insurance and therefore less flood resilience, as consumers are not protected from the financial risk of flooding. Discouraging NFIP policyholders from seeking private coverage also results in FEMA maintaining risk and exposure that the private sector could otherwise assume. Finally, to the extent that fewer property owners have flood insurance, reliance on federal disaster assistance could increase, ultimately increasing federal fiscal exposure.

## FEMA Has Released Detailed Information on Risk Rating 2.0, but Has Not Provided It to Policyholders

### FEMA Has Developed and Released Substantial Information on Risk Rating 2.0, Largely Targeted to Insurers

FEMA has developed and released substantial information to explain Risk Rating 2.0, relying primarily on WYO insurers to communicate the new methodology to policyholders. Specifically, FEMA developed guidance and training to enable WYO insurers to communicate with policyholders on Risk Rating 2.0. FEMA also developed two websites to describe the new methodology and make information available to NFIP insurers and policyholders. Such information includes overview material, summaries of changes, and detailed technical documents explaining the methodology, data sources, and premium calculation. FEMA also developed documents describing the specific characteristics and variables it uses to calculate premiums under Risk Rating 2.0 and the discounts policyholders could receive by undertaking actions to mitigate their flood risk. FEMA presented this information online in several formats, including video, interactive graphics, fact sheets, technical documents, and a frequently asked questions page.

FEMA also provided data on how premiums would change under Risk Rating 2.0, including the percentage of policies that would experience premium decreases and increases and the magnitude of the premium changes. These data included profiles tailored to individual states, as well as downloadable data at the county and zip code levels. Further, FEMA conducted training sessions and published training materials on its websites to inform insurers and agents who would be selling and servicing policies under Risk Rating 2.0 and interacting with policyholders.

## FEMA Has Not Provided Policyholders Complete Information about the New Methodology and Its Implications

FEMA has not provided policyholders with comprehensive information about Risk Rating 2.0 and its implications for mitigation and their individual premiums. Specifically, FEMA provided general policy information to policyholders, but according to FEMA officials, this information included only one minor reference to Risk Rating 2.0 as being a new ratemaking methodology. These mailings included a cover letter with a short introduction to flood insurance, the actual flood insurance policy, and policy declaration pages that summarize coverage and premiums. The policy declaration pages included information such as property characteristics; flood zone; replacement cost value; the full-risk premium; applicable premium discounts; policy assessments, surcharges, and fees; the total annual premium charged; and the history of the property's NFIP flood claims.

However, none of this information explained to policyholders the new methodology or its implications for mitigation and their individual premiums or referred policyholders to FEMA's Risk Rating 2.0 website where rate methodology documents and other resources could be found. Further, FEMA did not notify policyholders about the new ratemaking methodology before implementing it.

Instead, FEMA officials told us they relied on WYO insurers and insurance agents to communicate with policyholders and inform them about Risk Rating 2.0, which they said was consistent with how they communicated with policyholders before Risk Rating 2.0. FEMA officials said they focused on developing guidance and training to support WYO insurers and agents in policyholder communications. However, FEMA did not establish any requirements to ensure that insurers and agents communicated this information to policyholders on FEMA's behalf.

As a result, policyholders may be uncertain about the Risk Rating 2.0 methodology generally and about how it applies to them individually, including the justification for their individual premiums and the potential savings associated with mitigation options. Officials from two associations representing insurance agents told us policyholders have expressed concern over premium increases and generally do not understand Risk Rating 2.0, including how it produces premiums and what factors affect those premiums. Policyholders also had questions about potential savings associated with available mitigation options, such as elevation or floodproofing. For example, officials from insurance agent associations said policyholders asked agents how mitigating their flood risk could reduce their premium.

Furthermore, agent association officials told us some agents generally felt unequipped to explain Risk Rating 2.0 to policyholders and fully answer their questions. Although FEMA has disclosed details of its ratemaking methodology and the variables it uses on its website, association officials said agents and policyholders cannot use them to calculate the same information they could under FEMA's legacy ratemaking methodology.

Under the legacy methodology, agents could consult FEMA's rating manual to determine why premiums may have changed and how mitigation measures might affect premiums. However, Risk Rating 2.0 involves a more sophisticated modeling approach, which uses an automated ratemaking mechanism that did not exist under the legacy methodology.

As a result, Risk Rating 2.0 is more difficult for agents to explain to policyholders than the legacy methodology. The new methodology is complex and incorporates a greater number of flood risk variables. FEMA officials told us that this sophistication was necessary to be consistent with methods used by private insurers and to ensure that premiums reflect an individual property's flood risk. They added that because Risk Rating 2.0 allows agents to obtain an instant quote from an automated quoting system without consulting a detailed manual, insurance agents can obtain a premium and write a policy more easily.

One of FEMA's strategic objectives is empowering risk-informed decision- making.[109] To build long-term resilience, the strategic plan stresses the importance of individuals understanding risk and having resources and capacity to mitigate or reduce it. The strategic plan also notes the importance of accurate information about risk, and of data tools, guidance, and public messaging that ensure highly technical information is explained in easily understood, relatable ways. The plan states this will enable individuals and communities to better understand technical information to inform decision-making.

FEMA has not provided NFIP policyholders with comprehensive information about Risk Rating 2.0, or otherwise made them aware of it.

---

[109] Federal Emergency Management Agency, *2022–2026 FEMA Strategic Plan.*

Therefore, policyholders may not be fully informed about how Risk Rating 2.0 affects them and how they can reduce their premiums through mitigation. Enhancing communication with policyholders to improve their understanding of Risk Rating 2.0 as well as its implications for individual premiums and mitigation possibilities could help policyholders make more informed decisions about their flood risk and the risk-reducing effect of potential mitigation efforts, thus helping advance FEMA's resilience goals.

## Conclusion

FEMA's $36.5 billion in NFIP borrowing from Treasury since 2005 underscores the need for reforming the program. However, finding common ground on reform has been difficult, largely because of the competing goals of making the program solvent while keeping premiums affordable for policyholders. Our April 2017 report outlined a road map for comprehensive reform to help bridge that divide, but much-needed reform has yet to materialize.[110]

However, through Risk Rating 2.0, FEMA has taken an important step to help move the program toward solvency and actuarial soundness by better aligning premiums with the underlying flood risk of the individual properties it insures. Therefore, full implementation of this improved ratemaking methodology is essential. FEMA could take several steps to improve this effort, but addressing the program's broader solvency and affordability challenges will also require congressional action. Specifically, challenges remain in the following areas:

- *Additional policyholder charges.* Policyholders pay two charges that are not proportional to the risk of the insured property. Until Congress authorizes and requires FEMA to incorporate these charges into the full-risk premium, the total amounts paid by policyholders may not be actuarially justified, and some policyholders could be over- or underpaying.
- *CRS discounts.* CRS discounts are not actuarially justified because they are paid for by policyholders not receiving the discount and are not proportional to the risk reduction they provide. If FEMA were to adjust CRS to incorporate discounts into the full-risk premium based

[110] See GAO-17-425.

on the actuarial evaluation of risk reduction, it could ensure that full-risk premiums are actuarially sound and that policyholders are paying fair premiums. Further, if FEMA were to evaluate other means for incentivizing desirable community activities that cannot be actuarially justified, it could help ensure that such activities continue if they are no longer incentivized through CRS discounts.

- *Actuarial communication.* Congress does not have key information on Risk Rating 2.0, such as the loss levels that premiums are designed to cover, the associated uncertainty, and estimated revenue and shortfalls for the current and future years, as well as NFIP's fiscal outlook. By annually reporting on these items, FEMA could improve understanding of Risk Rating 2.0 and better enable Congress to oversee NFIP.
- *Affordability.* Addressing affordability through discounted premiums and caps on annual premium increases has several limitations. Specifically, this approach is not cost-effective because the discounts are not targeted based on need. The approach also addresses affordability poorly because some policyholders needing assistance are not receiving it, and it is temporary. In addition, this approach lacks transparency, and it hinders private-market growth by providing artificially low premiums. A means-based assistance program is one way Congress could address affordability more cost-effectively by targeting it based on need. This also would increase the transparency of the costs of affordability assistance by replacing discounted rates and premium shortfalls with full-risk premiums and explicit assistance in the budget. Further, replacing discounted premiums with assistance that also could be used for private policies would promote private- market growth. Finally, by addressing affordability needs more effectively, Congress could encourage more policyholders to maintain coverage, resulting in greater resilience to flood risk and less reliance on disaster assistance.
- *Program debt.* NFIP's debt to Treasury largely is a result of discounted premiums that FEMA has been statutorily required to provide. Charging current policyholders to repay the debt is not actuarially justified, and the associated costs exacerbate affordability concerns. Further, it is unlikely that FEMA will ever be able to repay the debt as currently structured. Attempts to do so likely would lead some policyholders to drop coverage altogether, leaving them

unprotected from flood risk, reducing resilience, and increasing reliance on federal disaster assistance. Without actions to address the legacy debt—for example, by canceling it or creating different repayment terms—and the potential for future debt, NFIP's debt likely will continue to grow, actuarial soundness will be delayed, and affordability concerns will increase.

- *NFIP rules affecting private insurers.* NFIP rules related to continuous coverage and cancellation refunds are barriers to private-sector growth. By authorizing and requiring FEMA to allow private coverage to satisfy NFIP's continuous coverage requirement and to offer risk-based partial refunds for midterm cancellations that are replaced by private policies, Congress could encourage policyholders to seek private coverage and thereby help to decrease federal fiscal exposure.
- *Policyholder communication.* Because FEMA has not communicated directly with policyholders about Risk Rating 2.0, policyholders may have questions about the methodology and its implications for their individual premiums and mitigation. By taking additional steps to improve policyholders' awareness and understanding of Risk Rating 2.0 and making available more detailed property-specific information about premiums and potential mitigation savings, FEMA could help policyholders make more informed decisions about their flood risk and promote mitigation and resilience.

For NFIP to achieve long-term solvency and other policy goals, it will be important for FEMA and Congress to take multiple actions to address a number of challenges. In particular, actions are needed to address the current and potential future debt as well as the conditions that caused the debt to accumulate over time. While actions to address the existing debt are essential, without elements such as full-risk premiums that are actuarially sound and an appropriated, means-based assistance program, NFIP's debt problems will likely persist. As NFIP's reauthorization approaches, Congress and FEMA have the opportunity to address the program's long-standing challenges and place it on a path to achieve fiscal solvency while addressing affordability.

## Matters for Congressional Consideration

We are recommending the following six matters for congressional consideration:

Congress should consider authorizing and requiring FEMA to incorporate the reserve fund assessment, to the extent necessary based on actuarial principles, into the risk charge within the full-risk premium. (Matter for Consideration 1)

Congress should consider repealing the HFIAA surcharge and authorizing and requiring FEMA to replace forgone revenue with actuarially determined premium adjustments. (Matter for Consideration 2)

Congress should consider providing any affordability assistance for flood insurance through a means-based program that is reflected in the federal budget rather than through statutorily discounted premiums. Options that Congress might consider include allowing assistance to be used for private policies and shortening or ending the period of discounted premiums for those that do not qualify for assistance. (Matter for Consideration 3)

Congress should consider addressing NFIP's legacy and potential future debt and should consider the best means for doing so. Options for addressing the legacy debt include canceling the debt or creating specific repayment terms funded by a transparent premium surcharge. Options for addressing future debt include providing funding to make up for the statutorily-generated premium shortfall, allowing immediate transition to full-risk rates accompanied by a means-based assistance program, changing the financing of catastrophic losses, and enabling FEMA to purchase additional reinsurance. (Matter for Consideration 4)

Congress should consider authorizing and requiring FEMA to allow private flood insurance coverage to satisfy NFIP's continuous coverage requirement. (Matter for Consideration 5)

Congress should consider authorizing and requiring FEMA to offer risk-based partial refunds for midterm cancellations of NFIP policies that are replaced by private flood insurance policies and authorizing and requiring FEMA to implement these refunds in an actuarially sound manner. (Matter for Consideration 6)

## Recommendations for Executive Action

We are making the following five recommendations to FEMA:

- The Assistant Administrator of FEMA's Federal Insurance Directorate should adjust CRS by calculating a community's rating based only on community activities that reduce flood risk and by incorporating discounts into the full-risk premium based on the actuarial evaluation of risk reduction. (Recommendation 1)
- The Assistant Administrator of FEMA's Federal Insurance Directorate should evaluate other means for incentivizing desirable community activities that cannot be actuarially justified but are currently a basis for discounts in CRS. (Recommendation 2)
- The Assistant Administrator of FEMA's Federal Insurance Directorate should publish an annual actuarial report that includes the loss levels that full-risk premiums are designed to cover and that current discounted premiums are able to cover, and the associated uncertainty; the estimated premium revenue and shortfall for current and future years; and an evaluation of NFIP's fiscal outlook, including projections of future debt. (Recommendation 3)
- The Assistant Administrator of FEMA's Federal Insurance Directorate should take steps to directly inform individual policyholders about Risk Rating 2.0 and make them aware of available information. (Recommendation 4)
- The Assistant Administrator of FEMA's Federal Insurance Directorate should take additional steps to make available to policyholders, agents, or both more detailed property-specific flood risk information to help them better understand the justification for individual premiums and potential savings associated with available mitigation options. (Recommendation 5)

## Agency Comments

We provided a draft of this report to the Department of Homeland Security for review and comment. In its comments, reproduced in appendix III, the Department of Homeland Security agreed with our recommendations, stating that it has proposed legislation to address some of the concerns noted in our report. This legislation includes a proposal to create a means-tested affordability program to assist low- and moderate-income policyholders. The department also stated that it would continue to enhance communication with policyholders directly and through NFIP insurers. The Department of Homeland Security also provided technical comments, which we incorporated as appropriate.

We are sending copies of this report to the appropriate congressional committees and the Secretary of Homeland Security. In addition, the report is available at no charge on the GAO website at https://www.gao.gov.

If you or your staff have any questions about this report, please contact Alicia Puente Cackley at (202) 512-8678 or cackleya@gao.gov, or Frank Todisco at (202) 512-2700 or todiscof@gao.gov. Contact points for our Offices of Congressional Relations and Public Affairs may be found on the last page of this report. GAO staff who made key contributions to this report are listed in appendix IV.

Alicia Puente Cackley
Director, Financial Markets and Community Investment

Frank Todisco
Chief Actuary, Applied Research and Methods

## Appendix I: Objectives, Scope, and Methodology

This report examines the Federal Emergency Management Agency's (FEMA) new methodology for setting premiums for the National Flood Insurance Program (NFIP), known as Risk Rating 2.0. Specifically, we examined (1) the actuarial soundness of the new methodology, (2) how premiums are changing for policyholders, (3) efforts to make flood insurance affordable for policyholders, (4) options for addressing program debt, (5) the potential implications of Risk Rating 2.0 for the private flood insurance market, and (6) FEMA's efforts to promote policyholder understanding of Risk Rating 2.0.

To address the first objective, our actuaries reviewed actuarial and other ratemaking documents provided by FEMA.[111] We also reviewed FEMA documents and statutory requirements on premiums, assessments, surcharges, and fees; reinsurance; historical rate reviews; and financial reports for NFIP. We reviewed all FEMA data sources used for developing the full-risk premiums and FEMA's methodology for selecting the data and ensuring data quality and credibility. To examine the actuarial soundness of premiums, we reviewed the actuarial assumptions and methods FEMA used to develop the target losses for the policy year.

We also reviewed FEMA's actuarial analysis on risk classifications, the rationale for actuarial assumptions applied, and the actuarial models used to develop rating factors, including commercial catastrophe models and FEMA models that use data from other government agencies, such as the U.S. Army Corps of Engineers. We reviewed the structure of the full-risk premium and the factors that affect the full-risk premium and the total policyholder payment. We also evaluated the reasonableness of FEMA's findings and conclusions included in its actuarial documents. We interviewed FEMA officials and an actuarial association. Finally, we compared the methodology and results against actuarial standards and principles.[112]

In performing this analysis, we relied on actuarial reports and documentation provided by FEMA. We reviewed the documents for reasonableness but did not audit them for accuracy. To the extent that there are material deficiencies in completeness and accuracy in FEMA's actuarial

---

[111] The actuarial analyses and reviews in this report were performed by Senior Actuary Lijia Guo, Ph.D., ASA, MAAA, and Chief Actuary Frank Todisco, FSA, MAAA. Collectively, the actuaries responsible for this review meet the American Academy of Actuaries' qualification standards with respect to their educational background, designated professional standing, and experience.

[112] Casualty Actuarial Society, *Statement of Principles Regarding Property and Casualty Ratemaking* (Arlington, Va.: May 7, 2021). The Actuarial Standards Board's relevant Actuarial Standards of Practice include 12 (Risk Classification for All Practice Areas); 23 (Data Quality); 25 (Credibility Procedures); 29 (Expense Provisions in Property/Casualty Insurance Ratemaking); 30 (Treatment of Profit and Contingency Provisions and the Cost of Capital in Property/Casualty Insurance Ratemaking); 36 (Statements of Actuarial Opinion Regarding Property/Casualty Loss and Loss Adjustment Expense Reserves); 38 (Catastrophe Modeling); 39 (Treatment of Catastrophe Losses in Property/Casualty Insurance Ratemaking); 41 (Actuarial Communications); 43 (Property/Casualty Unpaid Claim Estimates); 46 (Risk Evaluation in Enterprise Risk Management); 47 (Risk Treatment in Enterprise Risk Management); 53 (Estimating Future Costs for Prospective Property/Casualty Risk Transfer and Risk Retention); and 56 (Modeling).

reports, the actuarial premium estimates may be materially different from those shown in the reports had these deficiencies not been present. This review is not a technical review, and we did not verify the accuracy of the calculations performed by the actuaries who developed the full-risk premiums.

To address the second, third, and fourth objectives, we analyzed data from FEMA's PIVOT database on NFIP policies as of December 31, 2022.[113] We used these data to determine the premiums that FEMA was charging NFIP policyholders and compared them to the full-risk premiums that FEMA determined policyholders should be paying according to Risk Rating 2.0. We assessed the reliability of these data by interviewing FEMA officials and reviewing documentation on PIVOT. We also tested the data by identifying missing data, outliers, and any obvious errors, and comparing our results to published data. We determined that the data were sufficiently reliable for the purposes of our analyses.

Because FEMA does not collect income information for NFIP policyholders, we estimated policyholder household income using themedian household income of the census tract in which the insured property was located, according to data from the Census Bureau's 5-year American Community Survey for 2015–2019.

To further answer the second objective, we used a statistical technique called Bayesian Improved Surname Geocoding (BISG) to estimate the probability that existing NFIP policyholders identified with one of five racial and ethnic groups. These groups were

- Asian, Native Hawaiian, or Pacific Islander, non-Hispanic;
- Black or African American, non-Hispanic;
- Hispanic, any race;
- White, non-Hispanic; and
- all other groups.

Using this method, we combined data from two public release files from the 2010 Census of Population and Housing on racial and ethnic identification.

[113] For condominiums, NFIP offers a Residential Condominium Building Association Policy, which covers all units within a condominium. As such, it is necessary to adjust for the number of condominium units to determine the number of policies. We account for this when reporting the aggregate number of NFIP policies, but otherwise we treat these condominium policies as single policies. We also excluded from our definition of "commercial policy" a small number of nonresidential policies insuring mobile and manufactured homes.

We obtained aggregate data from the 2010 Census Surname File on the probability that a respondent having a given surname reported identifying with one of the groups above. We obtained aggregate data from Summary File 1 on the number of adults in each census block group who identified with each racial and ethnic group. We compared the racial and ethnic groups from each file to data with prior evidence of predictive accuracy, and we applied the BISG method as described in the literature.[114] We assessed the reliability of these estimates by conducting a literature review on the accuracy of BISG and by examining the completeness and distributions of the estimates for NFIP policyholders. Our prior work describes the BISG method in more detail.[115]

To answer the third objective, we reviewed legislative proposals and policy goals identified in our prior work.[116] We analyzed NFIP policy data to estimate the time it might take for FEMA to transition current policyholders to full-risk premiums and the continued unappropriated federal cost until the transition is completed. Our analysis focused on NFIP policies on the glidepath—those that had not yet reached full-risk premiums by December 31, 2022. Because new NFIP policies must pay full-risk premiums, we assumed that premium shortfalls would come from renewing NFIP policies on the glidepath from 2022 onwards.

To calculate premium shortfalls in calendar year 2022, we used PIVOT data to subtract actual premiums from estimated full-risk premiums for NFIP policies in force under Risk Rating 2.0 from January 1, 2022, to December 31, 2022. Because Risk Rating 2.0 was fully implemented after April 1, 2022, some NFIP policies had not yet renewed under Risk Rating 2.0 from January 1, 2022, to March 31, 2022, and did not renew under Risk Rating 2.0 until between January 1, 2023, and March 31, 2023. For calendar year 2023, we assumed that the average shortfalls and the time it will take these policies to reach full-risk premiums will be the same as the Risk Rating 2.0 policies we observed in 2022.

Our projection of premium shortfall from 2023 onward includes baseline and alternative scenarios on (1) future full-risk premiums, (2) future premiums

---

[114] Marc N. Elliott et al., "A New Method for Estimating Race/Ethnicity and Associated Disparities Where Administrative Records Lack Self-Reported Race/Ethnicity," *Health Services Research*, vol. 43, no. 5, part I (October 2008): 1730–1732, and Kosuke Imai and Kabir Khanna, "Improving Ecological Inference by Predicting Individual Ethnicity from Voter Registration Records," *Political Analysis*, vol. 24, no. 2 (Spring 2016): 263–272.

[115] GAO, *Tax Equity: Enhanced Evaluation Could Improve Outreach to Small Business Owners*, GAO-22-104582 (Washington, D.C.: Aug. 3, 2022).

[116] GAO, *Flood Insurance: Comprehensive Reform Could Improve Solvency and Enhance Resilience*, GAO-17-425 (Washington, D.C.: Apr. 27, 2017).

actually charged (which would be less than full risk while policies are still on the glidepath), and (3) the annual policy renewal rate. In our baseline projection, we assumed that policies on the glidepath would renew with NFIP each year until they reach full-risk premiums.

To project future premium shortfalls, we used inflation projections from the Congressional Budget Office and NFIP gross annual loss projections due to increased flood risks developed by the Office of Management and Budget. For the future full-risk premiums, we assumed they would increase with the projected annual inflation and annualized percent increase in flood risks. For future charged premiums, we assumed that the existing statutory annual premium increase caps would apply until policies on the glidepath reach their full-risk premiums. We analyzed the sensitivity of our estimates to our assumptions on inflation, flood risks, annual reductions in the number of policies due to nonrenewal, and annual premium increase caps by calculating the estimates using alternative assumptions. Our shortfall calculations do not account for assessments, surcharges, and fees. We calculated the total premium shortfall net of WYO expenses. In fiscal year 2023, FEMA agreed to pay WYO insurers 29.7 percent of premiums. We determined the present value of premium shortfalls using a discount rate of 2.82 percent, based on the 10-year average of Treasury spot rates, as of September 30, 2022.

We compared policyholders' estimated household income to the annual area median income of the area in which the property was located, as determined by the Department of Housing and Urban Development. We used these data and the property's full-risk premium from PIVOT to determine policyholders' eligibility for assistance and the amount of assistance they might receive under different potential means-based assistance criteria. We also reviewed studies on flood insurance affordability and legislative proposals for a means-based assistance program for NFIP.

The PIVOT data contained 9 months of policy renewal data under Risk Rating 2.0. We created our estimates of premium shortfall and the cost of means-based assistance by extrapolating values obtained from 9 months of data to 12 months, and assuming that declines in the number of policies observed from April through December 2022 continued for the period January through March 2023. To assess the need for and viability of a means-based assistance program, we compared effects of current affordability strategies to policy goals for flood insurance reform.[117]

---

[117] GAO-17-425.

To address the fourth objective, we analyzed NFIP policy data, reinsurance documents, and financial statements. We also reviewed our previous work on NFIP, as well as reports from the Congressional Budget Office, Congressional Research Service, FEMA, and others. We assessed the options for addressing program debt against actuarial standards and policy goals we established in prior work.[118]

To address the fifth objective, we assessed the size and makeup of the private flood insurance market using data from the National Association of Insurance Commissioners' (NAIC) data call on the number and total direct written premium of private flood insurance policies. We assessed the reliability of these data by comparing data elements, including private insurer direct written premium and number of policies sold, with totals from other NAIC publications, such as NAIC's annual industry report, and the raw data. We also interviewed NAIC officials about the accuracy and limitations of the data and their process for ensuring reliability of the data. We determined that the data were sufficiently reliable to determine the number and total direct written premium of private flood insurance policies in the United States.

We also interviewed six private flood insurers to obtain their views on how, if at all, the implementation of Risk Rating 2.0 might be affecting their companies and the overall private flood insurance market and any challenges to private insurer growth. We used the NAIC data to identify larger private flood insurers by direct written premium. We also used these data to identify insurers with a variety of experience writing residential and commercial policies, as well as those that did and did not participate in NFIP's Write Your Own program. Finally, we reviewed laws and regulations that affect private insurers' ability to provide flood insurance and assessed these laws and regulations against policy goals we established in prior work.[119]

To address the sixth objective, we reviewed materials available on FEMA's website related to Risk Rating 2.0, including FEMA's Flood Insurance Manual, rating methodology guide, and discount guide. We analyzed flood insurance policy materials that FEMA sends to policyholders to determine the extent to which FEMA notified policyholders of Risk Rating 2.0 changes. Further, we analyzed training materials FEMA created for agents and Write Your Own insurers to determine what information FEMA provided to these groups to inform them about Risk Rating 2.0 and assist policyholders with their policies. We compared these materials against several criteria,

---

[118] GAO-17-425.
[119] GAO-17-425.

including FEMA's strategic plan and policy goals we established in prior work.[120] In addition, to understand how FEMA communicated premium changes to insurers, agents, and policyholders, we interviewed FEMA officials and two associations representing insurance agents that work with NFIP policyholders.

For all objectives, we reviewed relevant laws and regulations, relevant FEMA documents, our prior reports, and academic publications on flood insurance, and we interviewed FEMA officials. We also attended the National Flood Conference in June 2022, which included discussion of a number of topics related to Risk Rating 2.0 and flood insurance reform.

We conducted this performance audit from March 2022 to July 2023 in accordance with generally accepted government auditing standards.

Those standards require that we plan and perform the audit to obtain sufficient, appropriate evidence to provide a reasonable basis for our findings and conclusions based on our audit objectives. We believe that the evidence obtained provides a reasonable basis for our findings and conclusions based on our audit objectives.

## Appendix II: Additional Data on Glidepath and Means-Based Assistance Estimates

We estimated the time it might take for the Federal Emergency Management Agency to transition current policyholders to full-risk premiums and the continued unappropriated federal cost until the transition is completed. Our estimates included four key inputs: annual premium increase caps, inflation rates, flood risk, and National Flood Insurance Program (NFIP) policy renewal. Changing each input resulted in different estimates (see table 3).

We estimated the cost and number of recipients of a means-based assistance program for which only current NFIP policyholders of primary single-family residences would be eligible (see table 4). We also estimated how these numbers would change by limiting eligibility to policyholders with properties in special flood hazard areas. We used two alternatives for determining the assistance amount. The first alternative would cover the amount of the premium that exceeded a certain percentage of household income (1 or 2 percent) and restrict eligibility to policyholders whose household income was below a certain percentage of the area median income

---

[120] GAO-17-425.

(80, 100, or 120 percent). The second alternative would provide premium discounts on a sliding scale, whereby the discount would increase (from 40 to 80 percent) as a policyholder's household income decreased relative to area median income (from 100 to 50 percent).

**Table 3.** Glidepath time and premium shortfall estimates

| Scenario | Year when 95 percent of policies reach full risk | Total shortfall (in billions) | Present value of total shortfall (in billions, 2022) |
|---|---|---|---|
| Baseline | 2037 | $26.7 | $22.9 |
| Alternate assumptions: statutory caps on annual premium increases | | | |
| Increase all premium increase caps to 25 percent | 2033 | 17.5 | 15.8 |
| Decrease 18 percent premium increase caps to 9 percent | 2055 | 67.2 | 46.4 |
| Decrease all premium increase caps to 9 percent | 2056 | 69.3 | 48.3 |
| Alternate assumptions: inflation | | | |
| Higher inflation | 2037 | 27.2 | 23.3 |
| Lower inflation | 2037 | 25.0 | 21.5 |
| Alternate assumptions: flood risk | | | |
| Higher flood risk | 2037 | 26.4 | 22.6 |
| Lower flood risk | 2037 | 25.8 | 22.1 |
| Alternate assumptions: policy nonrenewal | | | |
| 3 percent nonrenewal | 2036 | 22.1 | 19.2 |
| 6 percent nonrenewal | 2034 | 19.2 | 16.9 |

Source: GAO analysis of Federal Emergency Management Agency data. | GAO-23-105977.

Note: The baseline scenario assumes that all policies on the glidepath would renew National Flood Insurance Program coverage and that flood risk would increase by 0.31 percent annually. The alternate inflation scenarios assume that inflation would be 1 percentage point higher or lower in the first year and converge to the baseline over 5 years. The higher and lower flood risk scenarios change the annual increases in flood risk to 0.40 percent and 0.22 percent, respectively. The present value amounts were determined using a discount rate of 2.82 percent.

**Table 4.** Estimated participants and costs of alternative means-based assistance programs

| | | | *Alternative 1* | | | *Alternative 2* | |
|---|---|---|---|---|---|---|---|
| AMI eligibility threshold | ≤ 80% | ≤ 100% | ≤ 120% | ≤ 80% | ≤ 100% | ≤ 120% | ≤ 100% |
| Percentage of household income at which assistance begins | | 1% | | | 2% | | n/a |
| *All policies* | | | | | | | |
| Eligible policyholders | 756,159 | 1,236,585 | 1,555,816 | 473,894 | 718,359 | 875,569 | 1,549,904 |
| Total cost of federal assistance (first year, dollars in millions) | $907 | $1,556 | $2,030 | $585 | $969 | $1,237 | $1,308 |
| *Policies in special flood hazard areas only* | | | | | | | |
| Eligible policyholders | 378,710 | 632,449 | 795,342 | 259,556 | 410,009 | 508,641 | 721,209 |
| Total cost of federal assistance (first year, dollars in millions) | $559 | $977 | $1,287 | $383 | $646 | $840 | $752 |

Legend: AMI = area median income; n/a = not applicable.

Source: GAO analysis of Federal Emergency Management Agency data. | GAO-23-105977.

Note: This analysis assumes that a means-based assistance program would replace the glidepath, so any policy receiving assistance would immediately convert to the full-risk premium. The assistance would cover all costs of flood insurance, which include premiums as well as any assessments, surcharges, or fees.

# Appendix III: Comments from the Department of Homeland Security

U.S. Department of Homeland Security
Washington, DC 205284

Homeland Security

June 30, 2023

Alicia Puente Cackley
Director, Financial Markets and Community Investments
U.S. Government Accountability Office
441 G Street, NW
Washington, DC 20548

Frank Todisco
Chief Actuary, Applied Research and Methods
U.S. Government Accountability Office
441 G Street, NW
Washington, DC 20548

Re: Management Response to Draft Report GAO-23-105977, "FLOOD INSURANCE: FEMA's New Rate-setting Methodology Improves Actuarial Soundness but Highlights Need for Broader Program Reform"

Dear Ms. Puente Cackley and Mr. Todisco:

Thank you for the opportunity to comment on this draft report. The U.S. Department of Homeland Security (DHS or the Department) appreciates the U.S. Government Accountability Office's (GAO) work in planning and conducting its review and issuing this report.

DHS leadership is pleased to note GAO's recognition of the Federal Emergency Management Agency (FEMA) implementing the National Flood Insurance Program's (NFIP) Risk Rating 2.0 beginning in October 2021. As of April 1, 2023, FEMA has fully implemented Risk Rating 2.0, which leverages industry best practices, cutting-edge technology, and better data to enable FEMA to deliver rates that are actuarily sound, equitable, easier to understand, and better reflect a property's flood risk. GAO also acknowledged in the 2023 High-Risk report[1] that, with the implementation of Risk Rating 2.0, the NFIP moved from "partially met" to "met" in three of five categories on

[1]GAO, "High Risk: Efforts Made to Achieve Progress Need to Be Maintained and Expanded to Fully Address All Areas," dated April 20, 2023 (https://www.gao.gov/products/gao-23-106203).

its annual list of programs and operations that are vulnerable to waste, fraud, abuse, or mismanagement, or in need of transformation.

While GAO's draft report focused on options to address FEMA's NFIP debt, it is also important to note that FEMA is required to estimate flood insurance rates "based on consideration of the risk involved and accepted actuarial principles."[2] This premium is a prospective, actuarial measure of risk designed to cover expected future losses, not to recoup past unfavorable results or pay for earlier debt. FEMA does not factor into its premium an expense for debt or interest on the debt.[3]

The Department remains committed to achieving an equitable NFIP and has proposed legislation to, *inter alia*, (1) make flood insurance more affordable to low- and moderate-income policyholders though a means-tested assistance program, and (2) establish a framework to achieve solvency of NFIP. Additionally, FEMA remains committed to transparent and effective policyholder communication. While the NFIP has historically communicated with policyholders through the NFIP insurers, FEMA will continue to enhance communication both through the NFIP insurers and also more directly with the policyholders.

The draft report contained five recommendations with which the Department concurs. Enclosed find our detailed response to each recommendation. DHS previously submitted technical comments addressing several accuracy, contextual, and other issues under a separate cover for GAO's consideration.

Again, thank you for the opportunity to review and comment on this draft report. Please feel free to contact me if you have any questions. We look forward to working with you again in the future.

Sincerely,

JIM H CRUMPACKER Digitally signed by JIM H CRUMPACKER Date: 2023.06.30 12:18:51 -04'00'

JIM H. CRUMPACKER, CIA, CFE
Director
Departmental GAO-OIG Liaison Office

Enclosure

[2] 42 United States Code (USC) 4014 "Estimates of premium rates," (https://www.govinfo.gov/app/details/USCODE-2021-title42/USCODE-2021-title42-chap50-subchapI-sec4014)

[3] FEMA collects certain surcharges, such as the Homeowner Flood Insurance Affordability Act surcharge, and performs the Reserve Fund assessment which was implemented to better capitalize the NFIP before the introduction of the current rating system.

**Enclosure: Management Response to Recommendations Contained in GAO-23-105977**

GAO recommended that the Deputy Associate Administrator of FEMA's Federal Insurance and Mitigation Administration:

**Recommendation 1:** Adjust CRS [Community Rating System] by calculating a community's rating based only on community activities that reduce flood risk and by incorporating discounts into the full-risk premium based on the actuarial evaluation of risk reduction.

**Response:** Concur. FEMA Resilience (RSL) Mitigation Directorate (MD) Floodplain Management Division (FPMD) agrees that CRS rating should be based on community activities that reduce flood risk. Accordingly, FEMA's MD FPMD is undertaking a multi-year effort to redesign the CRS program to better align with its improved understanding of flood risk and flood risk reduction approaches. On February 1, 2023, FEMA RSL MD FPMD established a CRS redesign workgroup that includes representation from NFIP insurance, mitigation, and floodplain management to lead this effort and evaluate how the CRS program can better incentivize community-level action to reduce the loss of life and property due to flood risk. Additionally, FEMA RSL MD FPMD is exploring potential paths forward for the CRS program that will increase the nation's resilience to future flooding, support the sound financial framework of the NFIP, and result in a more customer-centric CRS program. These efforts will include the following actions:

| Actions | Estimated Completion Date (ECD) |
|---|---|
| Implement incremental program and process improvements for CRS | January 31, 2024 |
| Develop alternative program designs and initiate public input collection | September 30, 2024 |
| Finalize program design | September 30, 2025 |
| Develop strategy for implementing new program design | March 31, 2026 |
| Begin managing change and transition to new program design, including advance notice for NFIP program participants | June 30, 2026 |
| Begin implementation of new program design for CRS | December 31, 2027 |

Overall ECD: December 31, 2027.

**Recommendation 2:** Evaluate other means for incentivizing desirable community activities that cannot be actuarially justified but are currently a basis for discounts in CRS.

**Response:** Concur. FEMA RSL MD FPMD will evaluate other means for incentivizing community activities in the CRS program redesign previously described in this letter, and will also take the following actions:

| Actions | ECD |
|---|---|
| Implement incremental program and process improvements for CRS | January 31, 2024 |
| Initiate public input collection on incentivizing non-discount community activities | September 30, 2024 |
| Finalize report on public input | March 31, 2025 |
| Complete CRS Communities Incentives report | August 29, 2025 |

Overall ECD: August 29, 2025.

**Recommendation 3:** Conduct and publish an annual actuarial report that includes the loss levels that full-risk premiums are designed to cover and that current discounted premiums are able to cover, and the associated uncertainty; the estimated premium revenue and shortfall for current and future years; and an evaluation of NFIP's fiscal outlook, including projections of future debt.

**Response:** Concur. By no later than the end of fiscal year 2025, FEMA Resilience Federal Insurance Directorate (FID) will publish its first annual actuarial report for the current rating plan, to include the items discussed in this draft report. As part of this, FEMA FID will develop the necessary analysis, draft effective accompanying communication, and ensure the actuarial report is consistent with statutory reporting requirements and Actuarial Standards of Practice,[4] as appropriate.

These efforts will include the following actions:

| Actions | ECD |
|---|---|
| Develop analysis, draft communication, and ensure consistency with statutory reporting requirements and Actuarial Standards of Practice. | September 30, 2024 |
| Finalize Draft Report and Begin Clearance Process | March 31, 2025 |
| Publish Final Report | September 30, 2025 |

[4] Actuarial Standards of Practice, Actuarial Standards Board, http://www.actuarialstandardsboard.org/standards-of-practice/

It is also important to note that FEMA FID currently compiles multiple recurring reports related to the NFIP financial position, including:

- National Flood Insurance Program (NFIP) Fiscal Year Report to Congress: Biggert-Waters Flood Insurance Reform Act of 2012;
- National Flood Insurance Program Semi-Annual Debt Repayment Progress Report - Report to Congress and the Secretary of the Treasury;
- Quarterly Reserve Fund Report; and
- Quarterly Watermark - National Flood Insurance Program Financial Statement

These reports enable FEMA to satisfy existing statutory reporting requirements. However, comprehensive, stream-lined reports would more clearly communicate elements of the NFIP's financial position to Congress and the public. Accordingly, on April 21, 2023, DHS submitted to the 118th Congress 17 legislative proposals to reform FEMA's NFIP which will reduce reporting complexity. These legislative proposals include legislative reforms that would reduce the reporting complexity for the NFIP so that, in a two-year period, reports due to the Congress would be reduced from 15 to 4, while providing similar and more timely information.

Overall ECD: September 30, 2025.

**Recommendation 4:** Take steps to directly inform individual policyholders about Risk Rating 2.0 and make them aware of available information.

**Response:** Concur. Regardless of the rating methodology, FEMA agrees that individual policyholders should be informed about their flood risk and be able to obtain information about their flood insurance premium. FEMA FID will enhance policyholder communications, by reviewing the policyholder communication products and the public-facing websites to provide policyholders with more information about flood insurance.

With the implementation of Risk Rating 2.0, FEMA RSL FID Policyholder Services and Product Delivery Divisions updated policyholder communication products such as the policy declaration page, renewal notices, and annual Flood Insurance Reform Act notices that provide information about flood risk directly to policyholders. The updated declaration page provides information about the insured structure as well as itemized dollar amounts on the premiums, discounts, surcharges, and fees paid. The declaration page also refers policyholders to both a website and to their NFIP insurer to obtain more information about their flood risk. In addition, FEMA FID provides NFIP insurers with information for each quote provided to enable NFIP insurers and insurance agents to discuss flood risk with policyholders.

ECD: April 30, 2024.

**Recommendation 5:** Take steps to make available to policyholders, agents, or both more detailed property-specific flood risk information to help them better understand the justification for individual premiums and potential savings associated with available mitigation options.

**Response:** Concur. To support greater communication of the specific risk factors, FEMA FID created the Risk Rating 2.0 webpage on April 1, 2021[5] which provides state, county, and zip code level premium impact as well as technical documents, to include an overall explanation of Risk Rating 2.0, the premium calculation worksheet, the rating factors, and a detailed explanation for levees in Risk Rating 2.0. Currently, NFIP policyholders can obtain an understanding of the impact of mitigation options by working with their NFIP insurer or agent. NFIP insurers and agents are able to provide premium quotes based on the mitigation options in the quote. To help insurers and agents explain the benefits of mitigation and to support policyholder understanding, the NFIP highlights the mitigation discount as a separate line item. In addition, FEMA FID developed a public-facing Discount Explanation Guide[6] that provides information on the impact that mitigation options have on premiums.

FEMA FID recognizes both the challenges and the importance of communicating specific risk factors in a meaningful, simplified manner to agents and policyholders. These challenges are not unique to FEMA and are particularly inherent in any multi-variate rating system. Private market property and casualty carriers face similar hurdles and are still determining industry best practices. For example, private carriers have sought to pilot the ability to provide the top drivers of risk with an insurance quote but have struggled implementing this capability.

These efforts will include the following actions:

| Actions | ECD |
|---|---|
| Update floodsmart.gov | January 31, 2024 |
| Deploy a mitigation discount visualization tool | September 30, 2024 |
| Pilot online quoting tool | April 30, 2025 |

Overall ECD: August 29, 2025.

[5] https://www.fema.gov/flood-insurance/risk-rating
[6] https://agents.floodsmart.gov/sites/default/files/fema-Risk-Rating-2.0-discount-guide.pdf

6

# Appendix IV: GAO Contacts and Staff Acknowledgments

## GAO Contacts

Alicia Puente Cackley at (202) 512-8678 or cackleya@gao.gov.
Frank Todisco at (202) 512-2700 or todiscof@gao.gov.

## Staff Acknowledgments

In addition to the contacts named above, Patrick Ward (Assistant Director), Christopher Forys (Analyst in Charge), Xiang Bi, Dylan Desjardins, Lijia Guo, Jocelyn Kuo, Jill Lacey, Sailaja Ledalla, Matthew Levie, Scott McNulty, Marc Molino, Angela Pun, Steve Ruszczyk, Jessica Sandler, Jennifer Schwartz, and Jeff Tessin made key contributions to this report.

## GAO's Mission

The Government Accountability Office, the audit, evaluation, and investigative arm of Congress, exists to support Congress in meeting its constitutional responsibilities and to help improve the performance and accountability of the federal government for the American people. GAO examines the use of public funds; evaluates federal programs and policies, and provides analyses, recommendations, and other assistance to help Congress make informed oversight, policy, and funding decisions. GAO's commitment to good government is reflected in its core values of accountability, integrity, and reliability.

## Connect with GAO

Connect with GAO on Facebook, Flickr, Twitter, and YouTube. Subscribe to our RSS Feeds or Email Updates. Listen to our Podcasts. Visit GAO on the web at https://www.gao.gov.

## To Report Fraud, Waste, and Abuse in Federal Programs

Contact FraudNet:

Website: https://www.gao.gov/about/what-gao-does/fraudnet Automated answering system: (800) 424-5454 or (202) 512-7700.

## Congressional Relations

A. Nicole Clowers, Managing Director, ClowersA@gao.gov, (202) 512-4400, U.S. Government Accountability Office, 441 G Street NW, Room 7125, Washington, DC 20548.

## Public Affairs

Chuck Young, Managing Director, youngc1@gao.gov, (202) 512-4800 U.S. Government Accountability Office, 441 G Street NW, Room 7149 Washington, DC 20548.

## Strategic Planning and External Liaison

Stephen J. Sanford, Managing Director, spel@gao.gov, (202) 512-4707.

U.S. Government Accountability Office, 441 G Street NW, Room 7814, Washington, DC 20548.

## Chapter 9

# Options for Making the National Flood Insurance Program More Affordable*

**Diane P. Horn**


## Summary

Concerns about the affordability of flood insurance premiums have come to the fore as FEMA introduces a new pricing system known as Risk Rating 2.0, which represents the biggest change to the way the NFIP calculates flood insurance premiums since its inception. Nationally, 77% of policyholders will see an increase in their premiums in the first year, with 23% of policyholders seeing a decrease under Risk Rating 2.0. These impending rate raises, which vary from $120 to $240 or more annually, have increased congressional interest in reducing the cost burden of flood insurance on policyholders.

As full risk-based premiums are phased in under Risk Rating 2.0, some policyholders could be faced with large price increases either because they are currently buying coverage at subsidized rates and/or because the new rating system indicates that they now have a higher risk. Such increases raise issues of equity, as well as affordability. The NFIP currently insures just under 5 million structures in the United States, and most of the remaining structures do not have insurance to protect them against flood risk. This large insurance gap may increase if policyholders drop their coverage because they feel that premiums are too expensive.

The introduction of a means-tested NFIP affordability program has been under consideration by Congress for years. However, FEMA does not currently have the authority to implement an affordability program, nor


* This is an edited, reformatted and augmented version of Congressional Research Service Publication No. R47000, updated January 6, 2023.

In: The National Flood Insurance Program (NFIP)
Editor: Jolene Rivera
ISBN: 979-8-89530-612-3

does the NFIP's current rate structure provide the funding required to support one. If an affordability program were to be funded from NFIP funds, this would require either raising flood insurance rates for NFIP policyholders or diverting resources from another existing use. Alternatively, an affordability program could be funded fully or partially by congressional appropriations. A central question in any reform of the NFIP is who should bear the costs of floodplain occupancy in the future: individual policyholders (the insured), federal taxpayers, uninsured flood victims, or some combination of these.

A means-tested affordability program could be implemented in a number of different ways, which may differ in how to measure when a premium might impose a cost burden on a policyholder. Means-tested affordability assistance could take a capped-premiums approach, an income-based approach, a housing burden-based approach, a combined income- and housing burden-based approach, or a community characteristics approach.

In addition, an affordability program is only one possible way of reducing the cost burden to policyholders. This report outlines a range of policy options Congress could consider to reduce the amount that NFIP policyholders pay, such as

- reducing the amount that policyholders pay through the introduction of a mean-tested affordability program;
- reducing the amount that individual policyholders pay by increasing participation in the NFIP, which could distribute program costs amongst a larger population than at present;
- increasing income to the NFIP, which could be used to reduce policyholders' contributions to the costs of the program;
- reducing the NFIP debt and thus the amount that policyholders pay in interest on the debt; or
- increasing mitigation activities, which may reduce flood damages and thus flood claims, which could reduce the amount that policyholders have to pay for claims.

The report also includes a table summarizing past legislative proposals related to NFIP affordability.

## Introduction

Many Members and stakeholders have expressed concern about the perceived affordability of flood insurance premiums, concerns which have come to the fore as the Federal Emergency Management Agency (FEMA) introduces a new pricing system known as Risk Rating 2.0. This new rating system, which is designed to move all National Flood Insurance Program (NFIP) policies to risk-based pricing, represents the biggest change to the way the NFIP calculates flood insurance premiums since its inception.[1] Nationally, according to FEMA, in the first year 77% of policyholders will see an increase in their premiums and 23% of policyholders will see a decrease under Risk Rating 2.0.[2] These impending rate raises, which vary from $120 to $240 or more annually, have increased congressional interest in reducing the cost burden of flood insurance on policyholders.

The introduction of a means-tested NFIP affordability program has been under consideration by Congress for years. For example, certain bills for reauthorization and reform of the NFIP in the 115th Congress,[3] the 116th Congress,[4] and the 117th Congress[5] have contained provisions to establish an affordability program (see Table 1), as well as other provisions related to making NFIP premiums more affordable. The Build Back Better Act,[6] as passed by the House on November 19, 2021, would have appropriated funding to provide means-tested assistance to certain NFIP policyholders. However, a means-tested affordability program is only one possible way of reducing the cost burden to policyholders, and Congress could consider a range of other options that could reduce the amount that NFIP policyholders have to pay.

A central decision in any reform of the NFIP is who should bear the costs of floodplain occupancy in the future: individual policyholders (the insured), federal taxpayers, uninsured flood victims, or some combination of these. Increases in NFIP premiums under Risk Rating 2.0 may call further attention to the distribution of flood costs as an important policy concern.

---

[1] FEMA, *Risk Rating 2.0: Equity in Action*, https://www.fema.gov/flood-insurance/risk-rating.

[2] Ibid.

[3] H.R. 2874, the 21st Century Flood Reform Act; S. 1313, the Flood Insurance Affordability and Sustainability Act of 2017; and companion bills S. 1368 and H.R. 3285, the Sustainable, Fair, and Efficient (SAFE) Flood Insurance Program Reauthorization Act of 2017.

[4] .R. 3167, the National Flood Insurance Program Reauthorization Act of 2019; and companion bills S. 2187 and H.R. 3872, the National Flood Insurance Program Reauthorization and Reform Act of 2019.

[5] Companion bills S. 3128 and H.R. 5802, the National Flood Insurance Program Reauthorization and Reform Act of 2021.

[6] H.R. 5376.

## Affordability and Solvency of the National Flood Insurance Program

The NFIP is the primary source of flood insurance coverage for residential properties in the United States, with just under 5 million policies in more than 22,000 communities in all 56 states and jurisdictions.[7] The NFIP was created by the National Flood Insurance Act of 1968[8] (NFIA). The last long-term reauthorization of the NFIP ended at the end of FY2017. Since then, 22 short-term NFIP reauthorizations have been enacted,[9] and the NFIP is currently authorized until September 30, 2023.[10]

As a public insurance program, the objectives of the NFIP are different from the profit-maximization goals of private-sector companies. The NFIP has two main purposes: to provide access to primary flood insurance to properties with significant flood risk who might not otherwise be able to obtain insurance, and to reduce flood risk through the adoption of floodplain management standards. A longer-term objective of the NFIP is to reduce federal expenditure on disaster assistance after floods by substituting insurance payments for aid, with individual policyholders funding at least part of their recovery from flood damage.[11] For example, the U.S. Government Accountability Office (GAO) has argued that to the extent that more consumers have insurance to protect them from the financial effects of flooding, they may not need federal disaster assistance to help them recover from flood events. In addition, the receipt of federal disaster assistance generates the requirement to purchase flood insurance for properties located in special flood hazard areas. Removing the availability of federal disaster assistance to previous recipients of such assistance who live in a Special Flood Hazard Area (SFHA)[12] and who do not purchase flood insurance also reduces

---

[7] For more information on the NFIP, see CRS Report R44593, *Introduction to the National Flood Insurance Program (NFIP)*, by Diane P. Horn and Baird Webel.

[8] Title XIII of P.L. 90-448, as amended, 42 U.S.C. §4001 et seq.

[9] For additional information on NFIP reauthorizations since the end of FY2017, see CRS Insight IN10835, *What Happens If the National Flood Insurance Program (NFIP) Lapses?* by Diane P. Horn.

[10] P.L. 117-328. For more information on NFIP reauthorization, see CRS Insight IN10835, *What Happens If the National Flood Insurance Program (NFIP) Lapses?* by Diane P. Horn.

[11] National Research Council of the National Academies, *Affordability of National Flood Insurance Program Premiums: Report 1* (hereinafter *NRC Affordability Report 1*), 2015, pp. 31-33, http://www.nap.edu/catalog/21709/ affordability-of-national-flood-insurance-program-premiums-report-1.

[12] The Special Flood Hazard Area (SFHA) is defined by FEMA as an area with a 1% or greater risk of flooding every year.

federal disaster assistance expenditures.[13] Flood is one of the few natural hazards for which at-risk residents pay some of the costs after a disaster.

A key design feature of the NFIP is that policyholders' premiums, fees, and surcharges are intended to pay for all flood-related damages and program expenses,[14] with the option to borrow from the U.S. Treasury to pay claims for extreme events. From the inception of the NFIP, the program has been expected to set premiums that are simultaneously "risk-based" and "reasonable."[15] GAO notes that FEMA is tasked with two competing goals: keeping flood insurance affordable and keeping the program solvent.[16] The NFIP has been on the GAO high- risk list since 2006 because of concerns about its long-term fiscal solvency and related operational issues and, more recently, concerns about the NFIP's fiscal exposure to climate change.[17]

In a 2017 report, the Congressional Budget Office (CBO) estimated that the NFIP had an expected one-year actuarial shortfall[18] of $0.7 billion.[19] CBO also estimated that the cost of providing discounted rates to some NFIP policies was about $0.3 billion more than the receipts from surcharges created to help cover the costs of those discounts.[20] This shortfall arises primarily because premium rates do not fully reflect the full risk of its insured policies. This applies both to the risk of individual properties and also the risk of

---

[13] U.S. Government Accountability Office (GAO), *National Flood Insurance Program: Congress Should Consider Updating the Mandatory Purchase Requirement*, GAO-21-587, July 2021, p. 35, (hereinafter *GAO Mandatory Purchase Requirement*), https://www.gao.gov/assets/gao-21-578.pdf.

[14] Some types of properties receive subsidies, which are discussed in the section of this report on "Premium Subsidies and Cross-Subsidies."

[15] See 82 Stat. 573 for text in original statute (§1302(c) of P.L. 90-448). This language remains in statute (see 42 U.S.C.§4001(c)).

[16] GAO, *High-Risk Series: Dedicated Leadership Needed to Address Limited Progress in Most High-Risk Areas*, GAO-21-119SP, March 2, 2021, pp. 281-283, https://www.gao.gov/products/gao-21-119sp.

[17] GAO, *Climate Change: Opportunities to Reduce Federal Fiscal Exposure, Testimony Before the Committee on the Budget, House of Representatives*, GAO-19-625T, June 11, 2019, p. 7, https://www.gao.gov/products/gao-19-625t.

[18] An actuarial shortfall is when income from premiums, fees, and surcharges is too low to cover the costs associated with paying claims on existing policies and writing and servicing those policies. Congressional Budget Office (CBO), *The National Flood Insurance Program: Financial Soundness and Affordability* (hereinafter *CBO Affordability*), Washington, DC, September 1, 2017, p. 7. Note that this report was published before the introduction of Risk Rating 2.0.

[19] *CBO Affordability*, pp. 4-5. The actuarial shortfall estimated by CBO in this report excludes $0.7 billion for mapping floodplains, mitigating flood risk, and interest payment on the NFIP's debt to the Treasury.

[20] CBO Affordability, p. 8.

catastrophic losses to the program as a whole, which FEMA has traditionally managed by relying on its authority to borrow from the U.S. Treasury.[21]

GAO has been reporting since 1983 that the NFIP's premium rates do not reflect the full risk of loss because of various legislative requirements, which exacerbates the program's fiscal exposure.[22] GAO has also noted that while Congress has directed FEMA to provide subsidized premium rates for policyholders meeting certain requirements, it has not provided FEMA with funds to offset these subsidies and discounts, which has contributed to FEMA's need to borrow from the U.S. Treasury to pay NFIP claims.[23]

### *Premium Subsidies and Cross-Subsidies*

Except for certain subsidies, flood insurance rates in the NFIP are directed to be "based on consideration of the risk involved and accepted actuarial principles,"[24] meaning that the rate is reflective of the true flood risk to the property. FEMA determines full-risk rates[25] by estimating the probability of a given level of flooding, damage estimates based on that level of flooding, and accepted actuarial principles.[26] However, Congress has directed FEMA not to charge actuarial rates for certain categories of properties and to offer subsidies[27] or cross-subsidies to certain classes of properties in order to achieve the program's objectives so that owners of certain existing properties in flood zones[28] are able to afford flood insurance.

---

[21] GAO, *National Flood Insurance Program: Fiscal Exposure Persists Despite Property Acquisitions*, GAO-20-509, June 25, 2020, p. 32, https://www.gao.gov/assets/710/707821.pdf.

[22] Ibid., p. 29.

[23] GAO, *Flood Insurance: Comprehensive Reform Could Improve Solvency and Enhance Resilience* (hereinafter *GAO Solvency*), GAO-17-425, April 2017, p. 17, https://www.gao.gov/products/GAO-17-425.

[24] 42 U.S.C. §4014(a)(1).

[25] FEMA defines full-risk rates as those charged to a group of policies that generate premiums sufficient to pay the group's anticipated losses and expenses. See GAO, *National Flood Insurance Program: Continued Progress Needed to Fully Address Prior GAO Recommendations on Rate-Setting Methods*, GAO-16-59, March 2016, p. 8, http://www.gao.gov/assets/680/675855.pdf.

[26] For a brief explanation of accepted actuarial principles, see *NRC Affordability Report 1*, pp. 36-38.

[27] FEMA defines subsidized premium rates as those charged for a group of policies that results in aggregate premiums insufficient to pay for anticipated losses and expenses.

[28] Flood zones are geographic areas that FEMA has defined according to levels of flood risk and are depicted on a community's Flood Insurance Rate Map (FIRM). NFIP flood zones can be divided into three main categories: low- to moderate-risk areas (B, C, and X zones), high-risk areas (A zones), and high-risk coastal areas (V zones).

There are three main categories of properties which pay less than full risk-based rates:

- Pre-FIRM: Properties which were built or substantially improved[29] before December 31, 1974, or before FEMA published the first Flood Insurance Rate Map (FIRM) for their community, whichever was later.[30]
- Newly mapped: Properties newly mapped into an SFHA on or after April 1, 2015, if the applicant gets flood insurance coverage within a year of the mapping.
- Grandfathered: Properties that were built in compliance with the FIRM which was in effect at the time of construction.[31] FEMA allows owners of such
- properties to maintain their old flood insurance rate class if their property is remapped into a new flood rate class.[32]

As of September 2018, approximately 13% of NFIP policies received a pre-FIRM subsidy, 4% of NFIP policies received the newly mapped subsidy, and about 9% of NFIP policies were grandfathered.[33]

### *Fees and Surcharges*

In addition to the building and contents premium, NFIP policyholders pay a number of fees and surcharges mandated by law.

---

[29] 44 C.F.R. §59.1 defines substantial improvement as any reconstruction, rehabilitation, addition, or other improvement of a structure, the cost of which exceeds 50% of the market value of the structure before the start of construction of the improvement." For additional discussion of substantial improvement, see FEMA, *Substantial Improvement*, https://www.fema.gov/node/405414.

[30] 42 U.S.C. §4015(c).

[31] A property can be grandfathered due to a change in its flood zone or a change in its Base Flood Elevation (BFE), which is defined as the water-surface elevation of the base flood, which is the 1%-annual-chance flood, commonly called the 100-year flood. The probability is 1% that rising water will reach BFE height in any given year.

[32] An example of zone grandfathering would be a property that is initially mapped into a high-risk area (zone A) and is built to the proper building code and standards, and is later remapped into a higher-risk coastal area (zone V). If the policyholder has maintained continuous insurance coverage under the NFIP, the owner of this property can pay the flood insurance premium based on the prior lower-risk flood zone (zone A). Elevation grandfathering occurs when a new FIRM increases the BFE, but the property itself does not change flood zones.

[33] Email correspondence from FEMA Congressional Affairs staff, June 13, 2019. Note that FEMA has not collected updated information for rating categories since producing the September 2018 numbers.

- The *Federal Policy Fee* (FPF) was authorized by Congress in 1990 and helps pay for the administrative expenses of the program, including floodplain mapping and some of the insurance operations.[34] The amount of the Federal Policy Fee is set by FEMA and can increase or decrease year to year. Since October 2017, the FPF has been \$50 for Standard Flood Insurance Policies (SFIPs), \$25 for Preferred Risk Policies (PRPs),[35] and \$25 for contents-only policies.[36] The FPF is \$47 for all NFIP policies written under Risk Rating 2.0.[37]
- A *Reserve Fund Assessment* was authorized by Congress in the Biggert-Waters Flood Insurance Reform Act of 2012[38] to establish and maintain a reserve fund to cover future claim and debt expenses, especially those from catastrophic disasters.[39] FEMA charges every NFIP policyholder a reserve fund assessment of 18% of the premium.
- All NFIP policies are also assessed a *HFIAA Surcharge*[40] following the passage of the Homeowner Flood Insurance Affordability Act of 2014 (HFIAA).[41] The amount of the surcharge is dependent on the type of property being insured. For primary residences, the charge is \$25; for all other properties, the charge is \$250.[42]
- If a community is on probation from the NFIP,[43] all policyholders in that community will be charged a *Probation Surcharge* of \$50 for a

---

[34] 42 U.S.C. §4014(a)(1)(B)(iii).

[35] A Preferred Risk Policy is a Standard Flood Insurance Policy that offers low-cost coverage to owners and tenants of eligible buildings located in moderate- and low-risk flood zones in NFIP communities. PRP policies will no longer be offered under Risk Rating 2.0. See National Flood Services, *Risk Rating 2.0: What Is Changing*, https://nationalfloodservices.com/wp-content/uploads/2021/06/Risk-Rating-2.0-What-is-Changing.pdf.

[36] See FEMA, *Flood Insurance Manual, How to Write*, revised October 1, 2022, p. 3-51, https://www.fema.gov/sites/default/files/documents/fema_nfip-flood-insurance-full-manual_102022.pdf. Note that the FPF is higher for residential condominium buildings with more than 20 units.

[37] See FEMA, *Flood Insurance Manual: How to Write*, p. 3-50, revised October 1, 2022, https://www.fema.gov/sites/default/files/documents/fema_nfip-flood-insurance-full-manual_102022.pdf.

[38] Title II of P.L. 112-141.

[39] The Reserve Fund assessment was authorized by Congress in BW-12 to establish and maintain a Reserve Fund to cover future claim and debt expenses, especially those from catastrophic disasters (§100212 of P.L. 112-141, 126 Stat. 992, as codified at 42 U.S.C. §4017a).

[40] Section 8(a) of P.L. 113-89, 128 Stat. 1023.

[41] P.L. 112-141, §100236, 126 Stat. 957; as amended by P.L. 113-89, §16; 128 Stat. 1026.

[42] For a description of how the fee is applied to different policy types, see FEMA, *The HFIAA Surcharge Fact Sheet*, April 2015, https://www.fema.gov/media-library/assets/documents/105569.

[43] A community can be placed on probation by FEMA if it is found that it is failing to adequately enforce the floodplain management standards it has adopted. A community is given time to

full one-year period, even if the community brings its program into compliance and is removed from probation.

- Before the introduction of Risk Rating 2.0, FEMA charged a *Severe Repetitive Loss (SRL) Premium* of 15% on all SRL properties.[44] Revenues from these surcharges were deposited into the Reserve Fund.[45]

Currently, the categories of properties which pay less than the full risk-based rate are determined by the date when the structure was built relative to the date of adoption of the FIRM, rather than the flood risk or the ability of the policyholder to pay. GAO has suggested in a number of reports that linking subsidies to ability to pay rather than the existing approach, by which subsidies are linked to properties without regard to financial circumstances, would make premium assistance more transparent and thus more open to oversight by Congress and the public.[46]

***Legislative Reforms to Address NFIP Solvency and Affordability***

Competing aspects of the NFIP, particularly the desire to keep flood insurance affordable while making the program fiscally solvent, have made it challenging to reform the program.[47] Different Administrations and Congresses have placed varied emphases and priorities on affordability or solvency for premium setting. As these priorities change, the balance between actuarial objectives (financial soundness and alignment of individual premiums with risk) and encouraging participation (by keeping premiums affordable and offering subsidies to certain classes of policyholders) has also changed.[48]

The tension between solvency and affordability has been illustrated by legislative changes in the last decade. The Biggert-Waters Flood Insurance

---

rectify FEMA's concerns regarding their implementation of the floodplain management standards. Ultimately, if the community does not correct its cited deficiencies after given time periods described in regulations, the community will be suspended from the NFIP by FEMA. For additional details on probation, see 44 C.F.R. §59.24(b) and (c).

[44] FEMA, *April 1, 2021 and January 1, 2022 Program Changes*, W-20020, p. 22, https://nfipservices.floodsmart.gov/ sites/default/files/w-20020.pdf.

[45] The SRL premium will be incorporated into new premium rates as NFIP policyholders move to Risk Rating 2.0 rates in 2022 and 2023.

[46] *GAO Solvency*, p. 27.

[47] *GAO Solvency*, p. 1.

[48] American Academy of Actuaries, *The National Flood Insurance Program: Challenges and Solutions*, Washington, DC, September 25, 2019, p. 3, https://www.actuary.org/sites/default/files/2019-09/flood9.19.pdf.

Reform Act of 2012 (hereinafter BW-12)[49] moved the NFIP in the direction of better aligning policyholders' premiums with their actual flood risks by removing or accelerating phaseouts of discounted rates.[50] A core principle of BW- 12 was the eventual removal of subsidized policies.[51] Following the passage of BW-12, lawmakers received testimony and letters from constituents of multiple communities expressing concern that this would result in unreasonably high premiums that would create a financial burden on policyholders and could cause disruption to communities.

In response to these concerns, Congress passed the Homeowner Flood Insurance Affordability Act of 2014 (HFIAA),[52] which slowed or reversed some changes introduced in BW-12.[53] In particular, HFIAA slowed the rate of phaseout of subsidies for most primary residences, but retained the pace of the phaseout of the subsidy from BW-12 for business properties and secondary homes. In addition, HFIAA created a minimum and maximum increase in the amount for the phaseout of subsidies for all primary residences of 5%-18% annually. This permits individual property increases of up to 18%, but limits the rate class[54] increases to 15% per year.[55] In other words, the average annual premium rate increase for primary residences within a single risk classification rate may not be increased by more than 15% a year, while the individual premium rate increase for any individual policy may not be increased by more than 18% each year.[56]

Other categories of properties are required to have their premium increased by 25% per year until they reach full risk-based rates, including (1) nonprimary residences; (2) nonresidential properties; (3) business properties;

---

[49] Title II of P.L. 112-141.

[50] For more information on these changes, see Table 4 in CRS Report R44593, *Introduction to the National Flood Insurance Program (NFIP)*, by Diane P. Horn and Baird Webel.

[51] *NRC Affordability Report 1*, p. 1.

[52] See P.L. 112-141, §100236, 126 Stat. 957; as amended by P.L. 113-89, §16; 128 Stat. 1026.

[53] *CBO Affordability*, p. 4.

[54] A single rate class (or risk classification) is a group of properties with the same flood risk classification; for example, pre-FIRM properties or properties with the newly mapped subsidy.

[55] The chargeable risk premium rate for any property may not be increased by more than 18% per year (except in certain circumstances, which are listed); see 42 U.S.C. §4015(e)(1). The chargeable risk premium may not be increased by an amount that would result in the average of such rate increases for properties within the risk classification exceeding 15% of the average of the risk premium rate for properties within the risk classification; see 42 U.S.C.§4015(e)(3).

[56] The percentage increases are based on the current premium (e.g., a 15% annual increase from the prior year premium), rather than the percentage difference between the current premium and the actuarial rate (i.e., a rate increase of 25% does not mean the pre-FIRM subsidy is eliminated in four years).

(4) properties with severe repetitive loss;[57] (5) properties with substantial cumulative damage;[58] and properties with substantial damage[59] or substantial improvement after July 6, 2012. Actuarially sound rates, or full risk-based rates,[60] would help communicate risks to homeowners and could help to ensure the program's sustainability; however, for some policyholders this would mean a rate increase that could make premiums unaffordable or reduce their willingness to purchase flood insurance.[61] FEMA is moving toward charging full risk-based rates for all NFIP policies through the introduction of a new method for pricing NFIP policies, known as Risk Rating 2.0.

## Risk Rating 2.0

Risk Rating 2.0 represents the biggest change to the way the NFIP calculates flood insurance premiums since its inception. Under Risk Rating 2.0, premiums for individual properties will be based on their individual flood risk.

Risk Rating 2.0 went into effect on October 1, 2021, for new NFIP policies only. The new rates for existing policyholders took effect on April 1, 2022. All policies will move to Risk Rating 2.0 pricing when they renew after April 1, 2022.[62]

Under Risk Rating 2.0, premiums for an individual property are based on that property's specific flood risk, as opposed to being placed in a general risk category based on flood zones.[63] The premium is calculated based on the

---

[57] Severe repetitive loss properties are those that have incurred four or more claim payments exceeding $5,000 each, with a cumulative amount of such payments over $20,000; or at least two claims with a cumulative total exceeding the value of the property. See 42 U.S.C. §4014(h) and 44 C.F.R. §79.2(h).

[58] A property with substantial cumulative damage is any property that has incurred flood-related damage in which the cumulative amounts of payments under the NFIP equaled or exceeded the fair market value of such property. See 42U.S.C. §4014(a)(2)(C).

[59] 44 C.F.R. §59.1 defines "substantial damage" as damage of any origin sustained by a structure whereby the cost of restoring the structure to its before-damaged condition would equal or exceed 50% of the market value of the structure before the damage occurred. For additional discussion of substantial damage, see FEMA Fact Sheet, *NFIP "Substantial Damage"—What Does It Mean?* at https://www.fema.gov/press-release/20210318/fact-sheet-nfip-substantial-damage- what-does-it-mean-0.

[60] FEMA defines full risk-based rates expenses (rates intended to reflect the actual rate of flooding) as those charged to a group of policies that generate premiums sufficient to pay the group's anticipated losses and expenses.

[61] *CBO Affordability*, p. 21 and p. 4.

[62] FEMA, *Risk Rating 2.0: Equity in Action*, https://www.fema.gov/flood-insurance/risk-rating.

[63] For a more detailed explanation of flood zones, see CRS Report R44593, *Introduction to the National Flood Insurance Program (NFIP)*, by Diane P. Horn and Baird Webel.

specific features of the property, including structural variables such as the foundation type of the structure, the height of the lowest floor of the structure relative to base flood elevation, and the replacement cost value (RCV)[64] of the structure. Structures with higher replacement costs than current local or national averages should pay more for their NFIP coverage than structures that are below the average RCV, which should pay less.[65]

Risk Rating 2.0 also considers geographical variables such as the distance to water, the type and size of nearest bodies of water, flood frequency, and the elevation of the property relative to the flooding source. Risk Rating 2.0 also incorporates a broader range of flood frequencies and sources than the current system; in particular, pluvial flooding (flooding due to heavy rainfall).[66]

Risk Rating 2.0 will continue the overall policy of phasing out NFIP subsidies that began with BW-12 and continued with HFIAA, which slowed the rate at which subsidies were phased out for primary residences. If policyholders are currently paying less than the full risk-based rate for their property, their premium will increase over time until they reach the actuarial rate for their property. However, limitations on annual premium increases are set in statute,[67] and FEMA cannot increase rates annually beyond these caps. Although Risk Rating 2.0 will not be allowed to increase premiums for primary residences more than 18% annually, this will still represent a larger increase than policyholders have seen in years. Since HFIAA was passed in 2014, rate increases for primary residences have increased between 6% and 11% per year.[68]

Nationally, an estimated 77% of policyholders will see an increase in their premiums in the first year of Risk Rating 2.0, with 23% of policyholders

---

[64] Before Risk Rating 2.0, the premium for a property was based on the amount of insurance purchased for a structure rather than the replacement cost of the structure. In particular, structures whose value are above $250,000 paid less than they would if their rate was based on the RCV, because their rate was based on an average structure value that is much less than their actual structure value. For additional discussion of RCV, see CRS Report R45999, *National Flood Insurance Program: The Current Rating Structure and Risk Rating 2.0*, by Diane P. Horn.

[65] FEMA, *Risk Rating 2.0: Equity In Action*, https://www.fema.gov/flood-insurance/risk-rating.

[66] For additional information about Risk Rating 2.0, see CRS Report R45999, *National Flood Insurance Program: The Current Rating Structure and Risk Rating 2.0*, by Diane P. Horn; and CRS Insight IN11777, *National Flood Insurance Program Risk Rating 2.0: Frequently Asked Questions*, by Diane P. Horn.

[67] 42 U.S.C. §4015(e).

[68] See Table 1 in CRS Insight IN11777, *National Flood Insurance Program Risk Rating 2.0: Frequently Asked Questions*, by Diane P. Horn.

seeing a decrease.[69] The impending rate raises will vary from $120 to $240 or more annually. According to FEMA, 75% of primary residences would see an increase greater than 18% under Risk Rating 2.0 if the statutory limit did not exist.

FEMA estimates that 50% of policies will be at their full risk rate after five years and after 10 years, 90% of policies will be at their full risk rate.[70]

As full risk-based premiums are phased in under Risk Rating 2.0, some policyholders could be faced with large price increases either because they are currently buying coverage at subsidized rates, or because the new rating system indicates that they now have a higher risk, or both.

## Affordability of NFIP Premiums

The introduction of Risk Rating 2.0 has renewed concerns that full risk-based premiums could be unaffordable for some households and could lead property owners to either purchase lower amounts of coverage or choose not to purchase flood insurance at all. It has been suggested that some property owners might not be able to afford to remain in their homes if flood insurance premiums were too high.[71] Such increases raise issues of equity, as well as affordability. Premium increases under Risk Rating 2.0 may have the greatest effect on low- and moderate-income policyholders and communities,[72] as well as other potential impacts. For example, if homeowners and renters drop their insurance because of affordability issues, it may affect their ability to receive FEMA disaster assistance, for which they are required to obtain and maintain flood insurance. In addition, there may be locations where premium increases have adverse effects on a community as a whole if premiums increase for a large number of residents. For example, higher flood insurance rates could affect property values and the ability of property owners to sell their properties

---

[69] FEMA, *Risk Rating 2.0—National Rate Analysis*, https://www.fema.gov/sites/default/files/documents/fema_risk- rating-2.0-national-rate-analysis.pdf.

[70] Email from FEMA Congressional Affairs staff, April 16, 2021.

[71] GAO, *Flood Insurance: More Information Needed on Subsidized Properties*, GAO-13-607, July 3, 2013, p. 36, https://www.gao.gov/products/gao-13-607.

[72] See, for example, U.S. Congress, House Committee on Homeland Security, *Hearing on Ensuring Equity in Disaster Preparedness, Response, and Recovery*, Hearing Testimony of Chauncia Willis, Chief Executive Officer, Institute for Diversity and Inclusion in Emergency Management, 117th Cong., 1st sess., October 27, 2021, pp. 2-6, https://homeland.house.gov/imo/media/doc/2021-10-27-HRG-Testimony-Willis.pdf.

if potential buyers decide not to purchase a home in a high-risk area after determining the cost of flood insurance for the property.[73]

Higher premiums could potentially prevent achievement of the long-standing program objective of increasing the number of properties covered by flood insurance.[74] If NFIP policyholders were to cancel their policies, the federal government could face increased costs in the form of FEMA disaster assistance to these households.[75]

## Options to Reduce the Cost Burden on NFIP Policyholders

An ongoing area of congressional interest is how to reduce the cost burden of an individual NFIP policy.[76] Congress may consider several broad policy options which could reduce the cost of flood insurance to all policyholders through a variety of reforms to the structure of the NFIP. GAO noted that these options are not mutually exclusive and could potentially be combined,

depending on the policy priorities of Congress; however, the options all involve trade-offs and implementing any of them would likely be challenging.[77]

Congress could consider actions that would

- reduce the amount that policyholders pay through the introduction of a mean- tested affordability program;
- reduce the amount that individual policyholders pay by increasing participation in the NFIP, which could distribute program costs among a larger insured population;
- increase income to the NFIP, which could be used to reduce policyholders' contributions to the costs of the program;
- reduce the NFIP debt and thus the amount that policyholders pay in interest on the debt; or
- increase mitigation activities, which may reduce flood damages and thus flood claims, which could reduce the amount that policyholders have to pay for claims.

---

[73] GAO, *Overview of GAO's Past Work on the National Flood Insurance Program*, GAO-14-297R, April 9, 2014, p. 20, https://www.gao.gov/products/GAO-14-297R.

[74] *NRC Affordability Report 1*, p. 2.

[75] *NRC Affordability Report 1*, p. 64.

[76] GAO Solvency, p. 24.

[77] GAO Solvency, p. 10.

This report identifies potential options in the above categories that could lead to reductions in the amount that NFIP policyholders have to pay.

## Introduce a Means-Tested Affordability Program

Assistance through an affordability program could offset part or all of the cost of insurance through a number of approaches, which differ in the ways to measure when a premium might impose a cost burden on a policyholder. There are no objective definitions of affordability for flood insurance, nor are there objective thresholds to define "affordable" premiums either for an individual property owner or renter, or for any group of property owners or renters.[78] Although a lower insurance premium clearly is more affordable than a higher one, there is no objective threshold that separates affordable premiums from unaffordable premiums. The threshold for defining when an insurance program creates a cost burden requires making a policy judgment.[79] For example, GAO estimated that 47%-74% of policyholders could be eligible for subsidies if income eligibility was set at 80% or 140% of area median income (AMI), respectively.[80]

Policymakers will need to select which measure(s) will be used to target assistance to make flood insurance more affordable. They will also need to consider who will receive such assistance (e.g., only homeowners or also renters, only existing policyholders or also households that purchase flood insurance after the affordability program has begun). For example, if households without current NFIP insurance, who may have been deterred from buying insurance because of the cost, were not able to participate in an affordability program, it might exclude eligible low-income households. This could potentially raise questions of equity.

GAO has suggested in a number of reports that an affordability program that addresses the goals of encouraging consumer participation and promoting resilience could provide means-tested assistance through appropriations rather than through discounted premiums, and prioritize mitigation to reduce risk.[81] Such programs may differ in how to measure when a premium might impose a cost burden on a policyholder. Means-tested affordability assistance could be in the form of a capped-premiums approach, an income-based approach, a

---

[78] NRC Affordability Report 1, p. 80.
[79] NRC Affordability Report 1, pp. 79-80.
[80] GAO Affordability Assistance, pp. 22-23.
[81] GAO Solvency, p. 27.

housing-burden-based approach, a combined income- and housing burden-based approach, and a community characteristics approach.

In May 2022, FEMA submitted 17 legislative proposals to Congress outlining multiple reforms and actions to consider to reform the NFIP. One of these proposals was for a mean-tested assistance program to offer low- and moderate-income current and prospective policyholders a graduated premium discount.[82]

### *Options for a Means-Tested Affordability Program*

1) *Target premium discounts or subsidies to qualifying households.* NFIP subsidies are currently tied to a property. Implementing a means-tested approach could decouple the subsidy from the property and instead attach it to the policyholder or group of policyholders on the basis of financial need.[83] This could take the form of discounted rates or vouchers, where policyholders would be charged a full-risk premium but would receive a subsidy to cover the difference between what they are deemed able to pay and the full-risk rate premium. Policymakers might also choose to target assistance to households that are flood insurance cost-burdened and are required to purchase flood insurance. However, policyholders will also need to decide which properties are considered when determining a household's eligibility; for example, assistance could be limited to primary residences.[84]
   a) *Capped premiums approach.* Under a capped premium approach, a flood insurance premium is defined as unaffordable if it is greater than a specified percentage of the coverage of the policy.[85] For example, HFIAA directed FEMA to strive to minimize the number of policies with annual premiums that exceed 1% of the total coverage provided by the policy.[86] A capped premium approach does not consider policyholders' resources and other expenses, and this option could provide subsidies to households which may not have financial need.[87]

---

[82] FEMA, Legislative Proposals for the National Flood Insurance Program, https://www.fema.gov/sites/default/files/documents/fema_flood-insurance-reform-proposal_5242022.pdf.

[83] *GAO Affordability Assistance*, p. 11.

[84] Different options for an NFIP affordability program are discussed in more detail in "Introduce a Means-Tested Affordability Program."

[85] *NRC Affordability Report 1*, p. 81.

[86] 42 U.S.C. §4015(j).

[87] GAO Affordability Assistance, p. 18.

b) *Income-based approach.* An income-based approach to affordability assumes that flood insurance imposes a cost burden and thus is unaffordable for any household whose income is below a specified threshold. That standard could be based on median income for the area or federal poverty guidelines, or other criteria. For example, to be eligible for certain federal housing programs, individual households must meet specific income limits expressed as a percentage of the area median income (AMI).[88] An NFIP affordability program based on individuals' or households' income could use similar measures.[89] Means testing would add administrative complexity to the NFIP, but could be designed similarly to existing means-tested programs offered by the federal government.[90] Under an income-based approach, lower-income households would be responsible for paying for a portion of the premium, with FEMA covering the remainder of the premium amount. As household income levels rise, the portion of the premium that would be covered by FEMA would decrease.[91] FEMA noted that such a program would be relatively straightforward to implement; however, it could also provide benefits to households for which flood insurance is not unaffordable (e.g., households with low incomes but substantial assets).[92]

c) *Housing burden-based approach.* A housing cost approach considers not only a household's income but also housing costs, and assesses the ratio of housing costs to income when the NFIP premium is added to other housing costs. Under this approach, policymakers would have to select (or delegate selection of) a threshold, usually expressed as a percentage, at which the ratio of housing costs to income is judged to become unaffordable. One way to identify housing burden is through the use of the PITI ratio: the ratio of mortgage principal and interest (PI), property taxes (T), and insurance (I), including flood insurance, to

---

[88] See Department of Housing and Urban Development, *Methodology for Calculating FY2020 Medians*, https://www.huduser.gov/portal/datasets/il/il20/Medians-Methodology-FY20r.pdf.

[89] *GAO Affordability Assistance*, p. 12.

[90] *GAO Affordability Assistance*, pp. 11-15.

[91] FEMA, *An Affordability Framework for the National Flood Insurance Program*, 2018 (hereinafter *FEMA Affordability Framework*), p. 6, https://www.fema.gov/media-library/assets/documents/163171.

[92] *FEMA Affordability Framework*, p. 26.

household income. A comparable measure of housing burden for renters is the ratio of rent plus insurance to household income.[93] Previous work has shown that the PITI ratio is highly correlated with household income, so a program basing eligibility on the PITI ratio may effectively target lower-income households.[94] FEMA suggested in its Affordability Framework that it would consider flood insurance unaffordable if flood insurance causes the ratio of PITI to income to exceed 0.3 to 0.4, cutoffs that are taken from both HUD and private mortgage industry standards.[95] Based on an analysis of linked NFIP policy data and household income and Census Bureau American Community Survey (ACS) housing cost data,[96] FEMA found that the PITI ratio exceeded 0.4 for approximately 12% of homeowners with flood insurance policies in SFHAs.[97] FEMA's analysis found that the PITI ratio for renters (defined as gross rent over income) is higher than those for homeowners, with 33% of renters inside SFHAs and 27% of renters outside SFHAs with a PITI ratio over 0.47, and concluded that by this definition, flood insurance is unaffordable for a substantial percentage of renters.[98]

The housing cost burden approach might create some potentially perverse incentives by providing larger benefits for households potentially overextended on housing costs, and smaller benefits for households who were more frugal in making their choices. This approach may also miss some households that may be of concern to policymakers and could potentially steer benefits away from some low-income policyholders. For example, a household without a mortgage may have a low income but also a low PITI ratio and thus

---

[93] FEMA Affordability Framework, p. 15.

[94] Lloyd Dixon, Noreen Clancy, Benjamin M. Miller, et al., The Cost and Affordability of Flood Insurance in New York City: Economic Impacts of Rising Premiums and Policy Options for One- to Four- Family Homes, Rand Corporation, RAND RR1776, Santa Monica, CA, April 2017, pp. 25-26, https://www.rand.org/pubs/research_reports/RR1776.html.

[95] FEMA Affordability Framework, p. 15.

[96] United States Census Bureau, American Community Survey (ACS), https://www.census.gov/programs-surveys/acs.

[97] FEMA Affordability Framework, p. 6.

[98] FEMA Affordability Framework, pp. 16-18.

would be ineligible for assistance under this approach. In particular, it may not provide benefits to retirees who have paid off their mortgages or low-income households that have inherited a property mortgage-free. In general, households with access to credit would be more likely to qualify for assistance through the mortgage component of the PITI-ratio.

Another concern with a PITI-based approach is that households in regions with high costs of living (and mortgage payments) might be more likely to benefit from the program than households in regions with lower costs of living.[99] In addition, households would need to provide data on income and housing expenses, which may cause administrative burdens for both the policyholders to provide and FEMA to verify the data.

d) Income and housing burden-based approach. The FEMA affordability framework also considered an approach where benefits are targeted at households that are both income- and housing-burdened (which it noted is similar to HUD's Section 8 rental housing assistance program). It used the thresholds of 120% of AMI and housing burdens above 40% of income.[100]

2) Target premium discounts or subsidies based on community characteristics. Rather than determine eligibility for affordability assistance based on characteristics of individual households, community characteristics could be considered as eligibility criteria.[101] For example, policyholders could make all households in a community eligible for assistance if a specified percentage of them would likely be eligible on the basis of their individual characteristics. Alternatively, all homeowners in a community could be considered eligible for assistance if the community's poverty rate is sufficiently high or the median income is sufficiently low.[102] This could reduce administrative costs by removing the need to establish eligibility of every household. Another potential eligibility criterion could be the engagement of state and local governments in certain mitigation

[99] FEMA Affordability Framework, p. 31.

[100] FEMA Affordability Framework, p. 29.

[101] For example, this could potentially make use of FEMA's National Risk Index, which combines a community's hazard risk, social vulnerability, and resilience to calculate a relative risk assessment. See FEMA, National Risk Index for Natural Hazards (NRI), https://www.fema.gov/flood-maps/products-tools/national-risk-index.

[102] NRC Affordability Report 1, p. 95.

activities.[103] However, because this option does not consider financial need, some policyholders who do not face an affordability issue with their flood insurance premiums may receive assistance, while policyholders who have affordability issues but do not live in an eligible community would not receive assistance.[104]

3) Require recipients of affordability assistance to invest in FEMA-approved cost- effective mitigation measures. For example, property owners could receive grants or loans to help mitigate their flood risk and be charged a premium rate that reflects their lower risk. Another option could be to offer a multiyear loan that could cover both mitigation measures and the annual loan cost.[105] Vouchers could also be used to help policyholders cover the cost of repaying mitigation loans.[106] This approach could potentially be targeted at properties that are most costly to the NFIP, such as repetitive loss[107] (RL) and severe repetitive loss (SRL) properties.

The Build Back Better Act,[108] as passed by the House on November 19, 2021, would have appropriated $600 million, to remain available until the end of FY2026, for a means-tested affordability program to provide assistance in the form of graduated discounts for insurance costs for covered properties. NFIP policyholders with a household income not more than 120% of AMI would have been eligible to participate in the program. Covered properties were defined as primary residences for structures with one to four families, and primary residences of renters. The affordability assistance would have provided a discount on all premiums, fees, and surcharges.

103 NRC Affordability Report 1, p. 90.

104 GAO Affordability Assistance, p. 17.

105 Howard Kunreuther, "Improving the National Flood Insurance Program," Behavioural Public Policy, July 9, 2018, pp. 1-15.

106 GAO Affordability Assistance, p. 46.

107 The statutory definition of a repetitive loss structure is a structure covered by a contract for flood insurance that (a) has incurred flood-related damage on two occasions, in which the cost of repair, on the average, equaled or exceeded 25% of the value of the structure at the time of each such flood event; and (b) at the time of the second incidence of flood-related damage, the contract for flood insurance contains increased cost of compliance coverage. See 42 U.S.C.§4121(a)(7).

108 H.R. 5376, as passed by the House on November 19, 2021.

## Reduce the Amount That Policyholders Pay to the NFIP

A means-tested affordability program is only one possible way of reducing the cost burden to policyholders, and Congress could consider other changes to the NFIP to reduce the amount that policyholders pay.

### *Options to Reduce the Amount That Policyholders Pay to the NFIP*

1) *Reduce cross-subsidies.* Cross-subsidies are being phased out under Risk Rating 2.0. This should reduce premiums for policyholders who are paying more to cross-subsidize other policyholders. However, premiums for properties that are currently subsidized are expected to increase as cross-subsidies are reduced. Alternatively, the income to the NFIP will be reduced if the costs that are currently cross-subsidized are not passed on to other policyholders.
2) *Reduce or eliminate fees or surcharges paid by NFIP policyholders.* This would reduce flood insurance premiums but would also reduce income to the NFIP. Reduced fees and surcharges might encourage additional participation in the NFIP. However, FEMA does not have authority to eliminate all of these; elimination of some fees and surcharges[109] would require action by Congress.
3) *Reduce premiums or increase subsidies.* This could reduce the amount that policyholders pay to the NFIP but would also reduce income to the program unless Congress were to provide additional funding for the NFIP. In addition, increasing subsidies would run counter to the principles established by FEMA for Risk Rating 2.0.
4) *Eliminate the mandatory purchase requirement.* If the purchase of flood insurance were voluntary, those who could not afford NFIP premiums would not have to incur the expense. However, it is likely that take-up rates for NFIP policies would drop substantially if homeowners were not required to purchase flood insurance.[110] As a result, households would need to rely on their own financial resources or federal assistance for post-flood recovery. In addition, the presence of uninsured properties may reduce the resilience of a community more generally after a flood and may necessitate additional disaster assistance from the federal government.

---

[109] For example, the Federal Policy Fee, Reserve Fund Assessment, and the HFIAA surcharge.
[110] *NRC Affordability Report 1*, p. 113.

5) *Allow higher deductibles on NFIP policies.* The maximum deductible is currently $1,250 if the building coverage amount exceeds $100,000. Otherwise, the deductible is $1,000.[111] Congress could increase the maximum deductible or FEMA could encourage policyholders to choose a larger deductible.[112] According to FEMA, increasing the deductible to the maximum amount could reduce NFIP premiums by 40%.[113] However, although higher deductibles could decrease premium payments, in the event of a flood they might impose hardships on people. This could be a particular problem for low-income households who must pay for damage below the deductible amount, and could lead to an increase in demand for federal disaster assistance.
6) *Cap the rate at which NFIP premiums could increase.* The current maximum rate of allowable increase was set in HFIAA, with maximum rate increases for primary residences limited to 5%-18% per year. Premiums on other categories of properties can be increased at 25% annually.[114] Congress could set a lower cap on the rate at which premiums can be increased.[115]
7) *Cap NFIP premiums.* This could establish a ceiling beyond which premiums could not increase, and thus could help lower premiums of policyholders whose premiums are increasing.[116] However, this approach does not consider policyholders' income, assets, or other expenses and therefore does not necessarily take financial need into account.
8) *Allow communities to pay all or part of flood insurance premiums for their residents.* Community payment of individual policyholders' flood insurance premiums could shift the issue of affordability to the

---

[111] FEMA, *Flood Insurance Manual, 3. How to Write*, p. 3-42, revised October 1, 2022, https://www.fema.gov/sites/default/files/documents/fema_nfip-flood-insurance-full-manual_102022.pdf.

[112] CBO Affordability, p. 26.

[113] FEMA, Help Clients Pay Less for Flood Insurance, https://agents.floodsmart.gov/retention/costs.

[114] See the section of this report on "Risk Rating 2.0" for further information on the rates at which premiums can be increased.

[115] For example, S. 3128 and H.R. 5802 in the 117th Congress would cap annual premium increases at 9%.

[116] In the first year of Risk Rating 2.0, FEMA has capped the annual premium for a single-family primary residence at $12,125. Some of these properties have previously been paying as much as $45,925. This represents the first time that a dollar cap has been applied to the NFIP. FEMA, Briefing on Risk Rating 2.0 for CRS, March 29, 2021.

local level and allow each community to address it in the way that it sees fit. For example, a community could cross-subsidize the assessment of premiums, or use other community funds to offset high premiums for low-income or moderate-income households. A community could also recover all or part of the costs through measures such as special assessments levied on covered properties.

## Increase NFIP Participation

A long-standing objective of the NFIP has been to increase purchases of flood insurance policies, and this objective was one motivation for keeping NFIP premiums affordable when the program was established.[117] In designing the NFIP to help address floodplain management objectives,

Congress has generally emphasized the need for high policy take-up rates.[118] Adding new policyholders, however, would not improve the finances of the NFIP unless the new policies increase receipts more than they increase expected claims and other expenses.[119] GAO has noted that increased consumer participation could increase the size and scope of the NFIP and potentially increase federal fiscal exposure. However, it suggested, this could be reduced by implementing full-risk rates and balanced by an increasing number of lower-risk properties.[120]

### *The Mandatory Purchase Requirement*

Over time, the desire to increase take-up rates has led to a number of program changes, including the introduction of the mandatory purchase requirement (MPR). In a community that participates or has participated in the NFIP, owners of properties in the mapped SFHA are required to purchase flood insurance as a condition of receiving a federally backed mortgage. Under the MPR, federally backed or regulated lenders require borrowers to purchase and maintain a flood insurance policy when they provide a mortgage to properties in the SFHA. The MPR is enforced by lenders rather than FEMA, and FEMA

[117] See 82 Stat. 577 for text in the original statute (Section 1308(b)(2) of P.L. 90-448). This language remains in statute; see 42 U.S.C. §4015(b)(2).

[118] *NRC Affordability Report 1*, p. 31.

[119] *CBO Affordability*, p. 24.

[120] *GAO Solvency*, p. 33.

does not have authority to enforce lender compliance with the MPR.[121] At least 10 federal entities oversee lenders' compliance.[122]

Compliance with the MPR directly affects the number of properties that have flood insurance, although the full extent of noncompliance with the MPR is not known.[123] However, NFIP take-up rates for flood insurance are generally low, even in areas subject to the MPR,[124] and policies may not be maintained after purchase. For example, GAO found that about 28% of properties that were purchased in 2014 no longer had an NFIP policy by 2019.[125]

There is a large flood insurance gap in the United States, and many people that are exposed to flood risk are not covered by flood insurance. Currently the NFIP insures about 4.985 million structures in the United States,[126] and most of the remaining structures have no insurance to protect them from flood risk.[127] NFIP residential policies are nearly evenly divided between areas inside and outside the SFHA, but the majority of nonresidential policies are inside the SFHA. This is relevant to flood insurance affordability because flood insurance premiums are generally higher in SHFAs.[128] Expanding the MPR could increase premiums and create affordability concerns that could warrant having an affordability assistance program.[129]

In addition to the risk of uninsured losses to individual households and businesses, the NFIP could achieve greater financial stability with a wider policy base; in particular, through finding ways to increase coverage outside the SFHA. According to the American Academy of Actuaries, increasing the number of properties covered for flood, particularly in lower-risk areas, will not only protect consumers, lending institutions, and local communities, but

---

[121] GAO, GAO Mandatory Purchase Requirement, p. 9.

[122] GAO Mandatory Purchase Requirement, p. 4 and p. 10.

[123] GAO Mandatory Purchase Requirement, p. 35 and p. 45.

[124] Carolyn Kousky, Howard Kunreuther, Michael LaCour-Little, et al., "Flood Risk and the U.S. Housing Market," Journal of Housing Research, vol. 29, no. S.1 (November 30, 2020), pp. S3-S24.

[125] GAO Mandatory Purchase Requirement, p. 32.

[126] FEMA, Watermark, FY2021, Third Quarter, https://www.fema.gov/sites/default/files/documents/fema_fima- watermark-FY2021-Q3.pdf.

[127] American Academy of Actuaries, The National Flood Insurance Program: Challenges and Solutions, Washington, DC, September 25, 2019, p. 4, https://www.actuary.org/sites/default/files/2019-09/flood9.19.pdf.

[128] FEMA Affordability Framework, p. 8.

[129] FEMA Affordability Framework, p. 43.

will also improve the financial stability of the NFIP by achieving a better spread of risk.[130]

### *Options to Increase NFIP Participation*

1) *Ensure full compliance with the mandatory purchase requirement.* This option would require lenders to ensure that all mortgagees subject to the MPR purchase and maintain flood insurance. GAO's view is that measuring compliance with the MPR would require property- specific data on mortgage, flood zone determinations, and flood insurance policies compiled at loan origination and at various points during the life of the loan. GAO noted that this would entail establishing reporting requirements on lenders to provide relevant mortgage data, determining an appropriate authority to receive and compare these data, and determining the costs and benefits of obtaining these data.[131] In a recent report, GAO described challenges to understanding the full extent of noncompliance with the MPR.[132] Given the absence of a full understanding of compliance with the MPR, GAO suggested that there were a number of actions that FEMA could take, despite FEMA's limited statutory role related to the MPR, to examine trends and patterns related to consumer participation and potential noncompliance. Policy and claims data could be used to develop strategies for addressing noncompliance. For example, GAO recommended that FEMA could review its own data to identify patterns and trends and to develop policies for addressing noncompliance. In particular, an analysis of NFIP policy data could provide information on how long NFIP policies are maintained over time and when flood insurance policies are dropped. Further, an examination of the number and cost of claims associated with the policies that were dropped could help FEMA to understand some of the financial effects that noncompliance may be having on both consumers and the federal government. Finally, analysis of FEMA's policy data could provide information on the effectiveness of changes

[130] American Academy of Actuaries, The National Flood Insurance Program: Challenges and Solutions, Washington, DC, September 25, 2019, p. 82, https://www.actuary.org/sites/default/files/2019-09/flood9.19.pdf.

[131] GAO, *Flood Insurance: Extent of Noncompliance with Purchase Requirements Is Unknown*, GAO-02-39-6, June21, 2002, p. 4, https://www.gao.gov/products/GAO-02-396.

[132] GAO Mandatory Purchase Requirement, p. 29.

to the MPR, such as escrow requirements, in ensuring policies are maintained for the life of mortgage loans.[133]

2) *Require policyholders subject to the MPR to opt out rather than opt in.* Research in behavioral economics has found that, in many circumstances, individuals tend to stay with default options. It has been suggested that coupling flood insurance to homeowners' insurance as a default, while still giving individuals the option to decline coverage (opt out) if not required by the lender, might lead more people to purchase flood insurance.[134]
3) *Offer multiyear flood insurance policies.* The tendency to maintain the status quo is thought to increase the likelihood that insured individuals will maintain a multiyear policy for the length of the contract, whereas they may decide not to renew an annual policy after it expires.[135]
4) *Expand the MPR to all structures with federally backed mortgages in NFIP communities, not just those in the SFHA*. Both GAO and FEMA have suggested that the MPR could potentially be expanded to more (or all) mortgage loans made by federally regulated lending institutions for properties in communities participating in the NFIP. This would increase the consumer participation rate in the NFIP and potentially balance the NFIP portfolio with an increased number of lower-risk properties.[136] According to GAO, some private insurers have indicated that such a federal mandate could help achieve the level of consumer participation necessary to make the private sector comfortable with providing flood insurance coverage by increasing the number of policyholders, which would allow private insurers to diversify and manage the risk of their flood insurance portfolio and address concerns about adverse selection.[137] This would require congressional action to change the provision in the National Flood Insurance Act of 1968 that links the purchase of flood insurance to

---

[133] GAO Mandatory Purchase Requirement, pp. 31-32.

[134] Carolyn Kousky, Brett Lingle, Howard Kunreuther, et al., Moving the Needle on Closing the Flood Insurance Gap, Wharton Risk Management and Decision Processes Center, Issue Brief, Philadelphia, PA, February 13, 2019, p. 2, https://riskcenter.wharton.upenn.edu/wp-content/uploads/2019/02/Moving-the-Needle-on-Closing-the-Flood-Insurance-Gap.pdf.

[135] NRC Affordability Report 1, p. 62.

[136] GAO Solvency, p. 29 and p. 33.

[137] GAO, Flood Insurance: Strategies for Increasing Private Sector Involvement, GAO-47-127, January 2014, p. 23, https://www.gao.gov/products/GAO-14-127.

financial assistance.[138] Congressional action would not be needed to change the definition of an "area having special flood hazards," which is only defined in regulation[139] rather than in statute. This option would also require lenders to enforce the expanded MPR.

5) *Expand the MPR to all structures in the SFHA, not just those with federally backed mortgages.* The Association of State Floodplain Managers suggested that all properties within the SFHA should be required to have flood insurance, not just those with federally backed mortgages.[140] This would require every homeowner and business mapped into the SFHA to purchase flood insurance, whether or not they have a mortgage. This would require congressional action to change the provision in the NFIA that links the purchase of flood insurance to financial assistance in any area identified by the FEMA administrator as an area having special flood hazards.[141] This option would also require lenders to enforce the expanded MPR, or require the introduction of another method of enforcement.
6) *Require all structures in the floodplain (both the 1%-annual-chance floodplain and the 0.2%-annual-chance floodplain) to purchase flood insurance.* This would require all structures in the wider floodplain to purchase flood insurance. Currently, properties outside the SFHA are not required to purchase flood insurance but may voluntarily purchase a lower- cost NFIP policy. According to FEMA, on average about 40% of NFIP claims come from properties outside the SFHA.[142]
7) *Base the MPR on property-level expected damages instead of the boundary of the SFHA.* This approach could, for example, require the purchase of flood insurance for any properties with expected losses above a defined amount.
8) *Offer community flood insurance policies.* A community insurance option would allow a community to purchase a group flood insurance policy on behalf of all properties that are at risk of flooding. The community would pay a single premium for the group policy. Community insurance would increase take-up rates by automatically

[138] 42 U.S.C. §4012a(a).

[139] 44 C.F.R. §59.1.

[140] Association of State Floodplain Managers, Inc., *Rethinking the NFIP*, ASFPM Comments on NFIP Reform, January 11, 2011, p. 5, http://www.floods.org/ace-files/documentlibrary/National_Policy/Rethinking_the_NFIP_Comments_from_ASFPM_1-11-11.pdf.

[141] 42 U.S.C. §4012a(a).

[142] FEMA, *Answers to Questions About the NFIP*, p. 51, https://agents.floodsmart.gov/sites/default/files/fema-answers-to-questions-about-the-NFIP.pdf.

insuring all members of a participating community. This could potentially exacerbate affordability problems by forcing all members of a community to pay flood insurance premiums. However, if Congress believes that community flood insurance should be encouraged, it could choose to provide funds in order to offer discounted premiums, or to offer coverage to all properties in both the 1%-annual-chance floodplain and the 0.2%-annual-chance floodplain in order to promote resilience.[143]

9) *Require all homeowners and businesses that receive disaster assistance for flood damage to obtain and maintain flood insurance.* This requirement is already in place for properties that receive FEMA Public Assistance, FEMA Individuals and Households Program assistance, and Small Business Administration Disaster Loans. Recipients of funding from these programs are required to obtain and maintain flood insurance as a condition of receiving future disaster assistance for a flood event, or forfeit future disaster assistance for flooding. Similar requirements could be introduced for all residential and commercial properties that receive disaster assistance for flooding.

## Increase NFIP Income

The NFIP is different from other disaster assistance in that it is not directly funded by taxpayers. The majority of the NFIP's income is provided by policyholders' premiums, fees, and surcharges, which are used to pay claims for covered flood damages. In addition, there are charges added to the premium to cover the administrative costs of the program, including claims handling by private insurers, and to build up a financial reserve to cover catastrophic-loss years. As the NFIP currently operates, rates for full risk-based policies are intended to cover the expected cost associated with all potential flood events, including less likely, high-cost events.[144]

The NFIP has three sources of funding: (1) premiums, fees, and surcharges from NFIP policyholders; (2) annual appropriations for some of the

[143] See, for example, Carolyn Kousky and Leonard Shabman, *A Proposed Design for Community Flood Insurance*, Resources for the Future, Washington, DC, December 2015, pp. 21-23, https://media.rff.org/archive/files/document/file/RFF-Rpt-KouskyShabman-CommunityFloodIns.pdf.

[144] CBO Affordability, p. 26.

costs of flood mapping; and (3) borrowing from the U.S. Treasury when the balance of the National Flood Insurance Fund (NFIF) has been insufficient to pay claims. The only continuing direct appropriations to the NFIP are to supplement floodplain mapping activities; the remainder of flood mapping costs are paid by NFIP policyholders through the Federal Policy Fee (FPF). According to FEMA, in FY2020, 36.4% of spending on flood mapping came from the FPF and 63.6% from appropriations.[145] In recent years, appropriations to the NFIP for flood mapping have varied between $100 million and $275.5 million, an amount that represented 2.1% to 5.8% of the NFIP's income. These appropriations amounted to $1.79 billion between FY2015 and FY2021.[146]

In contrast, for example, the federal crop insurance program has permanent, indefinite funding authority: annual funding comes from both mandatory and discretionary appropriations.[147] The average cost of the program is projected at nearly $8 billion per year for FY2021 to FY2025 and to remain around that level for FY2026 to FY2030.[148] On average, the federal government pays roughly 60% of agricultural producers' insurance premiums.[149] CBO projects that the federal crop insurance program will cost almost $40 billion for the five-year period FY2021 to FY2025 and more than $80 billion for the 10-year period FY2021 to FY2030.[150]

Because close to 95% of the NFIP's costs are borne by policyholders, anything that increases NFIP income from sources other than policyholders, or that reduces NFIP costs paid by policyholders, ultimately reduces the amount that NFIP policyholders have to pay. In addition to paying NFIP claims, policyholders also pay the costs of many noninsurance activities in the public interest, such as flood mitigation grants and floodplain mapping and management.[151] The benefits of such tasks are not directly measured in the

---

[145] Email from FEMA Congressional Affairs staff, January 25, 2021.

[146] See Table 5 in CRS Report R44593, Introduction to the National Flood Insurance Program (NFIP), by Diane P. Horn and Baird Webel.

[147] For more information, see CRS Report R46686, *Federal Crop Insurance: A Primer*, by Stephanie Rosch.

[148] Ibid., pp. 3-4.

[149] CBO, *USDA Mandatory Farm Programs—CBO's Baseline as of March 6, 2020*, March 19, 2020, p. 1, https://www.cbo.gov/system/files/2020-03/51317-2020-03-usda.pdf.

[150] Ibid., p. 24.

[151] For example, in FY2022 NFIP policyholders paid $199 million for floodplain management and flood mapping and $175 million on flood mitigation assistance. See Table 5 in CRS Report R44593, *Introduction to the National Flood Insurance Program (NFIP)*, by Diane P. Horn and Baird Webel.

NFIP's financial results from underwriting flood insurance.[152] One way to reduce NFIP policyholders' cost burden would be for the federal government to pay some of the costs that are currently paid for by NFIP policyholders.[153] CBO noted that, like debt service, mapping and mitigation costs are not related to current NFIP policies, and suggested that Congress could shift those costs to taxpayers by funding those activities out of general revenue.[154]

## Options to Increase NFIP Income

1) *Charge actuarially sound rates for all policies and/or increase fees and surcharges.* Subsidies are being phased out under Risk Rating 2.0, but further reform of the rating system could be considered. This could be done by eliminating all subsidies or increasing the rate at which subsidies are phased out. Policyholders who are cross-subsidizing other policies could benefit from this. However, as long as the NFIP is primarily funded by policyholders, such an action could increase premiums for other policyholders.
2) *Reduce the number of Repetitive Loss and Severe Repetitive Loss properties.* To the extent that other NFIP policyholders are subsidizing RL and SRL properties, reducing the number of such properties, either through mitigation or other means, could reduce the cross- subsidy paid by other NFIP policyholders and thus their premiums.
3) *Prioritize sales of policies that are more likely to contribute to a net surplus.* CBO has suggested that FEMA could be directed to increase its marketing and publicity efforts, and to prioritize sales of particular types of policies; for example, commercial and nonresidential

152 American Academy of Actuaries Flood Insurance Work Group, *The National Flood Insurance Program: Challenges and Solutions*, April 2017, p. 79, http://www.actuary.org/files/publications/FloodMonograph.04192017.pdf.

153 The Infrastructure Investment and Jobs Act (IIJA), P.L. 117-58, in appropriated $3.5 billion for the Flood Mitigation Assistance (FMA) grant program, with $700 million for each of FY2022 to FY2026. NFIP policyholders contributed an additional $100 million towards the FMA program in FY2022. See Department of Homeland Security (DHS), *Notice of Funding Opportunity (NOFO), Fiscal Year 2022 Flood Mitigation Assistance*, August 5, 2022, p. 6, https://www.fema.gov/sites/default/files/documents/fema_fy22-fma-nofo_08052022_0.pdf.

154 CBO Affordability, p. 26.

properties that pay a higher HFIAA surcharge.[155] CBO noted that the success of such an approach would depend on FEMA's ability to target the growth in policies.[156]

4) *Increase appropriations to the NFIP.* The only direct annual appropriations for the NFIP are for a portion of the costs of the mapping and risk analysis program. Congress could appropriate additional funding to the NFIP, which would reduce the amount that policyholders would have to pay to cover the costs of the program.[157]

## Reduce NFIP Debt

The NFIP was not designed to retain funding to cover claims for truly extreme events; instead, the National Flood Insurance Act of 1968 allows the program to borrow money from the Treasury for such events. For most of the NFIP's history, the program has generally been able to cover its costs, borrowing relatively small amounts from the Treasury to pay claims and then repaying the loans with interest. Currently, Congress has authorized FEMA to borrow no more than \$30.425 billion from the U.S. Treasury to operate the NFIP.[158] The NFIP currently has \$9.9 billion of remaining borrowing authority.[159]

The NFIP was forced to borrow heavily to pay claims in the aftermath of three catastrophic flood seasons—the 2005 hurricane season (particularly Hurricanes Katrina, Rita, and Wilma), Hurricane Sandy in 2012, and the 2017 hurricane season (Hurricanes Harvey, Irma, and Maria).[160] On October 26, 2017, Congress cancelled \$16 billion of NFIP debt, making it possible for the program to pay claims for Hurricanes Harvey, Irma, and Maria.[161] This represents the first time that NFIP debt has been cancelled. The NFIP has not borrowed from the Treasury since November 2017.

---

[155] For information on the HFIAA surcharge, see the section in this report on "Fees and Surcharges."

[156] *CBO Affordability*, p. 24.

[157] See the discussion of the Infrastructure Investment and Jobs Act, P.L. 117-58, in point 36 in the section of this report on "Options to Encourage Community-Level Flood Risk Reduction Measures."

[158] P.L. 113-1.

[159] FEMA, *Watermark, FY2022, Third Quarter*, https://www.fema.gov/sites/default/files/documents/fema_fy22-q3- watermark.pdf.

[160] For details of NFIP borrowing, see CRS Insight IN10784, *National Flood Insurance Program Borrowing Authority*, by Diane P. Horn.

[161] P.L. 115-72, Title III, §308.

Only current and future participants in the NFIP are responsible for repaying NFIP debt, as the insurance program itself owes the debt to the Treasury and pays for accruing interest on that debt through the premium revenues of policyholders. Under its current authorization, the only means the NFIP has to pay off the debt is through the accrual of premium revenues in excess of outgoing claims, and from payments made out of the Reserve Fund.[162]

Reducing NFIP debt could lessen the need to raise premiums to pay interest and principal on existing debt. For example, from FY2006 to FY2016 (i.e., since the NFIP borrowed funds following Hurricane Katrina), the NFIP has paid $2.82 billion in principal repayments and $5.62 billion in interest to service the debt through the premiums collected on insurance policies.[163] Currently the NFIP is paying over $400 million a year—over $1 million in interest per day—on the debt accrued from past events.[164] For example, the NFIP paid $438 million in interest in FY2020[165] and $418 million in FY2019.[166] CBO estimated that retiring the debt would require increasing annual payments from policyholders. For example, paying off the debt over 30 years at an interest rate of 2.5% would entail annual payments of roughly $1.2 billion for principal and interest.[167]

In addition to charging policyholders enough to pay for their current risk of flood losses, FEMA has collected a reserve fund assessment since 2012, and an additional surcharge from all NFIP policyholders since 2014 to help repay program debt. This creates a potential inequity because policyholders are charged not only for the flood losses that they are expected to incur, but also for losses incurred by past policyholders. Charging current policyholders for debt incurred in past years runs contrary to generally accepted actuarial principles and private insurers' pricing practices.[168] According to actuarial principles, a premium rate is based on the risk of future losses and does not

162 42 U.S.C. §4017a.

163 FEMA, *Watermark, FY2022, Third Quarter*, https://www.fema.gov/sites/default/files/documents/fema_fy22-q3-watermark.pdf.

164 FEMA, *National Flood Insurance Program Debt Repayment Report as of September 30, 2019*, September 15, 2020, p. 10. Provided to CRS by FEMA Congressional Affairs Staff, January 4, 2020.

165 FEMA, *Watermark, FY2021, Third Quarter*, https://www.fema.gov/sites/default/files/documents/fema_fima-watermark-FY2021-Q3.pdf.

166 FEMA, *National Flood Insurance Program Debt Repayment Report as of September 30, 2019*, September 15, 2020, p. 10. Provided to CRS by FEMA Congressional Affairs Staff, January 4, 2020.

167 *CBO Affordability*, p. 26.

168 *GAO Solvency*, p. 16.

include past costs. For example, if in prior years a private insurance company's claims payments had exceeded the premiums collected, it would not recall those payments from current or future policyholders.[169]

GAO has considered the option of eliminating FEMA's debt to the Treasury, suggesting that if the debt were eliminated, FEMA could reallocate funds used for debt repayment for other purposes such as building a reserve fund and program operations, and arguing that this would also be more equitable for current policyholders and consistent with actuarial principles.[170] CBO suggested that forgiving the NFIP's debt would eliminate the need for large premium increases that would otherwise be required to repay the debt.[171]

An affordability report by the National Research Council (NRC) of the National Academy of Sciences considered the option of forgiving all or part of the NFIP debt within a larger affordability context, suggesting that after forgiving all or part of the NFIP debt, Congress could designate the Treasury as reinsurer for the NFIP. It proposed that Congress could, for example, explicitly state that when the total annual losses in the NFIP exceeded some designated threshold (e.g., $2 billion to $6 billion, perhaps on the basis of the average of noncatastrophic historical claims years), the Treasury could provide funds for the NFIP to honor all claims. The funds could be provided through the Disaster Relief Fund and, if needed, by an emergency supplemental appropriation. The NRC suggested that, taken together, those two actions could result in lower NFIP premiums, enhance affordability, and in turn lead to less spending on disaster assistance.

This would incur occasional costs by designating the Treasury as the source of funds for payment of claims above the defined threshold in high-loss years but would not need to draw on the Treasury each year to provide assistance to policyholders who face unaffordable premiums.[172]

The Build Back Better Act, as passed by the House on November 19, 2021, would have cancelled the full $20.525 billion debt owed by the NFIP to the Treasury and directed FEMA to spend an amount equal to the interest that the NFIP would have paid in servicing the cancelled debt for flood mapping

---

[169] Ibid.
[170] Ibid.
[171] CBO Affordability, p. 26.
[172] NRC Affordability Report 1, pp. 110-111.

in FY2022 and FY2023. FEMA's legislative proposals for the NFIP also suggested cancelling the NFIP debt.[173]

***Options to Reduce NFIP Debt***

1) *Eliminate NFIP interest payments to Treasury.* The NFIP is currently paying over $400 million a year in interest.[174] If these interest payments were eliminated, this money could be made available to reduce NFIP premiums, fund additional mitigation measures, or fund other actions that could benefit NFIP policyholders.[175]
2) *Cancel all or part of NFIP debt.* Eliminating the NFIP debt would require Congress to cancel debt outright, to appropriate funds for FEMA to repay the debt, or to change the law to eliminate the requirement that FEMA repay the accumulated debt.[176] GAO has suggested that if FEMA's debt to the Treasury were eliminated, FEMA could reallocate funds used for debt repayment for other purposes such as building a reserve fund for catastrophic-loss years and/or program operations, which would arguably be more equitable for current policyholders.[177]
3) *Change the way that losses from catastrophic storms are financed.* If Congress were to authorize supplements from the Treasury to be used for making NFIP claims payments in catastrophic-loss years, this would reduce the cost to policyholders in paying these claims. For example, FEMA's report to Congress on privatization of the NFIP concluded that it is difficult to imagine a practical system of flood insurance in which there is not some level of government involvement in the flood risk financing chain. The report argued that when low-frequency, high-magnitude events occur, the government will ultimately play a role in paying for the economic costs associated with a catastrophic flood, whether or not it chooses to underwrite the

---

173 FEMA, Legislative Proposals for the National Flood Insurance Program, https://www.fema.gov/sites/default/files/documents/fema_flood-insurance-reform-proposal_5242022.pdf.

174 For example, the NFIP paid $415 million in interest in FY2019 and $438 million in FY2020. See FEMA, Watermark, FY2021, Third Quarter, https://www.fema.gov/sites/default/files/documents/fema_fima-watermark- FY2021-Q3.pdf.

175 For example, S. 3128 and H.R. 5802 in the 117th Congress would prohibit the Treasury from charging interest to the NFIP for the five-year period beginning on the date of enactment.

176 42 U.S.C. §4016.

177 *GAO Solvency*, p. 16.

risk.[178] The NFIP currently has no financial structure in place, other than borrowing from the Treasury, to guarantee it can pay claims from a catastrophic-loss year.

The American Academy of Actuaries has argued that neither private insurers nor the NFIP can fully absorb any level of catastrophic loss and continue to operate. It suggested that there is a maximum amount of short-term loss that can be fully funded by NFIP revenue; Congress could set a threshold for the maximum amount of losses that the NFIP would be expected to fund fully. Beyond that threshold, the federal government would assume responsibility for losses.[179]

4) *Purchase additional reinsurance.* The purchase of private market reinsurance[180] reduces the likelihood of FEMA needing to borrow from the Treasury to pay claims.[181] In addition, as GAO noted, reinsurance allows FEMA to price some of its flood risk up front through the premiums it pays to the reinsurers rather than borrowing from Treasury after a flood.[182] From a risk management perspective, using reinsurance to cover losses in only the more extreme years could help the federal government manage and reduce the volatility of its losses over time. Transfer of risk to the private sector through reinsurance, however, is unlikely to lower the overall cost of the NFIP because reinsurers understandably charge premiums to compensate for the risk they assume. The primary benefit of reinsurance is to transfer and manage risk rather than to reduce the NFIP's long-term

---

178 FEMA, *National Flood Insurance Program Report to Congress on Reinsuring NFIP Insurance Risk and Options for Privatizing the NFIP*, August 13, 2015, p. 56, http://www.floods.org/ace-files/documentlibrary/2012_NFIP_Reform/Reinsuring_NFIP_Insurance_Risk_and_Options_for_Privatizing_the_NFIP_Report.pdf.

179 American Academy of Actuaries Flood Insurance Work Group, *The National Flood Insurance Program: Challenges and Solutions*, April 2017, pp. 28, 31, and 80, http://www.actuary.org/files/publications/FloodMonograph.04192017.pdf.

180 Reinsurance is defined as a transaction between a primary insurer and another licensed (re)insurer where the reinsurer agrees to cover all or part of the losses and/or loss adjustment expenses of the primary insurer. See National Association of Insurance Commissioners, *Glossary of Insurance Terms*, http://www.naic.org/ consumer_glossary.htm#R.

181 FEMA began large-scale purchases of reinsurance in 2017. The specifics of each reinsurance purchase has varied, but in general, the reinsurance has been designed to pay a certain percentage of the losses from a single, large-scale event, with a higher percentage if losses are higher. See FEMA, *National Flood Insurance Program's Reinsurance Program*, https://www.fema.gov/flood-insurance/work-with-nfip/reinsurance.

182 *GAO Solvency*, p. 19.

fiscal exposure,[183] and the purchase of reinsurance would reduce future debt rather than make the program more affordable at present.

## Reduce Flood Damage Through Mitigation

FEMA defines mitigation as any sustained action to reduce or eliminate long-term risk to both people and property from natural hazards and their effects.[184] Flood mitigation creates safer communities and can save money for individuals and taxpayers. The importance of FEMA's Hazard Mitigation Assistance (HMA) programs is illustrated by research findings that for every $1 invested by FEMA in flood mitigation between 1993 and 2003, society as a whole saved $7 due to reduced future flood losses.[185] If mitigation actions lead to lower damages and lower expected claims, they could make NFIP policies less expensive for households that implement them. An affordability program could be linked to mitigation loans or grants to reduce flood risk over time.[186] For example, homeowners could receive a loan or grant to make their property more resistant to flood damage, which could reduce flood risk and lower the cost of flood insurance premiums.

GAO suggested that instead of premium assistance, it would be preferable to address affordability by providing assistance for mitigation measures that would reduce flood risk and enhance resilience, and ultimately result in a lower premium rate.[187] GAO has suggested on numerous occasions that increasing mitigation activities would help to reduce flood risk and financial exposure,[188] including suggesting that FEMA could make mitigation activities mandatory, in conjunction with targeted financial assistance for policyholders.[189] In addition, property-level mitigation measures can reduce

---

[183] Ibid.

[184] FEM, *Hazard Mitigation Assistance Guidance*, Washington, DC, February 27, 2015, p. 1, https://www.fema.gov/ sites/default/files/2020-07/fy15_HMA_Guidance.pdf.

[185] National Institute of Building Sciences, *Natural Hazard Mitigation Saves: 2019 Report*, Washington, DC, 2019, p. 37, https://www.nibs.org/files/pdfs/NIBS_MMC_Mitigation Saves_2019.pdf. Note that the widely cited figure that $1 spent from federal grants saves $6 in future losses is an average across five hazards: riverine flood, hurricane surge, wind, earthquake, and wildland-urban interface fire. The study did not have enough data to calculate a benefit-cost ratio for federal grants for hurricane surge, but the benefit-cost ratio for federal grants for riverine flood is 7:1.

[186] GAO Solvency, p. 43.

[187] Ibid.

[188] See, for example, GAO Solvency, p. 25.

[189] GAO, Flood Insurance: More Information Needed on Subsidized Properties, GAO-13-607, July 3, 2013, p. 38, https://www.gao.gov/products/gao-13-607.

NFIP policyholders' premiums significantly. For example, FEMA estimates that elevating a property in the SFHA one foot above Base Flood Elevation (BFE) could result in a 30% reduction in annual premiums.[190] The Association of State Floodplain Managers calculated that elevating a property one foot above BFE could reduce annual flood insurance premiums by over $1,000, while elevating a property two or three feet above BFE could reduce premiums by over $1,400 and $1,500, respectively.[191] Insurance provisions could also provide incentives to limit flood damage by rewarding well-designed buildings with lower premiums, lower deductibles, or higher coverage limits. These incentives could also be made available to existing properties that implement new flood mitigation measures.

The NFIP offers three programs that encourage individuals or communities to reduce flood risk: Increased Cost of Compliance coverage, the Community Rating System, and the Flood Mitigation Assistance (FMA) grant program. These programs are funded by premiums, fees, and surcharges paid by NFIP policyholders. Reducing flood risk should lead to fewer NFIP claims over time and less financial support from NFIP policyholders. In addition, protection against flooding is in itself a benefit for households. Owners of mitigated properties may realize savings in a number of ways. In particular, they may escape damage during floods and avoid costs of repair and rebuilding.

Another way that the NFIP promotes mitigation is by requiring communities in the NFIP to adopt minimum floodplain management standards. According to FEMA, the program saves the nation an estimated $1.87 billion annually in flood losses avoided because of the NFIP's building and floodplain management regulations.[192] Internal FEMA studies have found that structures built to FEMA standards experience 65% less flood damage than structures not built to those standards, saving the nation $2.4 billion in avoided flood losses each year and $100 billion over the past 40 years.[193]

Communities play a key role in mitigating flood risk through planning and building requirements. FEMA does not regulate land use and does not have

---

[190] FEMA, Help Clients Pay Less for Flood Insurance, https://agents.floodsmart.gov/retention/costs.

[191] Association of State Floodplain Managers, *The Costs & Benefits of Building Higher*, June 30, 2017, p. 2, https://www.lfma.org/assets/docs/Benefits-and-Costs-of-Freeboard-flyer-6-30-17.pdf. Note that these estimates are for a single-family house, one floor, slab on grade foundation, with $200,000 of building coverage, $80,000 in contents coverage, and $1,000 deductible, at 2017 prices.

[192] GAO Solvency, p. 5.

[193] Email from FEMA Congressional Affairs staff, January 25, 2021.

authority over local development. Rather, it requires participating communities to adopt the minimum NFIP requirements through zoning, floodplain ordinances, and/or building codes. FEMA has set forth these minimum standards in federal regulations.[194] Communities are required to adopt these minimum floodplain management standards in order to participate in the NFIP.[195] NFIP minimum standards include, among many other conditions, that communities (1) require permits for development in SFHAs; (2) require elevation of the lowest floor of all new residential buildings in the SFHA to be at or above BFE; (3) restrict development in the regulatory floodway to prevent increasing the risk of flooding; and (4) require certain construction materials and methods that minimize future flood damage.[196] These requirements apply to new construction in the SFHA.

FEMA issued a request for public comment on revising the NFIP's floodplain management standards in October 2021, in response to a petition submitted by the Natural Resources Defense Council and the Association of State Floodplain Managers.[197] FEMA has not updated the NFIP criteria for building and land use in flood-prone areas since they were implemented in 1976,[198] despite growing flood risk and the existence of more protective standards at the state and local levels.[199]

### *Property-Level Mitigation*

The main source of funding for property-level mitigation measures is Increased Cost of Compliance (ICC) coverage, which is in effect a separate insurance policy to offset the expense of complying with more rigorous building code standards when local ordinances require them to do so. The

---

[194] See 44 C.F.R. Part 60, particularly 44 C.F.R. §60.3.

[195] 42 U.S.C. §4022(a)(1).

[196] 44 C.F.R. §60.3.

[197] Natural Resources Defense Council and the Association of State Floodplain Managers, Petition Requesting That the Federal Emergency Management Agency Amend Its Regulations Implementing the National Flood Insurance Program, Washington, DC, January 5, 2021, https://www.nrdc.org/sites/default/files/petition-fema-rulemaking-nfip-20210105.pdf.

[198] FEMA, "Request for Information on the National Flood Insurance Program's Floodplain Management Standards for Land Management and Use, and an Assessment of the Program's Impact on Threatened and Endangered Species and Their Habitats," 86(194) *Federal Register* 56713-56719, October 12, 2021.

[199] Natural Resources Defense Council and the Association of State Floodplain Managers, Petition Requesting That the Federal Emergency Management Agency Amend Its Regulations Implementing the National Flood Insurance Program, Washington, DC, January 5, 2021, p. 48, https://www.nrdc.org/sites/default/files/petition-fema-rulemaking-nfip- 20210105.pdf.

NFIP requires most policyholders[200] to purchase ICC coverage. ICC coverage is authorized in law, and rates for the coverage, as well as how much can be paid out for claims, are set by FEMA.[201] The ICC policy has a separate rate premium structure and provides an amount up to $30,000 in payments for certain eligible expenses. For example, ICC claims payments may be used toward the costs of elevating, demolishing, relocating, or flood-proofing nonresidential buildings, or any combination of these actions. According to ICC data, elevation is the most common form of mitigation.[202] Although the cost of elevating a structure depends on the type of building and elevation requirement, the average cost of elevating an existing property has been estimated at $33,239 to $91,732,[203] and suggestions have been made for years that the amount of ICC coverage should be raised.[204]

At the household level, there are currently few mitigation actions that lower premiums. The most commonly used interventions are structural elevation and flood-proofing (under certain circumstances).[205] However, even with the potential benefits of reduced future losses and decreased premiums, mitigation activities often require large upfront costs. Such risk reduction measures may be too expensive for many policyholders, and additional sources of funding may be needed, such as mitigation grants or loans. Such products could take the form of a stand-alone program or could be used in conjunction with other affordability approaches. The type of support for property-level mitigation activities could also be mixed: for example, grants could be made available for lower-income or cost-burdened households, and loans made available to households above this threshold.

---

[200] For example, ICC coverage is not required on condominium units and content-only policies.

[201] 42 U.S.C. §4011(b).

[202] See, for example, FEMA, *NFIP: Use of Increased Cost of Compliance Coverage*, FY2009 Report to Congress, October 2009, p. 6. Report provided to CRS by FEMA Congressional Affairs Staff, and Natural Resources Defense Council and the Association of State Floodplain Managers, *Petition Requesting That the Federal Emergency Management Agency Amend Its Regulations Implementing the National Flood Insurance Program*, Washington, DC, January 5, 2021, p. 48, https://www.nrdc.org/sites/default/files/petition-fema-rulemaking-nfip-20210105.pdf.

[203] Aerts, J.C.J.H., Botzen, W.J.W., Moel, H. de, et al., "Cost Estimates for Flood Resilience and Protection Strategies in New York City," *Annals of the New York Academy of Sciences*, vol. 1294, no. 1 (August 2013), pp. 22-26.

[204] See, for example, FEMA, *NFIP: Use of Increased Cost of Compliance Coverage*, FY2009 Report to Congress, October 2009, p. 32.

[205] See FEMA, *Flood Insurance Manual, 3. How to Write*, p. 3-41, revised October 1, 2022, https://www.fema.gov/sites/default/files/documents/fema_nfip-flood-insurance-full-manual_102022.pdf.

Risk Rating 2.0 currently provides credits for three mitigation actions: (1) installing flood openings according to the criteria in 44 C.F.R. §60.3;[206] (2) elevating onto posts, piles, and piers; and (3) elevating machinery and equipment above the lowest floor.[207]

### *Community-Level Mitigation and Floodplain Management Standards*

Some additional community-level mitigation measures could lead to lower NFIP premiums by removing properties from the SFHA, reducing the flood risk to individual properties, or by increasing a community's score in the Community Rating System (CRS).

The CRS is a voluntary incentive-based program that rewards communities for adopting floodplain management practices to a higher standard than the NFIP minimum standards by providing reduced-cost flood insurance premiums to policyholders in the community.[208] FEMA awards points that increase a community's "class" rating in the CRS on a scale of 1 to 10, with 1 being the highest ranking. Points are awarded for an array of improvements related to how the community informs its public on flood risk, maps and regulates its floodplain, reduces possible flood damage, and provides immediate warnings and responds to flooding incidents.[209] Starting at Class 9, policyholders in the SFHA within a CRS community receive a 5% discount on their SFIP premiums, with increasing discounts of 5% per class until reaching Class 1, at which those policyholders can receive a 45% discount.

Options that improve a community's CRS score will directly lower households' premiums by increasing the CRS discount on premiums. In addition, the CRS program provides an average 13.3% discount on SFIP premiums across the NFIP,[210] which is cross-subsidized into the NFIP program, such that the discount for one community ends up being offset by increased premium rates in all communities across the NFIP. Therefore, the

---

[206] 44 C.F.R. Part 60, *Criteria for Land Management and Use*, https://www.govinfo.gov/content/pkg/CFR-2012-title44- vol1/pdf/CFR-2012-title44-vol1-sec60-3.pdf.

[207] See FEMA, *Flood Insurance Manual: How to Write*, pp. 3-26 to 3-29, revised October 1, 2022, https://www.fema.gov/sites/default/files/documents/fema_nfip-flood-insurance-full-manual_102022.pdf.

[208] 42 U.S.C. §4022(b)(1).

[209] For a full listing of possible creditable activities in the Community Rating System, see FEMA, *NFIP Community Rating Coordinator's Manual 2017*, https://www.fema.gov/media-library-data/1493905477815-d794671adeed5beab6a6304d8ba0b207/633300_2017_CRS_Coordinators_Manual_508.pdf.

[210] Email correspondence from FEMA Congressional Affairs staff, October 22, 2020.

average 13.3% discount for CRS communities is cross-subsidized and shared across NFIP communities through a cost (or load) increase of 15.3% to overall premiums.[211]

The Flood Mitigation Assistance (FMA) Program[212] awards grants for a number of purposes, with the goal of mitigating flood-damaged properties to reduce or eliminate future NFIP claims, particularly from repetitive loss and severe repetitive loss properties. FMA funds mitigation activities such as state and local mitigation planning; the elevation, relocation, demolition, or flood proofing of structures; the acquisition of properties; and other activities.[213] FMA funding is available only to communities that participate in the NFIP. FMA grants are not available to individuals, although communities may apply for funding that benefits individual NFIP policyholders.

Providing increased federal funding for FMA could reduce flood risks and thus decrease the contributions to mitigation funding from NFIP policyholders. The annual amount available for FMA from FY2015 through FY2020 has varied between $150 and $200 million.[214]

The Infrastructure Investment and Jobs Act (IIJA)[215] appropriated $3.5 billion for the FMA program, with $700 million for each of FY2022 through FY2026. This represents a significant increase in the amount of funding available for flood mitigation, and the first time that funding has been appropriated for the FMA program.[216]

Other mitigation measures that reduce flood risk, particularly at the community level, may not lead directly to a reduction in flood insurance premiums for residents of that community, but may lead to reduced insurance claims, which would benefit NFIP finances as a whole.

### *Options to Encourage Property-Level Mitigation Activities*

1) Provide premium discounts for additional property-level mitigation activities. Congress could require FEMA to identify additional

---

[211] Ibid.

[212] 42 U.S.C. §4104c.

[213] For additional information on the FMA Program, see 44 C.F.R. Part 78, and FEMA's website at https://www.fema.gov/grants/mitigation/floods.

[214] See Table 5 in CRS Report R44593, *Introduction to the National Flood Insurance Program (NFIP)*, by Diane P. Horn and Baird Webel.

[215] P.L. 117-58.

[216] NFIP policyholders contributed an additional $100 million towards the FMA program in FY2022. See Department of Homeland Security (DHS), *Notice of Funding Opportunity (NOFO), Fiscal Year 2022 Flood Mitigation Assistance*, August 5, 2022, p. 6, https://www.fema.gov/sites/default/files/documents/fema_fy22-fma-nofo_08052022_0.pdf.

property-level mitigation activities for which NFIP policyholders could receive a reduced premium. To do this, FEMA would need to develop data and analyses that would link the measures' expected reduction in insurance losses to insurance premiums.[217]

2) Provide grants or loans to allow homeowners and businesses to introduce property- level mitigation activities. This could take the form of increasing funding available through the NFIP FMA program or FEMA's other Hazard Mitigation Assistance programs,[218] or by introducing new grant or loan programs for individuals and businesses. Currently, individuals and businesses cannot apply directly for mitigation funding. Mitigation grants or loans could be targeted to policyholders who meet defined criteria for affordability assistance, or targeted to certain types of properties. For example, mitigation funds could be targeted to those for whom the cost of NFIP premiums creates an affordability challenge, or for whom the cost of carrying out mitigation measures could be prohibitive, or to households that have little access to commercial credit.[219] Financial incentives could also be offered to encourage households in flood-prone areas to relocate outside the SFHA.
3) Provide grants or loans targeted at repetitive loss and severe repetitive loss properties. A relatively small number of NFIP properties that are repeatedly flooded contribute disproportionately to NFIP claims. Properties that have suffered multiple flood losses, known as repetitive loss (RL), and severe repetitive loss (SRL) properties are at greater risk than the average property insured by the NFIP. In the past 30 years, one out of every six dollars paid out in NFIP claims has gone to a building with a history of multiple floods; approximately $10.9 billion in claims have been paid on properties with two or more losses, accounting for over 15% of FEMA's total of $70.6 billion claims paid during the same period.[220] For such properties, the benefits of reduced flood risk and lower premiums may exceed the costs of mitigation. Targeting mitigation grants and/or loans at RL

---

[217] NRC *Affordability Report 1*, p. 108.

[218] See CRS Insight IN11187, *Federal Emergency Management Agency (FEMA) Hazard Mitigation Assistance*, by Diane P. Horn.

[219] NRC Affordability Report 1, p. 103.

[220] FEMA, "Request for Information on the National Flood Insurance Program's Floodplain Management Standards for Land Management and Use, and an Assessment of the Program's Impact on Threatened and Endangered Species and Their Habitats," 86(194) Federal Register 56713-56719, October 12, 2021.

and SRL properties could reduce both the premiums paid by these policyholders and the overall fiscal risk to the NFIP.[221]

4) Offer tax deductions or tax credits for mitigation activities. The cost burden of flood mitigation investments could be lowered through tax deductions and tax credits. At various times, Congress has passed legislation to provide tax relief to support recovery following disasters,[222] and such policy tools could be used to encourage mitigation activities. Tax credits generally provide greater financial assistance as they lower the actual amount of tax paid.[223] However, neither tax credits nor tax deductions may provide broad relief, and do not necessarily target those in need of financial assistance. Tax credits benefit only those owing tax, unless the credit is refundable and a refund is given if the filer owes less tax than the credit. A tax deduction benefits only those paying income tax, and the value of the deduction depends on the taxpayer's marginal tax rate. In addition, policyholders could face cash flow challenges because they would generally need to pay the full premium before they receive the tax benefit.[224]
5) Establish tax-deductible disaster savings accounts for mitigation activities. Pre-tax funds placed in disaster savings accounts could be used to cover hazard mitigation investments, or could cover disaster damages or flood insurance premiums. Funds could be contributed pre-tax, and amounts withdrawn for designated uses would not be taxed.[225] These accounts could also be used to cover homeowner expenses below their insurance policy deductible. This might encourage homeowners to increase the deductible, which would reduce the NFIP premium for that policy. As with tax deductions, the financial benefit to a household would depend on their marginal tax rate. In addition, a disaster savings account would not help those whose disposable income is not enough to allow them to put funds into a savings account.[226]

---

221 GAO, National Flood Insurance Program: Fiscal Exposure Persists Despite Property Acquisitions, GAO-20-509, June 25, 2020, p. 34, https://www.gao.gov/assets/710/707821.pdf.

222 See CRS Report R45864, Tax Policy and Disaster Recovery, by Molly F. Sherlock and Jennifer Teefy.

223 Ibid.

224 GAO Affordability Assistance, p. 2.

225 GAO Affordability Assistance, pp. 106-107.

226 GAO Affordability Assistance, p. 107.

***Options to Encourage Community-Level Flood Risk Reduction Measures***

1) *Improve a community's Community Rating System score.* A community could join the CRS or, if already participating in the CRS, carry out additional activities to improve its CRS class rating, thereby increasing the discount that residents receive on their flood insurance premiums. In particular, communities could focus on activities that receive a higher number of points, such as adoption of higher regulatory standards, open space preservation, flood protection, or acquisition and relocation of high-risk properties. For every step that a community's CRS rating increases, residents receive an additional 5% increase in their NFIP premium discount. Congress could also provide greater incentives for communities to participate in the CRS, perhaps by increasing the discounts for CRS class ratings. Congress could provide funding for technical assistance or staffing to small communities to enable them to join and participate in the CRS. Congress could direct FEMA to increase the CRS points for flood damage reduction activities that directly reduce flood risk.
2) *Encourage the use of green infrastructure and nature-based solutions to reduce flood risk.* Nature-based solutions make use of natural processes and ecosystem services for functional purposes, such as living shorelines, where natural habitats such as oyster reefs, mangroves, and salt marshes are used to hold the shoreline in place. FEMA recently elevated the CRS credits for nature-based solutions.[227] The number of points awarded for preserving open space is now among the highest given in the CRS. Credits are awarded according to the percentage of open space in a community's floodplain. The larger the percentage, the more credit is awarded.[228] Nature-based solutions may also provide benefits beyond mitigating the effects of natural hazards, such as improved water and air quality, healthier natural habitats, and added recreational space.
3) *Increase federal funding for flood mitigation.* Congress could appropriate funding for NFIP flood mitigation, rather than requiring

---

[227] FEMA, *Addendum to the 2017 CRS Coordinator's Manual*, January 2021, pp. A-6 to A-9, https://www.fema.gov/sites/default/files/documents/fema_community-rating-system_coordinator-manual_addendum-2021.pdf.

[228] FEMA, *Building Community Resilience with Nature-Based Solutions: A Guide for Local Communities*, Washington, DC, August 6, 2020, p. 18, https://www.fema.gov/sites/default/files/2020-08/fema_riskmap_nature-based-solutions- guide_2020.pdf.

the FMA program to be funded entirely by NFIP policyholders.[229] For example, the IIJA appropriated $3.5 billion for FMA, with $700 million for each of FY2022 through FY2026. Congress could also provide additional funding to other hazard mitigation programs,[230] which could potentially benefit NFIP communities.

4) *Increase the federal cost share of mitigation grants.* Congress could increase the federal cost share on mitigation grants, and could target this assistance toward particular types of communities. The cost share for the FMA program is usually 75% federal, 25% nonfederal. However, the cost share is 90% federal, 10% nonfederal for repetitive loss properties, and 100% federal for severe repetitive loss properties. Despite this, obtaining funding for the nonfederal cost share may be difficult for some communities, and Congress could increase the federal cost share to make it possible for such communities to carry out mitigation activities. For example, FEMA intends to reduce the FMA cost share for certain disadvantaged communities in FY2022, as part of the Justice40 Initiative,[231] by using the Centers for Disease Control and Prevention (CDC) Social Vulnerability Index (SVI)[232] at the census tract level at a threshold of 0.7501 or greater as a priority

---

[229] The Infrastructure Investment and Jobs Act (IIJA), P.L. 117-58, appropriates $3.5 billion for the NFIP Flood Mitigation Assistance Program, with $700 million for each of FY2022 through FY2026. This represents a significant increase in the amount of funding available for flood mitigation, and the first time that funding has been appropriated for the FMA program. NFIP policyholders contributed an additional $100 million towards the FMA program in FY2022. See Department of Homeland Security (DHS), *Notice of Funding Opportunity (NOFO), Fiscal Year 2022 Flood Mitigation Assistance*, August 5, 2022, p. 6, https://www.fema.gov/sites/default/files/documents/fema_fy22-fma-nofo_08052022_0.pdf.

[230] For more information about FEMA Hazard Mitigation Assistance, see CRS Report R46989, *FEMA Hazard Mitigation: A First Step Toward Climate Adaptation*, by Diane P. Horn and CRS Insight IN11733, *Recent Funding Increases for FEMA Hazard Mitigation Assistance*, by Diane P. Horn.

[231] Executive Office of the President, Office of Management and Budget, *Memorandum for the Heads of Departments and Agencies*, M-21-28, Washington, DC, July 20, 2021, p. 12, https://www.whitehouse.gov/wp-content/uploads/2021/ 07/M-21-28.pdf.

[232] The Centers for Disease Control and Prevention/Agency for Toxic Substances and Disease Registry (CDC/ATSDR) Social Vulnerability Index (SVI) uses United States Census Data to determine the social vulnerability of every census tract, ranked on 15 social factors. SVI scores range from 0 to 1, with 1 representing the highest level of social vulnerability. For example, a SVI ranking of 0.75 means that 75% of census tracts in the nation are less vulnerable than the tract of interest. See *CDC/ATSDR SVI Fact Sheet*, https://www.atsdr.cdc.gov/placeandhealth/svi/fact_sheet/fact_sheet.html, and *CDC SVI 2018 Documentation*, https://www.atsdr.cdc.gov/placeandhealth/svi/documentation/pdf/SVI2018Documentation-H.pdf.

scoring criterion.[233] In addition, the funding appropriated to FMA under the IIJA will provide a 90% federal cost share for a property that is (1) located in a census tract with a CDC SVI score of not less than 0.5001, or (2) that serves as a primary residence for individuals with a household income of not more than 100% of the applicable area median income.

5) *Require stronger building codes for new buildings and damaged buildings.* Flood risks can also be reduced at the building level. A 2019 study found that, on average, society saves $5 for every dollar spent on mitigation measures that exceed building code requirements for areas at risk of flooding from rivers, and $7 for areas at risk of hurricane surge flooding.[234] Although building codes are adopted and administered at a community level, the federal government can create incentives for communities to adopt and enforce up- to-date building codes and hazard-resistant design standards.[235] For example, FEMA's Mitigation Framework Leadership Group suggested that federal programs could be directed to promote the adoption of building codes and other mitigation requirements though incentives such as a higher federal cost share,[236] discounts on insurance premiums, tax credits, or access to additional grants or loans.[237] FEMA could also provide funding specifically for retrofitting existing buildings.

---

[233] DHS, *Notice of Funding Opportunity (NOFO), Fiscal Year 2021 Flood Mitigation Assistance,* p. 4, https://www.fema.gov/sites/default/files/documents/fema_nofo-fiscal-year-2021-flood-mitigation-assistance-grants.pdf.

[234] National Institute of Building Sciences, *Natural Hazard Mitigation Saves: 2019 Report*, Washington, DC, 2019, p. 37, https://www.nibs.org/files/pdfs/NIBS_MMC_MitigationSaves_2019.pdf.

[235] For example, FEMA defines a hazard-resistant building code as a "building code with provisions that provide a minimum level of building protection against natural hazards," and considers a community to be hazard resistant if it adopts either of the two most recent editions of building codes without weakening provisions related to flood, hurricane wind, and seismic hazards. FEMA, *Building Codes Saves: A Nationwide Study,* November 2020, p. xi and p. 3-4, https://www.fema.gov/sites/default/files/2020-11/fema_building-codes-save_study.pdf.

[236] See, for example, Section 20606 of the Bipartisan Budget Act of 2018 (P.L. 115-123) as it amends Stafford Act Section 406(b) to authorize an increased federal share for Public Assistance to provide incentives to governments to "invest in measures that increase readiness for, and resilience from, a major disaster," which may include "encouraging the adoption and enforcement of the latest published editions of relevant consensus-based codes, specifications, and standards."

[237] Department of Homeland Security, Mitigation Framework Leadership Group, *National Mitigation Investment Strategy*, Washington, DC, August 2019, p. 16, https://www.fema.gov/sites/default/files/2020-10/fema_national-mitigation-investment-strategy.pdf.

6) *Increase minimum floodplain management standards for NFIP participation*. When communities join the NFIP, they must adopt and enforce FEMA's minimum floodplain management standards, including those that regulate where and how structures may be built within the floodplain. These standards are minimum requirements for NFIP participation; states and communities can elect to adopt higher standards as a means of mitigating flood risk.[238] For example, FEMA minimum standards require that the elevation of the lowest floor of all new residential buildings in the SFHA to be at or above BFE.[239] However, approximately 38% of the U.S. population lives outside of areas with at least one foot of freeboard.[240] A community could require the elevation of the lowest floor to be above BFE, or to BFE plus a freeboard[241] of a defined number of feet above BFE. FEMA has found that the average annual losses avoided for freeboard structures was approximately $484 million.[242]
7) *Require stricter controls on development in the floodplain*. Communities play a key role in mitigating flood risk through planning requirements, particularly planning controls that restrict or eliminate new development in hazardous locations and discourage rebuilding in high-risk locations. The NFIP could require stricter standards related to floodplain development or provide greater incentives to limit development in the floodplain. For example, local governments could offer incentives to encourage developers to locate projects outside of the SFHA and/or to adopt flood mitigation measures that exceed those required by law. Another option is the use of conditional land use restrictions, which might require a landowner to restrict

---

[238] In October 2021, FEMA issued a request for information on the NFIP's floodplain management standards. The public comment period ended on January 27, 2022. See FEMA, "Request for Information on the NFIP's Floodplain Management Standards for Land Management and Use, and an Assessment of the Program's Impact on Threatened and Endangered Species and Their Habitats; Public Meeting; Extension of Comment Period," 86 (222) *Federal Register* 66329-66330, November 22, 2021.

[239] See 44 C.F.R. Part 60, particularly 44 C.F.R. §60.3.

[240] National Institute of Building Sciences, *Natural Hazard Mitigation Saves: 2019 Report*, Washington, DC, 2019, p. 69, https://www.nibs.org/files/pdfs/NIBS_MMC_MitigationSaves_2019.pdf.

[241] FEMA defines freeboard as an additional amount of height above the Base Flood Elevation used as a factor of safety in determining the level at which a structure's lowest floor must be elevated or floodproofed to be in accordance with the state or community floodplain management standards. See https://www.fema.gov/glossary/freeboard.

[242] FEMA, *Building Codes Saves: A Nationwide Study*, November 2020, p. 4-17, https://www.fema.gov/sites/default/files/2020-11/fema_building-codes-save_study.pdf.

future use of the land by allowing limited rebuilding, by totally prohibiting rebuilding or by allowing reconstruction with conditions (e.g., that they will remove structures when threatened by erosion or inundation). The NFIP could also require communities to delineate floodplains based on potential future development and apply higher standards for those areas.[243]

## Concluding Comments

FEMA does not currently have the authority to implement an affordability program, nor does the NFIP's current rate structure provide the funding required to support one. If an affordability program were to be funded from existing NFIP funds, it would require either raising flood insurance rates for NFIP policyholders or diverting resources from another existing use. If Congress were to appropriate funding for an affordability program,[244] either Congress or FEMA would face decisions on how to structure this program. Choosing among affordability program options, alone or in combination, requires an evaluation of their effects not only on premiums for households for which NFIP premiums create a cost burden, but also on NFIP net revenues, expenditures from federal general revenues, and take-up rates.[245]

Evaluation of policy options that would make NFIP premiums more affordable would require the ability to estimate the effect of each one on NFIP premium revenues and affordability. Some of the specific options discussed in this report may have conflicting or cascading impacts, so that movement toward one goal may make others harder to accomplish. For example, increased consumer participation could increase the size and scope of the NFIP, but could potentially increase federal fiscal exposure.[246] Congress and other stakeholders may want answers to questions with a specific focus on

---

[243] Natural Resources Defense Council and the Association of State Floodplain Managers, Petition Requesting That the Federal Emergency Management Agency Amend Its Regulations Implementing the National Flood Insurance Program, Washington, DC, January 5, 2021, pp. 46-47, https://www.nrdc.org/sites/default/files/petition-fema-rulemaking-nfip- 20210105.pdf.

[244] For example, the funding which would have been appropriated in the House-passed version of the Build Back Better Act.

[245] Carolyn Kousky, Brett Lingle, Howard Kunreuther, et al., *Moving the Needle on Closing the Flood Insurance Gap*, Wharton Risk Management and Decision Processes Center, Issue Brief, Philadelphia, PA, February 13, 2019, p. 9, https://riskcenter.wharton.upenn.edu/wp-content/uploads/2019/02/Moving-the-Needle-on-Closing-the-Flood-Insurance-Gap.pdf.

[246] *GAO Solvency*, p. 33.

location where premiums would change, such as "What are the effects in a particular congressional district for various groups of property owners?" or "Where are the effects concentrated?"[247]

Flooding is already the costliest natural disaster annually in the United States, and more frequent and intense flooding from climate change represents an increasing threat in the future.[248] The risk exposure of the NFIP will change over time, particularly due to the likelihood of increasing flood risk and continued development in flood-prone areas, with an increased number of properties likely to be identified as being at risk of flooding.[249] A 2013 report on the impact of climate change and population growth on the NFIP concluded that nationally, considering fluvial and coastal floods together, the SFHA is projected to be 40%-45% larger by 2100, with approximately 70% of this increase due to climate change.[250]

The decision about who pays for affordability assistance entails choices on the part of policymakers. For example, one choice relates to the degree to which costs are borne by federal taxpayers versus the NFIP policyholders who do not receive assistance but pay for assistance to others through a cross-subsidy. Another consideration is the degree to which affordability program costs are borne nationally versus more locally (by states, tribal nations, or communities) or are shared by federal and local governments.[251] A number of stakeholders have argued that an effective affordability program should be funded not by premium discounts or surcharges on other NFIP policyholders, but rather by a source external to the NFIP.[252] For example, GAO argued that providing premium assistance through appropriations rather than discounted

---

[247] National Research Council of the National Academies, *Affordability of National Flood Insurance Program Premiums: Report 2*, 2016, p. 26, http://www.nap.edu/catalog/21848/affordability-of-national-flood-insurance-program-premiums-report-2.

[248] U.S. Government Accountability Office, *FEMA Flood Maps: Better Planning and Analysis Needed to Address Current and Future Flood Hazards*, GAO-22-104079, October 25, 2021, p. 41, https://www.gao.gov/assets/gao-22- 104079.pdf.

[249] See, for example, Natural Resources Defense Council and the Association of State Floodplain Managers, Petition Requesting That the Federal Emergency Management Agency Amend Its Regulations Implementing the National Flood Insurance Program, Washington, DC, January 5, 2021, pp. 5-11, https://www.nrdc.org/sites/default/files/petition-fema-rulemaking-nfip-20210105.pdf.

[250] AECOM, in association with Michael Baker Jr., Inc., and Deloitte Consulting, LLP, *The Impact of Climate Change and Population Growth on the National Flood Insurance Program Through 2100*, Prepared for Federal Insurance and Mitigation Administration, FEMA, June 2013, pp. 5-12 and 5-13, https://aecom.com/content/wp-content/uploads/2016/06/Climate_Change_Report_AECOM_2013-06-11.pdf.

[251] *NRC Affordability Report 1*, p. 94.

[252] See, for example, *GAO Affordability Assistance*, p. 22, and *GAO Solvency*, p. 27.

premiums would address the policy goal of making the fiscal exposure more transparent because any affordability discounts on premium rates would be explicitly recognized in the budget each year,[253] and would make NFIP subsidy costs explicit by requiring Congress to appropriate funds for them.[254]

A central question in any reform of the NFIP is who should bear the costs of floodplain occupancy in the future. The 2015 National Research Council study on flood insurance affordability concluded that the costs of floods can be borne in three possible ways, or in some combination of them.

- Individual policyholders (whether NFIP or private) bear floodplain location cost in the form of insurance premiums paid and damages falling within policy deductible amounts.
- Federal taxpayers bear floodplain location costs if the federal government (1) develops a premium assistance program; (2) makes up for NFIP premium revenue shortfalls; (3) pays for pre-flood mitigation; or (4) makes post-flood disaster assistance payments to individual households.
- Property owners and other floodplain or coastal zone inhabitants bear the costs for losses that are uninsured or otherwise uncompensated.[255]

Reform of the NFIP would reallocate costs across these groups; Congress would face decisions on how that occurs.

---

[253] *GAO Solvency*, p. 27.

[254] *GAO Affordability Assistance*, p. 39.

[255] National Research Council of the National Academies, *Affordability of National Flood Insurance Program Premiums: Report 2*, 2016, p. 12, http://www.nap.edu/catalog/21848/affordability-of-national-flood-insurance- program-premiums-report-2.

**Table 1.** Legislative proposals related to NFIP affordability

| Congress | Increase Participation in the NFIP | Make NFIP Premiums More Affordable | Encourage Property-Level Flood Mitigation | Encourage Community-Level Flood Mitigation | Increase NFIP Income | Reduce NFIP Debt |
|---|---|---|---|---|---|---|
| 117th Congress | S. 3128 §108[a] | H.R. 4497 §308 | S. 3218 §§202, 204, 306 | H.R. 4497 §307 | S. 3128 §208, 303 | H.R. 4497 §307 |
| | | S. 3128 §§102, 103, 104, 106, 107, 209 | | S. 3128 §§201, 203, 204, 205, 206, 207, 210 | | S. 3128 §301 |
| | | H.R. 1449, §2 | | P.L. 117-58. | | H.R. 5376, §40104. |
| 116th Congress | H.R. 3167 §§305, 401, 408 | H.R. 3167 §§102, 103, 104, 106, 107, 209, 304, 402 | H.R. 3167 §§301, 303 | S. 3167 §§105, 302, 306, 307, 308 | H.R. 3167 §201 | H.R. 3167 §§301, 403 |
| | S. 2187[b] §108 | S. 2187 §§102, 103,104,106,107, 209 S. 2266 §3 | S. 2187 §§202, 204, 306 | S. 2187 §§201, 203, 204, 205, 206, 207, 210 | S. 2187 §§208, 303 | S. 2187 §301 |
| 115th Congress | H.R. 2874 §§507, 513 | H.R. 2874 §§102, 103, 111, 112, 202 | H.R. 2874 §§113, 403, 504 | | H.R. 2874 §504 | H.R. 2874 §§504, 505 |
| | S. 1313 §102 | S. 1313 §§205, 206, 207, 208, 401 | S. 1313 §§204, 206 | S. 1313 §201 | S. 1313 §§403, 404, 501 | |
| | S. 1368[c] §410 | S. 1368 §§102, 103, 204, 208 | S. 2168 §§201, 206 | S. 1368 §§202, 207, 422 | S. 1368 §§204, 303 | S. 1368 §301 |
| | S. 1571 §303 | S. 1571 §301 | S. 1571 §§103, 106 | S. 1571 §107 | S. 1571 §201 | |
| 114th Congress | H.R. 3297 §10 | | | | | |
| 113th Congress | | H.R. 3013 §6 | H.R. 1268 §2 | | | |
| | | H.R. 3294 §§3, 4 | H.R. 3298 §2 | | | |

Source: CRS analysis of legislation from https://www.congress.gov.

Notes: H.R. 5376 as passed by the House on November 19, 2021.

[a] S. 3128 and companion bill H.R. 5802

[b] S. 2187 and companion bill H.R. 3872

[c] S. 1368 and companion bill H.R. 3285

# Chapter 10

# The National Flood Insurance Program (NFIP), Reinsurance, and Catastrophe Bonds*

**Diane P. Horn**
**and Baird Webel**

Insurance transfers risk from one entity who does not want to bear that risk to another entity that does. An initial insurance purchase, such as homeowners buying a policy to cover damage to their home, is often only the first transfer of that risk. The initial (or *primary*) insurer may then transfer (or *cede*) some or all of this risk to another company or investor, such as a *reinsurer*. Reinsurers may also further transfer (or *retrocede*) risks to other reinsurers. Such transfers are, on the whole, a net cost for primary insurers, just as purchasing insurance is a net cost for homeowners.

The Homeowner Flood Insurance Affordability Act of 2014 (P.L. 113-89) revised the authority of the National Flood Insurance Program (NFIP) to secure reinsurance from "private reinsurance and capital markets." Risk transfer to the private market could reduce the likelihood of the Federal Emergency Management Agency (FEMA) borrowing from the Treasury to pay claims. In addition, it could allow the NFIP to recognize some of its flood risk up front through premiums it pays for risk transfers rather than after-the-fact borrowing, and could help the NFIP to reduce the volatility of its losses over time. However, because reinsurers charge premiums to compensate for the assumed risk as well as the reinsurers' costs and profit margins, the primary

* This is an edited, reformatted and augmented version of Congressional Research Service Publication No. IN10965, updated May 28, 2024.

In: The National Flood Insurance Program (NFIP)
Editor: Jolene Rivera
ISBN: 979-8-89530-612-3

benefit of reinsurance is to manage risk, not to reduce the NFIP's long- term fiscal exposure.

## Reinsurance

The most common form of risk transfer is a primary insurer purchasing coverage for its risks from another (re)insurer. Reinsurance is particularly important to smaller insurers who may not be large enough to spread correlated local risks, such as a storm hitting a specific area. Reinsurers generally have the size to diversify risks globally, as natural hazard events are assumed to be uncorrelated: a hurricane making landfall in Florida is assumed to be independent of a wildfire in California.

## NFIP Reinsurance Purchases

The NFIP's first large reinsurance purchase was in 2017, with additional purchases annually from 2018 to 2024. The details of these purchases have varied, but they have all covered losses from a single flooding event covering losses varying between $4 billion and $11 billion, with potential payouts of $1.042-$1.46billion and premiums of $90-$235 million. As of March 8, 2024, the NFIP has transferred $1.92 billion of the NFIP's flood risk to the private sector ahead of the 2024 hurricane season.

Claims from Hurricane Harvey exceeded $10 billion, triggering a full claim of $1.042 billion on the 2017 reinsurance. No reinsurance claims have been made since 2017. To date, the traditional reinsurance purchases have been a net fiscal negative for the NFIP, with a total of $2.275 billion in premiums paid and $1.042 billion received from claims.

## Catastrophe Bonds

In addition to reinsurance, new forms of "alternative" risk transfer have also developed. One category of such instruments are known as insurance linked securities (ILS)—financial instruments whose values are driven by insurance loss events and which transfer major natural disaster risks to capital market investors.

The most common form is catastrophe bonds, which operate somewhat like other bonds, but whose payout is dependent on the occurrence of a particular catastrophe.

Catastrophe bonds are structured so that payment depends on the occurrence of an event of a defined magnitude or that causes an aggregate insurance loss in excess of a stipulated amount. Only when these specific triggering conditions are met do investors begin to lose their investment. There are three main types of triggers:

- *Indemnity*—bonds triggered by the losses experienced by the sponsoring insurer following the occurrence of a specified event (e.g., if an insurer's residential property losses from a hurricane in Florida exceeds $25 million in 2024);
- *Industry Loss*—bonds triggered by a predetermined threshold of industry-wide losses following the occurrence of a specified event (e.g., if a total of all insurers' residential property losses from floods in 2024 exceeds $20 billion); or
- *Parametric*—bonds triggered by physical conditions occurring during a disaster such as wind speed or earthquake size (e.g., if a 25-foot storm surge hit New Orleans in 2024).

Catastrophe bonds were first used in the mid-1990s following Hurricane Andrew and the Northridge earthquake. The public sector has become increasingly interested in the use of catastrophe bonds. In 2009, Mexico became the first sovereign to issue catastrophe bonds, and the World Bank is one of the largest participants in the market. The New York City Metropolitan Transit Authority has issued four catastrophe bonds since 2013 to protect against storm surge. According to Swiss Re, $15.4 billion of ILS were issued in 2023, the highest recorded year of issuance since the inception of the catastrophe bond market.

## NFIP and Catastrophe Bonds

In August 2018, FEMA entered into its first transfer of NFIP risk through an ILS transaction in the form of a three-year agreement with the reinsurer Hannover Re, and in total has made seven capital market placements in 2019-2024. In each case, Hannover Re acts as a "transformer," transferring between

$0.3 and $0.575 billion of the NFIP's risk to capital markets by sponsoring issuance of an indemnity-triggered catastrophe bond. In the 2024 issuance, Hannover Re has indemnified FEMA for a single qualifying flooding event between March 7, 2024, and March 7, 2027. The 2024 agreement is structured to cover 10% of losses between $8 and $9 billion and 2.75% of losses between $9 and $11 billion. A storm comparable to Hurricane Katrina would result in a total loss for the catastrophe bond investors, while a storm comparable to Hurricanes Sandy or Harvey would erode the principal of both tranches but not cause a total payout.

Unlike the traditional reinsurance purchases, which cover NFIP losses for a single flood event anywhere in the United States and its territories, the catastrophe bonds apply only to flooding resulting directly or indirectly from a named storm and cover only the 50 states, the District of Columbia, Puerto Rico, and the U.S. Virgin Islands. The NFIP has not claimed on any of the catastrophe bonds.

## Chapter 11

# National Flood Insurance Program Borrowing Authority*

**Diane P. Horn**

This Insight evaluates the National Flood Insurance Program (NFIP) borrowing authority to receive loans from the Treasury and the current financial situation of the NFIP.

## NFIP Funding

Funding for the NFIP is primarily maintained in an authorized account called the National Flood Insurance Fund (NFIF). The NFIP is funded from receipts from the premiums of flood insurance policies, including fees and surcharges; direct annual appropriations for specific costs of the NFIP (only for flood mapping); and borrowing from the Treasury when the NFIF's balance has been insufficient to pay the NFIP's obligations (e.g., insurance claims). Since the end of FY2017, 30 short-term NFIP reauthorizations have been enacted. For further details of these reauthorizations, see CRS Insight IN10835, What Happens If the National Flood Insurance Program (NFIP) Lapses? The current reauthorization is set to expire on September 30, 2024. These extensions did not increase the NFIP's borrowing limit or provide additional funds to the NFIP.

---

* This is an edited, reformatted and augmented version of Congressional Research Service Publication No. IN10784, updated April 1, 2024.

In: The National Flood Insurance Program (NFIP)
Editor: Jolene Rivera
ISBN: 979-8-89530-612-3

## NFIP Borrowing Authority

The NFIP was not designed to retain funding to cover claims for truly extreme events; instead, the National Flood Insurance Act of 1968 allows the program to borrow money from the Treasury for such events. For most of the NFIP's history, the program has been able to cover its costs, borrowing relatively small amounts from the Treasury to pay claims and to repay the loans with interest. Only current and future participants in the NFIP are responsible for repaying NFIP debt, as the insurance program itself owes the debt to the Treasury and pays for accruing interest on that debt through the premium revenues of policyholders. Since 2005, the NFIP has made six principal repayments totaling $2.82 billion and has paid $6.17 billion in interest. The program paid $309 million in interest in FY2023, accruing $1.7 million in interest daily.

Table 1 shows NFIP borrowing, repayments, and debt from FY1980 to FY2024. Comparable figures are not available before 1980. When the NFIP was established, the borrowing limit was $250 million. In 1973, the borrowing limit was increased to $500 million, or $1 billion with Presidential approval. The borrowing limit was increased to $1.5 billion in 1996; however, borrowing at that level was not required before 2005. The largest debt was $917 million in 1997, which was reduced to zero by the end of FY2003. Congress increased the level of borrowing to pay claims in the aftermath of the 2005 hurricane season (particularly Hurricanes Katrina, Rita, and Wilma). Congress increased the borrowing limit to $18.5 billion in November 2005 and further increased the borrowing limit to $20.775 billion in March 2006. In July 2010, the borrowing limit was decreased to $20.725 billion. In 2013, following Hurricane Sandy, Congress increased the borrowing limit to the current $30.425 billion.

**Table 1.** NFIP borrowing FY1980 to FY2024

(nominal dollars)

| Fiscal Year | Amount Borrowed | Amount Repaid | Cumulative Debt |
|---|---|---|---|
| 1980 | 917,406,008 | 0 | 917,406,008 |
| 1981 | 164,614,526 | 624,970,099 | 457,050,435 |
| 1982 | 13,915,000 | 470,965,435 | 0 |
| 1983 | 50,000,000 | 0 | 50,000,000 |
| 1984 | 200,000,000 | 36,879,123 | 213,120,877 |
| 1985 | 0 | 213,120,877 | 0 |
| 1986 | 0 | 0 | 0 |

| Fiscal Year | Amount Borrowed | Amount Repaid | Cumulative Debt |
|---|---|---|---|
| 1987 | 0 | 0 | 0 |
| 1988 | 0 | 0 | 0 |
| 1989 | 0 | 0 | 0 |
| 1990 | 0 | 0 | 0 |
| 1991 | 0 | 0 | 0 |
| 1992 | 0 | 0 | 0 |
| 1993 | 0 | 0 | 0 |
| 1994 | 100,000,000 | 100,000,000 | 0 |
| 1995 | 265,000,000 | 0 | 265,000,000 |
| 1996 | 423,600,000 | 62,000,000 | 626,600,000 |
| 1997 | 530,000,000 | 239,600,000 | 917,000,000 |
| 1998 | 0 | 395,000,000 | 522,000,000 |
| 1999 | 400,000,000 | 381,000,000 | 541,000,000 |
| 2000 | 345,000,000 | 541,000,000 | 600,000,000 |
| 2001 | 600,000,000 | 345,000,000 | 600,000,000 |
| 2002 | 50,000,000 | 640,000,000 | 10,000,000 |
| 2003 | 0 | 10,000,000 | 0 |
| 2004 | 0 | 0 | 0 |
| 2005 | 300,000,000 | 75,000,000 | 225,000,000 |
| 2006 | 16,600,000,000 | 0 | 16,885,000,000 |
| 2007 | 650,000,000 | 0 | 17,735,000,000 |
| 2008 | 50,000,000 | 225,000,000 | 17,360,000,000 |
| 2009 | 1,987,988,421 | 347,988,421 | 19,000,000,000 |
| 2010 | 0 | 500,000,000 | 18,500,000,000 |
| 2011 | 0 | 750,000,000 | 17,750,000,000 |
| 2012 | 0 | 0 | 17,750,000,000 |
| 2013 | 6,250,000,000 | 0 | 24,000,000,000 |
| 2014 | 0 | 1,000,000,000 | 23,000,000,000 |
| 2015 | 0 | 0 | 23,000,000,000 |
| 2016 | 0 | 0 | 23,000,000,000 |
| 2017 | 7,425,000,000 | 0 | 30,425,000,000 |
| 2018 | 6,100,000,000 | 16,000,000,000[a] | 20,525,000,000 |
| 2019 | 0 | 0 | 20,525,000,000 |
| 2020 | 0 | 0 | 20,525,000,000 |
| 2021 | 0 | 0 | 20,525,000,000 |
| 2022 | 0 | 0 | 20,525,000,000 |
| 2023 | 0 | 0 | 20,525,000,000 |
| 2024 | 0 | 0 | 20,525,000,000 |

Sources: CRS analysis: data 1980-2017 provided by FEMA Congressional Affairs, November 20, 2017. Data since 2017 from NFIP Watermark financial statements.

[a] The $16 billion of debt was cancelled rather than repaid (P.L. 115-72, Title III, §308).

In January 2017, the NFIP borrowed $1.6 billion for flood losses in 2016 and debt repayments. On September 22, 2017, FEMA borrowed the remaining $5.825 billion from the Treasury, reaching the NFIP's authorized borrowing limit of $30.425 billion. On October 26, 2017, $16 billion of NFIP debt was cancelled to make it possible for the program to pay claims for Hurricanes Harvey, Irma, and Maria. This represents the first time NFIP debt has been cancelled, although Congress appropriated funds between 1980 and 1985 to repay NFIP debt. FEMA borrowed another $6.1 billion on November 9, 2017, to fund estimated 2017 losses, including those incurred by Hurricanes Harvey, Irma, and Maria, increasing the debt to $20.525 billion. The NFIP has not borrowed from Treasury since 2017.

The NFIP currently has $9.9 billion of remaining borrowing authority. As of March 13, 2024, the NFIP had $3.739 billion available to pay claims, with $760 million in the NFIF and $2.979 billion in the Reserve Fund.

The NFIP transfers a portion of its risk to the private sector through the purchase of reinsurance and the issuance of catastrophe bonds. The NFIP's first large reinsurance purchase was in January 2017, when FEMA purchased $1.042 billion of reinsurance, structured to pay 26% of losses between $4 billion and $8 billion arising from a single flooding event. Claims for Hurricane Harvey exceeded $9 billion, triggering a full reinsurance claim. Since then, the NFIP has not claimed any reinsurance, as no storms have reached the threshold for claims.

The NFIP could claim over $1.9 billion in reinsurance in 2024. In order for the NFIP to claim on these policies, losses for a single named storm would have to reach $7 billion for the2024 traditional reinsurance, $6 billion for the 2021 and 2022 catastrophe bonds, $7 billion for the 2023 catastrophe bond, and $8 billion for the 2024 catastrophe bond.

# Chapter 12

# National Flood Insurance Program Risk Rating 2.0: Frequently Asked Questions*

**Diane P. Horn**

This Insight answers some frequently asked questions about Risk Rating 2.0, which came fully into effect on April 1, 2022, changing the way the National Flood Insurance Program (NFIP) calculates flood insurance premiums. For additional information, see CRS Report R45999, *National Flood Insurance Program: The Current Rating Structure and Risk Rating 2.0*.

## What Is Risk Rating 2.0?

Risk Rating 2.0 is a new pricing methodology and represents the biggest change to the way the NFIP calculates flood insurance premiums since the program began in 1968. Premiums calculated under Risk Rating 2.0 reflect an individual property's specific flood risk, as opposed to being placed in a general risk category based on location and property type.

## Why Did the NFIP Introduce Risk Rating 2.0?

The NFIP updated its rating methodology to calculate flood insurance premiums for individual properties based on actual flood risk. This is intended

* This is an edited, reformatted and augmented version of Congressional Research Service Publication No. IN11777, updated May 28, 2024.

In: The National Flood Insurance Program (NFIP)
Editor: Jolene Rivera
ISBN: 979-8-89530-612-3

to produce rates that are more equitable, and to inform policyholders of their true flood risk.

## How Have Flood Insurance Premiums Been Calculated Previously?

The NFIP's rating structure followed the general insurance practices in place when the NFIP was established and had not fundamentally changed since the 1970s. It used several basic characteristics to classify properties and assign rates. Structures were evaluated by location within a flood zone on a Flood Insurance Rate Map (FIRM), occupancy type, and elevation relative to the Base Flood Elevation (BFE). This rating system did not take into account the individual flood risk or the cost to rebuild, and considered only two sources of flood risk: river flooding and coastal flooding.

## How Are Premiums Calculated Under Risk Rating 2.0?

Premiums are calculated based on specific features of an individual property, including distance from water, type of flooding, flood frequency, structure foundation type, height of the lowest floor relative to BFE, prior claims, and the structure's replacement cost value. FEMA has provided a Rate Explanation Guide, Discount Explanation Guide, and Flood Insurance Mitigation Discount Tool to illustrate how certain rating variables affect premiums. Risk Rating 2.0 also adds pluvial flood risk—flooding from heavy rainfall.

## Will Subsidized Premiums Increase Under Risk Rating 2.0?

Risk Rating 2.0 continues the phase-out of NFIP subsidies, which began with the Biggert-Waters Flood Insurance Reform Act of 2012 (BW-12) and continued with the Homeowner Flood Insurance Affordability Act of 2014 (HFIAA). Properties currently grandfathered will see their premiums move towards a full risk-based rate. All new policies pay the full risk-based rate. New policies and those renewed under Risk Rating 2.0 are limited by statutory rate increases.

## How Much Can Premiums Increase Annually?

The NFIP is not able to increase rates beyond statutory limits set in HFIAA, which allow premium increases of up to 18% annually for primary residences. Other categories of property are required to have their premium increased by 25% per year until they reach full risk-based rates, including (1) non-primary residences; (2) non-residential properties, (3) business properties; (4) properties with severe repetitive loss; (5) properties with substantial cumulative damage; and (6) properties with substantial damage or substantial improvement after July 6, 2012.

## Are There Discounts for Flood Mitigation Activities?

Policyholders can receive mitigation credits for elevating a property, elevating machinery and equipment above the lowest floor, and installing flood openings below BFE. All policyholders in communities in the Community Rating System (CRS) receive discounts of 5%-45%, based on the community's CRS score.

## How Have Average NFIP Premiums Changed in Recent Years?

Since HFIAA and before the introduction of Risk Rating 2.0, NFIP average premiums increased between 6% and 11% per year (see Table 1).

**Table 1.** Percentage increases in selected NFIP premiums, 2015-2021

| Rate Category | 2015 | 2016 | 2017 | 2018 | 2019 | 2020 | 2021 |
|---|---|---|---|---|---|---|---|
| Pre-FIRM Subsidized | 14.0% | 5.0% | 5.0% | 5.0% | 7.3% | 7.9% | 7.7% |
| V zone | 9.0% | 10.0% | 7.0% | 11.0% | 6.0% | 5.9% | 0.3% |
| A zone | 12.0% | 9.0% | 1.0% | 1.0% | 4.0% | 4.1% | 1.7% |
| X zone | 11.0% | 3.0% | 2.0% | 1.0% | 1.0% | 3.5% | 1.4% |
| Average | 9.9% | 9.0% | 6.3% | 8.0% | 8.2% | 11.3% | 10.2% |

Source: Compiled by CRS from annual WYO Company Bulletins.

Note: Rate increases for 2021 do not include changes from Risk Rating 2.0. Post-2022 rate increases are not determined by flood zone.

## Does Being Mapped into a Different Flood Zone Affect Premiums?

No, flood zones are no longer used in calculating a property's premium under Risk Rating 2.0. Instead, premiums are calculated based on the specific features of an individual property. FIRMs are still used for the mandatory purchase requirement and floodplain management.

## How Does Being Behind a Levee Affect My Premium?

FEMA uses data from the U.S. Army Corps of Engineers National Levee Database Levee Screening Tool (LST) to determine a levee's level of risk reduction. Currently, 20% of levees have been screened and have information to fulfill all levee data needs for Risk Rating 2.0.

## Does Risk Rating 2.0 Change Requirements to Buy Flood Insurance?

No, if a property is in a Special Flood Hazard Area (SFHA), the owner is required to buy flood insurance to secure a federally backed mortgage. Lenders use FIRMs to make this determination.

## Can New Premiums Under Risk Rating 2.0 Be Appealed?

No appeal procedure has been established for changes under Risk Rating 2.0. Policyholders can appeal against NFIP flood maps, but this will not change insurance premiums.

## How Are Premiums Changing in My State Under Risk Rating 2.0?

FEMA has posted state profiles showing changes under Risk Rating 2.0, and data at the county and zip code level can be downloaded. FEMA has also provided information on the cost of flood insurance for single family homes under Risk Rating 2.0, showing the number and percentage of policies by price range at the state, zip code, and county level, including the average replacement cost value in each price range and the percentage of policyholders facing different types of flood peril.

## Are Premiums Under Risk Rating 2.0 Affected by Changing Flood Risk Under Climate Change?

Premiums for a single year will not increase due to future climate change. However, if flood risk increases over time, premiums will increase to reflect the increased risk.

# Index

## S

## T



## U



## V



## W



## Y